Lord Lytton

Ernest Maltravers

Lord Lytton

Ernest Maltravers

ISBN/EAN: 9783742839107

Manufactured in Europe, USA, Canada, Australia, Japa

Cover: Foto ©Andreas Hilbeck / pixelio.de

Manufactured and distributed by brebook publishing software (www.brebook.com)

Lord Lytton

Ernest Maltravers

"THE WORLD," SAID HE, KISSING THE HAND THAT YET LAY ON HIS ARM
"THE WORLD WILL——"

ERNEST MALTRAVERS.

BY THE

RIGHT HON. LORD LYTTON.

With Coloured Illustrations by Jules Despres.

LONDON:
WALTER SCOTT, 14 PATERNOSTER SQUARE,
AND NEWCASTLE-UPON-TYNE.

A WORD TO THE READER.

PREFIXED TO THE FIRST EDITION OF 1837.

THOU must not, my old and partial friend, look into this work for that species of interest which is drawn from stirring adventures and a perpetual variety of incident. To a Novel of the present day are necessarily forbidden the animation, the excitement, the bustle, the pomp, and the stage-effect which History affords to Romance. Whatever merits, in thy gentle eyes, *Rienzi*, or *The Last Days of Pompeii*, may have possessed, this Tale, if it please thee at all, must owe that happy fortune to qualities widely different from those which won thy favour to pictures of the Past. Thou must sober down thine imagination, and prepare thyself for a story not dedicated to the narrative of extraordinary events—nor the elucidation of the characters of great men. Though there is scarcely a page in this work episodical to the main design, there may be much that may seem to thee wearisome and prolix, if thou wilt not lend thyself, in a kindly spirit and with a generous trust, to the guidance of the Author. In the hero of this tale thou wilt find neither a majestic demigod, nor a fascinating demon. He is a man with the weaknesses derived from humanity, with the strength that we inherit from the soul; not often obstinate in error, more often irresolute in virtue; sometimes too aspiring, sometimes too despondent; influenced by the circumstances to which he yet struggles to be superior, and changing in character with the changes of time and fate; but never wantonly rejecting those great principles by which alone we can work out the Science of Life—a desire for the Good, a passion for the Honest, a yearning after the True. From such principles, Experience, that severe Mentor, teaches us at length the safe and practical philosophy, which consists of Fortitude to bear, Serenity to enjoy, and Faith to look beyond!

It would have led, perhaps, to more striking incidents, and have furnished an interest more intense, if I had cast Maltravers, the Man of Genius, amidst those fierce but ennobling struggles with poverty and want to which genius is so often condemned. But wealth and lassitude have their temptations as well as penury and toil. And for the rest—I have taken much of my tale and many of my characters from real life, and would not unnecessarily seek other fountains when the Well of Truth was in my reach.

The Author has said his say, he retreats once more into silence and into shade; he leaves you alone with the creations he has called to life—the representatives of his emotions and his thoughts—the intermediators between the individual and the crowd—Children not of the clay, but of the spirit, may they be faithful to their origin!—so should they be monitors, not loud but deep, of the world into which they are cast, struggling against the obstacles that will beset them, for the heritage of their parent—the right to survive the grave!

London, *12th August 1837.*

PREFACE TO THE EDITION OF 1840.

HOWEVER numerous the works of fiction with which, my dear Reader, I have trespassed on your attention, I have published but three, of any account, in which the plot has been cast amidst the events, and coloured by the manner, of our own times. The first of these, *Pelham*, composed when I was little more than a boy, has the faults, and perhaps the merits, natural to a very early age—when the novelty itself of life quickens the observation—when we see distinctly, and represent vividly, what lies upon the surface of the world—and when, half sympathising with the follies we satirise, there is a gusto in our paintings which atones for their exaggeration. As we grow older we observe less, we reflect more; and, like Frankenstein, we dissect in order to create.

The second novel of the present day,* which, after an interval of some years, I submitted to the world, was one I now, for the first time, acknowledge, and which (revised and corrected) will be included in this series—viz, *Godolphin*—a work devoted to a particular portion of society, and the development of a peculiar class of character. The third,

---

* For *The Disowned* is cast in the time of our grandfathers, and *The Pilgrims of the Rhine* has nothing to do with actual life, and is not, therefore, to be called a novel.

which I now reprint, is *Ernest Maltravers*,* the most mature, and, on the whole, the most comprehensive of all that I have hitherto written.

For the original idea, which, with humility, I will venture to call the philosophical design, of a moral education or apprenticeship, I have left it easy to be seen that I am indebted to Goethe's *Wilhelm Meister*. But in *Wilhelm Meister* the apprenticeship is rather that of theoretical art. In the more homely plan that I set before myself, the apprenticeship is rather that of practical life. And, with this view, it has been especially my study to avoid all those attractions lawful in romance, or tales of pure humour or unbridled fancy—attractions that, in the language of reviewers, are styled under the head of "most striking descriptions," "scenes of extraordinary power," etc.; and are derived from violent contrasts and exaggerations pushed into caricature. It has been my aim to subdue and tone down the persons introduced, and the general agencies of the narrative, into the lights and shadows of life as it is. I do not mean by "life as it is," the vulgar and the outward life alone, but life in its spiritual and mystic, as well as its more visible and fleshly characteristics. The idea of not only describing, but developing character under the ripening influences of time and circumstance, is not confined to the apprenticeship of Maltravers alone, but pervades the progress of Cesarini, Ferrers, and Alice Darvil.

The original conception of Alice is taken from real life—from a person I never saw but twice, and then she was no longer young—but whose history made on me a deep impression. Her early ignorance and home—her first love—the strange and affecting fidelity that she maintained, in spite of new ties—her final re-meeting, almost in middle age, with

---

* At the date of this preface *Night and Morning* had not appeared.

one lost and adored almost in childhood—all this, as shown in the novel, is but the imperfect transcript of the true adventures of a living woman.

In regard to Maltravers himself, I must own that I have but inadequately struggled against the great and obvious difficulty of representing an author living in our own times, with whose supposed works or alleged genius, and those of any one actually existing, the reader can establish no identification, and he is therefore either compelled constantly to humour the delusion by keeping his imagination on the stretch, or lazily driven to confound the Author *in* the Book with the Author *of* the Book.* But I own, also, I fancies', while aware of this objection, and in spite of it, that so much not hitherto said might be conveyed with advantage through the lips or in the life of an imaginary writer of our own time, that I was contented, on the whole, either to task the imagination, or submit to the suspicions of the reader. All that my own egotism appropriates in the book are some occasional remarks, the natural result of practical experience. With the life or the character, the adventures or the humours, the errors or the good qualities, of Maltravers himself, I have nothing to do, except as the narrator and inventor.

E. B. L.

---

* In some foreign journal I have been much amused by a credulity of this latter description, and seen the various adventures of Mr. Maltravers gravely appropriated to the embellishment of my own life, including the attachment to the original of poor Alice Darvil; who now, by-the-way, must be at least seventy years of age, with a grandchild nearly as old as myself.

ERNEST MALTRAVERS.

BOOK I.

CHAPTER I.

"My meaning in't, I protest, was very honest in the behalf of the maid . . . . yet, who would have suspected an ambush where I was taken!"
—*All's Well that Ends Well*, Act iv. Sc. 3.

SOME four miles distant from one of our northern manufacturing towns, in the year 18—, was a wide and desolate common; a more dreary spot it is impossible to conceive—the herbage grew up in sickly patches from the midst of a black and stony soil. Not a tree was to be seen in the whole of the comfortless expanse. Nature herself had seemed to desert the solitude, as if scared by the ceaseless din of the neighbouring forges; and even Art, which presses all things into service, had disdained to cull use or beauty from these unpromising demesnes. There was something weird and primeval in the aspect of the place; especially when, in the long nights of winter you beheld the distant fires and lights, which give to the vicinity of certain manufactories so preternatural an appearance, streaming red and wild over the waste. So abandoned by man appeared the spot, that you found it difficult to imagine that it was only from human fires that its bleak and barren desolation was illumined. For miles along the moor you detected no vestige of any habitation; but as you approached the verge nearest to the town, you could just perceive, at a little distance from the main road by which the common was intersected, a small, solitary, and miserable hovel.

Within this lonely abode, at the time in which my story opens, were seated two persons. The one was a man of about fifty years of age, and in a squalid and wretched garb, which was yet relieved by an affectation of ill-assorted finery. A silk handkerchief, which boasted the ornament of a large brooch of false stones, was twisted jauntily round a muscular but meagre throat; his tattered breeches were also decorated by buckles, one of pinchbeck, and one of steel. His frame was lean, but broad and sinewy, indicative of considerable strength. His countenance was prematurely marked by deep furrows, and his grizzled hair waved over a low, rugged, and forbidding brow, on which there hung an everlasting frown that no smile from the lips (and the man smiled often) could chase away. It was a face that spoke of long-continued and hardened vice—it was one in which the Past had written indelible characters. The brand of the hangman could not have stamped it more plainly, nor have more unequivocally warned the suspicion of honest or timid men.

He was employed in counting some few and paltry coins, which, though an easy matter to ascertain their value, he told and retold, as if the act would increase the amount. "There must be some mistake here, Alice," he said in a low and muttered tone; "we can't be so low—you know I had two pounds in the drawer but Monday, and now—Alice you must have stolen some of the money—curse you."

The person thus addressed sat at the opposite side of the smouldering and sullen fire; she now looked quietly up—and her face singularly contrasted that of the man.

She seemed about fifteen years of age, and her complexion was remarkably pure and delicate, even despite the sunburnt tinge which her habits of toil had brought it. Her auburn hair hung in loose and natural curls over her forehead, and its luxuriance was remarkably even in one so young. Her countenance was beautiful, nay, even faultless, in its small and child-like features, but the expression pained you—it was so vacant. In repose it was almost the expression of an idiot—but when she spoke, or smiled, or even moved a muscle, the eyes, colour, lips, kindled into a life which proved that the intellect was still there, though but imperfectly awakened.

"I did not steal any, father," she said in a quiet voice; "but I should like to have taken some, only I knew you would beat me if I did."

"And what do you want money for?"

"To get food when I'm hungered."

"Nothing else?"

"I don't know."

The girl paused.—"Why don't you let me," she said after a while, "why don't you let me go and work with the other girls at the factory? I should make money there for you and me both."

The man smiled—such a smile—it seemed to bring into sudden play all the revolting characteristics of his countenance. "Child," he said, "you are just fifteen, and a sad fool you are: perhaps if you went to the factory you would get away from me; and what should I do without you? No, I think, as you are so pretty, you might get more money another way."

The girl did not seem to understand this allusion; but repeated vacantly, "I should like to go to the factory."

"Stuff!" said the man, angrily, "I have three minds to——"

Here he was interrupted by a loud knock at the door of the hut.

The man grew pale. "Who can that be?" he muttered. "The hour is late—near eleven. Again—again! Ask who knocks, Alice."

The girl stood for a moment or so at the door; and as she stood, her form, rounded yet slight, her earnest look, her varying colour, her tender youth, and a singular grace of attitude and gesture, would have inspired an artist with the very ideal of rustic beauty.

After a pause, she placed her lips to a chink in the door, and repeated her father's question.

"Pray pardon me," said a clear, loud, yet courteous voice, "but seeing a light at your window, I have ventured to ask if any one within will conduct me to ——; I will pay the service handsomely."

"Open the door, Alley," said the owner of the hut.

The girl drew a large wooden bolt from the door; and a tall figure crossed the threshold.

The new comer was in the first bloom of youth, perhaps about eighteen years of age, and his air and appearance surprised both sire and daughter. Alone, on foot, at such an hour, it was impossible for any one to mistake him for other than a gentleman; yet his dress was plain, and somewhat soiled by dust, and he carried a small knapsack on his shoulder. As he entered, he lifted his hat with somewhat of foreign urbanity, and a profusion of fair brown hair fell partially over a high and commanding forehead. His features were handsome, without being eminently so, and his aspect was at once bold and prepossessing.

"I am much obliged by your civility," he said, advancing carelessly, and addressing the man, who surveyed him with a scrutinising eye: "and trust, my good fellow, that you will increase the obligation by accompanying me to ——."

"You can't miss well your way," said the man, surlily: "the lights will direct you."

"They have rather misled me, for they seem to surround the whole common, and there is no path across it that I can see; however, if you will put me in the right road, I will not trouble you further."

"It is very late," replied the churlish landlord, equivocally.

"The better reason why I should be at ——. Come, my good friend, put on your hat, and I will give you half-a-guinea for your trouble."

The man advanced, then halted, again surveyed his guest, and said, "Are you quite alone, sir?"

"Quite."

"Probably you are known at ——?"

"Not I. But what matters that to you? I am a stranger in these parts."

"It is full four miles."

"So far, and I am fearfully tired already!" exclaimed the young man with impatience. As he spoke, he drew out his watch. "Past eleven, too!"

The watch caught the eye of the cottager; that evil eye sparkled. He passed his hand over his brow. "I am thinking, sir," he said, in a more civil tone than he had yet assumed, "that as you are so tired, and the hour is so late, you might almost as well ——"

"What?" exclaimed the stranger, stamping somewhat petulantly.

"I don't like to mention it; but my poor roof is at your service, and I would go with you to —— at daybreak to-morrow."

The stranger stared at the cottager, and then at the dingy walls of the hut. He was about, very abruptly, to reject the hospitable proposal, when his eye rested suddenly on the form of Alice, who stood, eager-eyed and open-mouthed, gazing on the handsome intruder. As he caught her eye, she blushed deeply, and turned aside. The view seemed to change the intentions of the stranger. He hesitated a moment, then muttered between his teeth: and sinking his knapsack on the ground, he cast himself into a chair beside the fire, stretched his limbs, and cried gaily, "So be it, my host: shut up your house again. Bring me a cup of beer, and a crust of bread, and so much for supper! As for bed, this chair will do vastly well."

"Perhaps we can manage better for you than that chair," answered the host. "But our best accommodation must seem bad enough to a gentleman: we are very poor people—hard-working, but very poor."

"Never mind me," answered the stranger, busying himself in stirring the fire; "I am tolerably well accustomed to greater hardships than sleeping on a chair in an honest man's house; and though you are poor, I will take it for granted you are honest."

The man grinned; and turning to Alice, bade her spread what their larder would afford. Some crusts of bread, some cold potatoes, and some tolerably strong beer, composed all the fare set before the traveller.

Despite his previous boasts, the young man made a wry face at these Socratic preparations, while he drew his chair to the board. But his look grew more gay as he caught Alice's eye; and as she lingered by the table, and faltered out some hesitating words of apology, he seized her hand, and pressing it tenderly—"Prettiest of lasses," said he—and while he spoke he gazed on her with undisguised admiration—"a man who has travelled on foot all day, through the ugliest country within the three seas, is sufficiently refreshed at night by the sight of so fair a face."

Alice hastily withdrew her hand, and went and seated herself in a corner of the room, whence she continued to look at the stranger with her usual vacant gaze, but with a half smile upon her rosy lips.

Alice's father looked hard first at one, then at the other.

"Eat, sir," said he, with a sort of chuckle, "and no fine words; poor Alice is honest, as you said just now."

"To be sure," answered the traveller, employing with great zeal a set of strong, even, and dazzling teeth at the tough crusts; "to be sure she is. I did not mean to offend you; but the fact is, that I am half a foreigner; and abroad, you know, one may say a civil thing to a pretty girl without hurting her feelings, or her father's either."

"Half a foreigner! why you talk English as well as I do," said the host, whose intonation and words were, on the whole, a little above his station.

The stranger smiled. "Thank you for the compliment," said he. "What I meant was, that I have been a great deal abroad; in fact, I have just returned from Germany. But I am English-born."

"And going home?"

"Yes."

"Far from hence?"

"About thirty miles, I believe."

"You are young, sir, to be alone."

The traveller made no answer, but finished his uninviting repast, and drew his chair again to the fire. He then thought he had sufficiently ministered to his host's curiosity to be entitled to the gratification of his own.

"You work at the factories, I suppose?" said he.

"I do, sir. Bad times."

"And your pretty daughter?"

"Minds the house."

"Have you no other children?"

"No; one mouth besides my own is as much as I can feed, and that scarcely. But you would like to rest now; you can have my bed, sir; I can sleep here."

"By no means," said the stranger, quickly; "just put a few more coals on the fire, and leave me to make myself comfortable."

The man rose, and did not press his offer, but left the room for a supply of fuel. Alice remained in her corner.

"Sweetheart," said the traveller, looking round and satisfying himself that they were alone; "I should sleep well if I could get one kiss from those coral lips."

Alice hid her face with her hands.

"Do I vex you?"

"Oh no, sir."

At this assurance the traveller rose, and approached Alice softly. He drew away her hands from her face, when she said gently, "Have you much money about you?"

"O the mercenary baggage!" said the traveller to himself; and then replied aloud, "Why, pretty one?—Do you sell your kisses so high then?"

Alice frowned, and tossed the hair from her brow. "If you have money," she said in a whisper, "don't say so to father. Don't sleep if you can help it. I'm afraid—hush—he comes!"

The young man returned to his seat with an altered manner. And as his host entered, he for the first time surveyed him closely. The imperfect glimmer of the half-dying and single candle threw into strong lights and shades the marked, rugged, and ferocious features of the cottager; and the eye of the traveller, glancing from the face to the limbs and frame, saw that whatever of violence the mind might design the body might well execute.

The traveller sank into a gloomy reverie. The wind howled—the rain beat—through the casement shone no solitary star—all was dark and sombre;—should he proceed alone—might he not suffer a greater danger upon that wide and desert moor—might not the host follow—assault him in the dark? He had no weapon, save a stick. But within, he had at least a rude resource in the large kitchen poker that was beside him. At all events, it would be better to wait for the present. He might at any time, when alone, withdraw the bolt from the door, and slip out unobserved.

Such was the fruit of his meditations while his host plied the fire.

"You will sleep sound to-night," said his entertainer, smiling.

"Humph! Why I am *over*-fatigued; I dare say it will be an hour or two before I fall asleep; but when I once *am* asleep, I sleep like a rock!"

"Come, Alice," said her father, "let us leave the gentleman. Good night, sir."

"Good night—good night," returned the traveller, yawning.

The father and daughter disappeared through a door in the corner of the room. The guest heard them ascend the creaking stairs—all was still.

"Fool that I am," said the traveller to himself, "will nothing teach me I am no longer a student at Gottingen, or cure me of these pedestrian adventures; had it not been for that girl's big blue eyes, I should be safe at —— by this time; if indeed the grim father had not murdered me by the road. However, we'll baulk him yet: another half-hour and I am on the moor: we must give him time. And in the meanwhile here is the poker. At the worst it is but one to one; but the churl is strongly built."

Although the traveller thus endeavoured to cheer his courage, his heart beat more loudly than its wont. He kept his eyes stationed on the door by which the cottagers had vanished, and his hand on the massive poker.

While the stranger was thus employed below, Alice, instead of turning to her own narrow cell, went into her father's room.

The cottager was seated at the foot of his bed, muttering to himself, and with eyes fixed on the ground.

The girl stood before him, gazing on his face, and with her arms lightly crossed above her bosom.

"It must be worth twenty guineas," said the host, abruptly to himself.

"What is it to you, father, what the gentleman's watch is worth?" The man started.

"You mean," continued Alice, quietly, "you mean to do some injury to that young man; but you shall not.'

The cottager's face grew black as night. "How," he began in a loud voice, but suddenly dropped the tone into a deep growl—"how dare you talk to me so?—go to bed—go to bed."

"No, father."

"No?"

"I will not stir from this room until daybreak."

"We will soon see that," said the man, with an oath.

"Touch me, and I will alarm the gentleman, and tell him that——"

"What?"

The girl approached her father, placed her lips to his ear, and whispered, "That you intend to murder him."

The cottager's frame trembled from head to foot; he shut his eyes, and gasped painfully for breath. "Alice," said he, gently, after a pause—"Alice, we are often nearly starving."

"*I* am—*you* never!"

"Wretch, yes; if I do drink too much one day, I pinch for it the next. But go to bed, I say—I mean no harm to the young man. Think you I would twist myself a rope?—no, no;—go along, go along."

Alice's face, which had before been earnest and almost intelligent, now relapsed into its wonted vacant stare.

"To be sure, father, they would hang you if you cut his throat. Don't forget that—good-night;" and so saying, she walked to her own opposite chamber.

Left alone, the host pressed his hand tightly to his forehead, and remained motionless for nearly half-an-hour.

"If that cursed girl would but sleep," he muttered at last, turning round, "it might be done at once. And there's the pond behind, as deep as a well; and I might say at daybreak that the boy had bolted. He seems quite a stranger here—nobody 'll miss him. He must have plenty of blunt to give half-a-guinea to a guide across a common! I want money, and I won't work—if I can help it, at least."

While he thus soliloquised, the air seemed to oppress him; he

"THEY ARE IN THE SHED BEHIND," SHE WHISPERED.

opened the window, he leant out—the rain beat upon him. He closed the window with an oath; took off his shoes, stole to the threshold, and, by the candle which he shaded with his hand, surveyed the opposite door. It was closed. He then bent anxiously forward and listened.

"All's quiet," thought he, "perhaps he sleeps already. I will steal down. If Jack Walters would but come to-night, the job would be done charmingly."

With that he crept gently down the stairs. In a corner, at the foot of the staircase, lay sundry matters, a few faggots, and a cleaver. He caught up the last. "Aha," he muttered; "and there's the sledge-hammer somewhere for Walters." Leaning himself against the door, he then applied his eye to a chink, which admitted a dim view of the room within, lighted fitfully by the fire.

CHAPTER II.

"What have we here!
A carrion death!"
—*Merchant of Venice*, Act II. Sc. 7.

IT was about this time that the stranger deemed it advisable to commence his retreat. The slight and suppressed sound of voices, which at first he heard above in the conversation of the father and child, had died away. The stillness at once encouraged and warned him. He stole to the front door, softly undid the bolt, and found the door locked, and the key missing. He had not observed that, during his repast, and ere his suspicions had been aroused, his host, in replacing the bar, and relocking the entrance, had abstracted the key. His fears were now confirmed. His next thought was the window—the shutter only protected it half-way, and was easily removed; but the aperture of the lattice, which only opened in part, like most cottage casements, was far too small to admit his person. His only means of escape was in breaking the whole window; a matter not to be effected without noise, and consequent risk.

He paused in despair. He was naturally of a strong-nerved and gallant temperament, not unaccustomed to those perils of life and limb which German students delight to brave; but his heart wellnigh failed him at that moment. The silence became distinct and burdensome to him, and a chill moisture gathered on his brow. While he stood irresolute and in suspense, striving to collect his thoughts, his ear, preternaturally sharpened by fear, caught the faint muffled sound of creeping footsteps—he heard the stairs creak. The sound broke the spell. The previous vague apprehension gave way when the danger became actually at hand. His presence of mind returned at once. He went back quickly to the fireplace, seized the poker, and began stirring the fire, and coughing loud, indicating as vigorously as possible that he was wide awake.

He felt that he was watched—he felt that he was in extreme peril. He felt that the appearance of slumber would be the signal for a mortal conflict. Time passed, all remained silent; nearly half-an-hour had elapsed since he had heard the steps upon the stairs. His situation began to prey upon his nerves, it irritated them—it became intolerable. It was not, now, fear that he experienced, it was the overwrought sense of mortal enmity—the consciousness that a man may feel who knows that the eye of a tiger is on him, and who, while in suspense he has regained his courage, foresees that sooner or later the spring must come; the suspense itself becomes an agony, and he desires to expedite the deadly struggle he cannot shun.

Utterly incapable any longer to bear his own sensations, the traveller rose at last, fixed his eyes upon the fatal door, and was about to cry aloud to the listener to enter, when he heard a slight tap at the window; it was twice repeated; and at the third time a low voice pronounced the name of Darvil. It was clear, then, that accomplices had arrived; it was no longer against one man that he should have to contend. He drew his breath hard, and listened with throbbing ears. He heard steps without upon the plashing soil; they retired—all was still.

He paused a few minutes, and walked deliberately and firmly to the inner door, at which he fancied his host stationed; with a steady hand he attempted to open the door; it was fastened on the opposite side. "So!" said he, bitterly, and grinding his teeth; "I must die like a rat in a cage. Well, I'll die biting."

He returned to his former post, drew himself up to his full height, and stood grasping his homely weapon, prepared for the worst, and not altogether unelated with a proud consciousness of his own natural advantages of activity, stature, strength, and daring. Minutes rolled on, the silence was broken by some one at the inner door; he heard the bolt gently withdrawn. He raised his weapon with both hands, and started to find the intruder was only Alice. She came in, pale as marble, with her finger on her lips.

She approached—she touched him.

"They are in the shed behind," she whispered, "looking for the sledge-hammer—they mean to murder you; get you gone—quick."

"How?—the door is locked."

"Stay. I have taken the key from his room."

She gained the door, applied the key—the door yielded. The traveller threw his knapsack once more over his shoulder and made but one stride to the threshold. The girl stopped him. "Don't say anything about it; he is my father, they would hang him."

"No, no. But you?—are safe, I trust?—depend on my gratitude —I shall be at —— to-morrow—the best inn—seek me if you can! Which way now?"

"Keep to the left."

The stranger was already several paces distant; through the darkness, and in the midst of the rain, he fled on with the speed of youth. The girl lingered an instant, sighed, then laughed aloud; closed and re-barred the door, and was creeping back, when from the inner entrance advanced the grim father, and another man, of broad, short, sinewy frame, his arms bare, and wielding a large hammer.

"How?" asked the host; "Alice here, and—hell and the devil! have you let him go?"

"I told you that you should not harm him."

With a violent oath, the ruffian struck his daughter to the ground, sprang over her body, unbarred the door, and, accompanied by his comrade, set off in vague pursuit of his intended victim.

CHAPTER III.

"You knew—none so well, of my daughter's flight."
—*Merchant of Venice*, Act iii. Sc. 1.

THE day dawned; it was a mild, damp, hazy morning; the sod sank beneath the foot, the roads were heavy with mire, and the rain of the past night lay here and there in broad shallow pools. Towards the town, waggons, carts, pedestrian groups were already moving; and now and then you caught the sharp horn of some early coach, wheeling its be-cloaked outside and be-nightcapped inside passengers along the northern thoroughfare.

A young man bounded over a stile into the road just opposite to the mile-stone, that declared him to be one mile from ———.

"Thank heaven!" he said, almost aloud. "After spending the night wandering about morasses like a will-o'-the-wisp, I approach a town at last. Thank heaven, again, and for all its mercies this night! I breathe freely. I AM SAFE."

He walked on somewhat rapidly; he passed a slow waggon—he passed a group of mechanics—he passed a drove of sheep, and now he saw walking leisurely before him a single figure. It was a girl, in a worn and humble dress, who seemed to seek her weary way with pain and languor. He was about also to pass her, when he heard a low cry. He turned, and beheld in the wayfarer his preserver of the previous night.

"Heavens! it is indeed you? Can I believe my eyes?"

"I was coming to seek you, sir," said the girl, faintly. "I, too, have escaped; I shall never go back to father; I have no roof to cover my head now."

"Poor child! but how is this? Did they ill-use you for releasing me?"

"Father knocked me down, and beat me again when he came back; but that is not all," she added, in a very low tone.

"What else?"

The girl grew red and white by turns. She set her teeth rigidly, stopped short, and then walking on quicker than before, replied—"It don't matter; I will never go back—I'm alone now. What, what shall I do?" and she wrung her hands.

The traveller's pity was deeply moved. "My good girl," said he, earnestly, "you have saved my life, and I am not ungrateful. Here" (and he placed some gold in her hand), "get yourself a lodging, food, and rest; you look as if you wanted them; and see me again this evening when it is dark, and we can talk unobserved."

The girl took the money passively, and looked up in his face while he spoke; the look was so unsuspecting, and the whole countenance was so beautifully modest and virgin-like, that had any evil passion prompted the traveller's last words, it must have fled scared and abashed as he met the gaze.

"My poor girl," said he, embarrassed, and after a short pause;— "you are very young, and very, very pretty. In this town you will be exposed to many temptations : take care where you lodge ; you have, no doubt, friends here?"

"Friends?—what are friends?" answered Alice.

"Have you no relations ; no *mother's kin?*"

"None."

"Do you know where to ask shelter?"

"No, sir ; for I can't go where father goes, lest he should find me out."

"Well, then, seek some quiet inn, and meet me this evening, just here, half-a-mile from the town, at seven. I will try and think of something for you in the meanwhile. But you seem tired, you walk with pain ; perhaps it will fatigue you to come—I mean, you had rather perhaps rest another day."

"Oh, no, no ! it will do me good to see you again, sir."

The young man's eyes met hers, and hers were not withdrawn ; their soft blue suffused with tears—they penetrated his soul.

He turned away hastily, and saw that they were already the subject of curious observation to the various passengers that overtook them. "Don't forget!" he whispered, and strode on with a pace that soon brought him to the town.

He inquired for the principal hotel—entered it with an air that bespoke that nameless consciousness of superiority which belongs to those accustomed to purchase welcome wherever welcome is bought and sold—and before a blazing fire and no unsubstantial breakfast, forgot all the terrors of the past night, or rather felt rejoiced to think he had added a new and strange hazard to the catalogue of adventures already experienced by Ernest Maltravers.

CHAPTER IV.

"Con una Dama tenia
Un galan conversacion."*
—MORATIN : *El Teatro Espanol.*--Num. 15.

MALTRAVERS was first at the appointed place. His character was in most respects singularly energetic, decided, and premature in its development ; but not so in regard to women : with them he was the creature of the moment ; and, driven to and fro by whatever impulse, or whatever passion, caught the

* With a dame he held a gallant conversation.

caprice of a wild, roving, and all-poetical imagination, Maltravers was, half unconsciously, a poet—a poet of action, and woman was his muse.

He had formed no plan of conduct towards the poor girl he was to meet. He meant no harm to her. If she had been less handsome, he would have been equally grateful; and her dress, and youth, and condition, would equally have compelled him to select the hour of dusk for an interview.

He arrived at the spot. The winter night had already descended; but a sharp frost had set in: the air was clear, the stars were bright, and the long shadows slept, still and calm, along the broad road, and the whitened fields beyond.

He walked briskly to and fro, without much thought of the interview, or its object, half chanting old verses, German and English, to himself, and stopping to gaze every moment at the silent stars.

At length he saw Alice approach: she came up to him timidly and gently. His heart beat more quickly; he felt that he was young and alone with beauty. "Sweet girl," he said, with involuntary and mechanical compliment, "how well this light becomes you! how shall I thank you for not forgetting me?"

Alice surrendered her hand to his without a struggle.

"What is your name?" said he, bending his face down to hers.

"Alice Darvil."

"And your terrible father—*is* he, in truth, your father?"

"Indeed he is my father and mother too!"

"What made you suspect his intention to murder me? Has he ever attempted the like crime?"

"No: but lately he has often talked of robbery. He is very poor, sir. And when I saw his eye, and when afterwards, while your back was turned, he took the key from the door, I felt that— that you were in danger."

"Good girl—go on."

"I told him so when we went upstairs. I did not know what to believe, when he said he would not hurt you; but I stole the key of the front door, which he had thrown on the table, and went to my room. I listened at my door; I heard him go downstairs; he stopped there for some time; and I watched him from above. The place where he was opened to the field by the backway. After some time, I heard a voice whisper him: I knew the voice, and then they both went out by the backway; so I stole down, and went out and listened; and I knew the other man was John

Walters. I'm afraid of *him*, sir. And then Walters said, says he, 'I will get the hammer, and sleep or wake, we'll do it.' And father said, 'It's in the shed.' So I saw there was no time to be lost, sir, and—and—but you know all the rest."

"But how did you escape?"

"Oh, my father, after talking to Walters, came to my room, and beat and—and—frightened me; and when he was gone to bed, I put on my clothes, and stole out; it was just light; and I walked on till I met you."

"Poor child, in what a den of vice have you been brought up!"

"Anan, sir."

"You don't understand me. Have you been taught to read and write?"

"Oh, no!"

"But I suppose you have been taught, at least, to say your catechism—and you pray sometimes?"

"I have prayed to father not to beat me."

"But to God?"

"God, sir!—what is that?"*

Maltravers drew back, shocked and appalled. Premature philosopher as he was, this depth of ignorance perplexed his wisdom. He had read all the disputes of schoolmen, whether or not the notion of a Supreme Being is innate; but he had never before been brought face to face with one who was unconscious of a God.

After a pause, he said—"My poor girl, we misunderstand each other. You know that there is a God?"

"No, sir."

"Did no one ever tell you who made the stars you now survey—and the earth on which you tread?"

"No."

"And have you never thought of it yourself?"

"Why should I? What has that to do with being cold and hungry?"

Maltravers looked incredulous—"You see that great building, with the spire rising in the starlight?"

---

* This ignorance—indeed the whole sketch of Alice—is from the life; nor is such ignorance, accompanied by what almost seems an instinctive or intuitive notion of wright or wrong, very uncommon, as our police courts can testify. In the *Examiner* for, I think, the year 18 5, will be found the case of a young girl ill-treated by her father, whose answers to the interrogatories of the magistrate are very similar to those of Alice to the questions of Maltravers.

"Yes, sir, sure."

"What is it called?"

"Why, a church."

"Did you never go into it?"

"No."

"What do people do there?"

"Father says one man talks nonsense, and the other folk listen to him."

"Your father is——; no matter. Good heavens! what shall I do with this unhappy child?"

"Yes, sir, I am very unhappy," said Alice, catching at the last words: and the tears rolled silently down her cheeks.

Maltravers never was more touched in his life. Whatever thoughts of gallantry might have entered his young head, had he found Alice such as he might reasonably have expected, he now felt there was a kind of sanctity in her ignorance; and his gratitude and kindly sentiment towards her took almost a brotherly aspect.

"You know, at least, what school is?" he asked.

"Yes, I have talked with girls who go to school."

"Would you like to go there too?"

"Oh, no, sir—pray not!"

"What should you like to do, then?—Speak out, child. I owe you so much, that I should be too happy to make you comfortable and contented in your way."

"I should like to live with you sir." Maltravers started, and half smiled, and coloured. But looking on her eyes, which were fixed earnestly on his, there was so much artlessness in their soft, unconscious gaze, that he saw she was wholly ignorant of the interpretation that might be put upon so candid a confession.

I have said that Maltravers was a wild, enthusiastic, odd being— he was, in fact, full of strange German romance and metaphysical speculations. He had once shut himself up for months to study astrology—and been even suspected of a serious hunt after the philosopher's stone; another time he had narrowly escaped with life and liberty from a frantic conspiracy of the young republicans of his university, in which, being bolder and madder then most of them, he had been an active ringleader; it was, indeed, some such folly that had compelled him to quit Germany sooner than himself or his parents desired. He had nothing of the sober Englishman about him. Whatever was strange and eccentric had an irresistible charm for Ernest Maltravers. And agreeably to this disposition, he now revolved an idea that enchanted his mobile and fantastic philosophy. He himself would educate this charming girl—he would write fair and heavenly characters upon this blank page—he would act the Saint Preux to this Julie of Nature. Alas, he did not think of the result which the parallel should have suggested! At that age, Ernest Maltravers never damped the ardour of an experiment by the anticipation of consequences.

"So," he said, after a short reverie, "so you would like to live with me? But, Alice, we must not fall in love with each other."

"I don't understand, sir."

"Never mind," said Maltravers, a little disconcerted.

"I always wished to go into service."

"Ha!"

"And you would be a kind master."

Maltravers was half disenchanted.

"No very flattering preference," thought he: "so much the safer for us. Well, Alice, it shall be as you wish. Are you comfortable where you are, in your new lodging?"

"No."

"Why, they do not insult you?"

"No, but they make a noise, and I like to be quiet, to think of you."

The young philosopher was reconciled again to his scheme.

"Well, Alice—go back—I will take a cottage to-morrow, and you shall be my servant, and I will teach you to read and write, and say your prayers, and know that you have a Father above who loves you better than he below. Meet me again at the same hour to-morrow. Why do you cry, Alice? why do you cry?"

"Because—because," sobbed the girl, "I am so happy, and I shall live with you and see you."

"Go, child—go, child," said Maltravers, hastily; and he walked away with a quicker pulse than became his new character of master and preceptor.

He looked back, and saw the girl gazing at him; he waved his hand, and she moved on and followed him slowly back to the town.

Maltravers, though not an elder son, was the heir of affluent fortunes; he enjoyed a munificent allowance that sufficed for the whims of a youth who had learned in Germany none of the extravagant notions common to young Englishmen of similar birth and prospects. He was a spoiled child, with no law but his own fancy—his return home was not expected—there was nothing to prevent the indulgence of his new caprice. The next day he hired a cottage in the neighbourhood, which was one of those pretty thatched edifices, with verandahs and monthly roses, a conservatory and a lawn, which justify the English proverb about a cottage and love. It had been built by a mercantile bachelor for some fair Rosamond, and did credit to his taste. An old woman, let with the house, was to cook and do the work. Alice was but a nominal servant. Neither the old woman nor the landlord comprehended the Platonic intentions of the young stranger. But he paid his rent in advance, and they were not particular. He, however, thought it prudent to conceal his name. It was one sure to be known in a town not very distant from the residence of his father, a wealthy and long-descended country gentleman. He adopted, therefore, the common name of Butler; which, indeed, belonged to one of his maternal connections, and by that name alone was he known both in the neighbourhood and to Alice. From her he would not have sought concealment—but somehow or other no occasion ever presented itself to induce him to talk much to her of his parentage or birth.

CHAPTER V.

"Thought would destroy their Paradise."—GRAY.

MALTRAVERS found Alice as docile a pupil as any reasonable preceptor might have desired. But still, reading and writing—they are very uninteresting elements! Had the groundwork been laid, it might have been delightful to raise the fairy palace of knowledge; but the digging the foundations and the constructing the cellars is weary labour. Perhaps he felt it so—for in a few days Alice was handed over to the very oldest and ugliest writing-master that the neighbouring town could afford. The poor girl at first wept much at the exchange; but the grave remonstrances and solemn exhortations of Maltravers reconciled her at last, and she promised to work hard, and pay every attention to her lessons. I am not sure, however, that it was the tedium of the work that deterred the idealist—perhaps he felt its danger—and at the bottom of his sparkling dreams and brilliant follies lay a sound, generous, and noble heart. He was fond of pleasure, and had been already the darling of the sentimental German ladies. But he was too young, and too vivid, and too romantic, to be what is called a sensualist. He could not look upon a fair face, and a guileless smile, and all the ineffable symmetry of a woman's shape, with the eye of a man buying cattle for base uses. He very easily fell in love, or fancied he did, it is true—but then he could not separate desire from fancy, or calculate the game of passion without bringing the heart or the imagination into the matter. And though Alice was very pretty and very engaging, he was not yet in love with her, and he had no intention of becoming so.

He felt the evening somewhat long, when for the first time Alice discontinued her usual lesson; but Maltravers had abundant resources in himself. He placed Shakspeare and Schiller on his table, and lighted his German meerschaum—he read till he became inspired, and then he wrote—and when he had composed a few stanzas he was not contented till he had set them to music, and tried their melody with his voice. For he had all the passion of a German for song and music—that wild Maltravers !— and his voice was sweet, his taste consummate, his science profound. As the sun puts out a star, so the full blaze of his imagination, fairly kindled, extinguished for the time his fairy fancy for his beautiful pupil.

It was late that night when Maltravers went to bed—and as he passed through the narrow corridor that led to his chamber, he heard a light step flying before him, and caught the glimpse of a female figure escaping through a distant door. "The silly child!" thought he, at once divining the cause; "she has been listening to my singing. I shall scold her." But he forgot that resolution.

The next day, and the next, and many days passed, and Maltravers saw but little of the pupil for whose sake he had shut himself up in a country cottage, in the depth of winter. Still he did not repent his purpose, nor was he in the least tired of his seclusion—he would not inspect Alice's progress, for he was certain he should be dissatisfied with its slowness—and people, however handsome, cannot learn to read and write in a day. But he amused himself, notwithstanding. He was glad of an opportunity to be alone with his own thoughts, for he was at one of those periodical epochs of life when we like to pause and breathe awhile, in brief respite from that methodical race in which we run to the grave. He wished to re-collect the stores of his past experience, and repose on his own mind, before he started afresh upon the active world. The weather was cold and inclement; but Ernest

Maltravers was a hardy lover of nature, and neither snow nor frost could detain him from his daily rambles. So about noon, he regularly threw aside books and papers, and took his hat and staff, and went whistling or humming his favourite airs through the dreary streets, or along the bleak waters, or amidst the leafless woods, just as the humour seized him; for he was not an Edwin or Harold, who reserved speculation only for lonely brooks and pastoral hills. Maltravers delighted to contemplate nature in men as well as in sheep or trees. The humblest alley in a crowded town had something poetical for him; he was ever ready to mix in a crowd, if it were only gathered round a barrel-organ or a dog-fight, and listen to all that was said, and notice all that was done. And this I take to be the true poetical temperament essential to every artist who aspires to be something more than a scene-painter. But, above all things, he was most interested in any display of human passions or affections; he loved to see the true colours of the heart, where they are most transparent—in the uneducated and poor—for he was something of an optimist, and had a hearty faith in the loveliness of our nature. Perhaps, indeed, he owed much of the insight into and mastery over character that he was afterwards considered to display, to his disbelief that there is any wickedness so dark as not to be susceptible of the light in some place or another. But Maltravers had his fits of unsociability, and then nothing but the most solitary scenes delighted him. Winter or summer, barren waste or prodigal verdure, all had beauty in his eyes; for their beauty lay in his own soul, through which he beheld them. From these walks he would return home at dusk, take his simple meal, rhyme or read away the long evenings with such alteration as music or the dreamy thoughts of a young man with gay life before him could afford. Happy Maltravers!—youth and genius have luxuries all the Rothschilds cannot purchase! And yet, Maltravers, you are ambitious!—life moves too slowly for you!—you would push on the wheels of the clock!—Fool—brilliant fool!—you are eighteen, and a poet!—What more can you desire?—Bid time stop for ever!

One morning Ernest rose earlier than his wont, and sauntered carelessly through the conservatory which adjourned his sitting-room; observing the plants with placid curiosity (for besides being a little of a botanist, he had odd visionary notions about the life of plants, and he saw in them a hundred mysteries which the herbalists do not teach us), when he heard a low and very musical voice singing at a little distance. He listened, and recognised, with surprise, words of his own, which he had lately set to music, and was sufficiently pleased with to sing nightly.

When the song ended, Maltravers stole softly through the conservatory, and as he opened the door which led into the garden, he saw at the open window of a little room which was apportioned to Alice, and jutted out from the building in the fanciful irregularity common to ornamental cottages, the form of his discarded pupil. She did not observe him, and it was not till he twice called her by name that she started from her thoughtful and melancholy posture.

"Alice," said he, gently, "put on your bonnet, and walk with me in the garden; you look pale, child; the fresh air will do you good."

Alice coloured and smiled, and in a few minutes was by his side. Maltravers, meanwhile, had gone in and lighted his meerschaum, for it was his great inspirer whenever his thoughts were perplexed, or he felt his usual fluency likely to fail him, and such was the case now. With this faithful ally he awaited Alice in the little walk that circled the lawn, amidst shrubs and evergreens.

"Alice," said he, after a pause; but he stopped short.

Alice looked up to him with grave respect.

"Tush!" said Maltravers; "perhaps the smoke is unpleasant to you. It is a bad habit of mine."

"No, sir," answered Alice; and she seemed disappointed. Maltravers paused and picked up a snowdrop.

"It is pretty," he said; "do you love flowers?"

"Oh, dearly," answered Alice, with some enthusiasm; "I never saw many till I came here."

"Now then, I can go on," thought Maltravers; why, I cannot say, for I do not see the *sequiter;* but on he went *in medias res.* "Alice, you sing charmingly."

"Ah! sir, you—you—" she stopped abruptly, and trembled visibly.

"Yes, I overheard you, Alice."

"And you are angry?"

"I I—Heaven forbid! It is a *talent*, but you don't know what that is; I mean it is an excellent thing to have an ear, and a voice, and a heart for music; and you have all three."

He paused, for he felt his hand touched; Alice suddenly clasped and kissed it. Maltravers thrilled through his whole frame;

but there was something in the girl's look that showed she was wholly unaware that she had committed an unmaidenly or forward action.

"I was so afraid you would be angry," she said, wiping her eyes as she dropped his hand; "and now I suppose you know all."

"All!"

"Yes; how I listened to you every evening, and lay awake the whole night, with the music ringing in my ears, till I tried to go over it myself; and so at last I ventured to sing aloud. I like that much better than learning to read."

All this was delightful to Maltravers; the girl had touched upon one of his weak points; however, he remained silent. Alice continued—

"And now, sir, I hope you will let me come and sit outside the door every evening, and hear you. I will make no noise—I will be so quiet."

"What, in that cold corridor, these bitter nights?"

"I am used to cold, sir. Father would not let me have a fire when he was not at home."

"No, Alice, but you shall come into the room while I play, and I will give you a lesson or two. I am glad you have so good an ear; it may be a means of your earning your own honest livelihood when you leave me."

"When I——; but I never intend to leave you, sir!" said Alice, beginning fearfully, and ending calmly.

Maltravers had recourse to the meerschaum.

Luckily, perhaps, at this time, they were joined by Mr. Simcox, the old writing-master. Alice went in to prepare her books; but Maltravers laid his hand upon the preceptor's shoulder.

"You have a quick pupil, I hope, sir," said he.

"Oh, very, very, Mr. Butler. She comes on famously. She practises a great deal when I am away, and I do my best."

"And," asked Maltravers, in a grave tone, "have you succeeded in instilling into the poor child's mind some of those more sacred notions of which I spoke to you in our first meeting?"

"Why, sir, she was, indeed, quite a heathen—quite a Mahometan, I may say; but she is a little better now."

"What have you taught her?"

"That God made her."

"That is a great step."

"And that He loves good girls, and will watch over them."

"Bravo! you beat Plato."

"No, sir, I never beat anyone, except little Jack Turner; but he is a dunce."

"Bah! What else do you teach her?"

"That the devil runs away with bad girls, and——"

"Stop there, Mr. Simcox. Never mind the devil yet awhile. Let her first learn to do good, that God may love her; the rest will follow. I would rather make people religious through their best feelings than their worst—through their gratitude and affections, rather than their fears and calculations of risk and punishment."

Mr. Simcox stared.

"Does she say her prayers?"

"I have taught her a short one."

"Did she learn it readily?"

"Lord love her, yes! When I told her she ought to pray to God to bless her benefactor, she would not rest till I had repeated a prayer out of our Sunday-school book, and she got it by heart at once."

"Enough, Mr. Simcox. I will not detain you longer."

Forgetful of his untasted breakfast, Maltravers continued his meerschaum and his reflections; he did not cease till he had convinced himself that he was but doing his duty to Alice, by teaching her to cultivate the charming talent she evidently possessed, and through which she might secure her own independence. He fancied that he should thus relieve himself of a charge and responsibility which often perplexed him. Alice would leave him, enabled to walk the world in an honest professional path. It was an excellent idea. "But there is danger," whispered Conscience. "Ay," answered Philosophy and Pride, those wise dupes that are always so solemn, and always so taken in; "but what is virtue without trial?"

And now every evening, when the windows were closed, and the hearth burnt clear, while the winds stormed, and the rain beat without, a lithe and lovely shape hovered about the student's chamber; and his wild songs were sung by a voice which Nature had made even sweeter than his own.

Alice's talent for music was indeed surprising; enthusiastic and quick as he himself was in all he undertook, Maltravers was amazed at her rapid progress. He soon taught her to play by ear; and Maltravers could not but notice that her hand, always delicate in shape, had lost the rude colour and roughness of labour. He thought of that pretty hand more often than he ought to have done, and guided it over the keys, when it could have found its way very well without him.

On coming to the cottage, he had directed the old servant to provide suitable and proper clothes for Alice; but now that she was admitted "to sit with the gentleman," the crone had the sense, without waiting for new orders, to buy the "pretty young woman" garments, still, indeed, simple, but of better materials and less rustic fashion; and Alice's redundant tresses were now carefully arranged into orderly and glossy curls, and even the texture was no longer the same; and happiness and health bloomed on her downy cheeks, and smiled from the dewy lips, which never quite closed over the fresh white teeth, except when she was sad;—but that seemed never, now she was not banished from Maltravers.

To say nothing of the unusual grace and delicacy of Alice's form and features, there is nearly always something of Nature's own gentility in very young women (except, indeed, when they get together and fall a-giggling); it shames us men to see how much sooner they are polished into conventional shape than our rough, masculine angles. A vulgar boy requires, Heaven knows what assiduity, to move three steps—I do not say like a gentleman, but like a body that has a soul in it; but give the least advantage of society or tuition to a peasant girl, and a hundred to one but she will glide into refinement before the boy can make a bow without upsetting the table. There is sentiment in all women, and sentiment gives delicacy to thought, and tact to manner. But sentiment with men is generally acquired, an offspring of the intellectual quality, not, as with the other sex, of the moral.

In the course of his musical and vocal lessons, Maltravers gently took the occasion to correct poor Alice's frequent offences against grammar and accent; and her memory was prodigiously quick and retentive. The very tones of her voice seemed altered in the ear of Maltravers; and, somehow or other, the time came when he was no longer sensible of the difference in their rank.

The old woman-servant, when she had seen how it would be from the first, and taken a pride in her own prophecy, as she ordered Alice's new dresses, was a much better philosopher than Maltravers; though he was already up to his ears in the moonlit abyss of Plato; and had filled a dozen common-place books with criticisms on Kant.

CHAPTER VI.

"Young man, I fear thy blood is rosy red,
Thy heart is soft."
—D'AGUILAR's *Fiesco*, Act iii. Sc. 1.

AS education does not consist in reading and writing only, so Alice, while still very backward in those elementary arts, forestalled some of their maturest results in her intercourse with Maltravers. Before the inoculation took effect, she caught knowledge in the natural way. For the refinement of a graceful mind and a happy manner is very contagious. And Maltravers was encouraged by her quickness in music to attempt such instruction in other studies as conversation could afford. It is a better school than parents and masters think, for there was a time when all information was given orally; and probably the Athenians learned more from hearing Aristotle than we do from reading him. It was a delicious revival of Academe—in the walks, or beneath the rustic porticoes of that little cottage—the romantic philosopher and the beautiful disciple! And his talk was much like that of a sage of the early world, with some wistful and earnest savage for a listener: of the stars and their courses—of beasts, and birds, and fishes, and plants, and flowers—the wide family of Nature—of the beneficence and power of God—of the mystic and spiritual history of Man.

Charmed by her attention and docility, Maltravers at length diverged from lore into poetry; he would repeat to her the simplest and most natural passages he could remember in his favourite poets; he would himself compose verses elaborately adapted to her understanding; she liked the last the best, and learned them the easiest. Never had young poet a more gracious inspiration, and never did this inharmonious world more complacently resolve itself into soft dreams, as if to humour the novitiate of the victims it must speedily take into its joyless priesthood. And Alice had now quietly and insensibly carved out her own avocations—the tenor of her service. The plants in the conservatory had passed under her care, and no one else was privileged to touch Maltravers' books, or arrange the sacred litter of a student's apartment. When he came down in the morning, or returned from his walks, everything was in order, yet by a kind of magic, just as he wished it; the flowers he loved best bloomed, fresh-gathered, on his table; the very position of the large chair, just in that corner by the fireplace, whence, on entering the room, its hospitable arms opened with the most cordial air of welcome, bespoke the presiding genius of a woman; and then, precisely as the clock struck eight, Alice entered, so pretty and smiling, and happy-looking, that it was no wonder the single hour at first allotted to her extended into three.

Was Alice in love with Maltravers?— She certainly did not exhibit the symptoms in the ordinary way—she did not grow more reserved, and agitated, and timid—there was no worm in the bud of her damask cheek; nay, though from the first she had been tolerably bold, she was more free and confidential, more at her ease every day; in fact she never for a moment suspected that she ought to be otherwise; she had not the conventional and sensitive delicacy of girls, who, whatever their rank of life, had been taught that there is a mystery and a peril in love; she had a vague idea about girls going wrong, but she did not know that love had anything to do with it; on the contrary, according to her father, it had connection with money, not love; all that she felt was so natural and so very sinless. Could she help being so delighted to listen to him, and so grieved to depart? What thus she felt she expressed, no less simply and no less guilelessly: and the candour sometimes completely blinded and misled him. No, she could not be in love, or she could not so frankly own that she loved him—it was a sisterly and grateful sentiment.

"The dear girl—I am rejoiced to think so," said Maltravers to himself; "I knew there would be no danger."

Was he not in love himself?—the reader must decide.

"Alice," said Maltravers, one evening, after a long pause of thought and abstraction on his side, while she was unconsciously practising her last lesson on the piano—"Alice—no don't turn round—sit where you are, but listen to me. We cannot live always in this way."

Alice was instantly disobedient—she did turn round, and those great blue eyes were fixed on his own with such anxiety and alarm, that he had no resource but to get up and look round for the meerschaum. But Alice, who divined by an instinct his lightest wish, brought it to him, while he was yet hunting, amidst the further corners of the room, in places were it was not certain to be. There it was, already filled with the fragrant Salonica, glittering with the gilt pastile, which, not too healthfully, adulterates the seductive weed with odours that pacify the repugnant censure of the fas-

tidious—for Maltravers was an epicurean even in his worst habits;
—there it was, I say, in that pretty hand which he had to touch as
he took it; and while he lit the weed, he had again to blush and
shrink beneath those great blue eyes.

"Thank you, Alice," he said; "thank you. Do sit down—there
—out of the draught. I am going to open the window, the night is
so lovely."

He opened the casement, overgrown with creepers, and the
moonlight lay fair and breathless upon the smooth lawn. The
calm and holiness of the night soothed and elevated his thoughts,
he had cut himself off from the eyes of Alice, and he proceeded
with a firm, though gentle voice—

"My dear Alice, we cannot always live together in this way;
you are now wise enough to understand me, so listen patiently.
A young woman never wants a fortune as long as she has a good
character; she is always poor and despised without one. Now,
a good character in this world is lost as much by imprudence as
guilt; and if you were to live with me much longer, it would be
imprudent, and your character would suffer so much that you
would not be able to make your own way in the world; far, then,
from doing you a service, I should have done you a deadly injury,
which I could not atone for: besides, heaven knows what may
happen worse than imprudence; for, I am very sorry to say,"
added Maltravers, with great gravity, "that you are much too pretty
and engaging to—to—in short, it won't do. I must go home; my
friends will have a right to complain of me if I remain thus lost to
them many weeks longer. And you, my dear Alice, are now sufficiently advanced to receive better instruction than I or Mr.
Simcox can give you. I therefore propose to place you in some
respectable family, where you will have more comfort, and a higher
station than you have here. You can finish your education, and
instead of being taught, you will be thus enabled to become a
teacher to others. With your beauty, Alice" (and Maltravers
sighed), "and natural talents, and amiable temper, you have only
to act well and prudently, to secure at last a worthy husband and a
happy home. Have you heard me, Alice! Such is the plan I
have formed for you."

The young man thought as he spoke, with honest kindness and
upright honour; it was a bitterer sacrifice than perhaps the reader
thinks for. But Maltravers, if he had an impassioned, had not a
selfish heart; and he felt, to use his own expression, more emphatic

than eloquent, that "it would not do" to live any longer alone with this beautiful girl, like the two children whom the good Fairy kept safe from sin and the world in the Pavilion of Roses.

But Alice comprehended neither the danger to herself, nor the temptations that Maltravers, if he could not resist, desired to shun. She rose, pale and trembling—approached Maltravers, and laid her hand gently on his arm.

"I will go away, when and where you wish—the sooner the better—to-morrow—yes, to-morrow ; you are ashamed of poor Alice ; and it has been very silly of me to be so happy." (She struggled with her emotion for a moment, and went on.) "You know heaven can hear me, even when I am away from you, and when I know more I can pray better ; and heaven will bless you, sir, and make you happy, for I never can pray for anything else."

With those words she turned away, and walked proudly towards the door. But when she reached the threshold, she stopped and looked round, as if to take a last farewell. All the associations and memories of that beloved spot rushed upon her—she gasped for breath—tottered—and fell to the ground insensible.

Maltravers was already by her side ; he lifted her light weight in his arms ; he uttered wild and impassioned exclamations—"Alice, beloved Alice—forgive me ; we will never part!" He chafed her hands in his own, while her head lay on his bosom, and he kissed again and again those beautiful eyelids, till they opened slowly upon him, and the tender arms tightened round him involuntarily.

"Alice," he whispered—"Alice, dear Alice, I love thee." Alas, it was true : he loved—and forgot all but that love. He was eighteen.

CHAPTER VII.

"How like a younker or a prodigal,
The scarfed bark puts from her native bay!"
—*Merchant of Venice.*

WE are apt to connect the voice of conscience with the stillness of midnight. But I think we wrong that innocent hour. It is that terrible "NEXT MORNING," when reason is wide awake, upon which remorse fastens its fangs. Has a man gambled away his all, or shot his friend in a duel—has he committed a crime, or incurred a laugh—it is the *next morning*, when the irretrievable Past rises before him like a spectre; then doth the churchyard of memory yield up its grisly dead—then is the witching hour when the foul fiend within us can least tempt perhaps, but most torment. At night we have one thing to hope for, one refuge to fly to—oblivion and sleep! But at morning, sleep is over, and we are called upon coldly to review, and re-act, and live again the waking bitterness of self-reproach. Maltravers rose a penitent and unhappy man—remorse was new to him, and he felt as if he had committed a treacherous and fraudulent, as well as guilty deed. This poor girl, she was so innocent, so confiding, so unprotected, even by her own sense of right. He went downstairs listless and dispirited. He longed yet dreaded to encounter Alice. He heard her step in the conservatory—paused, irresolute, and at length joined her. For the first time she blushed and trembled, and her eyes shunned his. But when he kissed her hand in silence, she whispered, "And am I now to leave you?" And Maltravers answered fervently, "Never!" and then her face grew so radiant with joy, that Maltravers was comforted despite himself. Alice knew no remorse, though she felt agitated and ashamed; as she had not comprehended the danger, neither was she aware of the fall. In fact, she never thought of herself. Her whole soul was with him; she gave him back in love the spirit she had caught from him in knowledge.

And they strolled together through the garden all that day, and Maltravers grew reconciled to himself. He had done wrong, it is true; but then perhaps Alice had already suffered as much as she could in the world's opinion, by living with him alone, though innocent, so long. And now she had an everlasting claim to his protection—she should never know shame or want. And the love that had led to the wrong, should, by fidelity and devotion, take from it the character of sin.

Natural and commonplace sophistries! *L'homme se pique!* as old Montaigne said; Man is his own sharper! The conscience is the most elastic material in the world. To-day you cannot stretch it over a mole-hill, to-morrow it hides a mountain.

O how happy they were now—that young pair! How the days flew like dreams! Time went on, winter passed away, and the early spring, with its flowers and sunshine, was like a mirror to their own youth. Alice never accompanied Maltravers in his walks abroad, partly because she feared to meet her father, and partly because Maltravers himself was fastidiously averse to all publicity. But then they had all that little world of three acres—lawn and fountain, shrubbery and terrace, to themselves, and Alice never asked if there was any other world without. She was now quite a scholar, as Mr. Simcox himself averred. She could read aloud and fluently to Maltravers, and copied out his poetry in a small, fluctuating hand, and he had no longer to chase throughout his vocabulary for short Saxon monosyllables to make the bridge of intercourse between their ideas. Eros and Psyche are ever united, and Love opens all the petals of the soul. On one subject alone Maltravers was less eloquent than of yore. He had not succeeded as a moralist, and he thought it hypocritical to preach what he did not practise. But Alice was gentler and purer, and as far as she knew, sweet fool! better than ever—she had invented a new prayer for herself; and she prayed as regularly and as fervently as if she were doing nothing amiss. But the code of heaven is gentler than that of earth, and does not declare that ignorance excuseth not the crime.

CHAPTER VIII.

"Some clouds sweep on as vultures for their prey.
 . . . .
No azure more shall robe the firmament,
Nor spangled stars be glorious."
—BYRON, *Heaven and Earth.*

IT was a lovely evening in April, the weather was unusually mild and serene for the time of the year, in the northern districts of our isle, and the bright drops of a recent shower sparkled upon the buds of the lilac and laburnum that clustered round the cottage of Maltravers. The little fountain that played in the centre of a circular basin, on whose clear surface the broad-leaved water-lily cast its fairy shadow, added to the fresh green of the lawn—

"And softè as velvèt the yongè grass,"

on which the rare and early flowers were closing their heavy lids. That twilight shower had given a racy and vigorous sweetness to the air which stole over many a bank of violets, and slightly stirred the golden ringlets of Alice as she sat by the side of her entranced and silent lover. They were seated on a rustic bench just without the cottage, and the open windows behind them admitted the view of that happy room—with its litter of books and musical instruments—eloquent of the POETRY OF HOME.

Maltravers was silent, for his flexile and excitable fancy was conjuring up a thousand shapes along the transparent air, or upon those shadowy violet banks. He was not thinking, he was imagining. His genius reposed dreamily upon the calm but exquisite sense of his happiness. Alice was not absolutely in his thoughts, but unconsciously she coloured them all—if she had left his side, the whole charm would have been broken. But Alice, who was not a poet or a genius, *was* thinking, and thinking only of Maltravers. . . . His image was "the broken mirror" multiplied in a thousand faithful fragments over everything fair and soft in that lovely microcosm before her. But they were both alike in one thing—they were not with the Future, they were sensible of the Present—the sense of the actual life, the enjoyment of the breathing time, was strong within them. Such is the privilege of the extremes of our existence—Youth and Age. Middle life is never with to-day, its home is in to-morrow. . . . anxious, and scheming, and desiring, and wishing this plot ripened and that hope fulfilled, while every wave of the forgotten Time brings it nearer and nearer to the end of all things. Half our life is consumed in longing to be nearer death.

"Alice," said Maltravers, waking at last from his reverie, and drawing that light, childlike form nearer to him, "you enjoy this hour as much as I do."

"Oh, much more!"

"More! and why so?"

"Because I am thinking of you, and perhaps you are not thinking of yourself."

Maltravers smiled and stroked those beautiful ringlets, and kissed that smooth, innocent forehead, and Alice nestled herself in his breast.

"How young you look by this light, Alice!" said he, tenderly looking down

"Would you love me less if I were old?" asked Alice.

"I suppose I should never have loved you in the same way if you had been old when I first saw you."

"Yet I am sure I should have felt the same for you if you had been—oh! ever so old!"

"What, with wrinkled cheeks, and palsied head, and a brown wig, and no teeth, like Mr. Simcox?"

"Oh, but you could never be like that! You would always look young—your heart would be always in your face. That dear smile—ah, you would look beautiful to the last!"

"But Simcox, though not very lovely now, has been, I dare say, handsomer than I am, Alice; and I shall be contented to look as well when I am as old!"

"I should never know you were old, because I can see you just as I please. Sometimes, when you are thoughtful, your brows meet, and you look so stern that I tremble; but then I think of you when you last smiled, and look up again, and though you are frowning still, you seem to smile. I am sure you are different to other eyes than to mine. . . . and time must kill *me* before, in my sight, it could alter *you*."

"Sweet Alice, you talk eloquently, for you talk love."

"My heart talks to you. Ah! I wish it could say all it felt. I wish it could make poetry like you, or that words were music—I would never speak to you in anything else. I was so delighted to learn music, because when I played I seemed to be talking to you. I am sure that whoever invented music did it because he loved dearly and wanted to say so. I said '*he*,' but I think it was a woman. Was it?"

"The Greeks I told you of, and whose life was music, thought it was a god."

"Ah, but you say the Greeks made Love a god. Were they wicked for it?"

"Our own God above is Love," said Ernest, seriously, "as our own poets have said and sung. But it is a love of another nature—divine, not human. Come, we will go within, the air grows cold for you."

They entered, his arm round her waist. The room smiled upon them its quiet welcome; and Alice, whose heart had not half vented its fulness, sat down to the instrument, still to "talk love" in her own way.

But it was Saturday evening. Now, every Saturday Maltravers received from the neighbouring town the provincial newspaper—it was his only medium of communication with the great world. But it was not for that communication that he always seized it with avidity, and fed on it with interest. The county in which his father resided bordered on the shire in which Ernest sojourned, and the paper included the news of that familiar district in its comprehensive columns. It, therefore, satisfied Ernest's conscience and soothed his filial anxieties to read from time to time, that "Mr. Maltravers was entertaining a distinguished party of friends at his noble mansion of Lisle Court;" or that "Mr. Maltravers' foxhounds had met on such a day at something copse;" or that "Mr. Maltravers, with his usual munificence, had subscribed twenty guineas to the new county goal." ... And as now Maltravers saw the expected paper laid beside the hissing urn, he seized it eagerly, tore the envelope, and hastened to the well-known corner appropriated to the paternal district. The very first words that struck his eyes were these:

"ALARMING ILLNESS OF MR. MALTRAVERS.

"We regret to state that this exemplary and distinguished gentleman was suddenly seized, on Wednesday night, with a severe spasmodic affection. Dr. —— was immediately sent for, who pronounced it to be gout in the stomach—the first medical assistance from London has been summoned.

"Postscript.—We have just learned, in answer to our inquiries at Lisle Court, that the respected owner is considerably worse: but slight hopes are entertained of his recovery. Captain Maltravers, his eldest son and heir, is at Lisle Court. An express has been despatched in search of Mr. Ernest Maltravers, who, involved by his high English spirit in some dispute with the authorities of a despotic government, had suddenly disappeared from Gottingen, where his extraordinary talents had highly distinguished him. He is supposed to be staying at Paris."

The paper dropped on the floor. Ernest threw himself back on the chair, and covered his face with his hands.

Alice was beside him in a moment. He looked up, and caught her wistful and terrified gaze. "Oh, Alice!" he cried, bitterly, and almost pushing her away, "if you could but guess my remorse!" Then springing on his feet, he hurried from the room.

Presently the whole house was in commotion. The gardener, who was always in the house about supper time, flew to the town for post-horses. The old woman was in despair about the laundress, for her first and only thought was for "master's shirts." Ernest locked himself in his room. Alice! poor Alice!

In little more than twenty minutes the chaise was at the door, and Ernest, pale as death, came into the room where he had left Alice.

She was seated on the floor, and the fatal paper was on her lap.

She had been endeavouring, in vain, to learn what had so sensibly affected Maltravers, for, as I said before, she was unacquainted with his real name, and therefore the ominous paragraph did not even arrest her eye.

He took the paper from her, for he wanted again and again to read it; some little word of hope or encouragement must have escaped him. And then Alice flung herself on his breast. "Do not weep," said he; "heaven knows I have sorrow enough of my own! My father is dying! So kind, so generous, so indulgent! O God, forgive me! Compose yourself, Alice. You will hear from me in a day or two."

He kissed her; but the kiss was cold and forced. He hurried away. She heard the wheels grate on the pebbles. She rushed to the window; but that beloved face was not visible. Maltravers had drawn the blinds, and thrown himself back to indulge his grief. A moment more, and even the vehicle that bore him away was gone. And before her were the flowers, and the starlit lawn, and the playful fountain, and the bench where they had sat in such heartfelt and serene delight. He was gone; and often—oh, how often, did Alice remember that his last words had been uttered in estranged tones—that his last embrace had been without love!

CHAPTER IX.

> "Thy due from me
> Is tears: and heavy sorrows of the blood,
> Which nature, love, and filial tenderness,
> Shall, O dear father, pay thee plenteously!"
> —*Second Part of Henry IV.*, Act iv. Sc. 4.

IT was late at night when the chaise that bore Maltravers stopped at the gates of a park lodge. It seemed an age before the peasant within was aroused from the deep sleep of labour-loving health. "My father," he cried, while the gate creaked on its hinges; "my father—is he better? Is he alive?"

"Oh, bless your heart, Master Ernest, the squire was a little better this evening."

"Thank heaven! On—on!"

The horses smoked and galloped along a road that wound through venerable and ancient groves. The moonlight slept soft upon the sward, and the cattle, disturbed from their sleep, rose lazily up, and gazed upon the unseasonable intruder.

It is a wild and weird scene, one of those noble English parks at midnight, with its rough forest-ground broken into dell and valley, its never-innovated and mossy grass, overrun with fern, and its immemorial trees, that have looked upon the birth, and look yet upon the graves, of a hundred generations. Such spots are the last proud and melancholy trace of Norman knighthood and old romance, left to the laughing landscapes of cultivated England. They always throw something of shadow and solemn gloom upon minds that feel their associations, like that which belongs to some ancient and holy edifice. They are the cathedral aisles of Nature, with their darkened vistas, and columned trunks, and arches of mighty foliage. But in ordinary times the gloom is pleasing, and more delightful than all the cheerful lawns and sunny slopes of the modern taste. *Now* to Maltravers it was ominous and oppressive; the darkness of death seemed brooding in every shadow, and its warning voice moaning in every breeze.

The wheels stopped again. Lights flitted across the basement storey; and one above, more dim than the rest, shone palely from the room in which the sick man slept. The bell rang shrilly out from amidst the dark ivy that clung around the porch. The heavy door swung back—Maltravers was on the threshold. His father lived—was better—was awake. The son was in the father's arms.

CHAPTER X.

"The guardian oak
Mourned o'er the roof it sheltered: the thick air
Laboured with doleful sounds.
—ELLIOTT *of Sheffield.*

MANY days had passed, and Alice was still alone; but she had heard twice from Maltravers. The letters were short and hurried. One time his father was better, and there were hopes; another time, and it was not expected that he could survive the week. They were the first letters Alice had ever received from him. Those *first* letters are an event in a girl's life—in Alice's life they were a very melancholy one. Ernest did not ask her to write to him; in fact, he felt, at such an hour, a repugnance to disclose his real name, and receive the letters of clandestine love in the house in which a father lay in death. He might have given the feigned address he had previously assumed, at some distant post-town, where his person was not known. But, then, to obtain such letters he must quit his father's side for hours. The thing was impossible. These difficulties Maltravers did not explain to Alice.

She thought it singular he did not wish to hear from her; but Alice was humble. What could she say worth troubling him with, and at such an hour? But how kind in him to write! how precious those letters! and yet they disappointed her, and cost her floods of tears: they were so short—so full of sorrow—there was so little love in them; and "dear," or even "*dearest* Alice," that uttered by the voice was so tender, looked cold upon the lifeless paper. If she but knew the exact spot where he was, it would be some comfort; but she only knew that he was away, and in grief; and though he was little more than thirty miles distant, she felt as if immeasurable space divided them. However, she consoled herself as she could: and strove to shorten the long, miserable day by playing over all the airs he liked, and reading all the passages he had commended. She should be so improved when he returned; and how lovely the garden would look: for every day its trees and bosquets caught a new smile from the deepening spring. Oh, they would be so happy once more! Alice *now* learned the life that lies in the future; and her young heart had not, as yet, been taught that of that future there is any prophet but Hope!

Maltravers, on quitting the cottage had forgotten that Alice was without money, and now that he found his stay would be indefinitely prolonged, he sent a remittance. Several bills were unpaid—some portion of the rent was due; and Alice, as she was desired, entrusted the old servant with a bank note, with which she was to discharge these petty debts. One evening, as she brought Alice the surplus, the good dame seemed greatly discomposed. She was pale and agitated; or, as she expressed it, "had a terrible fit of the shakes."

"What is the matter, Mrs. Jones? you have no news of him—of —of my—of your master?"

"Dear heart, miss—no," answered Mrs. Jones; "how should I? But I'm sure I don't wish to frighten you; there has been two sitch robberies in the neighbourhood!"

"Oh, thank heaven, that's all!" exclaimed Alice.

"Oh, don't go for to thank heaven for that, miss; it's a shocking thing for two lone females like us, and them ere windows all open to the ground! You sees, as I was taking the note to be changed at Mr. Harris's, the great grocer's shop, where all the poor folk was a buying agin to-morrow" (for it was Saturday night, the second Saturday after Ernest's departure; from that hegira Alice dated all chronology), "and everybody was a talking about the robberies last night. La, miss, they bound old Betty—you know Betty—a most respectable 'oman, who has known sorrows, and drinks tea with me once a week. Well, miss, they (only think!) bound Betty to the bed-post, with nothing on her but her shift—poor old soul! And as Mr. Harris gave me the change (please to see, miss, it's all right), and I asked for half gould, miss, it's more convenient, sitch an ill-looking fellow was by me, a buying o' baccy, and he did so stare at the money, that I vows I thought he'd have rin away with it from the counter; so I grabbled it up and went away. But, would you believe, miss, just as I got into the lane, afore you turns through the gate, I chanced to look back, and there, sure enough, was that ugly fellow close behind, a running like mad. Oh, I set up such a skreetch; and young Dobbins was a taking his cow out of the field, and he perked up over the hedge when he heard me; and the cow, too, with her horns, Lord bless her! So the fellow stopped, and I bustled through the gate, and got home. But la, miss, if we are all robbed and murdered?"

Alice had not heard much of this harangue; but what she did hear very slightly affected her strong, peasant-born nerves; not half so much, indeed, as the noise Mrs. Jones made in double-locking all the doors and windows—which operation occupied at least an hour and a half.

And at last all was still. Mrs. Jones had gone to bed—in the arms of sleep she had forgotten her terrors—and Alice had crept upstairs, and undressed, and said her prayers, and wept a little; and, with the tears yet moist upon her dark eyelashes, had glided into dreams of Ernest. Midnight was passed—the stroke of One sounded unheard from the clock at the foot of the stairs. The moon was gone—a slow, drizzling rain was falling upon the flowers, and cloud and darkness gathered fast and thick around the sky.

About this time, a low, regular, grating sound commenced at the thin shutters of the sitting-room below, preceded by a very faint noise, like the tinkling of small fragments of glass on the gravel without. At length it ceased, and the cautious and partial gleam of a lanthorn fell along the floor; another moment, and two men stood in the room.

"Hush, Jack!" whispered one; "hang out the glim, and let's look about us."

The dark-lanthorn, now fairly unmuffled, presented to the gaze of the robbers nothing that could gratify their cupidity. Books and music, chairs, tables, carpet, and fire-irons, though valuable enough in a house-agent's inventory, are worthless to the eyes of a housebreaker. They muttered a mutual curse.

"Jack," said the former speaker, "we must make a dash at the spoons and forks, and then hey for the money. The old girl had thirty shiners, besides flimsies."

The accomplice nodded consent; the lanthorn was again partially shaded, and with noiseless and stealthy steps the men quitted the apartment. Several minutes elapsed, when Alice was awakened from her slumber by a loud scream: she started, all was again silent: she must have dreamt it: her little heart beat violently at first, but gradually regained its tenor. She rose, however, and the kindness of her nature being more susceptible than her fear—she imagined Mrs. Jones might be ill—she would go to her. With this idea she began partially dressing herself, when she distinctly heard heavy footsteps and a strange voice in the room beyond. She was now thoroughly alarmed—her first impulse was to escape from the house—her next to bolt the door, and call aloud for assistance. But who would hear her cries? Between the two purposes she halted irresolute . . . and remained, pale and trembling, seated at the foot of the bed, when a broad light streamed through the chinks of the door—an instant more, and a rude hand seized her.

"Come, mem; don't be fritted, we won't harm you; but where's the gold-dust—where's the money?—the old girl says you've got it. Fork it over."

"O mercy, mercy! John Walters, is that you?"

"Damnation!" muttered the man, staggering back, "so you knows me, then: but you shan't peach; you shan't scrag me, b—t you."

While he spoke, he again seized Alice, held her forcibly down with one hand, while with the other he deliberately drew from a side pouch a long case-knife. In that moment of deadly peril, the second ruffian, who had been hitherto delayed in securing the servant, rushed forward. He had heard the exclamation of Alice, he heard the threat of his comrade; he darted to the bedside, cast a hurried gaze upon Alice, and hurled the intended murderer to the other side of the room.

"What, man, art mad?" he growled between his teeth. "Don't you know her? It is Alice;—it is my daughter."

Alice had sprung up when released from the murderer's knife, and now, with eyes strained and starting with horror, gazed upon the dark and evil face of her deliverer.

"O God! it is—it is my father!" she muttered, and fell senseless.

"Daughter or no daughter," said John Walters, "I shall not put my scrag in her power; recollect how she fritted us before, when she run away."

Darvil stood, thoughtful and perplexed—and his associate approached doggedly, with a look of such settled ferocity as it was impossible for even Darvil to contemplate without a shudder.

"You say right," muttered the father, after a pause; but fixing his strong gripe on his comrade's shoulder—"the girl must not be left here—the cart has a covering. We are leaving the country; I have a right to my daughter—she shall go with us. There, man, grab the money—it's on the table . . . you've got the spoons. Now then——" as Darvil spoke he seized his daughter in his arms; threw over her a shawl and a cloak that lay at hand, and was already on the threshold.

"I don't half like it," said Walters, grumblingly; "it been't safe."

"At least it is as safe as murder!" answered Darvil, turning round, with a ghastly grin. "Make haste."

When Alice recovered her senses, the dawn was breaking slowly along desolate and sullen hills. She was lying upon rough straw—the cart was jolting over the ruts of a precipitous, lonely road—and by her side scowled the face of that dreadful father.

CHAPTER XI.

"Yet he beholds her with the eyes of mind—
He sees the form which he no more shall meet—
She like a passionate thought is come and gone,
While at his feet the bright rill bubbles on."
—ELLIOTT *of Sheffield.*

IT was a little more than three weeks after that fearful night, when the chaise of Maltravers stopped at the cottage door—the windows were shut up; no one answered the repeated summons of the post-boy. Maltravers himself, alarmed and amazed, descended from the vehicle: he was in deep mourning. He went impatiently to the back entrance; that also was locked; round to the French windows of the drawing-room, always hitherto half-opened, even in the frosty days of winter—they were now closed like the rest. He shouted in terror, "Alice, Alice!"—no sweet voice answered in breathless joy, no fairy step bounded forward in welcome. At this moment, however, appeared the form of the gardener coming across the lawn. The tale was soon told; the house had been robbed—the old woman at morning found gagged and fastened to her bed-post—Alice flown. A magistrate had been applied to—suspicion fell upon the fugitive. None knew anything of her origin or name, not even the old woman. Maltravers had naturally and sedulously ordained Alice to preserve that secret, and she was too much in fear of being detected and claimed by her father not to obey the injunction with scrupulous caution. But it was known, at least, that she had entered the house a poor peasant girl; and what more common than for ladies of a certain description to run away from their lover, and take some of his property by mistake? And a poor girl like Alice, what else could be expected? The magistrate smiled, and the constables laughed. After all it was a good joke at the young gentleman's expense! Perhaps, as they had no orders from Maltravers, and they did not know where to find him, and thought he would be little inclined to prosecute, the search was not very rigorous. But two houses had been robbed the night before. Their owners were more on the alert. Suspicion fell upon a man of infamous character, John Walters; he had disappeared from the place. He had been last seen with an idle, drunken fellow, who was said to have known better days, and who at one time had been a skilful and well-paid mechanic, till his habits of theft and drunkenness threw him out of employ; and he had been since accused of connection with a gang of coiners—tried—and escaped from want of sufficient evidence against him. That man was Luke Darvil. His cottage was searched; but he also had fled. The trace of cart-wheels by the gate of Maltravers gave a faint clue to pursuit, and after an active search of some days, persons answering to the description of the suspected burglars—with a young female in their company—were tracked to a small inn, notorious as a resort for smugglers, by the sea-coast. But there every vestige of their supposed whereabouts disappeared.

And all this was told to the stunned Maltravers; the garrulity of the gardener precluded the necessity of his own inquiries, and the name of Darvil explained to him all that was dark to others. And Alice was suspected of the basest and the blackest guilt! Obscure, beloved, protected as she had been, she could not escape the calumny from which he had hoped everlastingly to shield her. But did *he* share that hateful thought? Maltravers was too generous and too enlightened.

"Dog!" said he, grinding his teeth, and clenching his hands at the startled menial, "dare to utter a syllable of suspicion against her, and I will trample the breath out of your body!"

The old woman, who had vowed that for the 'varsal world she would not stay in the house after such a "night of shakes," had now learned the news of her master's return, and came hobbling up to him. She arrived in time to hear his menace to her fellow-servant.

"Ah, that's right; give it him, your honour, bless your good heart—that's what I says. Miss rob the house! says I—Miss run away. Oh no—depend on it they have murdered her and buried the body."

Maltravers gasped for breath, and without uttering another word he re-entered the chaise, and drove to the house of the magistrate. He found that functionary a worthy and intelligent man of the world. To him he confided the secret of Alice's birth and his own. The magistrate concurred with him in believing that Alice had been discovered and removed by her father. New search was made—gold was lavished. Maltravers himself headed the search in person. But all came to the same result as before, save that by the descriptions he heard of the person—the dress—the tears of the young female who had accompanied the men supposed to be Darvil and Walters, he was satisfied that Alice yet lived; he hoped she might yet escape and return. In that hope he lingered for weeks—for months, in the neighbourhood; but time passed and no tidings. . . . He was forced at length to quit a neighbourhood at once so saddened and endeared. But he secured a friend in the magistrate, who promised to communicate with him if Alice returned, or her father was discovered. He enriched Mrs. Jones for life, in gratitude for her vindication of his lost and early love; he promised the amplest rewards for the smallest clue. And with a crushed and desponding spirit, he obeyed at last the repeated and anxious summons of the guardian to whose care, until his majority was attained, the young orphan was now entrusted.

CHAPTER XII.

"Sure there are poets that did never dream
Upon Parnassus."—DENHAM.

"Walk sober off, before a sprightlier age
Come tittering on, and shove you from the stage."—POPE.

"Hence to repose your trust in me was wise."
—DRYDEN'S *Absalom and Achitophel*.

MR. FREDERICK CLEVELAND, a younger son of the Earl of Byrneham, and therefore entitled to the style and distinction of "Honourable," was the guardian of Ernest Maltravers. He was now about the age of forty-three; a man of letters and a man of fashion, if the last half-obsolete expression be permitted to us, as being at least more classical and definite than any other which modern euphuism has invented to convey the same meaning. Highly educated, and with natural abilities considerably above mediocrity, Mr. Cleveland early in life had glowed with the ambition of an author. . . . He had written well and gracefully, but his success, though respectable, did not satisfy his aspirations. The fact is, that a new school of literature ruled the public, despite the critics—a school very different from that in which Mr. Cleveland had formed his unimpassioned and polished periods. And as that old earl, who in the time of Charles the First was the reigning wit of the court, in the time of Charles the Second was considered too dull even for a butt, so every age has its own literary stamp and coinage, and consigns the old circulation to its shelves and cabinets, as neglected curiosities. Cleveland could not become the fashion with the public as an author, though the coteries cried him up and the reviewers adored him—and the ladies of quality and the amateur dilettanti bought and bound his volumes of careful poetry and cadenced prose. But Cleveland had high birth and a handsome competence—his manners were delightful, his conversation fluent—and his disposition was as amiable as his mind was cultured. He became, therefore, a man greatly sought after in society—both respected and beloved. If he had not genius, he had great good sense—he did not vex his urbane temper and kindly heart with walking after a vain shadow, and disquieting himself in vain. Satisfied with an honourable and unenvied reputation, he gave up the dream of that higher fame which he clearly saw was denied to his aspirations—and maintained his good-humour with the world, though in his secret soul he thought it was very wrong in its literary caprices. Cleveland never married ; he lived partly in town, but principally at Temple Grove, a villa not far from Richmond. Here, with an excellent library, beautiful grounds, and a circle of attached and admiring friends, which comprised all the more refined and intellectual members of what is termed, by emphasis, *Good Society*—this accomplished and elegant person passed a life, perhaps much happier than he would have known had his young visions been fulfilled, and it had become his stormy fate to lead the rebellious and fierce Democracy of Letters.

Cleveland was indeed, if not a man of high and original genius, at least very superior to the generality of patrician authors. In retiring himself from frequent exercise in the arena, he gave up his mind with renewed zest to the thoughts and masterpieces of others. From a well-read man he became a deeply-instructed one. Metaphysics, and some of the material sciences, added new treasures to information more light and miscellaneous, and contributed to impart weight and dignity to a mind that might otherwise have become somewhat effeminate and frivolous. His social habits, his clear sense, and benevolence of judgment, made him also an exquisite judge of all those indefinable nothings or little things, that, formed into a total, become knowledge of the Great World. I say the Great World—for of the world without the circle of the great Cleveland naturally knew but little. But of all that related to that subtle orbit in which gentlemen and ladies move in elevated and ethereal order, Cleveland was a profound philosopher. It was the mode with many of his admirers to style him the Horace Walpole of the day. But though in some of the more external and superficial points of character they were alike, Cleveland had considerably less cleverness and infinitely more heart.

The late Mr. Maltravers, a man not indeed of literary habits, but an admirer of those who were—an elegant, high-bred, hospitable *seigneur de province*—had been one of the earliest of Cleveland's friends—Cleveland had been his fag at Eton—and he found Hal Maltravers—(Handsome Hal !)—had become the darling of the clubs, when he made his own *début* in society. They were inseparable for a season or two—and when Mr. Maltravers married, and enamoured of country pursuits, proud of his old hall, and sensibly enough conceiving that he was a greater man in his own broad lands than in the republican aristocracy of London, settled peaceably at Lisle Court. Cleveland corresponded with him regularly, and visited him twice a-year. Mrs. Maltravers died in giving birth to Ernest, her second son. Her husband loved her tenderly, and was long inconsolable for her loss. He could not bear the sight of the child that had cost him so dear a sacrifice. Cleveland and his sister, Lady Julia Danvers, were residing with him at the time of this melancholy event; and with judicious and delicate kindness, Lady Julia proposed to place the unconscious offender amongst her own children for some months. The proposition was accepted, and it was two years before the infant Ernest was restored to the paternal mansion. During the greater part of that time he had gone through all the events and revolutions of baby life, under the bachelor roof of Frederick Cleveland. The result of this was, that the latter loved the child like a father. Ernest's first intelligible word hailed Cleveland as "papa;" and when the urchin was at length deposited at Lisle Court, Cleveland talked all the nurses out of breath with admonitions, and cautions, and injunctions, and promises, and threats, which might have put many a careful mother to the blush. This circumstance formed a new tie between Cleveland and his friend. Cleveland's visits were now three times a-year instead of twice. Nothing was done for Ernest without Cleveland's advice. He was not even breeched till Cleveland gave his grave consent. Cleveland chose his school, and took him to it—and he spent a week of every vacation in Cleveland's house. The boy never got into a scrape, or won a prize, or wanted a *tip*, or coveted a book, but what Cleveland was the first to know of it. Fortunately, too, Ernest manifested by times tastes which the graceful author thought similar to his own. He early developed very remarkable talents, and a love for learning—though these were accompanied with a vigour of life and soul—an energy—a daring—which gave Cleveland some uneasiness, and which did not appear to him at all congenial with the moody shyness of an embryo genius, or the regular placidity of a precocious scholar. Meanwhile, the relation between father and son was rather a singular one. Mr. Maltravers had overcome his first, not unnatural, repugnance to the innocent cause of his irremediable loss. He was now fond and proud of his boy—as he was of all things that belonged to him. He spoiled and petted him even more than Cleveland did. But he interfered very little with his education or pursuits. His eldest son, Cuthbert, did not engross all his heart, but occupied all his care. With Cuthbert he connected the heritage of his ancient name, and the succession of his ancestral estates. Cuthbert was not a genius, nor intended to be one; he was to be an accomplished gentleman, and a great proprietor. The father understood Cuthbert, and could see clearly both his character and career. He had no scruple in managing his education, and forming his growing mind. But Ernest puzzled him. Mr. Maltravers was even a little embarrassed in the boy's society; he never quite overcame that feeling of strangeness towards him which he had experienced when he first received him back from Cleveland, and took Cleveland's directions about his health and so forth. It always seemed to him as if his friend shared his right to the child; and he thought it a sort of presumption to scold Ernest, though he very often swore at Cuthbert. As the younger son grew up, it certainly was evident that Cleveland did understand him better than his own father did; and so, as I have before said, on Cleveland the father was not displeased passively to shift the responsibility of the rearing.

Perhaps Mr. Maltravers might not have been so indifferent had Ernest's prospects been those of a younger son in general. If a profession had been necessary for him, Mr. Maltravers would have been naturally anxious to see him duly fitted for it. But from a maternal relation Ernest inherited an estate of about four thousand pounds a-year: and he was thus made independent of his father. This loosened another tie between them; and so by degrees Mr. Maltravers learned to consider Ernest less as his own son, to be advised or rebuked, praised or controlled, than as a very affectionate, promising, engaging boy, who, somehow or other, without any trouble on his part, was very likely to do great credit to his family, and indulge his eccentricities upon four thousand pounds a-year. The first time that Mr. Maltravers was seriously perplexed about him was when the boy, at the age of sixteen, having taught himself German, and intoxicated his wild fancies with "Werter," and "The Robbers," announced his desire, which sounded very like a demand, of going to Gottingen instead of to Oxford. Never were Mr. Maltravers' notions of a proper and gentleman-like finish to education more completely and rudely assaulted. He stammered out a negative, and hurried to his study to write a long letter to Cleveland, who, himself an Oxford prize-man, would, he was persuaded, see the matter in the same light. Cleveland answered the letter in person: listened in silence to all the father had to say, and then strolled through the park with the young man. The result of the latter conference was, that Cleveland declared in favour of Ernest.

"But, my dear Frederick," said the astonished father, "I thought the boy was to carry off all the prizes at Oxford?"

"I carried off some, Maltravers; but I don't see what good they did me."

"O, Cleveland!"

"I am serious."

"But it is such a very odd fancy."

"Your son is a very odd young man."

"I fear he is so—I fear he is, poor fellow! But what will he learn at Gottingen?"

"Languages and Independence," said Cleveland.

"And the classics—the classics—you are such an excellent Grecian!"

"There are great Grecians in Germany," answered Cleveland; "and Ernest cannot well unlearn what he knows already. My dear Maltravers, the boy is not like most clever young men. He must either go through action, and adventure, and excitement, in his own way, or he will be an idle dreamer, or an impracticable enthusiast all his life. Let him alone.—So Cuthbert is going into the Guards?"

"But he went first to Oxford."

"Humph! What a fine young man he is!"

"Not so tall as Ernest, but——"

"A handsomer face," said Cleveland. "He is a son to be proud of in one way, as I hope Ernest will be in another. Will you show me your new hunter?"

· · · · · ·

It was to the house of this gentleman, so judiciously made his guardian, that the student of Gottingen now took his melancholy way.

CHAPTER XIII.

> "But if a little exercise you choose,
> Some zest for ease, 'tis not forbidden here;
> Amid the groves you may indulge the Muse,
> Or tend the blooms and deck the vernal year."
> —*Castle of Indolence.*

THE house of Mr. Cleveland was an Italian villa adapted to an English climate. Through an Ionic arch you entered a domain of some eighty or a hundred acres in extent, but so well planted and so artfully disposed, that you could not have supposed the unseen boundaries enclosed no ampler a space. The road wound through the greenest sward, in which trees of venerable growth were relieved by a profusion of shrubs and flowers, gathered into baskets intertwined with creepers, or blooming from classic vases, placed with a tasteful care in such spots as required the *filling up*, and harmonised well with the object chosen. Not an old ivy-grown pollard, not a modest and bending willow, but was brought out, as it were, into a peculiar feature by the art of the owner. Without being overloaded, or too minutely elaborate (the common fault of the rich man's villa), the whole place seemed one diversified and cultivated garden; even the air almost took a different vegetation with each winding of the road; and the colours of the flowers and foliage varied with every view.

At length, when, on a lawn sloping towards a glassy lake, overhung by limes and chestnuts, and backed by a hanging wood, the house itself came in sight, the whole prospect seemed suddenly to receive its finishing and crowning feature. The house was long and low. A deep peristyle that supported the roof extended the whole length, and being raised above the basement, had the appearance of a covered terrace; broad flights of steps, with massive balustrades, supporting vases of aloes and orange-trees, led to the lawn; and under the peristyle were ranged statues, Roman antiquities, and rare exotics. On this side the lake another terrace, very broad, and adorned, at long intervals, with urns and sculpture, contrasted the shadowy and sloping bank beyond; and commanded, through unexpected openings in the trees, extensive views of the distant landscape, with the stately Thames winding through the midst. The interior of the house corresponded with the taste without.

All the principal rooms, even those appropriated to sleep, were on the same floor. A small but lofty and octagonal hall conducted to a suite of four rooms. At one extremity was a moderately-sized dining-room, with a ceiling copied from the rich and gay colours of Guido's "Hours;" and landscapes painted by Cleveland himself, with no despicable skill, were let into the walls. A single piece of sculpture, copied from the Piping Faun, and tinged with a flesh-like glow by purple and orange draperies behind it, relieved without darkening the broad and arched window which formed its niche. This communicated with a small picture room, not indeed rich with those immortal gems for which princes are candidates; for Cleveland's fortune was but that of a private gentleman, though, managed with a discreet if liberal economy, it sufficed for all his elegant desires. But the pictures had an interest beyond that of art, and the subjects were within the reach of a collector of ordinary opulence. They made a series of portraits—some originals, some copies (and the copies were often the best) of Cleveland's favourite authors. And it was characteristic of the man, that Pope's worn and thoughtful countenance looked down from the central place of honour. Appropriately enough this room led into the library, the largest room in the house, the only one, indeed, that was noticeable from its size as well as its embellishments. It was nearly sixty feet in length. The book-cases were crowned with bronze busts, while at intervals, statues, placed in open arches, backed with mirrors, gave the appearance of galleries, opening from the book-lined walls, and introduced an inconceivable air of classic lightness and repose into the apartment; with these arches the windows harmonised so well, opening on the peristyle, and bringing into delightful view the sculpture, the flowers, the terraces, and the lake without, that the actual prospects half seduced you into the belief that they were designs by some master-hand of the poetical gardens that yet crown the hills of Rome. Even the colouring of the prospects on a sunny day favoured the delusion, owing to the deep, rich hues of the simple draperies, and the stained glass of which the upper panes of the windows were composed. Cleveland was especially fond of sculpture; he was sensible, too, of the mighty impulse which that art has received in Europe within the last half century. He was even capable of asserting the doctrine, not yet sufficiently acknowledged in this country, that Flaxman surpassed Canova. He loved sculpture, too, not only for its own beauty, but for the beautifying and intellectual effect that it produces wherever it is admitted. It is a great mistake, he was wont to say, in collectors of statues, to arrange them *pêle mêle* in one long, monotonous gallery. The single relief, or statue, or bust, or simple urn, introduced appropriately in the smallest apartment we inhabit, charms us infinitely more than those gigantic museums, crowded into rooms never entered but for show, and without a chill, uncomfortable shiver. Besides, this practice of galleries, which the herd consider orthodox, places sculpture out of the patronage of the public. There are not a dozen people who can afford galleries. But every moderately affluent gentleman can afford a statue or a bust. The influence, too, upon a man's mind and taste, created by the constant and habitual view of monuments of the only imperishable art which resorts to physical materials, is unspeakable. Looking upon the Greek marble, we become acquainted, almost insensibly, with the character of the Greek life and literature. That Aristides, that Genius of Death, that fragment of the unrivalled Psyche, are worth a thousand Scaligers!

"Do you ever look at the Latin translation when you read Æschylus?" said a school-boy once to Cleveland.

"That is my Latin translation," said Cleveland, pointing to the Laocoon.

The library opened, at the extreme end, to a small cabinet for curiosities and medals, which, still in a straight line, conducted to a long belvidere, terminating in a little circular summer-house, that, by a sudden wind of the lake below, hung perpendicularly over its transparent tide, and, seen from the distance, appeared almost suspended on air, so light were its slender columns and arching dome. Another door from the library opened upon the corridor, which conducted to the principal sleeping-chambers; the nearest door was that of Cleveland's private study, communicating with his bedroom and dressing-closet. The other rooms were appropriated to, and named after, his several friends.

Mr. Cleveland had been advised by a hasty line of the movements of his ward, and he received the young man with a smile of welcome, though his eyes were moist and his lips trembled—for the boy was like his father!—a new generation had commenced for Cleveland!

"Welcome, my dear Ernest," said he; "I am so glad to see you, that I will not scold you for your mysterious absence. This is your room, you see your name over the door; it is a larger one than you used to have, for you are a man now; and there is your German sanctum adjoining—Schiller and the meerschaum!—a bad habit, that, the meerschaum! but not worse than the Schiller, perhaps! You see you are in the peristyle immediately. The meerschaum is good for flowers, I fancy, so have no scruple. Why, my dear boy, how pale you are! Be cheered—be cheered. Well, I must go myself, or you will infect me."

Cleveland hurried away; he thought of his lost friend. Ernest sank upon the first chair, and buried his face in his hands. Cleveland's valet entered, and bustled about, and unpacked the portmanteau, and arranged the evening dress. But Ernest did not look up nor speak; the first bell sounded; the second tolled unheard upon his ear. He was thoroughly overcome by his emotions. The first notes of Cleveland's kind voice had touched upon a soft chord, that months of anxiety and excitement had strained to anguish, but had never woke to tears. His nerves were shattered—those strong, young nerves! He thought of his dead father when he first saw Cleveland; but when he glanced round the room prepared for him, and observed the care for his comfort, and the tender recollection of his most trifling peculiarities everywhere visible, Alice, the watchful, the humble, the loving, the lost Alice, rose before him. Surprised at his ward's delay, Cleveland entered the room; there sat Ernest still, his face buried in his hands. Cleveland drew them gently away, and Maltravers sobbed like an infant. It was an easy matter to bring tears to the eyes of that young man: a generous or a tender thought, an old song, the simplest air of music, sufficed for that touch of the mother's nature. But the vehement and awful passion which belongs to manhood when thoroughly unmanned—this was the first time in which the relief of that stormy bitterness was known to him!

CHAPTER XIV.

"Musing full sadly in his sullen mind."—SPENSER.

"There forth issued from under the altar-smoke
A dreadful fiend."—*Ibid.*, *on Superstition*.

NINE times out of ten it is over the Bridge of Sighs that we pass the narrow gulf from Youth to Manhood. That interval is usually occupied by an ill-placed or disappointed affection. We recover, and we find ourselves a new being. The intellect has become hardened by the fire through which it has passed. The mind profits by the wrecks of every passion, and we may measure our road to wisdom by the sorrows we have undergone. But Maltravers was yet *on* the bridge, and, for a time, both mind and body were prostrate and enfeebled. Cleveland had the sagacity to discover that the affections had their share in the change that he grieved to witness, but he had also the delicacy not to force himself into the young man's confidence. But by little and little his kindness so completely penetrated the heart of his ward, that Ernest one evening told him his whole tale. As a man of the world, Cleveland perhaps rejoiced that it was no worse, for he had feared some existing entanglement, perhaps, with a married woman. But as a man who was better than the world in general, he sympathised with the unfortunate girl, whom Ernest pictured to him in faithful and unflattered colours, and he long forebore consolations which he foresaw would be unavailing. He felt, indeed, that Ernest was not a man "to betray the noon of manhood to a myrtle-shade;" that with so sanguine, buoyant, and hardy a temperament, he would at length recover from a depression which, if it could bequeath a warning, might as well not be wholly divested of remorse. And he also knew that few become either great authors or great men (and he fancied Ernest was born to be one or the other) without the fierce emotions and passionate struggles through which the Wilhelm Meister of Real Life must work out his apprenticeship, and attain the Master-Rank. But at last he had serious misgivings about the health of his ward. A constant and spectral gloom seemed bearing the young man to the grave. It was in vain that Cleveland, who secretly desired him to thirst for a public career, endeavoured to arouse his ambition—the boy's spirit seemed quite broken—and the visit of a political character, the mention of a political work, drove him at once into his solitary chamber. At length his mental disease took a new turn. He became, of a sudden, most morbidly and fanatically—I was about to say, religious: but that is not the word; let me call it pseudo-religious. His strong sense and cultivated taste did not allow him to delight in the raving tracts of illiterate fanatics—and yet, out of the benign and simple elements of the Scripture, he conjured up for himself a fanaticism quite as gloomy and intense. He lost sight of God the Father, and night and day dreamed only of God the Avenger. His vivid imagination was perverted to raise out of its own abyss phantoms of colossal terror. He shuddered aghast at his own creations, and earth and heaven alike seemed black with the everlasting wrath. These symptoms completely baffled and perplexed Cleveland. He knew not what remedy to administer—and to his unspeakable grief and surprise, he found that Ernest, in the true spirit of his strange bigotry, began to regard Cleveland—the amiable, the benevolent Cleveland—as one no less out of the pale of grace than himself. His elegant pursuits, his cheerful studies, were considered by the young but stern enthusiast as the miserable recreations of Mammon and the world. There seemed every probability that Ernest Maltravers would die in a madhouse, or, at best, succeed to the delusions, without the cheerful intervals, of Cowper.

CHAPTER XV.

"Sagacious, bold, and turbulent of wit,
Restless—unfixed in principles and place."—DRYDEN.

"Whoever acquires a very great number of ideas interesting to the society in which he lives, will be regarded in that society as a man of abilities."
—HELVETIUS.

IT was just when Ernest Maltravers was so bad that he could not be worse, that a young man visited Temple Grove. The name of this young man was Lumley Ferrers, his age about twenty-six, his fortune about eight hundred a-year—he followed no profession. Lumley Ferrers had not what is usually called genius; that is, he had no enthusiasm; and if the word talent be properly interpreted as meaning the talent of doing something better than others, Ferrers had not much to boast of on that score. He had no talent for writing, nor for music, nor painting, nor the ordinary round of accomplishments; neither at present had he displayed much of the hard and useful talent for action and business. But Ferrers had what is often better than either genius or talent; he had a powerful and most acute mind. He had, moreover, great animation of manner, high physical spirits, a witty, odd, racy vein of conversation, determined assurance, and profound confidence in his own resources. He was fond of schemes, stratagems, and plots—they amused and excited him—his power of sarcasm and of argument, too, was great, and he usually obtained an astonishing influence over those with whom he was brought in contact.

His high spirits, and a most happy frankness of bearing, carried off and disguised his leading vices of character, which were callousness to whatever was affectionate, and insensibility to whatever was moral. Though less learned than Maltravers, he was, on the whole, a very instructed man. He mastered the surface of many sciences, became satisfied of their general principles, and threw the study aside never to be forgotten (for his memory was like a vice), but never to be prosecuted any further. To this he added a general acquaintance with whatever is most generally acknowledged as standard in ancient or modern literature. What is admired only by a few, Lumley never took the trouble to read. Living amongst trifles, he made them interesting and novel by his mode of viewing and treating them. And here, indeed, was *a* talent—it was the talent of social life—the talent of enjoyment to the utmost with the least degree of trouble to himself. Lumley Ferrers was thus exactly one of those men whom everybody calls exceedingly clever, and yet it would puzzle one to say in what he was so clever. It was, indeed, that nameless power which belongs to ability, and which makes one man superior, on the whole, to another, though in many details by no means remarkable. I think it is Goethe who says somewhere, that, in reading the life of the greatest genius, we always find that he was acquainted with some men superior to himself, who yet never attained to general distinction. To the class of these mystical superior men, Lumley Ferrers might have belonged ; for though an ordinary journalist would have beaten him in the arts of composition, few men of genius, however eminent, could have felt themselves above Ferrers in the ready grasp and plastic vigour of natural intellect. It only remains to be said of this singular young man, whose character as yet was but half developed, that he had seen a great deal of the world, and could live at ease and in content with all tempers and ranks ; fox-hunters or scholars, lawyers or poets, patricians or *parvenus*.

Ernest was, as usual, in his own room, when he heard, along the corridor without, all that indefinable bustling noise which announces an arrival. Next came a most ringing laugh, and then a sharp, clear, vigorous voice, that ran through his ears like a dagger. Ernest was immediately aroused to all the majesty of indignant sullenness. He walked out on the terrace of the portico to avoid the repetition of the disturbance, and once more settled back into his broken and hypochondriacal reveries. Pacing to and fro that part of the peristyle which occupied the more retired wing of the house, with his arms folded, his eyes downcast, his brows knit, and all the angel darkened on that countenance, which formerly looked as if, like truth, it could shame the devil and defy the world, Ernest followed the evil thought that mastered him through the Valley of the Shadow. Suddenly he was aware of something—some obstacle which he had not previously encountered. He started, and saw before him a young man, of plain dress, gentleman-like appearance, and striking countenance.

"Mr. Maltravers, I think," said the stranger, and Ernest recognised the voice that had so disturbed him: "this is lucky; we can now introduce ourselves, for I find Cleveland means us to be intimate. Mr. Lumley Ferrers, Mr. Ernest Maltravers. There now, I am the elder, so I first offer my hand, and grin properly. People always grin when they make a new acquaintance! Well, that's settled. Which way are you walking?"

Maltravers could, when he chose it, be as stately as if he had never been out of England. He now drew himself up in displeased astonishment; extricated his hand from the gripe of Ferrers, and saying, very coldly, "Excuse me, sir, I am busy," stalked back to his chamber. He threw himself into his chair, and was presently forgetful of his late annoyance, when, to his inexpressible amazement and wrath, he heard again the sharp, clear voice close to his elbow.

Ferrers had followed him through the French casement into the room. "You are busy, you say, my dear fellow. I want to write some letters: we shan't interrupt each other—don't disturb yourself;" and Ferrers seated himself at the writing table, dipped a pen into the ink, arranged blotting-book and paper before him in due order, and was soon employed in covering page after page with the most rapid and hieroglyphical scrawl that ever engrossed a mistress or perplexed a dun.

"The presuming puppy!" growled Maltravers, half audibly, but effectually roused from himself; and examining with some curiosity so cool an intruder, he was forced to own that the countenance of Ferrers was not that of a puppy.

A forehead compact and solid as a block of granite, overhung small, bright, intelligent eyes of a light hazel; the features were handsome, yet rather too sharp and fox-like; the complexion, though not highly coloured, was of that hardy, healthy hue which generally betokens a robust constitution and high animal spirits; the jaw was massive, and, to a physiognomist, betokened firmness and strength of character; but the lips, full and large, were those of a sensualist, and their restless play, and habitual half-smile, spoke of gaiety and humour, though when in repose there was in them something furtive and sinister.

Maltravers looked at him in grave silence; but when Ferrers, concluding his fourth letter before another man would have got through his first page, threw down the pen, and looked full at Maltravers, with a good-humoured but penetrating stare, there was something so whimsical in the intruder's expression of face, and indeed in the whole scene, that Maltravers bit his lip to restrain a smile, the first he had known for weeks.

"I see you read, Maltravers," said Ferrers, carelessly turning over the volumes on the table. "All very right: we should begin life with books; they multiply the sources of employment; so does capital; but capital is of no use, unless we live on the interest— books are waste-paper, unless we spend in action the wisdom we get from thought. Action, Maltravers, action, that is the life for us. At our age we have passion, fancy, sentiment; we can't read them away, nor scribble them away; we must live upon them generously, but economically."

Maltravers was struck; the intruder was not the empty bore he had chosen to fancy him. He roused himself languidly to reply. "Life, *Mr.* Ferrers——"

"Stop, *mon cher*, stop; don't call me Mister; we are to be friends; I hate delaying that which *must* be, even by a superfluous dissyllable; you are Maltravers, I am Ferrers. But you were going to talk about life. Suppose we *live* a little while, instead of talking about it. It wants an hour to dinner: let us stroll into the grounds; I want to get an appetite; besides, I like nature when there are no Swiss mountains to climb before one can arrive at a prospect. *Allons!*"

"Excuse—" again began Maltravers, half interested, half annoyed.

"I'll be shot if I do. Come."

Ferrers gave Maltravers his hat, wound his arm into that of his new acquaintance, and they were on the broad terrace by the lake before Ernest was aware of it.

How animated, how eccentric, how easy was Ferrers' talk (for talk it was, rather than conversation, since he had the ball to himself); books, and men, and things—he tossed them about and played with them like shuttlecocks; and then his egotistical narrative of half a hundred adventures, in which he had been the hero, told so, that you laughed *at* him and laughed with him.

CHAPTER XVI.

"Now the bright morning star, day's harbinger,
Comes dancing from the east."—MILTON.

HITHERTO Ernest had never met with any mind that had exercised a strong influence over his own. At home, at school, at Gottingen—everywhere he had been the brilliant and wayward leader of others, persuading or commanding wiser and older heads than his own . even Cleveland always yielded to him, though not aware of it. In fact, it seldom happens that we are very strongly influenced by those *much* older than ourselves. It is the Senior, of from two to ten years, that most seduces and enthrals us. He has the same pursuits, views, objects, pleasures, but more art and experience in them all. He goes with us in the path we are ordained to tread, but from which the elder generation desires to warn us off. There is very little influence where there is not great sympathy. It was now an epoch in the intellectual life of Maltravers. He met for the first time with a mind that controlled his own. Perhaps the physical state of his nerves made him less able to cope with the half-bullying but thoroughly good-humoured imperiousness of Ferrers. Every day this stranger became more and more potential with Maltravers. Ferrers, who was an utter egotist, never asked his new friend to give him his confidence; he never cared three straws about other peoples' secrets, unless useful to some purpose of his own. But he talked with so much zest about himself—about women and pleasure, and the gay, stirring life of cities—that the young spirit of Maltravers was roused from its dark lethargy without an effort of its own. The gloomy phantoms vanished gradually—his sense broke from its cloud—he felt once more that God had given the sun to light the day, and even in the midst of darkness had called up the host of stars.

Perhaps no other person could have succeeded so speedily in curing Maltravers of his diseased enthusiasm ; a crude or sarcastic unbeliever he would not have listened to; a moderate and enlightened divine he would have disregarded, as a worldly and cunning adjuster of laws celestial with customs earthly. But Lumley Ferrers, who, when he argued, never admitted a sentiment or a simile in reply, who wielded his plain iron logic like a hammer, which, though its metal seemed dull, kindled the ethereal spark

with every stroke—Lumley Ferrers was just the man to resist the
imagination, and convince the reason, of Maltravers, and the
moment the latter came to argument, the cure was soon completed;
for, however we may darken and puzzle ourselves with fancies and
visions, and the ingenuities of fanatical mysticism, no man can
mathematically or syllogistically contend that the world which a
God made, and a Saviour visited, was designed to be damned!

And Ernest Maltravers one night softly stole to his room and
opened the New Testament, and read its heavenly moralities with
purged eyes; and when he had done, he fell upon his knees, and
prayed the Almighty to pardon the ungrateful heart that, worse than
the Atheist's, had confessed His existence but denied His goodness.
His sleep was sweet and his dreams were cheerful. Did he rise to
find that the penitence which had shaken his reason would henceforth suffice to save his life from all error? Alas! remorse overstrained has too often reactions as dangerous; and homely Luther
says well, that "the mind, like the drunken peasant on horseback,
when propped on one side nods and falls on the other." All that
can be said is, that there are certain crises in life which leave us
long weaker; from which the system recovers with frequent revul-
sion and weary relapse—but from which, looking back, after years
have passed on, we date the foundation of strength or the cure of
disease. It is not to mean souls that creation is darkened by a fear
of the anger of heaven.

CHAPTER XVII.

"There are times when we are diverted out of errors, but could not be
preached out of them. There are practitioners who can cure us of one disorder,
though, in ordinary cases, they be but poor physicians—nay, dangerous
quacks."—STEPHEN MONTAGUE.

LUMLEY FERRERS had one rule in life; and it was this—
to make all things and all persons subservient to himself.
And Ferrers now intended to go abroad for some years.
He wanted a companion, for he disliked solitude; besides, a companion shared the expenses, and a man of eight hundred a-year,
who desires all the luxuries of life, does not despise a partner
in the taxes to be paid for them. Ferrers, at this period, rather
liked Ernest than not: it was convenient to choose friends from
those richer than himself, and he resolved, when he first came to

Temple Grove, that Ernest should be his travelling companion. This resolution formed, it was very easy to execute it.

Maltravers was now warmly attached to his new friend, and eager for change. Cleveland was sorry to part with him; but he dreaded a relapse, if the young man were again left upon his hands. Accordingly, the guardian's consent was obtained; a travelling-carriage was bought, and fitted up with every imaginable imperial and *malle*. A Swiss (half valet and half courier) was engaged; one thousand a-year was allowed to Maltravers; and one soft and lovely morning, towards the close of October, Ferrers and Maltravers found themselves midway on the road to Dover.

"How glad I am to get out of England," said Ferrers: "it is a famous country for the rich; but here, eight hundred a-year, without a profession, save that of pleasure, goes upon pepper and salt; it is a luxurious competence abroad."

"I think I have heard Cleveland say that you will be rich some day or other."

"Oh yes; I have what are called expectations! You must know that I have a kind of settlement on two stools, the Well-born and the Wealthy; but between two stools—you recollect the proverb! The present Lord Saxingham, once plain Frank Lascelles, and my father, Mr. Ferrers, were first cousins. Two or three relations good-naturedly died, and Frank Lascelles became an earl; the lands did not go with the coronet: he was poor, and married an heiress. The lady died; her estate was settled on her only child, the handsomest little girl you ever saw. Pretty Florence, I often wish I could look up to you! Her fortune will be nearly all at her own disposal, too, when she comes of age; now she's in the nursery, 'eating bread and honey.' My father, less lucky and less wise than his cousin, thought fit to marry a Miss Templeton—a nobody. The Saxingham branch of the family politely dropped the acquaintance. Now, my mother had a brother, a clever, plodding fellow, in what is called 'business:' he became rich and richer: but my father and mother died, and were never the better for it. And I came of age, and *worth* (I like that expression) not a farthing more or less than this often-quoted eight hundred pounds a-year. My rich uncle is married, but has no children I am, therefore, heir-presumptive—but he is a saint, and close, though ostentatious. The quarrel between Uncle Templeton and the Saxinghams still continues. Templeton is angry if I see the Saxinghams—and the Saxinghams—my Lord, at least—is by no means so sure that I shall be Templeton's heir as not to feel a doubt lest I should, some day or other, sponge upon his lordship for a place. Lord Saxingham is in the administration, you know. Somehow or other I have an equivocal, amphibious kind of place in London society, which I don't like; on one side I am a patrician connection, whom the *parvenu* branches always incline lovingly to—and on the other side I am a half-dependent cadet, whom the noble relations look civilly shy at. Some day, when I grow tired of travel and idleness, I shall come back and wrestle with these little difficulties, conciliate my methodistical uncle, and grapple with my noble cousin. But now I am fit for something better than getting on in the world. Dry chips, not green wood, are the things for making a blaze! How slow this fellow drives! Hollo, you sir! get on! mind, twelve miles to the hour! You shall have sixpence a mile. Give me your purse, Maltravers; I may as well be cashier, being the elder and the wiser man; we can settle accounts at the end of the journey. By Jove, what a pretty girl!"

BOOK II.

CHAPTER I.

"*Il y eut certainement quelque chose de singulier dans mes sentimens pour cette charmante femme.*"*—ROUSSEAU.

IT was a brilliant ball at the Palazzo of the Austrian embassy at Naples, and a crowd of those loungers, whether young or old, who attach themselves to the reigning beauty, was gathered round Madame de Ventadour. Generally speaking, there is more caprice than taste in the election of a beauty to the Idalian throne. Nothing disappoints a stranger more than to see for the first time the woman to whom the world has given the golden apple. Yet he usually falls at last into the popular idolatry, and passes with inconceivable rapidity from indignant scepticism into superstitious veneration. In fact, a thousand things besides mere symmetry of feature go to make up the Cytherea of the hour . . . tact in society—the charm of manner—a nameless and piquant brilliancy. Where the world find the Graces they proclaim the Venus. Few persons attain pre-eminent celebrity for anything, without some adventitious and extraneous circumstances which have nothing to do with the thing celebrated. Some qualities or some circumstances throw a mysterious or personal charm about them.—"Is Mr. So-and-So really such a genius?"—"Is Mrs. Such-a-One really such a beauty?" you ask incredulously. "Oh, yes," is the answer. "Do you know all *about* him or her? Such a thing is said, or such a thing has happened." The idol is interesting in itself, and therefore its leading and popular attribute is worshipped.

* There certainly was something singular in my sentiments for this charming

Now Madame de Ventadour was at this time the beauty of Naples; and though fifty women in the room were handsomer, no one would have dared to say so. Even the women confessed her pre-eminence—for she was the most perfect dresser that even France could exhibit. And to no pretensions do ladies ever concede with so little demur, as those which depend upon that feminine art which all study, and in which few excel. Women never allow beauty in a face that has an odd-looking bonnet above it, nor will they readily allow any one to be ugly whose caps are unexceptionable. Madame de Ventadour had also the magic that results from intuitive high breeding, polished by habit to the utmost. She looked and moved the *grande dame*, as if Nature had been employed by Rank to make her so. She was descended from one of the most illustrious houses of France; had married at sixteen a man of equal birth, but old, dull, and pompous—a caricature rather than a portrait of that great French *noblesse*, now almost if not wholly extinct. But her virtue was without a blemish—some said from pride, some said from coldness. Her wit was keen and courtlike—lively, yet subdued; for her French high breeding was very different from the lethargic and taciturn imperturbability of the English. All silent people can seem conventionally elegant. A groom married a rich lady; he dreaded the ridicule of the guests whom his new rank assembled at his table—an Oxford clergyman gave him this piece of advice, "Wear a black coat and hold your tongue!" The groom took the hint, and is always considered one of the most gentleman-like fellows in the county. Conversation is the touchstone of the true delicacy and subtle grace which make the ideal of the moral mannerism of a court. And there sat Madame de Ventadour, a little apart from the dancers, with the silent English dandy, Lord Taunton, exquisitely dressed and superbly tall, bolt upright behind her chair; and the sentimental German Baron Von Schomberg, covered with orders, whiskered and wigged to the last hair of perfection, sighing at her left hand; and the French minister, shrewd, bland, and eloquent, in the chair at her right; and round on all sides pressed, and bowed, and complimented, a crowd of diplomatic secretaries and Italian princes, whose bank is at the gaming-table, whose estates are in their galleries, and who sell a picture, as English gentlemen cut down a wood, whenever the cards grow gloomy. The charming De Ventadour! she had attraction for them all! smiles for the silent, badinage for the gay, politics for the Frenchman, poetry for the

German—the eloquence of loveliness for all! She was looking her best—the slightest possible tinge of rouge gave a glow to her transparent complexion, and lighted up those large, dark, sparkling eyes (with a latent softness beneath the sparkle), seldom seen but in the French—and widely distinct from the unintellectual languish of the Spaniard, or the full and majestic fierceness of the Italian gaze. Her dress of black velvet, and graceful hat with its princely plume, contrasted the alabaster whiteness of her arms and neck. And what with the eyes, the skin, the rich colouring of the complexion, the rosy lips, and the small ivory teeth, no one would have had the cold hypercriticism to observe that the chin was too pointed, the mouth too wide, and the nose, so beautiful in the front face, was far from perfect in the profile.

"Pray, was Madame in the Strada Nuova to-day?" asked the German, with as much sweetness in his voice as if he had been vowing eternal love.

"What else have we to do with our mornings, we women?" replied Madame de Ventadour. "Our life is a lounge from the cradle to the grave; and our afternoons are but the type of our career. A promenade and a crowd—*voilà tout!* We never see the world except in an open carriage."

"It is the pleasantest way of seeing it," said the Frenchman, drily.

"I doubt it; the worst fatigue is that which comes without exercise."

"Will you do me the honour to waltz?" said the tall English lord, who had a vague idea that Madame de Ventadour meant she would rather dance than sit still. The Frenchman smiled.

"Lord Taunton enforces your own philosophy," said the minister.

Lord Taunton smiled because every one else smiled; and, besides, he had beautiful teeth; but he looked anxious for an answer.

"Not to-night—I seldom dance. Who is that very pretty woman? —What lovely complexions the English have! And who," continued Madame de Ventadour, without waiting for an answer to the first question, "who is that gentleman—the young one I mean—leaning against the door?"

"What, with the dark moustache?" said Lord Taunton—"he is a cousin of mine."

"Oh, no; not Colonel Bellfield; I know him—how amusing he is! —no; the gentleman I mean wears no moustache."

"Oh, the tall Englishman with the bright eyes and high forehead," said the French minister. "He is just arrived—from the East, I believe."

"It is a striking countenance," said Madame de Ventadour; "there is something chivalrous in the turn of the head. Without doubt, Lord Taunton, he is '*noble*.'"

"He is what you call '*noble*,'" replied Lord Taunton—"that is, what we call 'a gentleman'—his name is Mr. Maltravers. He lately came of age; and has, I believe, rather a good property."

"Monsieur Maltravers; only Monsieur!" repeated Madame de Ventadour.

"Why," said the French minister, "you understand that the English *gentilhomme* does not require a De or a title to distinguish him from the *roturier*."

"I know that; but he has an air above a simple *gentilhomme*. There is something *great* in his look; but it is not, I must own, the conventional greatness of rank; perhaps he would have looked the same had he been born a peasant."

"You don't think him handsome!" said Lord Taunton, almost angrily (for he was one of the Beauty-men, and Beauty-men are sometimes jealous).

"Handsome! I did not say that," replied Madame de Ventadour, smiling; "it is rather a fine head than a handsome face. Is he clever, I wonder?—but all you English, milord, are well educated."

"Yes, profound—profound: we are profound, not superficial," replied Lord Taunton, drawing down his wristbands.

"Will Madame de Ventadour allow me to present to her one of my countrymen?" said the English minister, approaching—"Mr. Maltravers."

Madame de Ventadour half smiled and half blushed, as she looked up, and saw bent admiringly upon her the proud and earnest countenance she had remarked.

The introduction was made—a few monosyllables exchanged. The French diplomatist rose and walked away with the English one. Maltravers succeeded to the vacant chair.

"Have you been long abroad?" asked Madame de Ventadour.

"Only four years; yet long enough to ask whether I should not be most abroad in England."

"You have been in the East—I envy you. And Greece, and Egypt—all the associations! You have travelled back into the Past; you have escaped, as Madame D'Epinay wished, out of civilisation and into romance."

"Yet Madame D'Epinay passed her own life in making pretty romances out of a very agreeable civilisation," said Maltravers, smiling.

"You know her memoirs, then," said Madame de Ventadour, slightly colouring. "In the current of a more exciting literature, few have had time for the second-rate writings of a past century."

"Are not those second-rate performances often the most charming," said Maltravers, "when the mediocrity of the intellect seems almost as if it were the effect of a touching, though too feeble, delicacy of sentiment? Madame D'Epinay's memoirs are of this character. She was not a virtuous woman—but she felt virtue and loved it; she was not a woman of genius—but she was tremblingly alive to all the influences of genius. Some people seem born with the temperament and the tastes of genius without its creative power; they have its nervous system, but something is wanting in the intellectual. They feel acutely, yet express tamely. These persons always have in their character an unspeakable kind of pathos—a court civilisation produces many of them—and the French memoirs of the last century are particularly fraught with such examples. This is interesting—the struggle of sensitive minds against the lethargy of a society, dull, yet brilliant, that *glares* them, as it were, to sleep. It comes home to us! for," added Maltravers, with a slight change of voice, "how many of us fancy we see our own image in the mirror!"

And where was the German baron?—flirting at the other end of the room. And the English lord?—dropping monosyllables to dandies by the doorway. And the minor satellites?—dancing, whispering, making love, or sipping lemonade. And Madame de Ventadour was alone with the young stranger in a crowd of eight hundred persons; and their lips spoke of sentiment, and their eyes involuntarily applied it!

While they were thus conversing, Maltravers was suddenly startled by hearing close behind him, a sharp, significant voice, saying in French, "Hein, hein! I've my suspicions—I've my suspicions."

Madame de Ventadour looked round with a smile. "It is only my husband," said she, quietly; "let me introduce him to you."

Maltravers rose and bowed to a little thin man, most elaborately dressed, with an immense pair of spectacles upon a long sharp nose.

"Charmed to make your acquaintance, sir!" said Monsieur de

Ventadour. "Have you been long in Naples?... Beautiful weather—won't last long—hein, hein, I've my suspicions! No news as to your parliament—be dissolved soon! Bad opera in London this year—hein, hein, I've my suspicions."

This rapid monologue was delivered with appropriate gesture. Each new sentence Mons. de Ventadour began with a sort of bow, and when it dropped in the almost invariable conclusion affirmative of his shrewdness and incredulity, he made a mystical sign with his fore-finger by passing it upward in a parallel line with his nose, which at the same time performed its own part in the ceremony by three convulsive twitches, that seemed to shake the bridge to its base.

Maltravers looked with mute surprise upon the connubial partner of the graceful creature by his side, and Mons. de Ventadour, who had said as much as he thought necessary, wound up his eloquence by expressing the rapture it would give him to see Mons. Maltravers at his hotel. Then, turning to his wife, he began assuring her of the lateness of the hour, and the expediency of departure. Maltravers glided away, and as he regained the door was seized by our old friend, Lumley Ferrers. "Come, my dear fellow," said the latter; "I have been waiting for you this half hour. *Allons.* But, perhaps, as I am dying to go to bed, you have made up your mind to stay supper. Some people have no regard for other people's feelings."

"No, Ferrers, I'm at your service;" and the young man descended the stairs and passed along the Chiaje towards their hotel. As they gained the broad and open space on which it stood, with the lovely sea before them, sleeping in the arms of the curving shore, Maltravers, who had hitherto listened in silence to the volubility of his companion, paused abruptly.

"Look at that sea, Ferrers.... What a scene!—what delicious air! How soft this moonlight! Can you not fancy the old Greek adventurers, when they first colonised this divine Parthenope—the darling of the ocean—gazing along those waves, and pining no more for Greece!"

"I cannot fancy anything of the sort," said Ferrers.... "And, depend upon it, the said gentlemen, at this hour of the night, unless they were on some piratical excursion—for they were cursed ruffians, those old Greek colonists—were fast asleep in their beds."

"Did you ever write poetry, Ferrers?"

"To be sure; all clever men have written poetry once in their lives—small-pox and poetry—they are our two juvenile diseases."

"And did you ever *feel* poetry?"

"Feel it!"

"Yes; if you put the moon into your verses, did you first feel it shining into your heart?"

"My dear Maltravers, if I put the moon into my verses, in all probability it was to rhyme to noon. 'The night was at her noon'—is a capital ending for the first hexameter—and the moon is booked for the next stage. Come in."

"No, I shall stay out."

"Don't be nonsensical."

"By moonlight there is no nonsense like common-sense."

"What! we—who have climbed the Pyramids, and sailed up the Nile, and seen mag c at Cairo, and been nearly murdered, bagged, and Bosphorized at Constantinople, is it for us, who have gone through so many adventures, looked on so many scenes, and crowded into four years events that would have satisfied the appetite of a cormorant in romance, if it had lived to the age of a phœnix;—is it for us to be doing the pretty and sighing to the moon, like a black-haired apprentice without a neckcloth, on board of the Margate hoy? Nonsense, I say—we have lived too much not to have lived away our green sickness of sentiment."

"Perhaps you are right, Ferrers," said Maltravers, smiling. "But I can still enjoy a beautiful night."

"Oh, if you like flies in *your* soup, as the man said to his guest, when he carefully replaced those entomological blackamoors in the tureen, after helping himself—if you like flies in your soup, well and good—*buona notte.*"

Ferrers certainly was right in his theory, that when we have known real adventures we grow less morbidly sentimental. Life is a sleep in which we dream most at the commencement and the close—the middle part absorbs us too much for dreams. But still, as Maltravers said, we can enjoy a fine night, especially on the shores of Naples.

Maltravers paced musingly to and fro for some time. His heart was softened—old rhymes rang in his ear—old memories passed through his brain. But the sweet, dark eyes of Madame de Ventadour shone forth through every shadow of the past. Delicious intoxication—the draught of the rose-coloured phial—which is fancy, but seems love!

CHAPTER II.

*"Then 'gan the Palmer thus—' Most wretched man
That to affections dost the bridle lend:
In their beginning they are weak and wan,
But soon, through suff'rance, growe to fearfull end;
While they are weak, betimes with them contend.'"*
—Spenser.

MALTRAVERS went frequently to the house of Madame de Ventadour—it was open twice a-week to the world, and thrice a-week to friends. Maltravers was soon of the latter class. Madame de Ventadour had been in England in her childhood, for her parents had been *émigrés*. She spoke English well and fluently, and this pleased Maltravers; for though the French language was sufficiently familiar to him, he was like most who are more vain of the mind than the person, and proudly averse to hazarding his best thoughts in the domino of a foreign language. We don't care how faulty the accent, or how incorrect the idiom, in which we talk nothings; but if we utter any of the poetry within us, we shudder at the risk of the most trifling solecism.

This was especially the case with Maltravers; for, besides being now somewhat ripened from his careless boyhood into a proud and fastidious man, he had a natural love for the Becoming. This love was unconsciously visible in trifles; it is the natural parent of Good Taste. And it was indeed an inborn good taste which redeemed Ernest's natural carelessness in those personal matters, in which young men usually take a pride. An habitual and soldier-like neatness, and a love of order and symmetry, stood with him in the stead of elaborate attention to equipage and dress.

Maltravers had not thought twice in his life whether he was handsome or not; and, like most men who have a knowledge of the gentler sex, he knew that beauty had little to do with engaging the love of women. The air, the manner, the tone, the conversation, the something that interests, and the something to be proud of—these are the attributes of the man made to be loved. And the Beauty-man is, nine times of ten, little more than the oracle of his aunts, and the "*sitch* a love" of the housemaids!

To return from this digression, Maltravers was glad that he could talk in his own language to Madame de Ventadour; and the con-vi

whi
and,
hith

Fo
to ca
appre
inde
Meist
In th
ticesh
it ha
lawfu
fancy
styled
of ex
contra
been
and t
shado
vulgar
mystic
The i
under
not o
pervad

The
from
longer
sion.
strang
new

the dead, often so useless, has an inexpressible charm when it is applied to the places where the Dead lived. We care nothing about the ancients on Highgate Hill—but at Baiæ, Pompeii, by the Virgilian Hades, the ancients are society with which we thirst to be familiar. To the animated and curious Frenchwoman what a cicerone was Ernest Maltravers! How eagerly she listened to accounts of a life more elegant than that of Paris!—of a civilisation which the world never can know again! So much the better—for it was rotten at the core, though most brilliant in the complexion. Those cold names and unsubstantial shadows which Madame de Ventadour had been accustomed to yawn over in skeleton histories, took from the eloquence of Maltravers the breath of life—they glowed and moved—they feasted and made love —were wise and foolish, merry and sad, like living things. On the other hand, Maltravers learned a thousand new secrets of the existing and actual world from the lips of the accomplished and observant Valerie. What a new step in the philosophy of life does a young man of genius make when he first compares his theories and experience with the intellect of a clever woman of the world! Perhaps it does not elevate him, but how it enlightens and refines! —what numberless minute yet important mysteries in human character and practical wisdom does he drink unconsciously from the sparkling *persiflage* of such a companion! Our education is hardly ever complete without it.

"And so you think these stately Romans were not, after all, so dissimilar to ourselves?" said Valerie, one day, as they looked over the same earth and ocean along which roved the eyes of the voluptuous but august Lucullus.

"In the last days of their Republic, a *coup-d'œil* of their social date might convey to us a general notion of our own. Their system, like ours—a vast aristocracy heaved and agitated, but kept ambitious and intellectual by the great democratic ocean which roared below and around it. An immense distinction between rich and poor—a nobility sumptuous, wealthy, cultivated, yet scarcely elegant or refined—a people with mighty aspirations for more perfect liberty, but always liable, in a crisis, to be influenced and subdued by a deep-rooted veneration for the very aristocracy against which they struggled—a ready opening, through all the walls of custom and privilege, for every description of talent and ambition; but so strong and universal a respect for wealth, that the finest spirit grew avaricious, griping and corrupt, almost

unconsciously; and the man who rose from the people did not
scruple to enrich himself out of the abuses he affected to lament;
and the man who would have died for his country could not help
thrusting his hands into her pockets. Cassius, the stubborn and
thoughtful patriot, with his heart of iron, had, you remember, an
itching palm. Yet, what a blow to all the hopes and dreams of a
world was the overthrow of the free party after the death of Cæsar!
What generations of freemen fell at Philippi! In England, perhaps, we may have ultimately the same struggle; in France, too
(perhaps a larger stage, with far more inflammable actors), we
already perceive the same war of elements which shook Rome to
her centre, which finally replaced the generous Julius with the
hypocritical Augustus, which destroyed the colossal patricians to
make way for the glittering dwarfs of a court, and cheated a people
out of the substance with the shadow of liberty. How it may end
in the modern world, who shall say? But while a nation has
already a fair degree of constitutional freedom, I believe no
struggle so perilous and awful as that between the aristocratic and
the democratic principle. A people against a despot—*that* contest
requires no prophet; but the change from an aristocratic to a
democratic commonwealth is indeed the wide, unbounded prospect
upon which rest shadows, clouds, and darkness. If it fail—for
centuries is the dial hand of Time put back; if it succeed——"

Maltravers paused.

"And if it succeed?" said Valerie.

"Why, then, man will have colonised Utopia!" replied Maltravers.

"But at least, in modern Europe," he continued, "there will be
fair room for the experiment. For we have not that curse of
slavery which, more than all else, vitiated every system of the
ancients, and kept the rich and poor alternately at war; and we
have a press, which is not only the safety-valve of the passions of
every party, but the great note-book of the experiments of every
hour—the homely, the invaluable ledger of losses and of gains.
No; the people who keep that tablet well never can be bankrupt.
And the society of those old Romans; their daily passions—occupations—humours!—why, the satire of Horace is the glass of our
own follies! We may fancy his easy pages written in the Chaussée
d'Antin, or May-fair; but there was one thing that will ever keep
the ancient world dissimilar from the modern."

"And what is that?"

"The ancients knew not that delicacy in the affections which characterises the descendants of the Goths," said Maltravers, and his voice slightly trembled; "they gave up to the monopoly of the senses what ought to have had an equal share in the reason and the imagination. Their love was a beautiful and wanton butterfly; but not the butterfly which is the emblem of the soul."

Valerie sighed. She looked timidly into the face of the young philosopher, but his eyes were averted.

"Perhaps," she said, after a short pause, "we pass our lives more happily without love than with it. And in our modern social system" (she continued, thoughtfully, and with profound truth, though it is scarcely the conclusion to which a woman often arrives), "I think we have pampered Love to too great a preponderance over the other excitements of life. As children, we are taught to dream of it; in youth, our books, our conversation, our plays, are filled with it. We are trained to consider it the essential of life; and yet, the moment we come to actual experience, the moment we indulge this inculcated and stimulated craving, nine times out of ten we find ourselves wretched and undone. Ah, believe me, Mr. Maltravers, this is not a world in which we should preach up, too far, the philosophy of Love!"

"And does Madame de Ventadour speak from experience?" asked Maltravers, gazing earnestly upon the changing countenance of his companion.

"No; and I trust that I never may!" said Valerie, with great energy.

Ernest's lip curled slightly, for his pride was touched.

"I could give up many dreams of the future," said he, "to hear Madame de Ventadour revoke that sentiment."

"We have outridden our companions, Mr. Maltravers," said Valerie, coldly, and she reined in her horse. "Ah, Mr. Ferrers," she continued, as Lumley and the handsome German baron now joined her, "you are too gallant; I see you imply a delicate compliment to my horsemanship, when you wish me to believe you cannot keep up with me: Mr. Maltravers is not so polite."

"Nay," returned Ferrers, who rarely threw away a compliment without a satisfactory return, "nay, you and Maltravers appeared lost among the old Romans; and our friend the baron took that opportunity to tell me of all the ladies who adored him."

"Ah, Monsieur Ferrare, *que vous êtes malin!*" said Schomberg, looking very much confused.

"*Malin!* no; I spoke from no envy: *I* never was adored, thank heaven! What a bore it must be!"

"I congratulate you on the sympathy between yourself and Ferrers," whispered Maltravers to Valerie.

Valerie laughed; but during the rest of the excursion she remained thoughtful and absent, and for some days their rides were discontinued. Madame de Ventadour was not well.

CHAPTER III.

"O Lord, forsake me not;
Mine were a lone dark lot
Bereft of thee."
—Hemans, *Genius singing in Love.*

FEAR that as yet Ernest Maltravers had gained little from Experience, except a few current coins of worldly wisdom (and not very valuable those!), while he had lost much of that nobler wealth with which youthful enthusiasm sets out on the journey of life. Experience is an open giver, but a stealthy thief. There is, however, this to be said in her favour, that we retain her gifts; and if ever we demand restitution in earnest, 'tis ten to one but what we recover her thefts. Maltravers had lived in lands where public opinion is neither strong in its influence, nor rigid in its canons; and that does not make a man better. Moreover, thrown headlong amidst the temptations that make the first ordeal of youth, with ardent passions and intellectual superiority, he had been led by the one into many errors, from the consequences of which the other had delivered him; the necessity of roughing it through the world—of resisting fraud to-day, and violence to-morrow—had hardened over the surface of his heart, though at bottom the springs were still fresh and living. He had lost much of his chivalrous veneration for women, for he had seen them less often deceived than deceiving. Again, too, the last few years had been spent without any high aims or fixed pursuits. Maltravers had been living on the capital of his faculties and affections in a wasteful, speculating spirit. It is a bad thing for a clever and ardent man not to have from the onset some paramount object of life.

All this considered, we can scarcely wonder that Maltravers

should have fallen into an involuntary system of pursuing his own amusements and pursuits, without much forethought of the harm or the good they were to do to others or himself. The moment we lose forethought, we lose sight of a duty; and though it seems like a paradox, we can seldom be careless without being selfish.

In seeking the society of Madame de Ventadour, Maltravers obeyed but the mechanical impulse that leads the idler towards the companionship which most pleases his leisure. He was interested and excited; and Valerie's manners, which to-day flattered, and to-morrow piquèd him, enlisted his vanity and pride on the side of his fancy. But although Monsieur de Ventadour, a frivolous and profligate Frenchman, seemed utterly indifferent as to what his wife chose to do—and in the society in which Valerie lived almost every lady had her cavalier—yet Maltravers would have started with incredulity or dismay had any one accused him of a systematic design on her affections. But he was living with the world, and the world affected him as it almost always does every one else. Still he had, at times, in his heart, the feeling that he was not fulfilling his proper destiny and duties; and when he stole from the brilliant resorts of an unworthy and heartless pleasure, he was ever and anon haunted by his old familiar aspirations for the Beautiful, the Virtuous, and the Great. However, hell is paved with good intentions; and so, in the meanwhile, Ernest Maltravers surrendered himself to the delicious presence of Valerie de Ventadour.

One evening, Maltravers, Ferrers, the French minister, a pretty Italian, and the Princess di ——, made the whole party collected at Madame de Ventadour's. The conversation fell upon one of the tales of scandal relative to English persons, so common on the continent.

"Is it true, Monsieur," said the French minister, gravely, to Lumley, "that your countrymen are much more immoral than other people? It is very strange, but in every town I enter, there is always some story in which *les Anglais* are the heroes. I hear nothing of French scandal—nothing of Italian—*toujours les Anglais.*"

"Because we are shocked at these things, and make a noise about them, while you take them quietly. Vice is our episode—your epic."

"I suppose it is so," said the Frenchman, with affected seriousness. "If we cheat at play, or flirt with a fair lady, we do it with decorum, and our neighbours think it no business of theirs. But you treat every frailty you find in your countrymen as a public concern, to be discussed and talked over, and exclaimed against, and told to all the world."

"I like the system of scandal," said Madame de Ventadour, abruptly, "say what you will; the policy of fear keeps many of us virtuous. Sin might not be odious, if we did not tremble at the consequence even of appearances."

"Hein, hein," grunted Monsieur de Ventadour, shuffling into the room. "How are you?—how are you? Charmed to see you. Dull night—I suspect we shall have rain. Hein, hein. Aha, Monsieur Ferrers, *comment ça va-t-il?* will you give me my revenge at *écarté?* I have my suspicions that I am in luck to-night. Hein, hein."

"*Écarté!*—well, with pleasure," said Ferrers.

Ferrers played well.

The conversation ended in a moment. The little party gathered round the table—all, except Valerie and Maltravers. The chairs that were vacated left a kind of breach between them; but still they were next to each other, and they felt embarrassed, for they felt alone.

"Do you never play?" asked Madame de Ventadour, after a pause.

"I *have* played," said Maltravers, "and I know the temptation. I dare not play now. I love the excitement, but I have been humbled at the debasement: it is a moral drunkenness that is worse than the physical."

"You speak warmly."

"Because I feel keenly. I once won of a man I respected, who was poor. His agony was a dreadful lesson to me. I went home, and was terrified to think I had felt so much pleasure in the pain of another. I have never played since that night."

"So young and so resolute!" said Valerie, with admiration in her voice and eyes; "you are a strange person. Others would have been cursed by losing, you were cured by winning. It is a fine thing to have principle at your age, Mr. Maltravers."

"I fear it was rather pride than principle," said Maltravers. "Error is sometimes sweet; but there is no anguish like an error of which we feel ashamed. I cannot submit to blush for myself."

"Ah!" muttered Valerie; "this is the echo of my own heart!" She rose and went to the window. Maltravers paused a moment, and followed her. Perhaps he half thought there was an invitation in the movement.

There lay before them the still street, with its feeble and unfrequent lights; beyond, a few stars, struggling through an atmosphere unusually clouded, brought the murmuring ocean partially into sight. Valerie leaned against the wall, and the draperies of the window veiled her from all the guests, save Maltravers; and between her and himself was a large marble vase filled with flowers; and by that uncertain light Valerie's brilliant cheek looked pale, and soft, and thoughtful. Maltravers never before felt so much in love with the beautiful Frenchwoman.

"Ah, madam!" said he softly; "there is one error, if it be so, that never can cost me shame."

"Indeed!" said Valerie, with an unaffected start, for she was not aware he was so near her. As she spoke she began plucking (it is a common woman's trick) the flowers from the vase between her and Ernest. That small, delicate, almost transparent hand!—Maltravers gazed upon the hand, then on the countenance, then on the hand again. The scene swam before him, and involuntarily, and as by an irresistible impulse, the next moment that hand was in his own.

"Pardon me—pardon me," said he, falteringly: "but that error is in the feelings that I know for you."

Valerie lifted on him her large and radiant eyes, and made no answer.

Maltravers went on. "Chide me, scorn me, hate me if you will. Valerie, I love you!"

Valerie drew away her hand, and still remained silent.

"Speak to me," said Ernest, leaning forward; "one word, I implore you—speak to me!"

He paused—still no reply; he listened breathlessly—he heard her sob. Yes; that proud, that wise, that lofty woman of the world, in that moment, was as weak as the simplest girl that ever listened to a lover. But how different the feelings that made her weak?—what soft and what stern emotions were blent together!

"Mr. Maltravers," she said, recovering her voice, though it sounded hollow, yet almost unnaturally firm and clear—"the die is cast, and I have lost for ever the friend for whose happiness I cannot live, but for whose welfare I would have died; I should have foreseen this, but I was blind. No more—no more; see me to-morrow, and leave me now!"

"But Valerie——"

"Ernest Maltravers," said she, laying her hand lightly on his own, "*there is no anguish like an error of which we feel ashamed!*"

Before he could reply to this citation from his own aphorism, Valerie had glided away; and was already seated at the card-table, by the side of the Italian princess.

Maltravers also joined the group. He fixed his eyes on Madame de Ventadour, but her face was calm—not a trace of emotion was discernible. Her voice, her smile, her charming and courtly manner, all were as when he first beheld her.

"These women—what hypocrites they are!" muttered Maltravers to himself; and his lip writhed into a sneer, which had of late often forced away the serene and gracious expression of his earlier years, ere he knew what it was to despise. But Maltravers mistook the woman he had dared to scorn.

He soon withdrew from the palazzo, and sought his hotel. There, while yet musing in his dressing-room, he was joined by Ferrers. The time had passed when Ferrers had exercised an influence over Maltravers; the boy had grown up to be the equal of the man, in the exercise of that two-edged sword—the reason. And Maltravers now felt, unalloyed, the calm consciousness of his superior genius. He could not confide to Ferrers what had passed between him and Valerie. Lumley was too *hard* for a confidant in matters where the heart was at all concerned. In fact, in high spirits, and in the midst of frivolous adventures, Ferrers was charming. But in sadness, or in the moments of deep feeling, Ferrers was one whom you would wish out of the way.

"You are sullen to-night, *mon cher*," said Lumley, yawning; "I suppose you want to go to bed—some persons are so ill-bred, so selfish, they never think of their friends. Nobody asks me what I won at *écarté*. Don't be late to-morrow—I hate breakfasting alone, and *I* am never later than a quarter before nine—I hate egotistical, ill-mannered people. Good-night."

With this, Ferrers sought his own room; there, as he slowly undressed, he thus soliloquised:—"I think I have put this man to all the use I can make of him. We don't pull well together any longer; perhaps I myself am a little tired of this sort of life. That is not right. I shall grow ambitious by-and-by; but I think it a bad calculation not to make the most of youth. At four or five-and-thirty it will be time enough to consider what one ought to be at fifty."

CHAPTER IV.

> "Most dangerous
> Is that temptation that does goad us on
> To sin, in loving virtue."
> —*Measure for Measure.*

"SEE her to-morrow!—that morrow is come!" thought Maltravers, as he rose the next day from a sleepless couch. Ere yet he had obeyed the impatient summons of Ferrers, who had thrice sent to say that "*he* never kept people waiting," his servant entered with a packet from England, that had just arrived by one of those rare couriers who sometimes honour that Naples, which *might* be so lucrative a mart to English commerce, if Neapolitan kings cared for trade, or English senators for "foreign politics." Letters from stewards and bankers were soon got through; and Maltravers reserved for the last an epistle from Cleveland. There was much in it that touched him home. After some dry details about the property, to which Maltravers had now succeeded, and some trifling comments upon trifling remarks in Ernest's former letters, Cleveland went on thus:—

"I confess, my dear Ernest, that I long to welcome you back to England. You have been abroad long enough to *see* other countries; do not stay long enough to prefer them to your own. You are at Naples, too—I tremble for you. I know well that delicious, dreaming, holiday-life of Italy, so sweet to men of learning and imagination—so sweet, too, to youth—so sweet to pleasure! But, Ernest, do you not feel already how it enervates?—how the luxurious *far niente* unfits us for grave exertion? Men may become too refined and too fastidious for useful purposes; and nowhere can they become so more rapidly than in Italy. My dear Ernest, I know you well; you are not made to sink down into a virtuoso, with a cabinet full of cameos and a head full of pictures; still less are you made to be an indolent cicesbeo to some fair Italian, with one passion and two ideas; and yet I have known men as clever as you, whom that bewitching Italy has sunk into one or other of these insignificant beings. Don't run away with the notion that you have plenty of time before you. You have no such thing. At your age, and with your fortune (I wish you were not so rich!), the holiday of one year becomes the custom of the next. In England, to be a useful or a distinguished man, you must labour. Now, labour itself is sweet, if we take to it early. We are a hardy race, but we are a manly one; and our stage is the most exciting in Europe for an able and an honest ambition. Perhaps you will tell me you are not ambitious now; very possibly—but ambitious you will be; and believe me, there is no unhappier wretch than a man who is ambitious but disappointed—who has the desire for fame, but has lost the power to achieve it—who longs for the goal, but will not, and cannot, put away his slippers to walk to it. What I most fear for you is one of these two evils—an early marriage or a fatal *liaison* with some married woman. The first evil is certainly the least, but for *you* it would still be a great one. With your sensitive romance, with your morbid cravings for the ideal, domestic happiness would soon grow trite and dull. You would demand new excitement, and become a restless and disgusted man. It is necessary for you to get rid of all the false fever of life before you settle down to everlasting ties. You do not yet know your own mind; you would choose your partner from some visionary caprice, or momentary impulse, and not from the deep and accurate knowledge of those qualities which would most harmonise with your own character. People, to live happily with each other, must *fit in*, as it were—the proud be mated with the meek, the irritable with the gentle, and so forth. No, my dear Maltravers, do not think of marriage yet awhile; and if there is any danger of it, come over to me immediately. But if I warn you against a lawful tie, how much more against an illicit one? You are precisely of the age, and of the disposition, which render the temptation so strong and so deadly. With you it might not be the sin of an hour, but the bondage of a life. I know your chivalric honour—your tender heart; I know how faithful you would be to one who had sacrificed for you. But that fidelity, Maltravers, to what a life of wasted talent and energy would it not compel you! Putting aside for the moment (for that needs no comment) the question of the grand immorality—what so fatal to a bold and proud temper as to be at war with society at the first entrance into life? What so withering to manly aims and purposes as the giving into the keeping of a woman, who has interest in your love, and interest against your career, which might part you at once from her side—the control of your future destinies? I could say more, but I trust what I have said is superfluous; if so, pray assure me of it. Depend upon this, Ernest Maltravers, that if you do not fulfil what nature intended for your fate, you will be a morbid misanthrope, or an indolent voluptuary—wretched and listless in manhood, repining and joyless in old age. But if you do fulfil your fate, you must enter soon into your apprenticeship. Let me see you labour and aspire—no matter what in—what to. Work, work—that is all I ask of you!

"I wish you could see your old country-house; it has a venerable and picturesque look, and during your minority they have let the ivy cover three sides of it. Montaigne might have lived there.

"Adieu, dearest Ernest,

"Your anxious and affectionate guardian,

"FREDERICK CLEVELAND.

"*P.S.*—I am writing a book—it shall last me ten years—it occupies me, but does not fatigue. Write a book yourself."

Maltravers had just finished this letter when Ferrers entered impatiently. "Will you ride out?" said he. "I have sent the breakfast away; I saw that breakfast was a vain hope to-day—indeed, *my* appetite is gone."

"Pshaw!" said Maltravers.

"Pshaw! humph! for my part I like well-bred people."

"I have had a letter from Cleveland."

"And what the deuce has that got to do with the chocolate, my dear fellow?"

"Oh, Lumley, you are insufferable; you think of nothing but yourself, and self with you means nothing that is not animal."

"Why, yes; I believe I have some sense," replied Ferrers, complacently. "I know the philosophy of life. All unfledged bipeds are animals, I suppose. If Providence had made me graminivorous, I should have eaten grass; if ruminating, I should have chewed the cud; but as it has made me a carnivorous, culinary, and cachinnatory animal, I eat a cutlet, scold about the sauce, and laugh at you; and that is what *you* call being selfish!"

It was late at noon when Maltravers found himself at the palazzo of Madame de Ventadour. He was surprised, but agreeably so, that he was admitted, for the first time, into the private sanctum which bears the hackneyed title of boudoir. But there was little enough of the fine lady's boudoir in the simple morning-room of Madame de Ventadour. It was a lofty apartment, stored with books, and furnished, not without claim to grace, but with very small attention to luxury.

Valerie was not there; and Maltravers, left alone, after a hasty glance around the chamber, leaned abstractedly against the wall, and forgot, alas! all the admonitions of Cleveland. In a few moments the door opened, and Valerie entered. She was unusually pale, and Maltravers thought her eyelids betrayed the traces of tears. He was touched, and his heart smote him.

"I have kept you waiting, I fear," said Valerie, motioning him to a seat at a little distance from that on which she placed herself; "but you will forgive me," she added, with a slight smile. Then, observing he was about to speak, she went on rapidly, "Hear me, Mr. Maltravers—before you speak, hear me! You uttered words last night that ought never to have been addressed to me. You professed to—love me."

"Professed!"

"Answer me," said Valerie, with abrupt energy, "not as man to woman, but as one human creature to another. From the bottom of your heart, from the core of your conscience, I call on you to speak the honest and the simple truth. Do you love me as your heart, your genius, must be capable of loving?"

"I love you truly—passionately!" said Maltravers, surprised and confused, but still with enthusiasm in his musical voice and earnest eyes. Valerie gazed upon him as if she sought to penetrate into his soul. Maltravers went on—"Yes, Valerie, when we first met you aroused a long dormant and delicious sentiment. But, since then, what deep emotions has that sentiment called forth? Your graceful intellect—your lovely thoughts, wise yet womanly—have completed the conquest your face and voice began. Valerie, I love you. And you—you, Valerie—ah! I do not deceive myself—you also——"

"Love!" interrupted Valerie, deeply blushing, but in a calm voice. "Ernest Maltravers, I do not deny it; honestly and frankly I confess the fault. I have examined my heart during the whole of the last sleepless night, and I confess that I love you. Now, then, understand me; we meet no more."

"What!" said Maltravers, falling involuntarily at her feet, and seeking to detain her hand, which he seized. "What! now, when you have given life a new charm, will you as suddenly blast it? No, Valerie; no, I will not listen to you."

Madame de Ventadour rose and said, with a cold dignity—"Hear me calmly, or I quit the room; and all I would now say rests for ever unspoken."

Maltravers rose also, folded his arms haughtily, bit his lip, and stood erect, and confronting Valerie rather in the attitude of an accuser than a suppliant.

"Madame," said he, gravely, "I will offend no more; I will trust to your manner, since I may not believe your words."

"You are cruel," said Valerie, smiling mournfully; "but so are all men. Now let me make myself understood. I was betrothed to Monsieur de Ventadour in my childhood. I did not see him till a month before we married. I had no choice. French girls have none! We were wed. I had formed no other attachment. I was proud and vain: wealth, ambition, and social rank for a time satisfied my faculties and my heart. At length I grew restless and unhappy. I felt that something of life was wanting. Monsieur de Ventadour's sister was the first to recommend to me the common resource of our sex—at least, in France—a lover. I was shocked and startled, for I belong to a family in which women are chaste and men brave. I began, however, to look around me, and examine the truth of the philosophy of vice. I found that no woman who loved honestly and deeply an illicit lover was happy. I found, too, the hideous profundity of Rochefoucauld's maxim, that a woman—I speak of French women—may live without a lover; but, a lover once admitted, she never goes through life with *only* one. She is deserted; she cannot bear the anguish and the solitude; she fills up the void with a second idol. For her there is no longer a fall from virtue; it is a gliding and involuntary descent from sin to sin, till old age comes on and leaves her without love and without respect. I reasoned calmly, for my passions did not blind my reason. I could not love the egotists around me. I resolved upon my career; and now, in temptation, I will adhere to it. Virtue is my lover, my pride, my comfort, my life of life. Do you love me, and will you rob me of this treasure? I saw you, and for the first time I felt a vague and intoxicating interest in another; but I did not dream of danger. As our acquaintance advanced I formed to myself a romantic and delightful vision. I would be your firmest, your truest friend; your confidant, your adviser—perhaps, in some epochs of life, your inspiration and your guide. I repeat that I foresaw no danger in your society. I felt myself a nobler and a better thing. I felt more benevolent, more tolerant, more exalted. I saw life through the medium of purifying admiration for a gifted nature, and a profound and generous soul. I fancied we might be ever thus—each to each—one strengthened, assured, supported by the other. Nay, I even contemplated with pleasure the prospect of your future marriage with another—of your loving wife—of contributing with her to your happiness—my imagination made me forget that we are made of clay. Suddenly, all these visions were expelled—the fairy palace was overthrown, and I found myself awake, and on the brink of the abyss—you loved me, and in the moment of that fatal confession, the mask dropped from my soul, and I felt that you had become too dear to me. Be silent still, I implore you. I do not tell you of the emotions, of the struggles, through which I have passed the last few hours—the crisis of a life. I tell you only of the resolution I formed. I thought it due to you, nor unworthy of myself, to speak the truth. Perhaps it might be more womanly to conceal it; but my heart has something masculine in its nature. I have a great faith in your nobleness. I believe you can sympathise with whatever is best in human weakness. I tell you that I love you—I throw myself upon your generosity. I beseech you to assist my own sense of right—to think well of me, to honour me—and to leave me!"

During the last part of this strange and frank avowal, Valerie's voice had grown inexpressibly touching: her tenderness forced itself into her manner; and when she ceased, her lip quivered; her tears, repressed by a violent effort, trembled in her eyes—her hands were clasped—her attitude was that of humility, not pride.

Maltravers stood perfectly spell-bound. At length he advanced; dropped on one knee, kissed her hand with an aspect and air of reverential homage, and turned to quit the room in silence; for he would not dare to trust himself to speak.

Valerie gazed at him in anxious alarm. "Oh, no, no!" she exclaimed, "do not leave me yet; this is our last meeting—our last. Tell me, at least, that you understand me; that you see, if I am no weak fool, I am also no heartless coquette; tell me that you see I am not so hard as I have seemed; that I have not knowingly trifled with your happiness; that even now I am not selfish. Your love—I ask it no more! But your esteem—your good opinion. Oh, speak—speak, I implore you!"

"Valerie," said Maltravers, "if I was silent, it was because my heart was too full for words. You have raised all womanhood in my eyes. I did love you—I now venerate and adore. Your noble frankness, so unlike the irresolute frailty, the miserable wiles of your sex, has touched a chord in my heart that has been mute for years. I leave you to think better of human nature. Oh!" he continued, "hasten to forget all of me that can cost you a pang.

Let me still, in absence and in sadness, think that I retain in your friendship—let it be friendship only—the inspiration, the guide of which you spoke; and if, hereafter, men shall name me with praise and honour, feel, Valerie, feel that I have comforted myself for the loss of your love by becoming worthy of your confidence—your esteem. Oh, that we had met earlier, when no barrier was between us!"

"Go, go, *now*," faltered Valerie, almost choked with her emotions; "may heaven bless you! Go!"

Maltravers muttered a few inaudible and incoherent words, and quitted the apartment.

CHAPTER V.

"The men of sense, those idols of the shadow, are very inferior to the men of Passions. It is the strong passions which, rescuing us from sloth, can alone impart to us that continuous and earnest attention necessary to great intellectual efforts."—HELVETIUS.

WHEN Ferrers returned that day from his customary ride, he was surprised to see the lobbies and hall of the apartment which he occupied in common with Maltravers littered with bags and *malles*, boxes and books, and Ernest's Swiss valet directing porters and waiters in a mosaic of French, English, and Italian.

"Well!" said Lumley, "and what is all this?"

"Il signore va partir, sare, ah! mon Dieu!—*tout* of a sudden."

"O—h! and where is he now?"

"In his room, sare."

Over the chaos strode Ferrers, and opening the door of his friend's dressing-room without ceremony, he saw Maltravers buried in a fauteuil, with his hands drooping on his knees, his head bent over his breast, and his whole attitude expressive of dejection and exhaustion.

"What is the matter, my dear Ernest? You have not killed a man in a duel?"

"No."

"What then?—Why are you going away, and whither?"

"No matter; leave me in peace."

"Friendly!" said Ferrers; "very friendly! And what is to become of me—what companion am I to have in this cursed resort of antiquarians and lazzaroni? You have no feeling, Mr. Maltravers!"

"Will you come with me, then?" said Maltravers, in vain endeavouring to rouse himself.

"But where are you going?"

"Anywhere; to Paris—to London."

"No; I have arranged my plans for the summer. I am not so rich as some people. I hate change: it is so expensive."

"But, my dear fellow——"

"Is this fair dealing with me?" continued Lumley, who, for once in his life, was really angry. "If I were an old coat you had worn for five years, you could not throw me off with more nonchalance."

"Ferrers, forgive me. My honour is concerned. I must leave this place. I trust you will remain my guest here, though in the absence of your host. You know that I have engaged the apartments for the next three months."

"Humph!" said Ferrers; "as that is the case, I may as well stay here. But why so secret? Have you seduced Madame de Ventadour, or has her wise husband his suspicions? Hein, hein!"

Maltravers smothered his disgust at this coarseness; and, perhaps, there is no greater trial of temper than in a *he* friend's gross remarks upon the connections of the heart.

"Ferrers," said he, "if you care for me, breathe not a word disrespectful to Madame de Ventadour: she is an angel!"

"But why leave Naples?"

"Trouble me no more."

"Good day, sir," said Ferrers, highly offended, and he stalked out of the chamber; nor did Ernest see him again before his departure.

It was late that evening when Maltravers found himself alone in his carriage, pursuing by starlight the ancient and melancholy road to Mola di Gaëta.

His solitude was a luxury to Maltravers; he felt an inexpressible sense of release to be freed from Ferrers. The hard sense, the unpliant though humorous imperiousness, the animal sensuality of his companion, would have been a torture to him in his present state of mind.

The next morning, when he rose, the orange blossoms of Mola di Gaëta were sweet beneath the window of the inn where he rested. It was now the early spring, and the freshness of the odour, the breathing health of earth and air, it is impossible to describe. Italy itself boasts few spots more lovely than that same Mola di Gaëta—nor does that halcyon sea wear, even at Naples or Sorrento, a more bland and enchanting smile.

So, after a hasty and scarcely tasted breakfast, Maltravers strolled through the orange groves, and gained the beach; and there, stretched at idle length by the murmuring waves, he resigned himself to thought, and endeavoured, for the first time since his parting with Valerie, to collect and examine the state of his mind and feelings. Maltravers, to his own surprise, did not find himself so unhappy as he had expected. On the contrary, a soft and almost delicious sentiment, which he could not well define, floated over all his memories of the beautiful Frenchwoman. Perhaps the secret was, that while his pride was not mortified, his conscience was not galled—perhaps, also, he had not loved Valerie so deeply as he had imagined. The confession and the separation had happily come before her presence had grown—*the want of a life*. As it was, he felt as if, by some holy and mystic sacrifice, he had been made reconciled to himself and mankind. He woke to a juster and higher appreciation of human nature, and of woman's nature in especial. He had found honesty and truth where he might least have expected it—in a woman of a court—in a woman surrounded by vicious and frivolous circles—in a woman who had nothing in the opinion of her friends, her country, her own husband, the social system in which she moved, to keep her from the concessions of frailty—in a woman of the world—a woman of Paris!—yes, it was his very disappointment that drove away the fogs and vapours that, arising from the marshes of the great world, had gradually settled round his soul. Valerie de Ventadour had taught him not to despise her sex, not to judge by appearances, not to sicken of a low and hypocritical world. He looked in his heart for the love of Valerie, and he found there the love of Virtue. Thus, as he turned his eyes inward, did he gradually awaken to a sense of the true impressions engraved there. And he felt the bitterest drop of the deep fountains was not sorrow for himself, but for her. What pangs must that high spirit have endured ere it could have submitted to the avowal it had made! Yet, even in this affliction, he found at last a solace. A mind so strong could support and heal the weakness of the heart. He felt that Valerie de Ventadour was not a woman to pine away in the unresisted indulgence of morbid and unholy emotions. He could not flatter himself that she would not seek to eradicate a love she repented;

and he sighed with a natural selfishness, when he owned also that sooner or later she would succeed. "But be it so," said he, half aloud—"I will prepare my heart to rejoice when I learn that she remembers me only as a friend. Next to the bliss of her love is the pride of her esteem."

Such was the sentiment with which his reveries closed—and with every league that bore him further from the south the sentiment grew strengthened and confirmed.

Ernest Maltravers felt that there is in the Affections themselves so much to purify and exalt, that even an erring love, conceived without a cold design, and (when its nature is fairly understood) wrestled against with a noble spirit, leaves the heart more tolerant and tender, and the mind more settled and enlarged. The philosophy limited to the reason puts into motion the automata of the closet—but to those who have the world for a stage, and who find their hearts are the great actors, experience and wisdom must be wrought from the Philosophy of the Passions.

BOOK III.

CHAPTER I.

"Here will we sit, and let the sounds of music
Creep in our ears—soft stillness and the night
Become the touches of sweet harmony."—SHAKSPEARE.

BOAT SONG ON THE LAKE OF COMO.

1.

"The Beautiful Clime!—the Clime of Love!
  Thou beautiful Italy!
Like a mother's eyes, the earnest skies
  Ever have smiles for thee!
Not a flower that blows, not a beam that glows,
  But what is in love with thee!

2.

The beautiful lake, the Larian lake!
  Soft lake like a silver sea,
The Huntress Queen, with her nymphs of sheen,
  Never had bath like thee.
See, the Lady of Night and her maids of light,
  Even now are mid-deep in thee!

3.

Beautiful child of the lonely hills,
  Ever blest may thy slumbers be!
No mourner should tread by thy dreamy bed,
  No life bring a care to thee—
Nay, soft to thy bed, let the mourner tread—
  And life be a dream like thee!"

SUCH, though uttered in the soft Italian tongue, and now imperfectly translated—such were the notes that floated one lovely evening in summer along the lake of Como. The boat, from which came the song, drifted gently down the sparkling waters, towards the mossy banks of a lawn, whence on a little eminence gleamed the white walls of a villa, backed by vineyards. On that lawn stood a young and handsome woman, leaning on the arm of her husband, and listening to the song. But her delight was soon deepened into one of more personal interest, as the boatmen, nearing the banks, changed their measure, and she felt that the minstrelsy was in honour of herself.

SERENADE TO THE SONGSTRESS.

1.
CHORUS.

"Softly—oh, soft ! let us rest on the oar,
And vex not a billow that sighs to the shore—
For sacred the spot where the starry waves meet
With the beach, where the breath of the citron is sweet;
There's a spell on the waves that now waft us along
To the last of our Muses, the Spirit of Song.

RECITATIVE.

The Eagle of old renown,
And the Lombard's iron crown,
And Milan's mighty name are ours no more;
But by this glassy water,
Harmonia's youngest daughter,
Still from the lightning saves one laurel to our shore.

2.
CHORUS.

They heard thee, Teresa, the Teuton, the Gaul,
Who have raised the rude thrones of the North on our fall;
They heard thee, and bow'd to the might of thy song,
Like love went thy steps o'er the hearts of the strong,
As the moon to the air, as the soul to the clay,
To the void of this earth was the breath of thy lay.

RECITATIVE.

Honour for aye to her,
The bright interpreter
Of Art's great mysteries to the enchanted throng;
While tyrants heard thy strains,
Sad Rome forgot her chains :
The world the sword had lost was conquer'd back by song !"

"Thou repentest, my Teresa, that thou hast renounced thy dazzling career for a dull home, and a husband old enough to be thy father," said the husband to the wife, with a smile that spoke confidence in the answer.

"Ah, no! even this homage would have no music to me if thou didst not hear it."

She was a celebrated personage in Italy—the Signora Cesarini, now Madame de Montaigne! Her earlier youth had been spent upon the stage, and her promise of vocal excellence had been most brilliant. But after a brief though splendid career, she married a French gentleman of good birth and fortune, retired from the stage, and spent her life alternately in the gay saloons of Paris, and upon the banks of the dreamy Como, on which her husband had purchased a small but beautiful villa. She still, however, exercised in private her fascinating art; to which—for she was a woman of singular accomplishment and talent—she added the gift of the improvisatrice. She had just returned for the summer to this lovely retreat, and a party of enthusiastic youths from Milan had sought the lake of Como to welcome her arrival with the suitable homage of song and music. It is a charming relic, that custom of the brighter days of Italy; and I myself have listened, on the still waters of the same lake, to a similar greeting to a greater genius—the queen-like and unrivalled Pasta—the Semiramis of Song! And while my boat paused, and I caught something of the enthusiasm of the serenaders, the boatman touched me, and, pointing to a part of the lake on which the setting sun shed its rosiest smile, he said, "There, Signor, was drowned one of your countrymen—'bellissimo uomo! che fu bello!'"—yes, there, in the pride of his promising youth, of his noble and almost godlike beauty, before the very windows—the very eyes—of his bride—the waves, without a frown, had swept over the idol of many hearts—the graceful and gallant Locke.* And above his grave was the voluptuous sky, and over it floated the triumphant music. It was as the moral of the Roman poets—calling the living to a holiday over the oblivion of the dead.

As the boat now touched the bank, Madame de Montaigne accosted the musicians, thanked them with a sweet and unaffected earnestness for the compliment so delicately offered, and invited

---

* Captain William Locke of the Life Guards (the only son of the accomplished Mr. Locke of Norbury Park), distinguished by a character the most amiable, and by a personal beauty that certainly equalled, perhaps surpassed, the highest masterpiece of Grecian Sculpture. He was returning, in a boat, from the town of Como, to his villa on the banks of the lake, when the boat was upset by one of the mysterious under-currents to which the lake is dangerously subjected, and he was drowned in sight of his bride, who was watching his return from the terrace or balcony of their home.

them ashore. The Milanese, who were six in number, accepted the invitation, and moored their boat to the jutting shore. It was then that Monsieur de Montaigne pointed out to the notice of his wife a boat that had lingered under the shadow of a bank, tenanted by a young man, who had seemed to listen with rapt attention to the music, and who had once joined in the chorus (as it was twice repeated), with a voice so exquisitely attuned, and so rich in its deep power, that it had awakened the admiration even of the serenaders themselves.

"Does not that gentleman belong to your party?" De Montaigne asked of the Milanese.

"No, Signor, we know him not," was the answer; "his boat came unawares upon us as we were singing."

While this question and answer were going on, the young man had quitted his station, and his oars cut the glassy surface of the lake, just before the place where De Montaigne stood. With the courtesy of his country, the Frenchman lifted his hat; and by his gesture arrested the eye and oar of the solitary rower. "Will you honour us," he said, "by joining our little party?"

"It is a pleasure I covet too much to refuse," replied the boatman, with a slight foreign accent, and in another moment he was on shore. He was one of remarkable appearance. His long hair floated with a careless grace over a brow more calm and thoughtful than became his years; his manner was unusually quiet and self-collected, and not without a certain stateliness, rendered more striking by the height of his stature, a lordly contour of feature, and a serene, but settled expression of melancholy in his eyes and smile. "You will easily believe," said he, "that, cold as my countrymen are esteemed (for you must have discovered already that I am an Englishman), I could not but share in the enthusiasm of those about me, when loitering near the very ground sacred to the inspiration. For the rest, I am residing for the present in yonder villa, opposite to your own: my name is Maltravers, and I am enchanted to think that I am no longer a personal stranger to one whose fame has already reached me."

Madame de Montaigne was flattered by something in the manner and tone of the Englishman, which said a great deal more than his words; and in a few minutes, beneath the influence of the happy continental ease, the whole party seemed as if they had known each other for years. Wines, and fruits, and other simple and unpretending refreshments were brought out and arranged on a rude

THE FRENCHMAN LIFTED HIS HAT, AND, BY HIS GESTURE, ARRESTED THE EYE AND OAR OF THE SOLITARY ROWER.

table upon the grass, round which the guests seated themselves with their host and hostess, and the clear moon shone over them, and the lake slept below in silver. It was a scene for a Boccaccio or a Claude.

The conversation naturally fell upon music; it is almost the only thing which Italians in general can be said to know—and even that knowledge comes to them, like Dogberry's reading and writing, by nature—for of music, as an *art*, the unprofessional amateurs know but little. As vain and arrogant of the last wreck of their national genius as the Romans of old were of the empire of all arts and arms, they look upon the harmonies of other lands as barbarous; nor can they appreciate or understand appreciation of the mighty German music, which is the proper minstrelsy of a nation of *men*— a music of philosophy, of heroism, of the intellect and the imagination; beside which, the strains of modern Italy are indeed effeminate, fantastic, and artificially feeble. Rossini is the Canova of music, with much of the pretty, with nothing of the grand!

The little party talked, however, of music, with an animation and gusto that charmed the melancholy Maltravers, who for weeks had known no companion save his own thoughts, and with whom, at all times, enthusiasm for any art found a ready sympathy. He listened attentively, but said little; and from time to time, whenever the conversation flagged, amused himself by examining his companions. The six Milanese had nothing remarkable in their countenances or in their talk; they possessed the characteristic energy and volubility of their countrymen, with something of the masculine dignity which distinguishes the Lombard from the Southern, and a little of the French polish, which the inhabitants of Milan seldom fail to contract. Their rank was evidently that of the middle class; for Milan has a middle class, and one which promises great results hereafter. But they were noways distinguished from a thousand other Milanese whom Maltravers had met in the walks and cafés of their noble city. The host was somewhat more interesting. He was a tall, handsome man, of about eight-and-forty, with a high forehead, and features strongly impressed with the sober character of thought. He had but little of the French vivacity in his manner; and without looking at his countenance, you would still have felt insensibly that he was the oldest of the party. His wife was at least twenty years younger than himself, mirthful and playful as a child, but with a certain feminine and fascinating softness in her unrestrained gestures and sparkling gaiety, which seemed to subdue her natural joyousness into the form and method of conventual elegance. Dark hair carelessly arranged, an open forehead, large, black, laughing eyes, a small, straight nose, a complexion just relieved from the olive by an evanescent yet perpetually recurring blush ; a round, dimpled cheek, an exquisitely-shaped mouth, with small pearly teeth, and a light and delicate figure a little below the ordinary standard, completed the picture of Madame de Montaigne.

"Well," said Signor Tirabaloschi, the most loquacious and sentimental of the guests, filling his glass ; " these are hours to think of for the rest of life. But we cannot hope the Signora will long remember what *we* never can forget. Paris, says the French proverb, *est le paradis des femmes;* and, in paradise, I take it for granted, we recollect very little of what happened on earth."

"Oh," said Madame de Montaigne, with a pretty musical laugh, "in Paris it is the rage to despise the frivolous life of cities, and to affect *des sentimens romanesques.* This is precisely the scene which our fine ladies and fine writers would die to talk of and describe. Is it not so, *mon ami ?*" and she turned affectionately to De Montaigne.

"True," replied he ; " but you are not worthy of such a scene— you laugh at sentiment and romance."

"Only at French sentiment, and the romance of the Chaussée d'Antin. You English," she continued, shaking her head at Maltravers, " have spoiled and corrupted us ; we are not content to imitate you, we must excel you ; we out-horror horror, and rush from the extravagant into the frantic !"

"The ferment of the new school is, perhaps, better than the stagnation of the old," said Maltravers. "Yet even you," addressing himself to the Italians, "who first in Petrarch, in Tasso, and in Ariosto, set to Europe the example of the sentimental and the romantic ; who built among the very ruins of the classic school, amidst its Corinthian columns and sweeping arches, the spires and battlements of the Gothic—even you are deserting your old models, and guiding literature into newer and wilder paths. 'Tis the way of the world—eternal progress is eternal change."

"Very possibly," said Signor Tirabaloschi, who understood nothing of what was said. "Nay, it is extremely profound ; on reflection, it is beautiful—superb ; you English are so—so—in short, it is admirable. Ugo Foscolo is a great genius—so is Monti ; and as for Rossini—you know his last opera—*cosa stupenda !*"

Madame de Montaigne glanced at Maltravers, clapped her little hands, and laughed outright. Maltravers caught the contagion, and laughed also. But he hastened to repair the pedantic error he had committed of talking over the heads of the company. He took up the guitar, which, among their musical instruments, the serenaders had brought, and, after touching its chords for a few moments, said: "After all, Madame, in your society, and with this moonlit lake before us, we feel as if music were our best medium of conversation. Let us prevail upon these gentlemen to delight us once more."

"You forestall what I was going to ask," said the ex-singer; and Maltravers offered the guitar to Tirabaloschi, who was, in fact, dying to exhibit his powers again. He took the instrument with a slight grimace of modesty, and then, saying to Madame de Montaigne, "There is a song composed by a young friend of mine, which is much admired by the ladies; though, to me, it seems a little too sentimental," sang the following stanzas (as good singers are wont to do) with as much feeling as if he could understand them!—

NIGHT AND LOVE.

"When stars are in the quiet skies,
 Then most I pine for thee;
Bend on me, then, thy tender eyes,
 As stars look on the sea!

For thoughts, like waves that glide by night,
 Are stillest where they shine;
Mine earthly love lies hushed in light,
 Beneath the heaven of thine.

There is an hour when angels keep
 Familiar watch on men;
When coarser souls are wrapt in sleep—
 Sweet spirit, meet me then.

There is an hour when holy dreams,
 Through slumber, fairest glide;
And in that mystic hour it seems
 Thou should'st be by my side.

The thoughts of thee too sacred are
 For daylight's common beam—
I can but know thee as my star,
 My angel, and my dream."

And now, the example set, and the praises of the fair hostess exciting general emulation, the guitar circled from hand to hand,

and each of the Italians performed his part—you might have fancied yourself at one of the old Greek feasts, with the lyre and the myrtle-branch going the round.

But both the Italians and the Englishman felt the entertainment would be incomplete without hearing the celebrated vocalist and improvisatrice who presided over the little banquet; and Madame de Montaigne, with a woman's tact, divined the general wish, and anticipated the request that was sure to be made. So she took the guitar from the last singer, and, turning to Maltravers, said, "You have heard, of course, some of our more eminent improvisatori, and therefore if I ask you for a subject it will only be to prove to you that the talent is not general amongst the Italians."

"Ah," said Maltravers, "I have heard, indeed, some ugly old gentlemen, with immense whiskers, and gestures of the most alarming ferocity, pour out their vehement impromptus; but I have never yet listened to a young and a handsome lady. I shall only believe the inspiration when I hear it direct from the Muse."

"Well, I will do my best to deserve your compliments—you must give me the theme."

Maltravers paused a moment, and suggested the Influence of Praise on Genius.

The improvisatrice nodded assent, and after a short prelude broke forth into a wild and varied strain of verse, in a voice so exquisitely sweet, with a taste so accurate, and a feeling so deep, that the poetry sounded to the enchanted listeners like the language that Armida might have uttered. Yet the verses themselves, like all extemporaneous effusions, were of a nature both to pass from the memory and to defy transcription.

When Madame de Montaigne's song ceased, no rapturous plaudits followed—the Italians were too affected by the science, Maltravers by the feeling, for the coarseness of ready praise; and ere that delighted silence which made the first impulse was broken, a new-comer, descending from the groves that clothed the ascent behind the house, was in the midst of the party.

"Ah, my dear brother," cried Madame de Montaigne, starting up, and hanging fondly on the arm of the stranger, "why have you lingered so long in the wood? You, so delicate! And how are you? How pale you seem!"

"It is but the reflection of the moonlight, Teresa," said the intruder. "I feel well." So saying, he scowled on the merry party, and turned as if to slink away.

"No, no," whispered Teresa, "you must stay a moment and be presented to my guests; there is an Englishman here whom you will like—who will *interest* you."

With that she almost dragged him forward, and introduced him to her guests. Signor Cesarini returned their salutations with a mixture of bashfulness and *hauteur*, half-awkward, and half-graceful, and muttering some inaudible greeting, sank into a seat, and appeared instantly lost in reverie. Maltravers gazed upon him, and was pleased with his aspect—which, if not handsome, was strange and peculiar. He was extremely slight and thin—his cheeks hollow and colourless, with a profusion of black, silken ringlets, that almost descended to his shoulders. His eyes, deeply sunk into his head, were large and intensely brilliant; and a thin moustache, curling downward, gave an additional austerity to his mouth, which was closed with gloomy and half-sarcastic firmness. He was not dressed as people dress in general, but wore a frock of dark camlet, with a large shirt-collar turned down, and a narrow slip of black silk twisted rather than tied round his throat; his nether garment fitted tight to his limbs, and a pair of half-hessians completed his costume. It was evident that the young man (and he was very young—perhaps about nineteen or twenty) indulged that coxcombry of the Picturesque, which is the sign of a vainer mind than is the commoner coxcombry of the *Mode*.

It is astonishing how frequently it happens that the introduction of a single intruder upon a social party is sufficient to destroy all the familiar harmony that existed there before. We see it even when the intruder is agreeable and communicative—but in the present instance, a ghost could scarcely have been a more unwelcoming or unwelcome visitor. The presence of this shy, speechless, supercilious-looking man, threw a damp over the whole group. The gay Tirabaloschi immediately discovered that it was time to depart—it had not struck anyone before, but it certainly *was* late. The Italians began to bustle about, to collect their music, to make fine speeches and fine professions—to bow and to smile—to scramble into their boat, and to push off towards the inn at Como, where they had engaged their quarters for the night. As the boat glided away, and while two of them were employed at the oar, the remaining four took up their instruments and sang a parting glee. It was quite midnight—the hush of all things around had grown more intense and profound—there was a wonderful might of silence in the shining air and amidst the shadows thrown by the near banks and distant hills over the water. So that, as the music chiming in with the oars grew fainter and fainter, it is impossible to describe the thrilling and magical effect it produced.

The party ashore did not speak; there was a moisture, a grateful one, in the bright eyes of Teresa, as she leant upon the manly form of De Montaigne, for whom her attachment was, perhaps, yet more deep and pure for the difference of their ages. A girl who once loves a man, not indeed old, but much older than herself, loves him with such a *looking up* and venerating love! Maltravers stood a little apart from the couple, on the edge of the shelving bank, with folded arms and thoughtful countenance. "How is it," said he, unconscious that he was speaking half aloud, "that the commonest beings of the world should be able to give us a pleasure so unworldly? What a contrast between those musicians and this music! At this distance, their forms are dimly seen, one might almost fancy the creators of those sweet sounds to be of another mould from us. Perhaps even thus the poetry of the Past rings on our ears—the deeper and the diviner, because removed from the clay which made the poets. O Art, Art! how dost thou beautify and exalt us! what is nature without thee!"

"You are a poet, Signor," said a soft, clear voice beside the soliloquist; and Maltravers started to find that he had had unknowingly a listener in the young Cesarini.

"No," said Maltravers, "I cull the flowers, I do not cultivate the soil."

"And why not?" said Cesarini, with abrupt energy; "you are an Englishman—*you* have a public—you have a country—you have a living stage, a breathing audience; we Italians have nothing but the Dead."

As he looked on the young man, Maltravers was surprised to see the sudden animation which glowed upon his pale features.

"You asked me a question I would fain put to you," said the Englishman, after a pause. "*You*, methinks, are a poet?"

"I have fancied that I might be one. But poetry with us is a bird in the wilderness—it sings from an impulse—the song dies without a listener. Oh that I belonged to a *living* country—France, England, Germany, America—and not to the corruption of a dead giantess—for such is now the land of the ancient lyre."

"Let us meet again, and soon," said Maltravers, holding out his hand.

Cesarini hesitated a moment, and then accepted and returned

the proffered salutation. Reserved as he was, something in Maltravers attracted him; and, indeed, there was that in Ernest which fascinated most of those unhappy eccentrics who do not move in the common orbit of the world.

In a few moments more the Englishman had said farewell to the owners of the villa, and his light boat skimmed rapidly over the tide.

"What do you think of the *Inglese?*" said Madame de Montaigne to her husband, as they turned towards the house. (They said not a word about the Milanese.)

"He has a noble bearing for one so young," said the Frenchman, "and seems to have seen the world, and both to have profited and to have suffered by it."

"He will prove an acquisition to our society here," returned Teresa; "he interests me; and you, Castruccio?" turning to seek for her brother; but Cesarini had already, with his usual noiseless step, disappeared within the house.

"Alas, my poor brother!" she replied, "I cannot comprehend him. What does he desire?"

"Fame!" replied De Montaigne, calmly. "It is a vain shadow; no wonder that he disquiets himself in vain."

CHAPTER II.

"Alas! what boots it with incessant care
To strictly meditate the thankless Muse;
Were it not better done as others use,
To sport with Amaryllis in the shade,
Or with the tangles of Neæra's hair!"
—MILTON's *Lycidas.*

THERE is nothing more salutary to active men than occasional intervals of repose—when we look within, instead of without, and examine almost *insensibly* (for I hold strict and conscious self-scrutiny a thing much rarer than we suspect)—what we have done—what we are capable of doing. It is settling, as it were, a debtor and creditor account with the Past, before we plunge into new speculations. Such an interval of repose did Maltravers now enjoy. In utter solitude, so far as familiar companionship is concerned, he had for several weeks been making himself acquainted with his own character and mind. He read and thought much, but without any exact or definite object. I think it is Montaigne who says somewhere—"People talk about thinking—but for my part, I never think, except when I sit down to write." I believe this is not a very common case, for people who don't write think as well as people who do; but connected, severe, well-developed thought, in contradistinction to vague meditation, must be connected with some tangible plan or object; and, therefore, we must be either writing men or acting men, if we desire to test the logic, and unfold into symmetrical design, the fused colours of our reasoning faculty. Maltravers did not yet feel this, but he was sensible of some intellectual want. His ideas, his memories, his dreams crowded thick and confused upon him; he wished to arrange them in order, and he could not. He was overpowered by the unorganised affluence of his own imagination and intellect. He had often, even as a child, fancied that he was formed to do something in the world, but he had never steadily considered what it was to be, whether he was to become a man of books or a man of deeds. He had written poetry when it poured irresistibly from the fount of emotion within, but looked at his effusions with a cold and neglectful eye when the enthusiasm had passed away.

Maltravers was not much gnawed by the desire of fame—perhaps few men of real genius are, until artificially worked up to it. There is in a sound and correct intellect, with all its gifts fairly balanced, a calm consciousness of power, a certainty that when its strength is fairly put out, it must be to realise the usual result of strength. Men of second-rate faculties, on the contrary, are fretful and nervous, fidgeting after a celebrity which they do not estimate by their own talents, but by the talents of some one else. They see a tower, but are occupied only with measuring its shadow, and think their own height (which they never calculate) is to cast as broad a one over the earth. It is the short man who is always throwing up his chin, and is as erect as a dart. The tall man stoops, and the strong man is not always using the dumb-bells.

Maltravers had not yet, then, the keen and sharp yearning for reputation; he had not, as yet, tasted its sweets and bitters—fatal draught, which *once* tasted, begets too often an insatiable thirst! neither had he enemies and decriers whom he was desirous of abashing by merit. And that is a very ordinary cause for exertion in proud minds. He was, it is true, generally reputed clever, and fools were afraid of him; but as he actively interfered with no man's pretensions, so no man thought it necessary to call him a blockhead. At present, therefore, it was quietly and naturally that his mind was working its legitimate way to its destiny of exertion. He began idly and carelessly to note down his thoughts and impressions; what was once put on the paper begot new matter; his ideas became more lucid to himself; and the page grew a looking-glass, which presented the likeness of his own features. He began by writing with rapidity, and without method. He had no object but to please himself, and to find a vent for an overcharged spirit; and, like most writings of the young, the matter was egotistical. We commence with the small nucleus of passion and experience, to widen the circle afterwards; and, perhaps, the most extensive and universal masters of life and character have begun by being egotists. For there is in a man that has much in him a wonderfully acute and sensitive perception of his own existence. An imaginative and susceptible person has, indeed, ten times as much life as a dull fellow, "an' he be Hercules." He multiplies himself in a thousand objects, associates each with his own identity, lives in each, and almost looks upon the world, with its infinite objects, as a part of his individual being. Afterwards, as he tames down, he withdraws his forces into the citadel, but he still has a knowledge of, and an interest in, the land they once covered. He understands other people, for he has lived in other people—the dead and the living—fancied himself now Brutus and now Cæsar, and thought how *he* should act in almost every imaginable circumstance of life.

Thus, when he begins to paint human characters, essentially different from his own, his knowledge comes to him almost intuitively. It is as if he were describing the mansions in which he himself has formerly lodged, though for a short time. Hence, in great writers of History—of Romance—of the Drama—the *gusto* with which they paint their personages; their creations are flesh and blood, not shadows or machines.

Maltravers was at first, then, an egotist in the matter of his rude and desultory sketches—in the manner, as I said before, he was careless and negligent, as men will be who have not yet found that expression is an art. Still, those wild and valueless essays—those rapt and secret confessions of his own heart—were a delight to him. He began to taste the transport, the intoxication of an author. And oh, what a luxury is there in that first love of the Muse! that process by which we give a palpable form to the long-intangible visions which have flitted across us—the beautiful ghost of the Ideal within us, which we invoke in the Gadara of our still closets, with the wand of the simple pen!

It was early noon, the day after he had formed his acquaintance with the De Montaignes, that Maltravers sat in his favourite room—the one he had selected for his study, from the many chambers of his large and solitary habitation. He sat in a recess by the open window, which looked on the lake; and books were scattered on his table, and Maltravers was jotting down his criticisms on what he read, mingled with his impressions on what he saw. It is the pleasantest kind of composition—the note-book of a man who studies in retirement, who observes in society, who in all things can admire and feel. He was yet engaged in this easy task, when Cesarini was announced, and the young brother of the fair Teresa entered his apartment.

"I have availed myself soon of your invitation," said the Italian.

"I acknowledge the compliment," replied Maltravers, pressing the hand shyly held out to him.

"I see you have been writing—I thought you were attached to literature. I read it in your countenance, I heard it in your voice," said Cesarini, seating himself.

"I have been idly beguiling a very idle leisure, it is true," said Maltravers.

"But you do not write for yourself alone—you have an eye to the great tribunals—Time and the Public?"

"Not so, I assure you honestly," said Maltravers, smiling. "If you look at the books on my table, you will see that they are the great masterpieces of ancient and modern lore—these are studies that discourage tyros——"

"But inspire them."

"I do not think so. Models may form our taste as critics, but do not excite us to be authors. I fancy that our own emotions, our own sense of our destiny, make the great lever of the inert matter we accumulate. 'Look in my heart and write,' said an old English writer,[*] who did not, however, practice what he preached. And you, Signor——"

"Am nothing, and would be something," said the young man, shortly and bitterly.

[*] Sir Phillip Sidney.

"And how does that wish not realise its object?"

"Merely because I am Italian," said Cesarini. "With us there is no literary public—no vast reading class—we have dilettanti and literati, and students, and even authors; but these make only a coterie, not a public. I have written, I have published; but no one listened to me. I am an author without readers."

"It is no uncommon case in England," said Maltravers.

The Italian continued—"I thought to live in the mouths of men—to stir up thoughts long dumb—to awaken the strings of the old lyre! In vain. Like the nightingale, I sing only to break my heart with a false and melancholy emulation of other notes."

"There are epochs in all countries," said Maltravers, gently, "when peculiar veins of literature are out of vogue, and when no genius can bring them into public notice. But you wisely said there were two tribunals—the Public and Time. You have still the latter to appeal to. Your great Italian historians wrote for the unborn—their works not even published till their death. That indifference to living reputation has in it, to me, something of the sublime."

"I cannot imitate them—and they were not poets," said Cesarini, sharply. "To poets, praise is a necessary aliment; neglect is death."

"My dear Signor Cesarini," said the Englishman, feelingly, "do not give way to these thoughts. There ought to be in a healthful ambition the stubborn stuff of persevering longevity; it must live on, and hope for the day which comes slow or fast, to all whose labours deserve the goal."

"But perhaps mine do not. I sometimes fear so—it is a horrid thought."

"You are very young yet," said Maltravers; "how few at your age ever sicken for fame! That first step is, perhaps, the half-way to the prize."

I am not sure that Ernest thought exactly as he spoke; but it was the most delicate consolation to offer to a man whose abrupt frankness embarrassed and distressed him. The young man shook his head despondingly. Maltravers tried to change the subject—he rose and moved to the balcony, which overhung the lake—he talked of the weather—he dwelt on the exquisite scenery—he pointed to the minute and more latent beauties around, with the eye and taste of one who had looked at Nature in her details. The poet grew more animated and cheerful; he became more eloquent;

he quoted poetry and he talked it. Maltravers was more and more interested in him. He felt a curiosity to know if his talents equalled his aspirations; he hinted to Cesarini his wish to see his compositions—it was just what the young man desired. Poor Cesarini! It was much to him to get a new listener, and he fondly imagined every honest listener must be a warm admirer. But with the coyness of his caste, he affected reluctance and hesitation; he dallied with his own impatient yearnings. And Maltravers, to smooth his way, proposed an excursion on the lake.

"One of my men shall row," said he; "you shall recite to me, and I will be to you what the old housekeeper was to Molière."

Maltravers had deep good-nature where he was touched, though he had not a superfluity of what is called good-humour, which floats on the surface and smiles on all alike. He had much of the milk of human kindness, but little of its oil.

The poet assented, and they were soon upon the lake. It was a sultry day, and it was noon; so the boat crept slowly along by the shadow of the shore, and Cesarini drew from his breast-pocket some manuscripts of small and beautiful writing. Who does not know the pains a young poet takes to bestow a fair dress on his darling rhymes!

Cesarini read well and feelingly. Everything was in favour of the reader. His own poetical countenance—his voice, his enthusiasm, half-suppressed—the pre-engaged interest of the auditor—the dreamy loveliness of the hour and scene—(for there is a great deal as to time in these things!) Maltravers listened intently. It is very difficult to judge of the exact merit of poetry in another language, even when we know that language well—so much is there in the untranslatable magic of expression, the little subtleties of style. But Maltravers, fresh, as he himself had said, from the study of great and original writers, could not but feel that he was listening to feeble though melodious mediocrity. It was the poetry of words, not things. He thought it cruel, however, to be hypercritical, and he uttered all the commonplaces of eulogium that occured to him. The young man was enchanted. "And yet," said he with a sigh, "I have no Public. In England they would appreciate me." Alas! in England, at that moment, there were five hundred poets as young, as ardent, and yet more gifted, whose hearts beat with the same desire—whose nerves were broken by the same disappointments.

Maltravers found that his young friend would not listen to any

judgment not purely favourable. The archbishop in *Gil Blas*
was not more touchy upon any criticism that was not panegyric.
Maltravers thought it a bad sign, but he recollected Gil Blas, and
prudently refrained from bringing on himself the benevolent wish
of " beaucoup de bonheur et un peu plus de bon goût." When
Cesarini had finished his MS., he was anxious to conclude the
excursion—he longed to be at home, and think over the admiration
he had excited. But he left his poems with Maltravers, and
getting on shore by the remains of Pliny's villa, was soon out of
sight.

Maltravers that evening read the poems with attention. His
first opinion was confirmed. The young man wrote without knowledge. He had never felt the passions he painted—never been in
the situations he described. There was no originality in him, for
there was no experience: it was exquisite mechanism, his verse—
nothing more! It might well deceive him, for it could not but
flatter his ear—and Tasso's silver march rang not more musically
than did the chiming stanzas of Castruccio Cesarini.

The perusal of this poetry, and his conversation with the poet,
threw Maltravers into a fit of deep musing. "This poor Cesarini
may warn me against myself," thought he. "Better hew wood
and draw water, than attach ourselves devotedly to an art in which
we have not the capacity to excel. . . . It is to throw away the
healthful objects of life for a diseased dream—worse than the
Rosicrucians, it is to make a sacrifice of all human beauty for the
smile of a sylphid, that never visits us but in visions." Maltravers
looked over his own compositions, and thrust them into the fire.
He slept ill that night. His pride was a little dejected. He was
like a beauty who has seen a caricature of herself.

CHAPTER III.

"Still follow Sense, of every art the Soul."
—POPE: *Moral Essays—Essay iv.*

ERNEST MALTRAVERS spent much of his time with the
family of De Montaigne. There is no period of life in
which we are more accessible to the sentiment of friendship,
than in the intervals of moral exhaustion which succeed to the
disappointments of the passions. There is, then, something

inviting in those gentler feelings which keep alive, but do not fever, the circulation of the affections. Maltravers looked with the benevolence of a brother upon the brilliant, versatile, and restless Teresa. She was the last person in the world he could have been in love with—for his nature, ardent, excitable, yet fastidious, required something of repose in the manners and temperament of the woman whom he could love, and Theresa scarcely knew what repose was. Whether playing with her children (and she had two lovely ones—the eldest six years old), or teasing her calm and meditative husband, or pouring out extempore verses, or rattling over airs which she never finished, on the guitar or piano—or making excursions on the lake—or, in short, in whatever occupation she appeared as the Cynthia of the minute, she was always gay and mobile—never out of humour, never acknowledging a single care or cross in life—never susceptible of grief, save when her brother's delicate health or morbid temper saddened her atmosphere of sunshine. Even then, the sanguine elasticity of her mind and constitution quickly recovered from the depression; and she persuaded herself that Castruccio would grow stronger every year, and ripen into a celebrated and happy man. Castruccio himself lived what romantic poetasters call the "life of a poet." He loved to see the sun rise over the distant Alps—or the midnight moon sleeping on the lake. He spent half the day, and often half the night, in solitary rambles, weaving his airy rhymes, or indulging his gloomy reveries, and he thought loneliness made the element of a poet. Alas! Dante, Alfieri, even Petrarch might have taught him, that a poet must have intimate knowledge of men as well as mountains, if he desire to become the CREATOR. When Shelley, in one of his prefaces, boasts of being familiar with Alps and glaciers, and heaven knows what, the critical artist cannot help wishing that he had been rather familiar with Fleet Street or the Strand. Perhaps, then, that remarkable genius might have been more capable of realising characters of flesh and blood, and have composed corporeal and consummate wholes, not confused and glittering fragments.

Though Ernest was attached to Teresa, and deeply interested in Castruccio, it was De Montaigne for whom he experienced the higher and graver sentiment of esteem. This Frenchman was one acquainted with a much larger world than that of the Coteries. He had served in the army, been employed with distinction in civil affairs, and was of that robust and healthful moral constitution

which can bear with every variety of social life, and estimate calmly
the balance of our mortal fortunes. Trial and experience had left
him that true philosopher who is too wise to be an optimist, too just
to be a misanthrope. He enjoyed life with sober judgment, and
pursued the path most suited to himself, without declaring it to be
the best for others. He was a little hard, perhaps, upon the errors
that belong to weakness and conceit—not to those that have their
source in great natures or generous thoughts. Among his characteristics was a profound admiration for England. His own country
he half loved, yet half disdained. The impetuosity and levity of his
compatriots displeased his sober and dignified notions. He could
not forgive them (he was wont to say) for having made the two
grand experiments of popular revolution and military despotism in
vain. He sympathised neither with the young enthusiasts who
desired a republic, without well knowing the numerous strata of
habits and customs upon which that fabric, if designed for per-
manence, should be built—nor with the uneducated and fierce
chivalry that longed for a restoration of the warrior empire—nor
with the dull and arrogant bigots who connected all ideas of order
and government with the ill-starred and worn-out dynasty of the
Bourbons. In fact, GOOD SENSE was with him the *principium et
fons* of all theories and all practice. And it was this quality that
attached him to the English. His philosophy on this head was
rather curious.

"Good sense," said he one day to Maltravers, as they were
walking to and fro at De Montaigne's villa, by the margin of the
lake, "is not a merely intellectual attribute. It is rather the result
of a just equilibrium of all our faculties, spiritual and moral. The
dishonest, or the toys of their own passions, may have genius ; but
they rarely, if ever, have good sense in their conduct of life. They
may often win large prizes, but it is by a game of chance, not skill.
But the man whom I perceive walking an honourable and upright
career—just to others, and also to himself (for we owe justice to
ourselves—to the care of our fortunes, our character—to the
management of our passions)—is a more dignified representative of
his Maker than the mere child of genius. Of such a man we say,
he has GOOD SENSE ; yes, but he has also integrity, self-respect,
and self-denial. A thousand trials which his sense braves and
conquers, are temptations also to his probity—his temper—in a
word, to all the many sides of his complicated nature. Now, I do
not think he will have this *good sense* any more than a drunkard

will have strong nerves, unless he be in the constant habit of keeping his mind clear from the intoxication of envy, vanity, and the various emotions that dupe and mislead us. Good sense is not, therefore, an abstract quality or a solitary talent; but it is the natural result of the habit of thinking justly, and, therefore, seeing clearly, and is as different from the sagacity that belongs to a diplomatist or attorney, as the philosophy of Socrates differed from the rhetoric of Gorgias. As a mass of individual excellencies make up this attribute in a man, so a mass of such men thus characterised give a character to a nation. Your England is, therefore, renowned for its good sense; but it is renowned also for the excellencies which accompany strong sense in an individual, high honesty and faith in its dealings, a warm love of justice and fair play, a general freedom from the violent crimes common on the Continent, and the energetic perseverance in enterprise once commenced, which results from a bold and healthful disposition."

"Our Wars, our Debt——" began Maltravers.

"Pardon me," interrupted De Montaigne, "I am speaking of your People, not of your Government. A government is often a very unfair representative of a nation. But even in the wars you allude to, if you examine, you will generally find them originate in the love of justice (which is the basis of good sense), not from any insane desire of conquest or glory. A man, however sensible, must have a heart in his bosom, and a great nation cannot be a piece of selfish clockwork. Suppose you and I are sensible, prudent men, and we see in a crowd one violent fellow unjustly knocking another on the head, we should be brutes, not men, if we did not interfere with the savage; but if we thrust ourselves into a crowd with a large bludgeon, and belabour our neighbours, with the hope that the spectators would cry, 'See what a bold, strong fellow that is!'—then we should be only playing the madman from the motive of the coxcomb. I fear you will find, in the military history of the French and English, the application of my parable."

"Yet still, I confess, there is a gallantry, and a nobleman-like and Norman spirit in the whole French nation, which make me forgive many of their excesses, and think they are destined for great purposes, when experience shall have sobered their hot blood. Some nations, as some men, are slow in arriving at maturity; others seem men in their cradle. The English, thanks to their sturdy Saxon origin, elevated, not depressed, by the Norman infusion, never were children. The difference is striking, when you regard the representatives of both in their great men—whether writers or active citizens."

"Yes," said De Montaigne, "in Milton and Cromwell there is nothing of the brilliant child. I cannot say as much for Voltaire or Napoleon. Even Richelieu, the manliest of our statesmen, had so much of the French infant in him as to fancy himself a *beau garcon*, a gallant, a wit, and a poet. As for the Racine school of writers, they were not out of the leading-strings of imitation—cold copyists of a pseudo-classic—in which they saw the form, and never caught the spirit. What so little Roman, Greek, Hebrew, as their Roman, Greek, and Hebrew dramas? Your rude Shakspeare's Julius Cæsar—even his Troilus and Cressida—have the ancient spirit, precisely as they are imitations of nothing ancient. But our Frenchmen copied the giant images of old, just as the school-girl copies a drawing, by holding it up to the window, and tracing the lines on silver-paper."

"But your new writers—De Staël—Chateaubriand?" *

"I find no fault with the sentimentalists," answered the severe critic, "than that of exceeding feebleness—they have no bone and muscle in their genius—all is flaccid and rotund in its feminine symmetry. They seem to think that vigour consists in florid phrases and little aphorisms, and delineate all the mighty tempests of the human heart with the polished prettiness of a miniature-painter on ivory. No!—these two are children of another kind—affected, tricked-out, well-dressed children—very clever, very precocious—but children still. Their whinings, and their sentimentalities, and their egotism, and their vanity, cannot interest masculine beings, who know what life and its stern objects are."

"Your brother-in-law," said Maltravers, with a slight smile, "must find in you a discouraging censor."

"My poor Castruccio,' replied De Montaigne, with a half-sigh; "he is one of those victims whom I believe to be more common than we dream of—men whose aspirations are above their powers. I agree with a great German writer, that in the first walks of Art no man has a right to enter, unless he is convinced that he has strength and speed for the goal. Castruccio might be an amiable member of society, nay, an able and useful man, if he would apply the powers he possesses to the rewards they may obtain. He has

* At the time of this conversation, the later school, adorned by Victor Hugo, who, with notions of Art elaborately wrong, is still a man of extraordinary genius, had not risen into its present equivocal reputation.

talent enough to win him reputation in any profession but that of a poet."

"But authors who obtain immortality are not always first-rate."

"First-rate in their way, I suspect; even if that way be false or trivial. They must be connected with the *history* of their literature; you must be able to say of them, 'In this school, be it bad or good, they exerted such and such an influence;' in a word, they must form a link in the great chain of a nation's authors, which may be afterwards forgotten by the superficial, but without which the chain would be incomplete. And thus, if not first-rate for all time, they have been first-rate in their own day. But Castruccio is only the echo of others—he can neither found a school nor ruin one. Yet this" (again added De Montaigne, after a pause)—"this melancholy malady in my brother-in-law would cure itself, perhaps, if he were not Italian. In your animated and bustling country, after sufficient disappointment as a poet, he would glide into some other calling, and his vanity and craving for effect would find a rational and manly outlet. But in Italy, what can a clever man do, if he is not a poet or a robber? If he love his country, that crime is enough to unfit him for civil employment, and his mind cannot stir a step in the bold channels of speculation without falling foul of the Austrian or the Pope. No; the best I can hope for Castruccio is, that he will end in an antiquary, and dispute about ruins with the Romans. Better that than mediocre poetry."

Maltravers was silent, and thoughtful. Strange to say, De Montaigne's views did not discourage his own new and secret ardour for intellectual triumphs; not because he felt that he was now able to achieve them, but because he felt the iron of his own nature, and knew that a man who *has* iron in his nature must ultimately hit upon some way of shaping the metal into use.

The host and guest were now joined by Castruccio himself—silent and gloomy as indeed he usually was, especially in the presence of De Montaigne, with whom he felt his "self-love" wounded; for though he longed to despise his hard brother-in-law, the young poet was compelled to acknowledge that De Montaigne was not a man to be despised.

Maltravers dined with the De Montaignes, and spent the evening with them. He could not but observe that Castruccio, who affected in his verses the softest sentiments—who was, indeed, by original nature, tender and gentle—had become so completely warped by that worst of all mental vices—the eternally pondering on his own excellencies, talents, mortifications, and ill-usage, that he never contributed to the gratification of those around him; he had none of the little arts of social benevolence, none of the playful youth of disposition which usually belongs to the good-hearted, and for which men of a master-genius, however elevated their studies, however stern or reserved to the vulgar world, are commonly noticeable amidst the friends they love, or in the home they adorn. Occupied with one dream, centred in self, the young Italian was sullen and morose to all who did not sympathise with his own morbid fancies. From the children—the sister—the friend—the whole living earth, he fled to a poem on Solitude, or stanzas upon Fame. Maltravers said to himself, "I will never be an author—I will never sigh for renown—if I am to purchase shadows at such a price!"

CHAPTER IV.

"It cannot be too deeply impressed on the mind, that application is the price to be paid for mental acquisitions, and that it is as absurd to expect them without it, as to hope for a harvest where we have not sown the seed."

"In everything we do, we may be possibly laying a train of consequences, the operation of which may terminate only with our existence,"

—BAILEY: *Essays on the Formation and Publication of Opinions*.

TIME passed, and autumn was far advanced towards winter; still Maltravers lingered at Como. He saw little of any other family than that of the De Montaignes, and the greater part of his time was necessarily spent alone. His occupation continued to be that of making experiments of his own powers, and these gradually became bolder and more comprehensive. He took care, however, not to show his "Diversions of Como" to his new friends: he wanted no audience—he dreamt of no Public; he desired merely to practise his own mind. He became aware, of his own accord, as he proceeded, that a man can neither study with much depth, nor compose with much art, unless he has some definite object before him; in the first, some one branch of knowledge to master; in the last, some one conception to work out. Maltravers fell back upon his boyish passion for metaphysical speculation; but with what different results did he now wrestle with the subtle schoolmen—now that he had practically known mankind! How insensibly new lights broke in upon him, as he threaded the labyrinth of cause and effect, by which we seek to arrive at that curious and biform monster—our own nature. His mind became saturated, as it were, with these profound studies and meditations; and when at length he paused from them, he felt as if he had not been living in solitude, but had gone through a process of action in the busy world: so much juster, so much clearer, had become his knowledge of himself and others. But though these researches coloured, they did not limit his intellectual pursuits. Poetry and the lighter letters became to him, not merely a relaxation, but a critical and thoughtful study. He delighted to penetrate into the causes that have made the airy webs spun by men's fancies so permanent and powerful in their influence over the hard, work-day world. And what a lovely scene—what a sky—what an air wherein to commence the projects of that ambition which seeks to establish an empire in the hearts and memories of mankind! I believe it has a great effect on the future labours of a writer—the place where he first dreams that it is his destiny to write!

From these pursuits Ernest was aroused by another letter from Cleveland. His kind friend had been disappointed and vexed that Maltravers did not follow his advice and return to England. He had shown his displeasure by not answering Ernest's letter of excuses; but lately he had been seized with a dangerous illness which reduced him to the brink of the grave; and with a heart softened by the exhaustion of the frame, he now wrote in the first moments of convalescence to Maltravers, informing him of his attack and danger, and once more urging him to return. The thought that Cleveland—the dear, kind, gentle guardian of his youth—had been near unto death, that he might never more have hung upon that fostering hand, nor replied to that paternal voice, smote Ernest with terror and remorse. He resolved instantly to return to England, and made his preparations accordingly.

He went to take leave of the De Montaignes. Teresa was trying to teach her first-born to read;—and seated by the open window of the villa, in her neat, not precise, deshabille—with the little boy's delicate, yet bold and healthy countenance looking up fearlessly at hers, while she was endeavouring to initiate him—half gravely, half laughingly—into the mysteries of monosyllables, the pretty boy and the fair young mother made a delightful picture. De Montaigne was reading the Essays of his celebrated namesake, in whom he boasted, I know not with what justice, to claim an ancestor. From time to time he looked from the page to take a glance at the progress of his heir, and keep up with the march of intellect. But he did not interfere with the maternal lecture; he was wise enough to know that there is a kind of sympathy between a child and a mother, which is worth all the grave superiority of a father in making learning palatable to young years. He was far too clever a man not to despise all the systems of forcing infants under knowledge-frames, which are the present fashion. He knew that philosophers never made a greater mistake than in insisting so much upon beginning abstract education from the cradle. It is quite enough to attend to an infant's temper, and correct that cursed predilection for telling fibs which falsifies all Dr. Reid's absurd theory about innate propensities to truth, and makes the prevailing epidemic of the nursery. Above all, what advantage ever compensates for hurting a child's health or breaking his spirit? Never let him learn, more than you can help it, the crushing bitterness of fear. A bold child who looks you in the face, speaks the truth, and shames the devil; that is the stuff of which to make good and brave—ay, and wise men!

Maltravers entered, unannounced, into this charming family party, and stood unobserved for a few moments by the open door. The little pupil was the first to perceive him, and forgetful of monosyllables, ran to greet him; for Maltravers, though gentle rather than gay, was a favourite with children, and his fair, calm, gracious countenance did more for him with them, than if, like Goldsmith's Burchell, his pockets had been filled with gingerbread and apples. "Ah, fie on you, Mr. Maltravers!" cried Teresa, rising; "you have blown away all the characters I have been endeavouring this last hour to imprint upon sand."

"Not so, Signora," said Maltravers, seating himself, and placing the child on his knee; "my young friend will set to work again with a greater gusto after this little break in upon his labours."

"You will stay with us all day, I hope?" said De Montaigne.

"Indeed," said Maltravers, "I am come to ask permission to do so, for to-morrow I depart for England."

"Is it possible?" cried Teresa. "How sudden! How we shall miss you! But perhaps you have bad news from England?"

"I have news that summon me hence," replied Maltravers; "my guardian and second father has been dangerously ill. I am uneasy about him, and reproach myself for having forgotten him so long in your seductive society."

"I am really sorry to lose you," said De Montaigne, with greater warmth in his tones than in his words. "I hope heartily we shall meet again soon; you will come, perhaps, to Paris?"

"Probably," said Maltravers; "and you, perhaps, to England?"

"Ah, how I should like it!" exclaimed Teresa.

"No, you would not," said her husband; "you would not like England at all; you would call it *triste* beyond measure. It is one of those countries of which a nation should be proud, but which has no amusement for a stranger, precisely because full of such serious and stirring occupations to the citizens. The pleasantest countries for strangers are the worst countries for natives (witness Italy), and *vice versâ*."

Teresa shook her dark curls, and would not be convinced.

"And where is Castruccio?" asked Maltravers.

"In his boat on the lake," replied Teresa. "He will be inconsolable at your departure; you are the only person he can understand, or who understands him; the only person in Italy—I had almost said in the whole world."

"Well, we shall meet at dinner," said Ernest; "meanwhile, let me prevail on you to accompany me to the *Pliniana*. I wish to say farewell to that crystal spring."

Teresa, delighted at any excursion, readily consented.

"And I too, mamma," cried the child; "and my little sister?"

"Oh, certainly," said Maltravers, speaking for the parents.

So the party was soon ready, and they pushed off in the clear, genial noon-tide (for November in Italy is as early as September in the North), across the sparkling and dimpled waters. The children prattled, and the grown-up people talked on a thousand matters. It was a pleasant day that last day at Como! For the farewells of friendship have indeed something of the melancholy, but not the anguish, of those of love. Perhaps it would be better if we could get rid of love altogether. Life would go on smoother and happier without it. Friendship is the wine of existence, but love is the dram-drinking.

When they returned, they found Castruccio seated on the lawn. He did not appear so much dejected at the prospect of Ernest's departure as Teresa had anticipated; for Castruccio Cesarini was a very jealous man, and he had lately been chagrined and discontented with seeing the delight that the De Montaignes took in Ernest's society.

"Why is this?" he often asked himself; "why are they more

pleased with this stranger's society than mine? My ideas are as
fresh, as original; I have as much genius, yet even my dry
brother-in-law allows *his* talents, and predicts that *he* will be an
eminent man; while *I*—No!—one is not a prophet in one's own
country!"

Unhappy young man! his mind bore all the rank weeds of the
morbid poetical character, and the weeds choked up the flowers that
the soil, properly cultivated, should alone bear. Yet that crisis in
life awaited Castruccio, in which a sensitive and poetical man is
made or marred; the crisis in which a sentiment is replaced by the
passions—in which love for some real object gathers the scattered
rays of the heart into a focus; out of that ordeal he might pass a
purer and manlier being—so Maltravers often hoped. Maltravers
then little thought how closely connected with his own fate was to
be that passage in the history of the Italian! Castruccio contrived to take Maltravers aside, and as he led the Englishman
through the wood that backed the mansion, he said, with some
embarrassment, "You go, I suppose, to London?"

"I shall pass through it—can I execute any commission for
you?"

"Why, yes; my poems!—I think of publishing them in England;
your aristocracy cultivate the Italian letters; and, perhaps, I may
be read by the fair and noble—*that* is the proper audience of poets.
For the vulgar herd—I disdain it!"

"My dear Castruccio, I will undertake to see your poems published in London, if you wish it; but do not be sanguine. In
England we read little poetry, even in our own language, and we
are shamefully indifferent to foreign literature."

"Yes, foreign literature generally, and you are right; but *my*
poems are of another kind. They must command attention in
a polished and intelligent circle."

"Well! let the experiment be tried; you can let me have the
poems when we part."

"I thank you," said Castruccio, in a joyous tone, pressing his
friend's hand; and for the rest of that evening he seemed an
altered being; he even carressed the children, and did not sneer at
the grave conversation of his brother-in-law.

When Maltravers rose to depart, Castruccio gave him the packet;
and then, utterly engrossed with his own imagined futurity of fame,
vanished from the room to indulge his reveries. He cared no
longer for Maltravers—he had put him to use—he could not be

sorry for his departure, for that departure was the Avatar of HIS appearance to a new world!

A small, dull rain was falling, though at intervals the stars broke through the unsettled clouds, and Teresa did not therefore venture from the house; she presented her smooth cheek to the young guest to salute, pressed him by the hand, and bade him adieu with tears in her eyes. "Ah!" said she, "when we meet again I hope you will be married—I shall love your wife dearly. There is no happiness like marriage and home!" and she looked with ingenuous tenderness at De Montaigne.

Maltravers sighed—his thoughts flew back to Alice. Where now was that lone and friendless girl, whose innocent love had once brightened a home for *him?* He answered by a vague and mechanical commonplace, and quitted the room with De Montaigne, who insisted on seeing him depart. As they neared the lake, De Montaigne broke the silence.

"My dear Maltravers," he said, with a serious and thoughtful affection in his voice, "we may not meet again for years. I have a warm interest in your happiness and career—yes, *career*—I repeat the word. I do not habitually seek to inspire young men with ambition. Enough for most of them to be good and honourable citizens. But in your case it is different. I see in you the earnest and meditative, not rash and overweening youth, which is usually productive of a distinguished manhood. Your mind is not yet settled, it is true; but it is fast becoming clear and mellow from the first ferment of boyish dreams and passions. You have everything in your favour—competence, birth, connections; and, above all, you are an Englishman! You have a mighty stage, on which, it is true, you cannot establish a footing without merit and without labour—so much the better; in which strong, resolute rivals will urge you on to emulation, and then competition will task your keenest powers. Think what a glorious fate it is, to have an influence on the vast, but ever-growing mind of such a country—to feel, when you retire from the busy scene, that you have played an unforgotten part—that you have been the medium, under God's great will, of circulating new ideas throughout the world—of upholding the glorious priesthood of the Honest and the Beautiful. This is the true ambition; the desire of mere personal notoriety is vanity, not ambition. Do not, then, be lukewarm or supine. The trait I have observed in you," added the Frenchman, with a smile, "most prejudicial to your chances of distinction is, that you are *too* philosophical, too apt to *cui bono* all the exertions that interfere with the indolence of cultivated leisure. And you must not suppose, Maltravers, that an active career will be a path of roses. At present you have no enemies; but the moment you attempt distinction, you will be abused, calumniated, reviled. You will be shocked at the wrath you excite, and sigh for your old obscurity, and consider, as Franklin has it, that 'you have paid too dear for your whistle.' But, in return for individual enemies, what a noble recompense to have made the Public itself your friend; perhaps even Posterity your familiar! Besides," added De Montaigne, with almost a religious solemnity in his voice, "there is a conscience of the head as well as of the heart, and in old age we feel as much remorse, if we have wasted our natural talents, as if we have perverted our natural virtues. The profound and exultant satisfaction with which a man who knows that he has not lived in vain—that he has entailed on the world an heir-loom of instruction or delight—looks back upon departed struggles, is one of the happiest emotions of which the conscience can be capable. What, indeed, are the petty faults we commit as individuals, affecting but a narrow circle, ceasing with our own lives, to the incalculable and everlasting good we may produce as public men by one book or by one law? Depend upon it that the Almighty, who sums up all the good and all the evil done by his creatures in a just balance, will not judge the august benefactors of the world with the same severity as those drones of society, who have no great services to show in the eternal ledger, as a set-off to the indulgence of their small vices. These things rightly considered, Maltravers, you will have every inducement that can tempt a lofty mind and a pure ambition to awaken from the voluptuous indolence of the literary Sybarite, and contend worthily in the world's wide Altis for a great prize."

Maltravers never before felt so flattered—so stirred into high resolves. The stately eloquence, the fervid encouragement of this man, usually so cold and fastidious, roused him like the sound of a trumpet. He stopped short, his breath heaved thick, his cheek flushed. "De Montaigne," said he, "your words have cleared away a thousand doubts and scruples—they have gone right to my heart. For the first time I understand what fame is—what the object, and what the reward of labour! Visions, hopes, aspirations, I may have had before—for months a new spirit has been fluttering within me. I have felt the wings breaking from the shell. But all was confused, dim, uncertain. I doubted the wisdom of effort, with life so short, and the pleasures of youth so sweet. I now look no longer on life but as a part of the eternity to which I *feel* we were born; and I recognise the solemn truth that our objects, to be worthy life, should be worthy of creatures in whom the living principle never is extinct. Farewell! come joy or sorrow, failure or success, I will struggle to deserve your friendship."

Maltravers sprang into his boat, and the shades of night soon snatched him from the lingering gaze of De Montaigne.

BOOK IV.

CHAPTER I.

> "I, alas!
> Have lived but on this earth a few sad years;
> And so my lot was ordered, that a father
> First turned the moments of awakening life
> To drops, each poisoning youth's sweet hope."
> —CRNOI.

FROM accompanying Maltravers along the noiseless progress of mental education, we are now called awhile to cast our glances back at the ruder and harsher ordeal which Alice Darvil was ordained to pass. Along her path poetry shed no flowers, nor were her lonely steps towards the distant shrine at which her pilgrimage found its rest lighted by the mystic lamp of science, or guided by the thousand stars which are never dim in the heavens for those favoured eyes from which genius and fancy have removed many of the films of clay. Not along the aërial and exalted ways that wind far above the homes and business of common men—the solitary Alps of Spiritual Philosophy—wandered the desolate steps of the child of poverty and sorrow. On the beaten and rugged highways of common life, with a weary heart, and with bleeding feet, she went her melancholy course. But the goal which is the great secret of life, the *summum arcanum* of all philosophy, whether the Practical or the Ideal, was, perhaps, no less attainable for that humble girl than for the elastic step and aspiring heart of him who thirsted after the Great, and almost believed in the Impossible.

We return to that dismal night in which Alice was torn from the roof of her lover. It was long before she recovered her consciousness of what passed, and gained a full perception of the fearful revolution which had taken place in her destinies. It was then a grey and dreary morning twilight; and the rude but covered vehicle which bore her was rolling along the deep ruts of an unfrequented road, winding among the unenclosed and mountainous wastes that, in England, usually betoken the neighbourhood of the sea. With a shudder Alice looked round: Walters, her father's accomplice, lay extended at her feet, and his heavy breathing showed that he was fast asleep. Darvil himself was urging on the jaded and sorry horse, and his broad back was turned towards Alice; the rain, from which, in his position, he was but ill protected by the awning, dripped dismally from his slouched hat; and now, as he turned round, and his sinister and gloomy gaze rested upon the face of Alice, his bad countenance, rendered more haggard by the cold, raw light of the cheerless dawn, completed the hideous picture of unveiled and ruffianly wretchedness.

"Ho, ho! Alley, so you are come to your senses," said he, with a kind of joyless grin. "I am glad of it, for I can have no fainting fine ladies with me. You have had a long holiday, Alley; you must now learn once more to work for your poor father. Ah, you have been d—d sly; but never mind the past—I forgive it. You must not run away again without my leave; if you are fond of sweethearts, I won't balk you—but your old father must go shares, Alley."

Alice could hear no more: she covered her face with the cloak that had been thrown about her, and though she did not faint, her senses seemed to be locked and paralysed. By-and-by Walters woke, and the two men, heedless of her presence, conversed upon their plans. By degrees she recovered sufficient self-possession to listen, in the instinctive hope that some plan of escape might be suggested to her. But from what she could gather of the incoherent and various projects they discussed, one after another— disputing upon each with frightful oaths and scarce intelligible slang, she could only learn that it was resolved at all events to leave the district in which they were—but whither seemed yet all undecided. The cart halted at last at a miserable-looking hut, which the sign-post announced to be an inn that afforded good accommodation to travellers; to which announcement was annexed the following epigrammatic distich:—

"Old Tom, he is the best of gin;
Drink him once, and you'll drink him *agin!*"

The hovel stood so remote from all other habitations, and the waste around was so bare of trees, and even shrubs, that Alice saw with despair that all hope of flight in such a place would be indeed a chimera. But to make assurance doubly sure, Darvil himself, lifting her from the cart, conducted her up a broken and unlighted staircase, into a sort of loft rather than a room, and pushing her rudely in, turned the key upon her, and descended. The weather was cold, the livid damps hung upon the distained walls, and there was neither fire nor hearth; but thinly clad as she was—her cloak and shawl her principal covering—she did not feel the cold, for her heart was more chilly than the airs of heaven. At noon an old woman brought her some food, which, consisting of fish and poached game, was better than might have been expected in such a place, and what would have been deemed a feast under her father's roof. With an inviting leer, the crone pointed to a pewter measure of raw spirits that accompanied the viands, and assured her, in a cracked and maudlin voice, that "'Old Tom' was a kinder friend than any of the young fellars!" This intrusion ended, Alice was again left alone till dusk, when Darvil entered with a bundle of clothes, such as are worn by the peasants of that primitive district of England.

"There, Alley," said he, "put on this warm toggery; finery won't do now. We must leave no scent in the track; the hounds are after us, my little blowen. Here's a nice stuff gown for you, and a red cloak that would frighten a turkey-cock. As to the other cloak and shawl, don't be afraid; they shan't go to the pop-shop, but we'll take care of them against we get to some large town where there are young fellows with blunt in their pockets; for you seem to have already found out that your face is your fortune, Alley. Come, make haste, we must be starting. I shall come up for you in ten minutes. Tush; don't be faint-hearted: here, take 'Old Tom'— take it, I say. What, you won't? Well, here's to your health, and a better taste to you!"

And now, as the door once more closed upon Darvil, tears for the first time came to the relief of Alice. It was a woman's weakness that procured for her that woman's luxury. Those garments—they were Ernest's gift—Ernest's taste; they were like the last relic of that delicious life which now seemed to have fled for ever. All traces of that life—of him, the loving, the protecting, the adored! all trace of herself, as she had been re-created by love, was to be lost to her for ever. It was (as she had read somewhere, in the little elementary volumes that bounded her historic lore) like that last fatal ceremony in which those condemned for life to the mines of Siberia are clothed with the slave's livery, their past name and record eternally blotted out, and thrust into the vast wastes, from which even the mercy of despotism, should it ever re-awaken, cannot recall them; for all evidence of them—all individuality—all mark to distinguish them from the universal herd, is expunged from the world's calendar. She was still sobbing in vehement and unrestrained passion, when Darvil re-entered. "What, not dressed yet?" he exclaimed, in a voice of impatient rage; "harkye, this won't do. If in two minutes you are not ready, I'll send up John Walters to help you; and he is a rough hand, I can tell you."

This threat recalled Alice to herself. "I will do as you wish," said she, meekly.

"Well, then, be quick," said Darvil; "they are now putting the horse to. And mark me, girl, your father is running away from the gallows, and that thought does not make a man stand upon scruples. If you once attempt to give me the slip, or do or say anything that can bring the bulkies upon us—by the devil in hell—if, indeed, there be hell or devil—my knife shall become better acquainted with that throat—so look to it!"

And this was the father—this the condition—of her whose ear had for months drunk no other sound than the whispers of flattering love—the murmurs of Passion from the lips of Poetry.

They continued their journey till midnight; they then arrived at an inn, little different from the last; but here Alice was no longer consigned to solitude. In a long room, reeking with smoke, sat from twenty to thirty ruffians before a table, on which mugs and vessels of strong potations were formidably interspersed with sabres and pistols. They received Walters and Darvil with a shout of welcome, and would have crowded somewhat unceremoniously round Alice, if her father, whose well-known desperate and brutal ferocity made him a man to be respected in such an assembly, had not said, sternly, "Hands off, messmates, and make way by the fire for my little girl—she is meat for your masters."

So saying, he pushed Alice down into a huge chair in the chimney nook, and, seating himself near her, at the end of the table, hastened to turn the conversation.

"Well, captain," said he, addressing a small, thin man at the head of the table, "I and Walters have fairly cut and run—the land has a bad air for us, and we now want the sea-breeze to cure the rope fever. So, knowing this was your night, we have crowded sail, and here we are. You must give the girl there a lift, though I know you don't like such lumber, and we'll run ashore as soon as we can."

"She seems a quiet little body," replied the captain; "and we would do more than that to oblige an old friend like you. In half-an-hour Oliver* puts on his nightcap, and we must then be off."

"The sooner the better."

The men now appeared to forget the presence of Alice, who sat, faint with fatigue and exhaustion, for she had been too sick at heart to touch the food brought to her at their previous halting-place, gazing abstractedly upon the fire. Her father, before their departure, made her swallow some morsels of sea-biscuit, though each seemed to choke her; and then, wrapped in a thick boat-cloak, she was placed in a small, well-built cutter; and as the sea-winds whistled round her, the present cold and the past fatigues lulled her miserable heart into the arms of the charitable Sleep.

CHAPTER II.

"You are once more a free woman;
Here I discharge your bonds."
—*The Custom of the Country.*

AND many were thy trials, poor child; many that, were this book to germinate into volumes more numerous than monk ever composed upon the lives of saint or martyr (though a hundred volumes contained the record of two years only in the life of St. Anthony), it would be impossible to describe! We may talk of the fidelity of books, but no man ever wrote even his own biography without being compelled to omit at least nine-tenths of the most important materials. What are three—what six volumes? We live six volumes in a day! Thought, emotion, joy, sorrow, hope, fear, how prolix would they be, if they might each tell their hourly tale! But man's life itself is a brief epitome of that which is infinite and everlasting; and his most accurate confessions are a miserable abridgment of a hurried and confused compendium!

It was about three months, or more, from the night in which Alice wept herself to sleep amongst those wild companions, when she contrived to escape from her father's vigilant eye. They were then

* The Moon.

on the coast of Ireland. Darvil had separated himself from Walters—from his sea-faring companions; he had run through the greater part of the money his crimes had got together; he began seriously to attempt putting into execution his horrible design of depending for support upon the sale of his daughter. Now Alice might have been moulded into sinful purposes before she knew Maltravers; but from that hour her very error made her virtuous— she had comprehended, the moment she loved, what was meant by female honour; and by a sudden revelation she had purchased modesty, delicacy of thought and soul, in the sacrifice of herself. Much of our morality (prudent and right upon system) with respect to the first false step of women, leads us, as we all know, into barbarous errors as to individual exceptions. Where from pure and confiding love that first false step has been taken, many a woman has been saved, in after-life, from a thousand temptations. The poor unfortunates, who crowd our streets and theatres, have rarely, in the first instance, been corrupted by love; but by poverty, and the contagion of circumstance and example. It is a miserable cant phrase to call them the victims of seduction; they have been the victims of hunger, of vanity, of curiosity, of evil *female* counsels; but the seduction of love hardly ever conducts to a *life* of vice. If a woman has once really loved, the beloved object makes an impenetrable barrier between her and other men; their advances terrify and revolt—she would rather die than be unfaithful even to a memory. Though man loves the sex, woman loves only the individual; and the more she loves him, the more cold she is to the species. For the passion of woman is in the sentiment—the fancy—the heart. It rarely has much to do with the coarse images with which boys and old men—the inexperienced and the worn out—connect it.

But Alice, though her blood ran cold at her terrible father's language, saw in his very design the prospect of escape. In an hour of drunkenness he thrust her from the house, and stationed himself to watch her—it was in the city of Cork. She formed her resolution instantly—turned up a narrow street, and fled at full speed. Darvil endeavoured in vain to keep pace with her—his eyes dizzy, his steps reeling with intoxication. She heard his last curse dying from a distance on the air, and her fear winged her steps; she paused at last, and found herself on the outskirts of the town. She paused, overcome, and deadly faint; and then, for the first time, she felt that a strange and new life was stirring within her own. She had long since known that she bore in her womb the unborn offspring of Maltravers, and that knowledge had made her struggle and live on. But now, the embryo had quickened into being—it moved—it appealed to her—a thing unseen, unknown; but still it was a living creature appealing to a mother! Oh, the thrill, half of ineffable tenderness, half of mysterious terror, at that moment!—What a new chapter in the life of woman did it not announce!—Now, then, she must be watchful over herself—must guard against fatigue—must wrestle with despair. Solemn was the trust committed to her—the life of another—the child of the Adored. It was a summer night—she sat on a rude stone, the city on one side, with its lights and lamps—the whitened fields beyond, with the moon and the stars above: and *above* she raised her streaming eyes, and she thought that God the Protector smiled upon her from the face of the sweet skies. So, after a pause and a silent prayer, she rose and resumed her way. When she was wearied she crept into a shed in a farmyard, and slept, for the first time for weeks, the calm sleep of security and hope.

CHAPTER III.

> "How like a prodigal doth she return
> With over-weathered ribs and ragged sails."
> —*Merchant of Venice.*
>
> "*Mer.* What are these?
> *Uncle.* The tenants."
> —BEAUMONT AND FLETCHER.—*Wit without Money.*

IT was just two years from the night in which Alice had been torn from the cottage: and, at that time, Maltravers was wandering amongst the ruins of ancient Egypt, when, upon the very lawn where Alice and her lover had so often loitered hand in hand, a gay party of children and young people were assembled. The cottage had been purchased by an opulent and retired manufacturer. He had raised the low, thatched roof another storey high—and blue slate had replaced the thatch—and the pretty verandahs, overgrown with creepers, had been taken down, because Mrs. Hobbs thought they gave the rooms a dull look; and the little rustic doorway had been replaced by four Ionic pillars in stucco; and a new dining-room, twenty-two feet by eighteen, had been built out at one wing, and a new drawing-room had been built over the new dining-room. And the poor little cottage looked quite grand and villa-like. The fountain had been taken away, because it made the house damp; and there was such a broad carriage-drive from the gate to the house! The gate was no longer the modest, green, wooden gate, ever ajar with its easy latch; but a tall, cast-iron, well-locked gate, between two pillars to match the porch. And on one of the gates was a brass-plate, on which was graven, "Hobbs' Lodge— Ring the bell." The lesser Hobbses and the bigger Hobbses were all on the lawn—many of them fresh from school— for it was the half-holiday of a Saturday afternoon. There was mirth, and noise, and shouting, and whooping, and the respectable old couple looked calmly on. Hobbs the father smoking his pipe (alas, it was not the dear meerschaum!); Hobbs the mother talking to her eldest daughter (a fine young woman, three months married, for love, to a poor man), upon the proper number of days that a leg of mutton (weight ten pounds) should be made to last. "Always, my dear, have large joints, they are much the most saving. Let me see—what a noise the boys do make! No, my love, the ball's not here."

"Mamma, it is under your petticoats."

"La, child, how naughty you are!"

"Holla, you sir! it's my turn to go in now. Biddy, wait—girls have no innings—girls only fag out."

"Bob, you cheat."

"Pa, Ned says I cheat."

"Very likely, my dear; you are to be a lawyer."

"Where was I, my dear?" resumed Mrs. Hobbs, resettling herself, and readjusting the invaded petticoats. "Oh, about the leg of mutton!—yes, large joints are the best—the second day a nice hash, with dumplings; the third, broil the bone—your husband is sure to like broiled bones!—and then keep the scraps for Saturday's pie;—you know, my dear, your father and I were worse off than you when we began. But now we have everything that is handsome about us—nothing like management. Saturday pies are very nice things, and then you start clear with your joint on Sunday. A good wife like you should never neglect the Saturday's pie!"

"Yes," said the bride, mournfully; "but Mr. Tiddy does not like pies."

"Not like pies! that's very odd—Mr. Hobbs likes pies—perhaps you don't have the crust made thick eno'. Howsomever, you can make it up to him with a pudding. A wife should always study her husband's tastes—what is a man's home without love? Still, a husband ought not to be aggravating, and dislike pie on a Saturday!"

"Holla! I say, ma, do you see that 'ere gipsy? I shall go and have my fortune told."

"And I—and I!"

"Lor, if there ben't a tramper!" cried Mr. Hobbs, rising indignantly; "what can the parish be about?"

The object of these latter remarks, filial and paternal, was a young woman in a worn, threadbare cloak, with her face pressed to the open-work of the gate, and looking wistfully—oh, how wistfully!—within. The children eagerly ran up to her, but they involuntarily slackened their steps when they drew near, for she was evidently not what they had taken her for. No gipsy hues darkened the pale, thin, delicate cheek—no gipsy leer lurked in those large blue and streaming eyes—no gipsy effrontery bronzed that candid and childish brow. As she thus pressed her countenance with convulsive eagerness against the cold bars, the young people caught the contagion of inexpressible and half-fearful sadness—they approached almost respectfully—"Do you want anything here?" said the eldest and boldest of the boys.

"I—I—surely this is Dale Cottage?"

"It was Dale Cottage, it is Hobbs' Lodge now; can't you read?" said the heir of the Hobbs's honours, losing, in contempt at the girl's ignorance, his first impression of sympathy.

"And—and—Mr. Butler, is he gone *too*?"

Poor child! she spoke as if the cottage was gone, not improved; the Ionic portico had no charm for her!

"Butler!—no such person lives here. Pa, do you know where Mr. Butler lives?"

Pa was now moving up to the place of conference the slow artillery of his fair, round belly and portly calves. "Butler, no—I know nothing of such a name—no Mr. Butler lives here. Go along with you—ain't you ashamed to beg?"

"No Mr. Butler!" said the girl, gasping for breath, and clinging to the gate for support. "Are you sure, sir?"

"Sure, yes!—what do you want with him?"

"Oh, papa, she looks faint!" said one of the *girls*, deprecatingly—"do let her have something to eat, I'm sure she's hungry."

Mr. Hobbs looked angry; he had often been taken in, and no rich man likes beggars. Generally speaking, the rich man is in the right. But then Mr. Hobbs turned to the suspected tramper's sorrowful face, and then to his fair pretty child—and his good angel whispered something to Mr. Hobbs's heart—and he said, after a pause, "Heaven forbid that we should not feel for a poor fellow-creature not so well to do as ourselves! Come in, my lass, and have a morsel to eat."

The girl did not seem to hear him, and he repeated the invitation, approaching to unlock the gate.

"No, sir," said she, then; "no, I thank you. I could not come in now. I could not eat *here*. But tell me, sir, I implore you, can you not even guess where I may find Mr. Butler?"

"Butler!" said Mrs. Hobbs, whom curiosity had now drawn to the spot. "I remember that was the name of the gentleman who hired the place, and was robbed."

"Robbed!" said Mr. Hobbs, falling back and relocking the gate —"and the new tea-pot just come home," he muttered inly,—— "Come, be off, child—be off; we know nothing of your Mr. Butlers."

The young woman looked wildly in his face, cast a hurried glance over the altered spot, and then, with a kind of shiver, as if the wind had smitten her delicate form too rudely, she drew her cloak more closely round her shoulders, and, without saying another word, moved away. The party looked after her as, with trembling steps, she passed down the road, and all felt that pang of shame which is common to the human heart at the sight of a distress it has not sought to soothe. But this feeling vanished at once from the breast of Mrs. and Mr. Hobbs, when they saw the girl stop where a turn of the road brought the gate before her eyes; and for the first time they perceived, what the worn cloak had hitherto concealed, that the poor young thing bore an infant in her arms. She halted, she gazed fondly back. Even at that distance the despair of her eyes was visible; and then, as she pressed her lips to the infant's brow, they heard a convulsive sob—they saw her turn away, and she was gone!

"Well, I declare!" said Mrs. Hobbs.

"News for the parish," said Mr. Hobbs; "and she so young, too! —what a shame!"

"The girls about here are very bad now-a-days, Jenny," said the mother to the bride.

"I see now why she wanted Mr. Butler," quoth Hobbs, with a knowing wink—"the slut has come to swear!"

And it was for this that Alice had supported her strength—her courage—during the sharp pangs of child-birth; during a severe and crushing illness, which for months after her confinement had stretched her upon a peasant's bed (the object of the rude but kindly charity of an Irish shealing)—for this, day after day, she had whispered to herself, "I shall get well, and I will beg my way to the cottage, and find him there still, and put my little one into his arms, and all will be bright again"—for this, as soon as she could walk without aid, had she set out on foot from the distant land—for this, almost with a dog's instinct (for she knew not what way to turn—what county the cottage was placed in; she only knew the name of the neighbouring town; and that, populous as it was, sounded strange to the ears of those she asked; and she had often and often been directed wrong)—for this, I say, almost with a dog's faithful instinct, had she, in cold and heat, in hunger and in thirst, tracked to her old master's home her desolate and lonely way! And thrice had she over-fatigued herself—and thrice again been indebted to humble pity for a bed whereon to lay a feverish and broken frame. And once, too, her baby—her darling, her life of life, had been ill—had been near unto death, and she could not stir till the infant (it was a girl) was well again, and could smile in her face and crow. And thus many, many months had elapsed, since the day she set out on her pilgrimage, to that on which she found its goal. But never, save when the child was ill, had she desponded or abated heart and hope. She should see him again, and he would kiss her child. And now—no—I cannot paint the might of that stunning blow! She knew not, she dreamed not, of the kind precautions Maltravers had taken; and he had not sufficiently calculated on her thorough ignorance of the world. How could she divine that the magistrate, not a mile distant from her, could have told her all she sought to know? Could she but have met the gardener—or the old woman-servant—all would have been well! These last, indeed, she had the forethought to ask for. But the woman was dead, and the gardener had taken a strange service in some distant county. And so died her last gleam of hope. If one person who remembered the search of Maltravers had but met and recognised her! But she had been seen by so few—and now the bright, fresh girl was so sadly altered! Her race was not yet run, and many a sharp wind upon the mournful seas had the bark to brave before its haven was found at last.

CHAPTER IV.

*"Patience and sorrow strove
Which should express her goodliest."*—SHAKSPEARE.

"Je la plains, je la blame, et je suis son appui." *—VOLTAIRE.

AND now Alice felt that she was on the wide world alone with her child—no longer to be protected, but to protect; and after the first few days of agony, a new spirit, not indeed of hope, but of endurance, passed within her. Her solitary wanderings, with God her only guide, had tended greatly to elevate and confirm her character. She felt a strong reliance on His mysterious mercy—she felt, too, the responsibility of a mother. Thrown for so many months upon her own resources, even for the bread of life, her intellect was unconsciously sharpened, and a habit of patient fortitude had strengthened a nature originally clinging and femininely soft. She resolved to pass into some other country, for she could neither bear the thoughts that haunted the neighbourhood around, nor think, without a loathing horror, of the possibility of her father's return. Accordingly, one day she renewed her wanderings—and, after a week's travel, arrived at a small village. Charity is so common in England, it so spontaneously springs up everywhere, like the good seed by the road-side, that she had rarely wanted the bare necessaries of existence. And her humble manner, and sweet, well-tuned voice, so free from the professional whine of mendicancy, had usually its charm for the sternest. So she generally obtained enough to buy bread and a night's lodging, and, if sometimes she failed, she could bear hunger, and was not afraid of creeping into some shed, or, when by the sea-shore, even into some sheltering cavern. Her child throve too—for God tempers the wind to the shorn lamb! But now, so far as physical privation went, the worst was over.

It so happened that as Alice was drawing herself wearily along to the entrance of the village which was to bound her day's journey, she was met by a lady, past middle age, in whose countenance compassion was so visible, that Alice would not beg, for she had a strange delicacy or pride, or whatever it may be called, and rather begged of the stern than of those who looked kindly at her—she did not like to lower herself in the eyes of the last.

* I pity her, I blame her, and am her support.

The lady stopped.

"My poor girl, where are you going?"

"Where God pleases, madam," said Alice.

"Humph! and is that your own child?—you are almost a child yourself?"

"It is mine, madam," said Alice, gazing fondly at the infant; "it is my all!"

The lady's voice faltered. "Are you married?" she asked.

"Married!—Oh, no, madam!" replied Alice, innocently, yet without blushing, for she never knew that she had done wrong in loving Maltravers.

The lady drew gently back, but not in horror—no, in still deeper compassion; for that lady had true virtue, and she knew that the faults of her sex are sufficiently punished to permit Virtue to pity them without a sin.

"I am sorry for it," she said, however, with greater gravity. "Are you travelling to seek the father?"

"Ah, madam! I shall never see him again!" And Alice wept.

"What!—he has abandoned you—so young, so beautiful!" added the lady to herself.

"Abandoned me!—no, madam; but it is a long tale. Good evening—I thank you kindly for your pity."

The lady's eyes ran over.

"Stay," said she; "tell me frankly where you are going, and what is your object."

"Alas! madam, I am going anywhere, for I have no home; but I wish to live, and work for my living, in order that my child may not want for anything. I wish I could maintain myself—*he* used to say I could."

"He!—your language and manner are not those of a peasant. What can you do?—What do you know?"

"Music, and work, and—and—"

"Music!—this is strange! What were your parents?"

Alice shuddered, and hid her face with her hands.

The lady's interest was now fairly warmed in her behalf.

"She has sinned," said she to herself; "but at that age how can one be harsh?—She must not be thrown upon the world to make sin a habit. Follow me," she said, after a little pause; "and think you have found a friend."

The lady then turned from the high-road down a green lane

which led to a park lodge. This lodge she entered; and, after a short conversation with the inmate, beckoned to Alice to join her.

"Janet," said Alice's new protector to a comely and pleasant-eyed woman, "this is the young person—you will show her and the infant every attention. I shall send down proper clothing for her to-morrow, and I shall then have thought what will be best for her future welfare."

With that, the lady smiled benignly upon Alice, whose heart was too full to speak; and the door of the cottage closed upon her, and Alice thought the day had grown darker.

CHAPTER V.

> "Believe me, she has won me much to pity her.
> Alas! her gentle nature was not made
> To buffet with adversity."—ROWE.

> "Sober he was, and grave from early youth,
> Mindful of forms, but more intent on truth;
> In a light drab he uniformly dress'd,
> And look serene th' unruffled mind express'd.
>
> . . . . .
>
> Yet might observers in his sparkling eye
> Some observation, some acuteness spy;
> The friendly thought it keen, the treacherous deem'd it sly;
> Yet not a crime could foe or friend detect,
> His actions all were like his speech correct—
> Chaste, sober, solemn, and devout they named
> Him who was this, and not of *this* ashamed."—CRABBE.

> "I'll on and sound this secret."—BEAUMONT AND FLETCHER.

MRS. LESLIE, the lady introduced to the reader in the last chapter, was a woman of the firmest intellect combined (no unusual combination) with the softest heart. She learned Alice's history with admiration and pity. The natural innocence of the young mother spoke so eloquently in her words and looks, that Mrs. Leslie, on hearing her tale, found much less to forgive than she had anticipated. Still, she deemed it necessary to enlighten Alice as to the criminality of the connection she had formed. But here Alice was singularly dull—she listened in meek patience to Mrs. Leslie's lecture; but it evidently made but slight impression on her. She had not yet seen enough of the Social state to correct the first impressions of the Natural: and all she could say in answer to Mrs. Leslie was—" It may be all very true, madam, but I have been so much better since I knew him!"

But though Alice took humbly any censure upon herself, she would not hear a syllable insinuated against Maltravers. When, in a very natural indignation, Mrs. Leslie denounced him as a destroyer of innocence—for Mrs. Leslie could not learn all that extenuated his offence—Alice started up with flashing eyes and heaving heart, and would have hurried from the only shelter she had in the wide world—she would sooner have died—she would sooner even have seen her child die, than done that idol of her soul, who, in her eyes, stood alone on some pinnacle between earth and heaven, the wrong of hearing him reviled. With difficulty Mrs. Leslie could restrain, with still more difficulty could she pacify and soothe her; and for the girl's petulance, which others might have deemed insolent and ungrateful, the woman-heart of Mrs. Leslie loved her all the better. The more she saw of Alice, and the more she comprehended her story and her character, the more was she lost in wonder at the romance of which this beautiful child had been the heroine, and the more perplexed she was as to Alice's future prospects.

At length, however, when she became acquainted with Alice's musical acquirements, which were, indeed, of no common order, a light broke in upon her. Here was the source of her future independence. Maltravers, it will be remembered, was a musician of consummate skill as well as taste, and Alice's natural talent for the art had advanced her, in the space of months, to a degree of perfection which it cost others—which it had cost even the quick Maltravers—years to obtain. But we learn so rapidly when our teachers are those we love; and it may be observed that the less our knowledge, the less perhaps our genius in other things, the more facile are our attainments in music, which is a very jealous mistress of the mind. Mrs. Leslie resolved to have her perfected in this art, and so enable her to become a teacher to others. In the town of C——, about thirty miles from Mrs. Leslie's house, though in the same county, there was no inconsiderable circle of wealthy and intelligent persons; for it was a cathedral town, and the resident clergy drew around them a kind of provincial aristocracy. Here, as in most rural towns in England, music was much cultivated, both among the higher and middle classes. There were amateur concerts, and glee-clubs, and subscriptions for sacred music: and once every five years there was the great C—— Festival. In this town Mrs. Leslie established Alice: she placed her under the roof of a *ci-devant* music-master, who, having retired from his profession, was no longer jealous of rivals, but who, by handsome terms, was induced to complete the education of Alice. It was an eligible and comfortable abode, and the music-master and his wife were a good-natured, easy old couple.

Three months of resolute and unceasing perseverance, combined with the singular ductility and native gifts of Alice, sufficed to render her the most promising pupil the good musician had ever accomplished; and in three months more, introduced by Mrs. Leslie to many of the families in the place, Alice was established in a home of her own; and what with regular lessons, and occasional assistance at musical parties, she was fairly earning what her tutor reasonably pronounced to be "a very genteel independence."

Now, in these arrangements (for we must here go back a little) there had been one gigantic difficulty of conscience in one party, of feeling in another, to surmount. Mrs. Leslie saw at once that unless Alice's misfortune was concealed, all the virtues and all the talents in the world could not enable her to retrace the one false step. Mrs. Leslie was a woman of habitual truth and strict rectitude, and she was sorely perplexed between the propriety of candour and its cruelty. She felt unequal to take the responsibility of action on herself; and, after much meditation, she resolved to confide her scruples to one, who of all whom she knew, possessed the highest character for moral worth and religious sanctity. This gentleman, lately a widower, lived at the outskirts of the town selected for Alice's future residence, and at that time happened to be on a visit in Mrs. Leslie's neighbourhood. He was an opulent man, a banker; he had once represented the town in parliament, and retiring, from disinclination to the late hours and onerous fatigues even of an unreformed House of Commons, he still possessed an influence to return one, if not both, of the members for the city of C——. And that influence was always exerted so as best to secure his own interest with the powers that be, and advance certain objects of ambition (for he was both an ostentatious and ambitious man in his own way), which he felt he might more easily obtain by proxy than by his own votes and voice in parliament—an atmosphere in which his light did not shine. And it was with a wonderful address that the banker contrived at once to support the government, and yet, by the frequent expression of liberal opinions, to conciliate the Whigs and the Dissenters of his neighbourhood. Parties, political and sectarian, were not then so irreconcilable as they are now. In the whole county there was no one so respected as this eminent person, and yet he possessed no shining talents, though a laborious and energetic man of business. It was solely and wholly the force of moral character which gave him his position in society. He felt this; he was sensitively proud of it; he was painfully anxious not to lose an atom of a distinction that required to be vigilantly secured. He was a very *remarkable*, yet not (perhaps could we penetrate all hearts) a very *uncommon* character —this banker! He had risen from, comparatively speaking, a low origin and humble fortunes, and entirely by the scrupulous and sedate propriety of his outward conduct. With such a propriety he, therefore, inseparably connected every notion of worldly prosperity and honour. Thus, though far from a bad man, he was forced into being something of a hypocrite. Every year he had grown more starch and more saintly. He was conscience-keeper to the whole town; and it is astonishing how many persons hardly dared to make a will or subscribe to a charity without his advice. As he was a shrewd man of this world, as well as an accredited guide to the next, his advice was precisely of a nature to reconcile the Conscience and the Interest; and he was a kind of negotiator in the reciprocal diplomacy of earth and heaven. But our banker was really a charitable man, and a benevolent man, and a sincere believer. How, then, was he a hypocrite? Simply because he professed to be far *more* charitable, *more* benevolent, and *more* pious than he really was. His reputation had now arrived to that degree of immaculate polish, that the smallest breath, which would not have tarnished the character of another man, would have fixed an indelible stain upon his. As he affected to be more strict than the churchman, and was a great oracle with all who regarded churchmen as lukewarm, so his conduct was narrowly watched by all the clergy of the orthodox cathedral; good men, doubtless, but not affecting to be saints, who were jealous at being so luminously outshone by a layman and an authority of the sectarians. On the other hand, the intense homage, and almost worship he received from his followers, kept his goodness upon a stretch, if not beyond all human power, certainly beyond his own. For "admiration" (as it is well said somewhere) "is a kind of superstition which expects miracles." From nature this gentleman had received an inordinate share of animal propensities; he had strong passions, he was by temperament a sensualist. He loved good eating and good wine—he loved women. The two former blessings of the carnal life are not incompatible with canonisation; but St. Anthony has shown that women, however angelic, are not precisely that order of angels that saints may safely commune with. If, therefore, he ever yielded to temptations of a sexual nature, it was with profound secrecy and caution; nor did his right hand know what his left hand did.

This gentleman had married a woman much older than himself, but her fortune had been one of the necessary stepping-stones in his career. His exemplary conduct towards this lady, ugly as well as old, had done much towards increasing the odour of his sanctity. She died of an ague, and the widower did not shock probabilities by affecting too severe a grief.

"The Lord's will be done!" said he; "she was a good woman, but we should not set our affections too much upon His perishable creatures!"

This was all he was ever heard to say on the matter. He took an elderly gentlewoman, distantly related to him, to manage his house, and sit at the head of the table; and it was thought not impossible, though the widower was past fifty, that he might marry again.

Such was the gentleman called in by Mrs. Leslie, who, of the same religious opinions, had long known and revered him, to decide the affairs of Alice and of Conscience.

As this man exercised no slight or fugitive influence over Alice Darvil's destinies, his counsels on the point in discussion ought to be fairly related.

"And now," said Mrs. Leslie, concluding the history, "you will perceive, my dear sir, that this poor young creature has been less culpable than she appears. From the extraordinary proficiency she has made in music, in a time that, by her own account, seems incredibly short, I should suspect her unprincipled betrayer must have been an artist—a professional man. It is just possible that they may meet again, and (as the ranks between them cannot be so very disproportionate) that he may marry her. I am sure that he could not do a better or a wiser thing, for she loves him too fondly, despite her wrongs. Under these circumstances, would it be a—a—a culpable disguise of truth to represent her as a married woman—separated from her husband—and give her the name of her seducer? Without such a precaution you will see, sir, that all hope of settling her reputably in life—all chance of procuring her any creditable independence, is out of the question. Such is my dilemma. What is your advice?—palatable or not, I shall abide by it."

The banker's grave and saturnine countenance exhibited a slight degree of embarrassment at the case submitted to him. He began brushing away, with the cuff of his black coat, some atoms of dust that had settled on his drab small-clothes; and, after a slight pause, he replied, "Why, really, dear madam, the question is one of much delicacy—I doubt if men could be good judges upon it; your sex's tact and instinct on these matters are better—much better than our sagacity. There is much in the dictates of your own heart; for to those who are in the grace of the Lord, He vouchsafes to communicate his pleasure by spiritual hints and inward suggestions!"

"If so, my dear sir, the matter is decided; for my heart whispers me, that this slight deviation from truth would be a less culpable offence than turning so young and, I had almost said, so innocent a creature adrift upon the world. I may take your opinion as my sanction."

"Why, really, I can scarcely say so much as that," said the banker, with a slight smile. "A deviation from truth cannot be incurred without some forfeiture of strict duty."

"Not in any case? Alas, I was afraid so!" said Mrs. Leslie, despondingly.

"In any case! Oh, there *may* be cases! But had I not better see the young woman, and ascertain that your benevolent heart has not deceived you?"

"I wish you would," said Mrs. Leslie; "she is now in the house. I will ring for her."

"Should we not be alone?"

"Certainly, I will leave you together."

Alice was sent for, and appeared.

"This pious gentleman," said Mrs. Leslie, "will confer with you for a few moments, my child. Do not be afraid; he is the best of men." With these words of encouragement the good lady vanished, and Alice saw before her a tall dark man, with a head bald in front, yet larger behind than before, with spectacles upon a pair of shrewd, penetrating eyes, and an outline of countenance that showed he must have been handsome in earlier manhood.

"My young friend," said the banker, seating himself, after a deliberate survey of the fair countenance that blushed beneath his gaze, "Mrs. Leslie and myself have been conferring upon your temporal welfare. You have been unfortunate, my child?"

"Ah—yes."

"Well, well, you are very young; we must not be too severe upon youth. You will never do so again?"

"Do what, please you, sir?"

"What! Humph! I mean that you will be more rigid, more circumspect. Men are deceitful; you must be on your guard against them. You are handsome, child, very handsome—more's the pity." And the banker took Alice's hand and pressed it with great unction. Alice looked at him gravely, and drew the hand away instinctively.

The banker lowered his spectacles, and gazed at her without their aid; his eyes were still fine and expressive. "What is your name?" he asked.

"Alice—Alice Darvil, sir."

"Well, Alice, we have been considering what is best for you. You wish to earn your own livelihood, and perhaps marry some honest man hereafter."

"Marry, sir—never!" said Alice, with great earnestness, her eyes filling with tears.

"And why?"

"Because I shall never see *him* on earth, and they do not marry in heaven, sir."

The banker was moved, for he was not worse than his neighbours, though trying to make them believe he was so much better.

"Well, time enough to talk of that; but in the meanwhile you would support yourself?"

"Yes, sir. His child ought to be a burthen to none—nor I either. I once wished to die, but then who would love my little one? *Now* I wish to live."

"But what mode of livelihood would you prefer? Would you go into a family in some capacity?—not that of a servant—you are too delicate for that."

"Oh, no—no!"

"But, again, why?" asked the banker, soothingly, yet surprised.

"Because," said Alice, almost solemnly, "there are some hours when I feel I must be alone. I sometimes think I am not all right *here*," and she touched her forehead. "They called me an idiot before I knew *him!*—No, I could not live with others, for I can only cry when nobody but my child is with me."

This was said with such unconscious, and therefore with such pathetic simplicity, that the banker was sensibly affected. He rose, stirred the fire, resettled himself, and after a pause, said emphatically—"Alice, I will be your friend. Let me believe you will deserve it."

Alice bent her graceful head, and seeing that he had sunk into an abstracted silence, she thought it time for her to withdraw.

"She is, indeed, beautiful," said the banker, almost aloud, when he was alone; "and the old lady is right—she is as innocent as if she had not fallen. I wonder——." Here he stopped short, and walked to the glass over the mantel-piece, where he was still gazing on his own features when Mrs. Leslie returned.

"Well, sir," said she, a little surprised at this seeming vanity in so pious a man.

The banker started. "Madam, I honour your penetration as much as your charity; I think that there is so much to be feared in letting all the world know this young female's past error, that, though I dare not advise, I cannot blame your concealment of it."

"But, sir, your words have sunk deep into my thoughts; you said every deviation from truth was a forfeiture of duty."

"Certainly; but there are some exceptions. The world is a bad world, we are born in sin, and the children of wrath. We do not tell infants all the truth, when they ask us questions, the proper answers of which would mislead, not enlighten, them. In some things the whole world are infants. The very science of government is the science of concealing truth—so is the system of trade. We could not blame the tradesman for not telling the public, that if all his debts were called in he would be a bankrupt."

"And he may marry her after all—this Mr. Butler."

"Heaven forbid—the villain!—Well, madam, I will see to this poor young thing—she shall not want a guide."

"Heaven reward you. How wicked some people are to call you severe!"

"I can bear *that* blame with a meek temper, madam. Good day."

"Good day. You will remember how strictly confidential has been our conversation."

"Not a breath shall transpire. I will send you some tracts to-morrow—so comforting. Heaven bless you!"

This difficulty smoothed, Mrs. Leslie, to her astonishment, found that she had another to contend with in Alice herself. For, first,

Alice conceived that to change her name and keep her secret, was to confess that she ought to be ashamed, rather than proud, of her love to Ernest, and she thought that so ungrateful to him!—and, secondly, to take his name, to pass for his wife—what presumption —he would certainly have a right to be offended! At these scruples Mrs. Leslie well-nigh lost all patience; and the banker, to his own surprise, was again called in. We have said that he was an experienced and skilful adviser, which implies the faculty of persuasion. He soon saw the handle by which Alice's obstinacy might always be moved—her little girl's welfare. He put this so forcibly before her eyes; he represented the child's future fate as resting so much, not only on her own good conduct, but on her outward respectability, that he prevailed upon her at last; and, perhaps, one argument that he incidentally used, had as much effect on her as the rest. "This Mr. Butler, if yet in England, may pass through our town—may visit amongst us—may hear you spoken of, by a name similar to his own, and curiosity would thus induce him to seek you. Take his name, and you will always bear an honourable index to your mutual discovery and recognition. Besides, when you are respectable, honoured, and earning an independence, he may not be too proud to marry you. But take your own name, avow your own history, and not only will your child be an outcast, yourself a beggar, or, at best, a menial dependant, but you lose every hope of recovering the object of your too-devoted attachment."

Thus Alice was convinced. From this time she became close and reserved in her communications. Mrs. Leslie had wisely selected a town sufficiently remote from her own abode to preclude any revelations of her domestics; and, as Mrs. Butler, Alice attracted universal sympathy and respect from the exercise of her talents, the modest sweetness of her manners, the unblemished propriety of her conduct. Somehow or other, no sooner did she learn the philosophy of concealment, than she made a great leap in knowledge of the world. And, though flattered and courted by the young loungers of C——, she steered her course with so much address that she was never persecuted. For there are few men in the world who make advances where there is no encouragement.

The banker observed her conduct with silent vigilance. He met her often, he visited her often. He was intimate at houses where she attended to teach or perform. He lent her good books—he advised her—he preached to her. Alice began to look up to him— to like him—to consider him as a village girl in Catholic countries may consider a benevolent and kindly priest. And he—what was his object?—at that time it is impossible to guess:—he became thoughtful and abstracted.

One day an old maid and an old clergyman met in the High Street of C——.

"And how do you do, ma'am?" said the clergyman; "how is the rheumatism?"

"Better, thank you, sir. Any news?"

The clergyman smiled, and something hovered on his lips, which he suppressed.

"Were you," the old maid resumed, "at Mrs. Macnab's last night? Charming music!"

"Charming! How pretty that Mrs. Butler is! and how humble! Knows her station—so unlike professional people."

"Yes, indeed!—What attention a certain banker paid her!"

"He! he! he! yes; he is very fatherly—very!"

"Perhaps he will marry again; he is always talking of the holy state of matrimony—a holy state it may be—but heaven knows, his wife, poor woman, did not make it a pleasant one."

"There may be more causes for that than we guess of," said the clergyman, mysteriously. "I would not be uncharitable, but——"

"But what?"

"Oh, when he was young, our great man was not so correct, I fancy, as he is now."

"So I have heard it whispered; but nothing against him was ever known."

"Hem—it is very odd!"

"What's very odd?"

"Why, but it's a secret—I dare say it's all very right."

"Oh, I shan't say a word. Are you going to the cathedral?—don't let me keep you standing. Now, pray proceed!"

"Well, then, yesterday I was doing duty in a village more than twenty miles hence, and I loitered in the village to take an early dinner; and, afterwards, while my horse was feeding I strolled down the green."

"Well—well?"

"And I saw a gentleman muffled carefully up, with his hat slouched over his face, at the door of a cottage, with a little child in his arms, and he kissed it more fondly than, be we ever so good, we generally kiss other people's children; and then he gave it to a peasant woman standing near him, and mounted his horse, which was tied to the gate, and trotted past me; and who do you think this was?"

"Patience me—I can't guess!"

"Why, our saintly banker. I bowed to him, and I assure you he turned as red, ma'am, as your waistband."

"My!"

"I just turned into the cottage when he was out of sight, for I was thirsty, and asked for a glass of water, and I saw the child. I declare, I would not be uncharitable, but I thought it monstrous like—you know whom!"

"Gracious! you don't say——"

"I asked the woman 'if it was hers?' and she said 'No,' but was very short."

"Dear me, I *must* find this out!—What is the name of the village?"

"Covedale."

"Oh, I know—I know."

"Not a word of this; I dare say there's nothing in it. But I am not much in favour of your new lights."

"Nor I neither. What better than the old Church of England?"

Two days after this, three old maids made an excursion to the village of Covedale, and lo! the cottage in question was shut up—the woman and the child were gone. The people in the village knew nothing about them—had seen nothing particular in the woman or child—had always supposed them mother and daughter; and the gentleman identified by the clerical inquisitor with the banker had never but once been observed in the place.

"The vile old parson," said the eldest of the old maids, "to take away so good a man's character!—and the fly will cost one pound two, with the baiting!"

CHAPTER VI.

"In this disposition was I, when looking out of my window one day to take the air, I perceived a kind of peasant who looked at me very attentively."—*Gil Blas.*

A SUMMER'S evening in a retired country town has something melancholy in it. You have the streets of a metropolis without their animated bustle—you have the stillness of the country without its birds and flowers. The reader will please to bring before him a quiet street, in the quiet country town of C——, in a quiet evening in quiet June; the picture is not mirthful—two young dogs are playing in the street, one old dog is watching by a newly-painted door. A few ladies of middle age move noiselessly along the pavement, returning home to tea; they wear white muslin dresses, green spencers a little faded, straw poke bonnets, with green or coffee-coloured gauze veils. By twos and threes they have disappeared within the thresholds of small neat houses with little railings, enclosing little green plots. Threshold, house, railing, and plot, each as like to the other as are those small commodities called "nest tables," which, "even as a broken mirror multiplies," summon to the bewildered eye countless iterations of one four-legged individual. Paradise Place was a set of nest houses.

A cow had passed through the streets, with a milkwoman behind; two young and gay shopmen, "looking after the gals," had reconnoitred the street and vanished in despair. The twilight advanced —but gently; and though a star or two were up, the air was still clear. At the open window at one of the tenements in this street sat Alice Darvil. She had been working (that pretty excuse to women for thinking), and as the thoughts grew upon her, and the evening waned, the work had fallen upon her knee, and her hands dropped mechanically on her lap. Her profile was turned towards the street, but without moving her head or changing her attitude, her eyes glanced from time to time to her little girl, who nestled on the ground beside her, tired with play; and, wondering, perhaps, why she was not already in bed, seemed as tranquil as the young mother herself. And sometimes Alice's eyes filled with tears—and then she sighed, as if to sigh the tears away. But, poor Alice, if she grieved, hers was now a silent and a patient grief!

The street was deserted of all other passengers, when a man passed along the pavement on the side opposite to Alice's house. His garb was rude and homely, between that of a labourer and a farmer; but still there was an affectation of tawdry show about the bright scarlet silk handkerchief, tied in a sailor or smuggler fashion round the sinewy throat; the hat was set jauntily on one side, and, dangling many an inch from the gaily-striped waistcoat, glittered a watch-chain and seals, which appeared suspiciously out of character with the rest of the attire. The passenger was covered with dust; and as the street was in a suburb communicating with the high-road, and formed one of the entrances into the town, he had probably, after a long day's journey, reached his evening's destination. The looks of this stranger were anxious, restless, and perturbed. In his gait and swagger there was the recklessness of the professional blackguard; but in his vigilant, prying, suspicious eyes, there was a hang-dog expression of apprehension and fear. He seemed a man upon whom Crime had set its significant mark—and who saw a purse with one eye and a gibbet with the other. Alice did not note the stranger until she herself had attracted and centred all his attention. He halted abruptly as he caught a view of her face— shaded his eyes with his hand as if to gaze more intently—and at length burst into an exclamation of surprise and pleasure. At that instant Alice turned, and her gaze met that of the stranger. The fascination of the basilisk can scarcely more stun and paralyse its victim than the look of this stranger charmed, with the appalling glamoury of horror, the eye and soul of Alice Darvil. Her face became suddenly locked and rigid, her lips as white as marble, her eyes almost started from their sockets—she pressed her hands convulsively together, and shuddered—but still she did not move. The man nodded, and grinned, and then, deliberately crossing the street gained the door and knocked loudly. Still Alice did not stir—her senses seemed to have forsaken her—presently the stranger's loud, rough voice was heard below, in answer to the accents of the solitary woman-servant whom Alice kept in her employ; and his strong, heavy tread made the slight staircase creak and tremble. Then Alice rose as by an instinct, caught her child in her arms, and stood erect and motionless, facing the door. It opened—and the FATHER and DAUGHTER were once more face to face within the same walls.

"Well, Alley, how are you, my blowen?—glad to see your old dad again, I'll be sworn. No ceremony, sit down. Ha, ha! snug here—very snug—we shall live together charmingly. Trade on your own account—eh? sly;—well, can't desert your poor old father. Let's have something to eat and drink."

So saying, Darvil threw himself at length upon the neat, prim, little chintz sofa, with the air of a man resolved to make himself perfectly at home.

Alice gazed, and trembled violently, but still said nothing—the power of voice had indeed left her.

"Come, why don't you stir your stumps? I suppose I must wait on myself—fine manners!—But, ho, ho—a bell, by gosh—mighty grand—never mind—I am used to call for my own wants."

A hearty tug at the frail bell-rope sent a shrill alarum half-way through the long lath-and-plaster row of Paradise Place, and left the instrument of the sound in the hand of its creator.

Up came the maid-servant, a formal old woman, most respectable.

"Harkye, old girl!" said Darvil; "bring up the best you have to eat—not particular—let there be plenty. And I say—a bottle of brandy. Come, don't stand there staring like a stuck pig. Budge! Hell and furies! don't you hear me?"

The servant retreated, as if a pistol had been put to her head, and Darvil, laughing loud, threw himself again upon the sofa. Alice looked at him, and, still without saying a word, glided from the room—her child in her arms. She hurried downstairs, and in the hall met her servant. The latter, who was much attached to her mistress, was alarmed to see her about to leave the house.

"Why, marm, where be you going? Dear heart, you have no bonnet on! What is the matter? Who is this?"

"Oh!" cried Alice, in agony; "what shall I do?—where shall I fly?" The door above opened. Alice heard, started, and the next moment was in the street. She ran on breathlessly, and like one insane. Her mind was, indeed, for the time gone, and had a river flowed before her way, she would have plunged into an escape from a world that seemed too narrow to hold a father and his child.

But just as she turned the corner of a street that led into the more public thoroughfares, she felt her arm grasped, and a voice called out her name in surprised and startled accents.

"Heavens, Mrs. Butler! Alice! What do I see? What is the matter?"

"Oh, sir, save me!—you are a good man—a great man—save me—he is returned!"

"He! who?—Mr. Butler?" said the banker (for that gentleman it was), in a changed and trembling voice.

"No, no—ah, not he!—I did not say *he*—I said my father—my, my—ah—look behind—look behind—*is* he coming?"

"Calm yourself, my dear young friend—no one is near. I will go and reason with your father. No one shall harm you—I will protect you. Go back—go back, I will follow—we must not be seen together." And the tall banker seemed trying to shrink into a nutshell.

"No, no," said Alice, growing yet paler, "I cannot go back."

"Well, then, just follow me to the door—your servant shall get you your bonnet, and accompany you to my house, where you can wait till I return. Meanwhile I will see your father, and rid you, I trust, of his presence."

The banker, who spoke in a very hurried and even impatient voice, waited for no reply, but took his way to Alice's house. Alice herself did not follow, but remained in the very place where she was left, till joined by her servant, who then conducted her to the rich man's residence... But Alice's mind had not recovered its shock, and her thoughts wandered alarmingly.

CHAPTER VII.

> "*Miramont.*—Do they chafe roundly?
> *Andrew.*—As they were rubbed with soap, sir.
> And now they swear aloud, now calm again
> Like a ring of bells, whose sound the wind still utters,
> And then they sit in council what to do,
> And then they jar again what shall be done?"
> —BEAUMONT AND FLETCHER.

OH! what a picture of human nature it was when the banker and the vagabond sat together in that little drawing-room, facing each other—one in the arm-chair, one on the sofa! Darvil was still employed on some cold meat, and was making wry faces at the very indifferent brandy which he had frightened the formal old servant into buying at the nearest public-house; and opposite sat the respectable—highly respectable, man of forms and ceremonies, of decencies and quackeries, gazing gravely upon this low, dare-devil ruffian:—the well-to-do hypocrite—the penniless villain; —the man who had everything to lose—the man who had nothing in the wide world but his own mischievous, rascally life, a gold watch, chain, and seals, which he had stolen the day before, and thirteen shillings and threepence halfpenny in his left breeches-pocket!

The man of wealth was by no means well acquainted with the nature of the beast before him. He had heard from Mrs. Leslie (as we remember) the outline of Alice's history, and ascertained that their joint *protégé's* father was a great blackguard; but he expected to find Mr. Darvil a mere dull, brutish villain, a peasant-ruffian—a blunt serf, without brains, or their substitute, effrontery. But Luke Darvil was a clever, half-educated fellow: he did not sin from ignorance, but had wit enough to have bad principles, and he was as impudent as if he had lived all his life in the best society. He was not frightened at the banker's drab breeches and imposing air—not he! The Duke of Wellington would not have frightened Darvil, unless his grace had had the constables for his *aides-de-camp*.

The banker, to use a homely phrase, was "taken aback."

"Look you here, Mr. What's-your-name!" said Darvil, swallowing a glass of the raw alcohol as if it had been water—"look you now—you can't humbug me. What the devil do you care about my daughter's respectability or comfort, or anything else, grave old dog as you are!—It is my daughter herself you are licking your brown old chaps at!—and faith, my Alley is a very pretty girl—very—but queer as moonshine. You'll drive a much better bargain with me than with her."

The banker coloured scarlet—he bit his lips, and measured his companion from head to foot (while the latter lolled on the sofa), as if he were meditating the possibility of kicking him downstairs. But Luke Darvil would have thrashed the banker, and all his clerks into the bargain. His frame was like a trunk of thews and muscles, packed up by that careful dame, Nature, as tightly as possible; and a prize-fighter would have thought twice before he entered the ring against so awkward a customer. The banker was a man prudent to a fault, and he pushed his chair six inches back as he concluded his survey.

"Sir," then said he, very quietly, "do not let us misunderstand each other. Your daughter is safe from your control—if you molest her, the law will protect——"

"She is not of age," said Darvil. "Your health, old boy."

"Whether she is of age or not," returned the banker, unheeding the courtesy conveyed in the last sentence, "I do not care three straws—I know enough of the law to know, that if she have rich friends in this town, and you have none, she will be protected, and you will go to the treadmill."

"That is spoken like a sensible man," said Darvil, for the first time with a show of respect in his manner : "you now take a practical view of the matter, as we used to say at the spouting-club."

"If I were in your situation, Mr. Darvil, I tell you what I would do. I would leave my daughter and this town to-morrow morning, and I would promise never to return, and never to molest her, on condition she allowed me a certain sum from her earnings, paid quarterly."

[illegible] lived all his life in the best company [illegible] the banker's drab breeches and imposing [illegible] Wellington would not have frightened [illegible] had the constables for his under-[illegible]

[illegible]

[illegible] quietly, "do not let us misunderstand [illegible] is safe from your control—if you molest [illegible]—"

[illegible] Darvil. "Your health, old boy."

[illegible] or not," returned the banker, unheeding [illegible] the last sentence, "I do not care three [illegible] the law to know, that if she have rich [illegible] ou have none, she will be protected, and [illegible]ll."

[illegible] sensible man," said Darvil, for the first [illegible]ct in his manner: "you now take a prac-[illegible]s we used to say at the spouting-club. [illegible]ation, Mr. Darvil, I tell you what [illegible] aughter and this town to-morrow morning, [illegible]ever to return, and never to molest her, on [illegible] me a certain sum from her earnings, paid

"And if I preferred living with her?"

"In that case, I, as a magistrate of this town, would have you sent away as a vagrant, or apprehended——"

"Ha!"

"Apprehended on suspicion of stealing that gold chain and seals which you wear so ostentatiously."

"By goles, but you're a clever fellow," said Darvil, involuntarily; "you know human natur'."

The banker smiled: strange to say, he was pleased with the compliment.

"But," resumed Darvil, helping himself to another slice of beef, "you are in the wrong box—planted in Queer Street, as *we* say in London; for if you care a d—n about my daughter's respectability, you will never muzzle her father on suspicion of theft—and so there's tit for tat, my old gentleman!"

"I shall deny that you are her father, Mr. Darvil; and I think you will find it hard to prove the fact in any town where I am a magistrate."

"By goles, what a good prig you would have made! You are as sharp as a gimlet. Surely you were brought up at the Old Bailey!"

"Mr. Darvil, be ruled. You seem a man not deaf to reason, and I ask you whether, in any town in this country, a poor man in suspicious circumstances can do anything against a rich man whose character is established? Perhaps, you are right in the main: I have nothing to do with that. But I tell you that you shall quit this house in half-an-hour—that you shall never enter it again but at your peril: and if you do—within ten minutes from that time you shall be in the town gaol. It is no longer a contest between you and your defenceless daughter; it is a contest between——"

"A tramper in fustian and a gemman as drives a coach," interrupted Darvil, laughing bitterly, yet heartily. "Good—good!"

The banker rose. "I think you have made a very clever definition," said he. "Half-an-hour—you recollect—good evening."

"Stay," said Darvil; "you are the first man I have seen for many a year that I can take a fancy to. Sit down—sit down, I say, and talk a bit, and we shall come to terms soon, I dare say—that's right. Lord! how I should like to have you on the roadside instead of within these gimcrack walls. Ha! ha! the argufying would be all in *my* favour then."

The banker was not a brave man, and his colour changed

DAVID STARTED TO HIS FEET—HIS EYES GLARED—HE GRASPED THE CARVING KNIFE BEFORE HIM.

slightly at the intimation of this obliging wish. Darvil eyed him grimly and chucklingly.

The rich man resumed—"That may or may not be, Mr. Darvil, according as I might happen or not to have pistols about me. But to the point. Quit this house without further debate, without noise, without mentioning to any one else your claim upon its owner——"

"Well, and the return?"

"Ten guineas now, and the same sum quarterly, as long as the young lady lives in this town, and you never persecute her by word or letter."

"That is forty guineas a-year. I can't live upon it."

"You will cost less in the House of Correction, Mr. Darvil."

"Come, make it a hundred; Alley is cheap at that."

"Not a farthing more," said the banker, buttoning up his breeches-pockets with a determined air.

"Well, out with the shiners."

"Do you promise or not?"

"I promise."

"There are your ten guineas. If in half-an-hour you are not gone —why then——"

"Then?"

"Why then you have robbed me of ten guineas, and must take the usual consequences of robbery."

Darvil started to his feet—his eyes glared—he grasped the carving-knife before him.

"You are a bold fellow," said the banker, quietly; "but it won't do. It is not worth your while to murder me; and I am a man sure to be missed."

Darvil sunk down, sullen and foiled. The respectable man was more than a match for the villain.

"Had you been as poor as I—Gad! what a rogue you would have been!"

"I think not," said the banker; "I believe roguery to be a very bad policy. Perhaps once I *was* almost as poor as you are, but I never turned rogue."

"You never were in my circumstances," returned Darvil, gloomily. "I was a gentleman's son. Come, you shall hear my story. My father was well-born, but married a maid-servant when he was at college; his family disowned him, and left him to starve. He died in the struggle against a poverty he was not brought up to, and my dame went into service again; became housekeeper to an old bachelor—sent me to school—but mother had a family by the old bachelor, and I was taken from school and put to trade. All hated me—for I was ugly; d—n them! Mother cut me—I wanted money—robbed the old bachelor—was sent to gaol, and learned there a lesson or two how to rob better in future. Mother died—I was adrift on the world. The world was my foe—could not make it up with the world, so we went to war—you understand, old boy? Married a poor woman and pretty—wife made me jealous—had learned to suspect every one. Alice born—did not believe her mine; not like me—perhaps a gentleman's child. I hate—I loathe gentlemen. Got drunk one night—kicked my wife in the stomach three weeks after her confinement. Wife died—tried for my life—got off. Went to another country—having had a sort of education, and being sharp eno', got work as a mechanic. Hated work just as I hated gentlemen—for was I not by blood a gentleman? There was the curse. Alice grew up; never looked on her as my flesh and blood. Her mother was a w——! Why should not she be one? There, that's enough. Plenty of excuse, I think, for all I have ever done. Curse the world—curse the rich—curse the handsome—curse—curse all!"

"You have been a very foolish man," said the banker; "and seem to me to have had very good cards if you had known how to play them. However, that is your look-out. It is not yet too late to repent—age is creeping on you.—Man, there is another world."

The banker said the last words with a tone of solemn and even dignified adjuration.

"You think so—do you?" said Darvil, staring at him.

"From my soul I do."

"Then you are not the sensible man I took you for," replied Darvil, drily; "and I should like to talk to you on that subject."

But our Dives, however sincere a believer, was by no means one

> "At whose control
> Despair and anguish fled the struggling soul."

He had words of comfort for the pious, but he had none for the sceptic—he could soothe, but he could not convert. It was not in his way; besides, he saw no credit in making a convert of Luke Darvil. Accordingly, he again rose with some quickness, and said—

"No, sir; that is useless, I fear, and I have no time to spare; and so once more, good night to you."

"But you have not arranged where my allowance is to be sent."

"Ah! true; I will guarantee it. You will find my name sufficient security."

"At least, it is the best I can get," returned Darvil, carelessly; "and, after all, it is not a bad chance-day's work. But I'm sure I can't say where the money shall be sent. I don't know a man who would not grab it."

"Very well, then—the best thing (I speak as a man of business) will be to draw on me for ten guineas, quarterly. Wherever you are staying, any banker can effect this for you. But mind, if ever you overdraw, the account stops."

"I understand," said Darvil; "and when I have finished the bottle I shall be off."

"You had better," replied the banker, as he opened the door.

The rich man returned home hurriedly. "So Alice, after all, has some gentle blood in her veins," thought he. "But that father—no, it will never do. I wish he were hanged and nobody the wiser. I should very much like to arrange the matter without marrying; but then—scandal—scandal—scandal. After all, I had better give up all thoughts of her. She is monstrous handsome, and so—humph!—I shall never grow an old man."

CHAPTER VIII.

"Began to bend down his admiring eyes
On all her touching looks and qualities,
Turning their shapely sweetness every way,
Till 'twas his food and habit day by day."
—LEIGH HUNT.

THERE must have been a secret something about Alice Darvil singularly captivating, that (associated as she was with images of the most sordid and the vilest crimes) left her still pure and lovely alike in the eyes of a man as fastidious as Ernest Maltravers, and of a man as influenced by all the thoughts and theories of the world as the shrewd banker of C——. Amidst things foul and hateful had sprung up this beautiful flower, as if to preserve the inherent heavenliness and grace of human nature, and proclaim the handiwork of God in scenes where human nature had been most debased by the abuses of social art; and where the light of God himself was most darkened and obscured. That such contrasts, though rarely and as by chance, are found, every one who has carefully examined the wastes and deserts of life must own. I have drawn Alice Darvil scrupulously from life; and I can declare that I have not exaggerated hue or lineament in the portrait. I do not suppose, with our good banker, that she owed anything, unless it might be a greater delicacy of form and feature, to whatever mixture of gentle blood was in her veins. But, somehow or other, in her original conformation there was the happy bias of the plants towards the Pure and the Bright. For, despite Helvetius, a common experience teaches us that though education and circumstances may mould the mass, Nature herself sometimes forms the individual, and throws into the clay, or its spirit, so much of beauty or deformity, that nothing can utterly subdue the original elements of character. From sweets one draws poison—from poison another extracts but sweets. But I, often deeply pondering over the psychological history of Alice Darvil, think that one principal cause why she escaped the early contaminations around her, was in the slow and protracted development of her intellectual faculties. Whether or not the brutal violence of her father had in childhood acted through the nerves upon the brain, certain it is that until she knew Maltravers—until she loved—till she was cherished—her mind had seemed torpid and locked up. True, Darvil had taught her nothing, nor permitted her to be taught anything; but that mere ignorance would have been no preservation to a quick, observant mind. It was the bluntness of the senses themselves that operated like an armour between her mind and the vile things around her. It was the rough, dull covering of the chrysalis, framed to bear rude contact and biting weather, that the butterfly might break forth, winged and glorious, in due season. Had Alice been a quick child, she would have probably grown up a depraved and dissolute woman; but she comprehended, she understood little or nothing, till she found an inspirer in that affection which inspires both beast and man; which makes the dog (in his natural state one of the meanest of the savage race) a companion, a guardian, a protector, and raises Instinct half-way to the height of Reason.

The banker had a strong regard for Alice; and when he reached home, he heard with great pain that she was in a high state of fever. She remained beneath his roof that night, and the elderly gentlewoman, his relation and *gouvernante*, attended her. The banker slept but little; and the next morning his countenance was unusually pale.

Towards daybreak Alice had fallen into a sound and refreshing sleep; and when, on waking, she found, by a note from her host, that her father had left her house, and she might return in safety and without fear, a violent flood of tears, followed by long and grateful prayer, contributed to the restoration of her mind and nerves. Imperfect as this young woman's notions of abstract right and wrong still were, she was yet sensible to the claims of a father (no matter how criminal) upon his child: for feelings with her were so good and true, that they supplied in a great measure the place of principles. She knew that she could not have lived under the same roof with her dreadful parent; but she still felt an uneasy remorse at thinking he had been driven from that roof in destitution and want. She hastened to dress herself, and seek an audience with her protector; and the latter found, with admiration and pleasure, that he had anticipated her own instantaneous and involuntary design in the settlement made upon Darvil. He then communicated to Alice the compact he had already formed with her father, and she wept and kissed his hand when she heard, and secretly resolved that she would work hard to be enabled to increase the sum allowed. Oh, if her labours could serve to retrieve a parent from the necessity of darker resources for support! Alas! when crime has become a custom, it is like gaming or drinking—the excitement is wanting; and had Luke Darvil been suddenly made inheritor of the wealth of a Rothschild, he would either still have been a villain in one way or the other; or *ennui* would have awakened conscience, and he would have died of the change of habit.

Our banker always seemed more struck by Alice's moral feelings than even by her physical beauty. Her love for her child, for instance, impressed him powerfully, and he always gazed upon her with softer eyes when he saw her caressing or nursing the little fatherless creature, whose health was now delicate and precarious. It is difficult to say whether he was absolutely in love with Alice; the phrase is too strong, perhaps, to be applied to a man past fifty, who had gone through emotions and trials enough to wear away freshness from his heart. His feelings altogether for Alice, the designs he entertained towards her, were of a very complicated nature; and it will be long, perhaps, before the reader can thoroughly comprehend them. He conducted Alice home that day; but he said little by the way, perhaps because his female relation, for appearance' sake, accompanied them also. He, however, briefly cautioned Alice on no account to communicate to any one that it was her father who had been her visitor; and she still shuddered too much at the reminiscence to appear likely to converse on it. The banker also judged it advisable to be so far confidential with Alice's servant as to take her aside, and tell her that the inauspicious stranger of the previous evening had been a very distant relation of Mrs. Butler, who, from a habit of drunkenness, had fallen into evil and disorderly courses. The banker added, with a sanctified air, that he trusted, by a little serious conversation, he had led the poor man to better notions, and that he had gone home with an altered mind to his family. "But, my good Hannah," he concluded, "you know you are a superior person, and above the vulgar sin of indiscriminate gossip; therefore, mention what has occurred to no one; it can do no good to Mrs. Butler—it may hurt the man himself, who is well-to-do—better off than he seems, and who, I hope, with grace, may be a sincere penitent; and it will also—but that is nothing—very seriously displease me. By-the-by, Hannah, I shall be able to get your grandson into the Free School."

The banker was shrewd enough to perceive that he had carried his point; and he was walking home, satisfied, on the whole, with the way matters had been arranged, when he was met by a brother magistrate.

"Ha!" said the latter, "and how are you, my good sir? Do you know that we have had the Bow Street officers here, in search of a notorious villain who has broken from prison? He is one of the most determined and dexterous burglars in all England, and the runners have hunted him into our town. His very robberies have tracked him by the way. He robbed a gentleman the day before yesterday of his watch, and left him for dead on the road—this was not thirty miles hence."

"Bless me!" said the banker, with emotion; "and what is the wretch's name?"

"Why, he has as many *aliases* as a Spanish grandee; but I believe the last name he has assumed is Peter Watts."

"Oh!" said our friend, relieved—"well, have the runners found him?"

"No, but they are on his scent. A fellow answering to his description was seen by the man at the toll-bar, at daybreak this morning, on the way to F——: the officers are after him."

"I hope he may meet with his deserts—and crime is never unpunished, even in this world. My best compliments to your lady:—and how is little Jack?—Well! glad to hear it—fine boy, little Jack—good day."

"Good day, my dear sir. Worthy man, that!"

CHAPTER IX.

> "But who is this? thought he, a demon vile,
> With wicked meaning and a vulgar style;
> Hammond they call him—they can give the name
> Of man to devils——Why am I so tame?
> Why crush I not the viper? Fear replied,
> Watch him awhile, and let his strength be tried."—CRABBE.

THE next morning, after breakfast, the banker took his horse —a crop-eared, fast-trotting hackney—and merely leaving word that he was going upon business into the country and should not return to dinner, turned his back on the spires of C——.

He rode slowly, for the day was hot. The face of the country which was fair and smiling, might have tempted others to linger by the way: but our hard and practical man of the world was more influenced by the weather than the loveliness of the scenery. He did not look upon Nature with the eye of imagination; perhaps a railroad, had it then and there existed, would have pleased him better than the hanging woods, the shadowy valleys, and the changeful river that from time to time beautified the landscape on either side of the road. But, after all, there is a vast deal of hypocrisy in the affected admiration for Nature;—and I don't think one person in a hundred cares for what lies by the side of a road, so long as the road itself is good, hills levelled, and turnpikes cheap.

It was midnoon, and many miles had been passed, when the banker turned down a green lane and quickened his pace. At the end of about three-quarters of an hour he arrived at a little solitary inn, called "The Angler"—put up his horse, ordered his dinner at six o'clock—begged to borrow a basket to hold his fish—and it was then apparent that a longish cane he had carried with him was capable of being extended into a fishing rod. He fitted in the various joints with care, as if to be sure no accident had happened to the implement by the journey—pried anxiously into the contents of a black case of lines and flies—slung the basket behind his back, and while his horse was putting down his nose and whisking about his tail, in the course of those nameless coquetries that horses carry on with ostlers—our worthy brother of the rod strode rapidly through some green fields, gained the river side, and began fishing with much semblance of earnest interest in the sport. He had caught one trout, seemingly by accident—for the astonished fish was hooked up on the outside of its jaw—probably while in the act, not of biting, but of gazing at the bait—when he grew discontented with the spot he had selected; and, after looking round as if to convince himself that he was not liable to be disturbed or observed (a thought hateful to the fishing fraternity), he stole quickly along the margin, and finally, quitting the river side altogether, struck into a path that, after a sharp walk of nearly an hour, brought him to the door of a cottage. He knocked twice, and then entered of his own accord—nor was it till the summer sun was near its decline that the banker regained his inn. His simple dinner, which they had delayed in wonder at the protracted absence of the angler, and in expectation of the fishes he was to bring back to be fried, was soon despatched; his horse was ordered to the door, and the red clouds in the west already betokened the lapse of another day, as he spurred from the spot on the fast-trotting hackney, fourteen miles an hour.

"That ere gemman has a nice bit of blood," said the ostler, scratching his ear.

"Oiy—who be he?" said a hanger-on of the stables.

"I dooant know. He has been here twice afoar, and he never cautches anything to sinnify—he be mighty fond of fishing, sure*ly*."

Meanwhile, away sped the banker—milestone on milestone glided by—and still, scarce turning a hair, trotted gallantly out the good hackney. But the evening grew darker, and it began to rain; a drizzling, persevering rain, that wets a man through ere he is aware of it. After his fiftieth year, a gentleman who has a tender regard for himself does not like to get wet; and the rain inspired the banker, who was subject to rheumatism, with the resolution to make a short cut along the fields. There were one or two low hedges by this short way, but the banker had been there in the spring, and knew every inch of the ground. The hackney leaped easily—and the rider had a tolerably practised seat—and two miles saved might just prevent the menaced rheumatism: accordingly, our friend opened a white gate, and scoured along the fields without any misgivings as to the prudence of his choice. He arrived at his first leap—there was the hedge, its summit just discernible in the dim light. On the other side, to the right, was a haystack, and close by this haystack seemed the most eligible place for clearing the obstacle. Now, since the banker had visited this place, a deep ditch, that served as a drain, had been dug at the opposite base of the hedge, of which neither horse nor man was aware, so that the leap was far more perilous than was anticipated. Unconscious of this additional obstacle, the rider set off in a canter. The banker was high in air, his loins bent back, his rein slackened, his right hand raised knowingly—when the horse took fright at an object crouched by the haystack—swerved, plunged midway into the ditch, and pitched its rider two or three yards over its head. The banker recovered himself sooner than might have been expected; and, finding himself, though bruised and shaken, still whole and sound, hastened to his horse. But the poor animal had not fared so well as its master, and its off-shoulder was either put out or dreadfully sprained. It had scrambled its way out of the ditch, and there it stood disconsolate by the hedge, as lame as one of the trees that, at irregular intervals, broke the symmetry of the barrier. On ascertaining the extent of his misfortune, the banker became seriously uneasy; the rain increased—he was several miles yet from home—he was in the midst of houseless fields, with another leap before him—the leap he had just passed behind—and no other egress that he knew of into the main road. While these thoughts passed through his brain, he became suddenly aware that he was not alone. The dark object that had frightened his horse rose slowly from the snug corner it had occupied by the haystack, and a gruff voice, that made the banker thrill to the marrow of his bones, cried, "Holloa! who the devil are you?"

Lame as his horse was, the banker instantly put his foot into the stirrup; but before he could mount, a heavy gripe was laid on his shoulder—and, turning round with as much fierceness as he could assume, he saw—what the tone of the voice had already led him to forebode—the ill-omened and cut-throat features of Luke Darvil.

"Ha! ha! my old annuitant, my clever feelosofer—jolly old boy—how are you?—give us a fist. Who would have thought to meet you on a rainy night, by a lone haystack, with a deep ditch on one side and no chimney-pot within sight? Why, old fellow, I, Luke

Darvil—I, the vagabond—I, whom you would have sent to the treadmill for being poor, and calling on my own daughter—I am as rich as you are here—and as great, and as strong, and as powerful!"

And while he spoke, Darvil, who was really an undersized man, seemed to swell and dilate, till he appeared half a head taller than the shrinking banker, who was five feet eleven inches without his shoes.

"E—hem!" said the rich man, clearing his throat, which seemed to him uncommonly husky; "I do not know whether I insulted your poverty, my dear Mr. Darvil—I hope not; but this is hardly a time for talking—pray let me mount, and——"

"Not a time for talking!" interrupted Darvil, angrily; "it's just the time to my mind; let me consider—ay, I told you, that whenever we met by the roadside it would be my turn to have the best of the argufying."

"I dare say—I dare say, my good fellow."

"Fellow not me!—I won't be fellowed now. I say I have the best of it here—man to man, I am your match."

"But why quarrel with me?" said the banker, coaxingly; "I never meant you harm, and I am sure you cannot mean me harm."

"No!—and why?" asked Darvil, coolly;—"why do you think I can mean you no harm?"

"Because your annuity depends on me."

"Shrewdly put—we'll argufy that point. My life is a bad one, not worth more than a year's purchase; now, suppose you have more than forty pounds about you—it may be better worth my while to draw my knife across your gullet than to wait for the quarter-day's ten pounds a-time. You see it's all a matter of calculation, my *dear* Mr. What's-your-name!"

"But," replied the banker, and his teeth began to chatter, "I have not forty pounds about me."

"How do I know that?—you say so. Well, in the town yonder your word goes for more than mine: I never gainsayed you when you put that to me, did I? But here, by the haystack, my word is better than yours; and if I say you must and shall have forty pounds about you, let's see whether you dare contradict me!"

"Look you, Darvil," said the banker, summoning up all his energy and intellect, for his moral power began now to back his physical cowardice, and he spoke calmly, and even bravely, though his heart throbbed aloud against his breast, and you might have knocked him down with a feather—"the London runners are even now hot after you."

"Ha!—you lie!"

"Upon my honour, I speak the truth. I heard the news last evening. They tracked you to C——; they tracked you out of the town; a word from me would have given you into their hands. I said nothing—you are safe—you may yet escape. I will even help you to fly the country, and live out your natural date of years, secure and in peace."

"You did not say that the other day in the snug drawing-room · you see I have the best of it now—own that."

"I do," said the banker.

Darvil chuckled, and rubbed his hands.

The man of wealth once more felt his importance, and went on. "This is one side of the question. On the other, suppose you rob and murder me, do you think my death will lessen the heat of the pursuit against you? The whole country will be in arms, and before forty-eight hours are over you will be hunted down like a dog."

Darvel was silent, as if in thought; and, after a pause, replied— "Well, you are a 'cute one after all. What have you got about you? you know you drove a hard bargain the other day—now it's my market—fustian has riz—kersey has fell."

"All I have about me shall be yours," said the banker, eagerly.

"Give it me, then."

"There!" said the banker, placing his purse and pocket-book into Darvil's hands.

"And the watch?"

"The watch?—well, there!"

"What's that?"

The banker's senses were sharpened by fear, but they were not so sharp as those of Darvil; he heard nothing but the rain pattering on the leaves, and the rush of water in the ditch at hand. Darvil stooped and listened—till, raising himself again, with a deep-drawn breath, he said, "I think there are rats in the haystack; they will be running over me in my sleep; but they are playful creturs, and I like 'em. And now, my *dear* sir, I am afraid I must put an end to you!"

"Good heavens! what do you mean? How?"

"Man, there is another world!" quoth the ruffian, mimicking the banker's solemn tone in their former interview. "So much the better for you! In that world they don't tell tales."

"I swear I never will betray you."

"You do?—swear it, then."

"By all my hopes of earth and heaven!"

"What a d——d coward you be!" said Darvil, laughing scornfully. "Go—you are safe. I am in good humour with myself again. I crow over you, for no man can make *me* tremble. And villain as you think me, while you fear me you cannot despise—you respect me. Go, I say—go."

The banker was about to obey, when suddenly, from the haystack, a broad, red light streamed upon the pair, and the next moment Darvil was seized from behind, and struggling in the gripe of a man nearly as powerful as himself. The light, which came from a dark-lanthorn placed on the ground, revealed the forms of a peasant in a smock-frock, and two stout-built, stalwart men, armed with pistols—besides the one engaged with Darvil.

The whole of this scene was brought as by the trick of the stage —as by a flash of lightning—as by the change of a showman's phantasmagoria—before the astonished eyes of the banker. He stood arrested and spell-bound, his hand on his bridle, his foot on his stirrup. A moment more, and Darvil had dashed his antagonist on the ground; he stood at a little distance, his face reddened by the glare of the lanthorn, and fronting his assailants—that fiercest of all beasts, a desperate man at bay! He had already succeeded in drawing forth his pistols, and he held one in each hand—his eyes flashing from beneath his bent brows, and turning quickly from foe to foe! At last those terrible eyes rested on the late reluctant companion of his solitude.

"So *you* then betrayed me," he said, very slowly, and directed his pistol to the head of the dismounted horseman.

"No, no!" cried one of the officers, for such were Darvil's assailants; "fire away in this direction, my hearty—we're paid for it. The gentleman knew nothing at all about it."

"Nothing, by G——!" cried the banker, startled out of his sanctity.

"Then I shall keep my shot," said Darvil; "and mind, the first who approaches me is a dead man."

It so happened that the robber and the officers were beyond the distance which allows sure mark for a pistol-shot, and each party felt the necessity of caution.

"Your time is up, my swell cove!" cried the head of the detachment; "you have had your swing, and a long one it seems to have been—you must now give in. Throw down your barkers, or we must make mutton of you, and rob the gallows."

Darvil did not reply, and the officers, accustomed to hold life cheap, moved on towards him—their pistols cocked and levelled.

Darvil fired—one of the men staggered and fell. With a kind of instinct, Darvil had singled out the one with whom he had before wrestled for life. The ruffian waited not for the others—he turned and fled along the fields.

"Zounds, he is off!" cried the other two, and they rushed after him in pursuit. A pause—a shot—another—an oath—a groan—and all was still.

"It's all up with him now!" said one of the runners, in the distance; "he dies game."

At these words, the peasant, who had before skulked behind the haystack, seized the lanthorn from the ground and ran to the spot. The banker involuntarily followed.

There lay Luke Darvil on the grass—still living, but a horrible and ghastly spectacle. One ball had pierced his breast, another had shot away his jaw. His eyes rolled fearfully, and he tore up the grass with his hands.

The officers looked coldly on. "He was a clever fellow!" said one. "And has given us much trouble," said the other; "let us see to Will."

"But he's not dead yet," said the banker, shuddering.

"Sir, he cannot live a minute."

Darvil raised himself bolt upright—shook his clenched fist at his conquerors, and a fearful gurgling howl, which the nature of his wound did not allow him to syllable into a curse, came from his breast—with that he fell flat on his back—a corpse.

"I am afraid, sir," said the elder officer, turning away, "you had a narrow escape—but how came you here?"

"Rather, how came *you* here?"

"Honest Hodge there with the lanthorn had marked the fellow skulk behind the haystack, when he himself was going out to snare rabbits. He had seen our advertisement of Watt's person, and knew that we were then at a public-house some miles off. He came to us—conducted us to the spot—we heard voices—showed up the glim—and saw our man. Hodge, you are a good subject, and love justice."

"Yees; but I shall have the rewourd," said Hodge, showing his teeth.

"Talk o' that by-and-by," said the officer. "Will, how are you, man?"

"Bad," groaned the poor runner, and a rush of blood from the lips followed the groan.

It was many days before the ex-member for C—— sufficiently recovered the tone of his mind to think further of Alice; when he did, it was with great satisfaction that he reflected that Darvil was no more, and that the deceased ruffian was only known to the neighbourhood by the name of Peter Watts.

BOOK V.

CHAPTER I.

> . . . "My genius spreads her wing,
> And flies where Britain courts the western spring.
>
> . . . .
> Pride in their port, defiance in their eye,
> I see the lords of human kind pass by,
> Intent on high designs."
> —GOLDSMITH.

I HAVE no respect for the Englishman who re-enters London, after long residence abroad, without a pulse that beats quick and a heart that heaves high. The public buildings are few, and, for the most part, mean; the monuments of antiquity not comparable to those which the pettiest town in Italy can boast of; the palaces are sad rubbish; the houses of our peers and princes are shabby and shapeless heaps of brick. But what of all this? the spirit of London is in her thoroughfares—her population! What wealth—what cleanliness—what order—what animation! How majestic, and yet how vivid, is the life that runs through her myriad veins! How, as the lamps blaze upon you at night, and street after street glides by your wheels, each so regular in its symmetry, so equal in its civilisation—how all speak of the CITY OF FREEMEN!

Yes, Maltravers felt his heart swell within him, as the posthorses whirled on his dingy carriage—over Westminster Bridge—along Whitehall—through Regent Street—towards one of the quiet and private house-like hotels that are scattered round the neighbourhood of Grosvenor Square.

Ernest's arrival had been expected. He had written from Paris to Cleveland to announce it; and Cleveland had, in reply, informed him that he had engaged apartments for him at Mivart's. The smiling waiters ushered him into a spacious and well-aired room—the arm-chair was already wheeled by the fire—a score or so of letters strewed the table, together with two of the evening papers. And how eloquently of busy England do those evening papers speak! A stranger might have felt that he wanted no friend to welcome him—the whole room smiled on him a welcome.

Maltravers ordered his dinner and opened his letters; they were of no importance; one from his steward, one from his banker, another about the county races, a fourth from a man he had never heard of, requesting the vote and powerful interest of Mr. Maltravers for the county of B——, should the rumour of a dissolution be verified; the unknown candidate referred Mr. Maltravers to his "well-known public character." From these epistles Ernest turned impatiently, and perceived a little three-cornered note which had hitherto escaped his attention. It was from Cleveland, intimating that he was in town; that his health still precluded his going out, but that he trusted to see his dear Ernest as soon as he arrived.

Maltravers was delighted at the prospect of passing his evening so agreeably; he soon despatched his dinner and his newspapers, and walked in the brilliant lamplight of a clear, frosty evening of early December in London, to his friend's house in Curzon Street, a small house, bachelor-like and unpretending: for Cleveland spent his moderate though easy fortune almost entirely at his country villa. The familiar face of the old valet greeted Ernest at the door, and he only paused to hear that his guardian was nearly recovered to his usual health, ere he was in the cheerful drawing-room, and—since Englishmen do not embrace—returning the cordial gripe of the kindly Cleveland.

"Well, my dear Ernest," said Cleveland, after they had gone through the preliminary round of questions and answers, "here you are at last. Heaven be praised; and how well you are looking—how much you are improved! It is an excellent period of the year for your *début* in London. I shall have time to make you intimate with people before the whirl of 'the season' commences."

"Why, I thought of going to Burleigh, my country-place. I have not seen it since I was a child."

"No, no! you have had solitude enough at Como, if I may trust to your letter; you must now mix with the great London world; and you will enjoy Burleigh the more in the summer."

"I fancy this great London world will give me very little

pleasure; it may be pleasant enough to young men just let loose from college, but your crowded ball-rooms and monotonous clubs will be wearisome to one who has grown fastidious before his time. *J'ai vécu beaucoup dans peu d'années.* I have drawn in youth too much upon the capital of existence to be highly delighted with the ostentatious parsimony with which our great men economise pleasure."

"Don't judge before you have gone through the trial," said Cleveland; "there is something in the opulent splendour, the thoroughly sustained magnificence, with which the leaders of English fashion conduct even the most insipid amusements, that is above contempt. Besides, you need not necessarily live with the butterflies. There are plenty of bees that will be very happy to make your acquaintance. Add to this, my dear Ernest, the pleasure of being made of —of being of importance in your own country. For you are young, well-born, and sufficiently handsome to be an object of interest to mothers and to daughters; while your name, and property, and interest will make you courted by men who want to borrow your money and obtain your influence in your county. No, Maltravers, stay in London—amuse yourself your first year, and decide on your occupation and career the next; but reconnoitre before you give battle."

Maltravers was not ill pleased to follow his friend's advice, since by so doing he obtained his friend's guidance and society. Moreover, he deemed it wise and rational to see, face to face, the eminent men in England, with whom, if he fulfilled his promise to De Montaigne, he was to run the race of honourable rivalry. Accordingly, he consented to Cleveland's propositions.

"And have you," said he, hesitating, as he loitered by the door after the stroke of twelve had warned him to take his leave— "have you never heard anything of my—my—the unfortunate Alice Darvil?"

"Who?—Oh, that poor young woman; I remember!—not a syllable."

Maltravers sighed deeply, and departed.

CHAPTER II.

"Je trouve que c'est une folie de vouloir étudier le monde en simple spectateur. . . . Dans l'école du monde, comme dans celle de l'amour, il faut commencer par pratiquer ce qu'on veut apprendre." *—ROUSSEAU.

ERNEST MALTRAVERS was now fairly launched upon the wide ocean of London. Amongst his other property was a house in Seamore Place—that quiet, yet central street, which enjoys the air without the dust of the Park. It had been hitherto let, and the tenant now quitting very opportunely, Maltravers was delighted to secure so pleasant a residence; for he was still romantic enough to desire to look out upon trees and verdure rather than brick houses. He indulged only in two other luxuries. His love of music tempted him to an opera-box, and he had that English feeling which prides itself in the possession of beautiful horses—a feeling that enticed him into an extravagance on this head that baffled the competition and excited the envy of much richer men. But four thousand a-year goes a great way with a single man who does not gamble, and is too philosophical to make superfluities wants.

The world doubled his income, magnified his old country-seat into a superb chateau, and discovered that his elder brother, who was only three or four years older than himself, had no children. The world was very courteous to Ernest Maltravers.

It was, as Cleveland said, just at that time of year when people are at leisure to make new acquaintances. A few only of the most difficult houses in town were open; and their doors were cheerfully expanded to the accomplished ward of the popular Cleveland. Authors, and statesmen, and orators, and philosophers—to all he was presented—all seemed pleased with him, and Ernest became the fashion before he was conscious of the distinction. But he had rightly foreboded. He had commenced life too soon; he was disappointed; he found some persons he could admire, some whom he could like, but none with whom he could grow intimate, or for whom he could feel an interest. Neither his heart nor his imagination was touched; all appeared to him like artificial machines; he

---

* I find that it is a folly to wish to study the world like a simple spectator. . . . In the school of the world, as in that of love, it is necessary to begin by practising what we wish to learn.

was discontented with things like life, but in which something or other was wanting. He more than ever recalled the brilliant graces of Valerie de Ventadour, which had thrown a charm over the most frivolous circles; he even missed the perverse and fantastic vanity of Castruccio. The mediocre poet seemed to him at least less mediocre than the worldlings about him. Nay, even the selfish good spirits and dry shrewdness of Lumley Ferrers would have been an acceptable change to the dull polish and unrevealed egotism of jealous wits and party politicians. "If these are the flowers of the parterre, what must be the weeds?" said Maltravers to himself, returning from a party at which he had met half-a-score of the most orthodox lions.

He began to feel the aching pain of satiety.

But the winter glided away—the season commenced, and Maltravers was whirled on with the rest into the bubbling vortex.

CHAPTER III.

*"And crowds commencing mere vexation,
Retirement sent its invitation."*—SHENSTONE.

THE tench, no doubt, considers the pond in which he lives as the Great World. There is no place, however stagnant, which is not the great world to the creatures that move about in it. People who have lived all their lives in a village still talk of the world as if they had ever seen it! An old woman in a hovel does not put her nose out of her door on a Sunday without thinking that she is going amongst the pomps and vanities of the great world. *Ergo*, the great world is to all of us the little circle in which we live. But as fine people set the fashion, so the circle of fine people is called the Great World, *par excellence*. Now, this great world is not a bad thing when we thoroughly understand it; and the London great world is at least as good as any other. But then we scarcely *do* understand that or anything else in *beaux jour* —which, if they are sometimes the most exquisite, are also often the most melancholy and the most wasted portion of our life. Maltravers had not yet found out either *the set* that pleased him or the species of amusement that really amused. Therefore he drifted on and about the vast whirlpool, making plenty of friends—going to balls and dinners—and bored with both, as men are who have no object in society. Now the way society is enjoyed is to have a pursuit, a *métier* of some kind, and then to go into the world, either to make the individual object a social pleasure, or to obtain a reprieve from some toilsome avocation. Thus, if you are a politician, politics at once make an object in your closet, and a social tie between others and yourself when you are in the world. The same may be said of literature, though in a less degree; and though, as fewer persons care about literature than politics, your companions must be more select. If you are very young, you are fond of dancing; if you are very profligate, perhaps you are fond of flirtations with your friend's wife. These last are objects in their way: but they don't last long, and, even with the most frivolous, are not occupations that satisfy the whole mind and heart, in which there is generally an aspiration after something useful. It is not vanity alone that makes a man of the *mode* invent a new bit, or give his name to a new kind of carriage; it is the influence of that mystic yearning after utility, which is one of the master-ties between the individual and the species.

Maltravers was not happy—that is a lot common enough; but he was not amused—and that is a sentence more insupportable. He lost a great part of his sympathy with Cleveland, for, when a man is not amused, he feels an involuntary contempt for those who are. He fancies they are pleased with trifles which his superior wisdom is compelled to disdain. Cleveland was of that age when we generally grow social—for, by being rubbed long and often against the great loadstone of society, we obtain in a thousand little minute points an attraction in common with our fellows. Their petty sorrows and small joys—their objects of interest or employment, at some time or other, have been ours. We gather up a vast collection of moral and mental farthings of exchange; and we scarcely find any intellect too poor but what we can deal with it in some way. But in youth we are egotists and sentimentalists, and Maltravers belonged to the fraternity who employ

"The heart in passion and the head in rhymes."

At length—just when London begins to grow most pleasant—when flirtations become tender, and water-parties numerous—when birds sing in the groves of Richmond, and whitebait refresh the statesmen by the shores of Greenwich—Maltravers abruptly fled from the gay metropolis, and arrived, one lovely evening in July, at his own ivy-grown porch at Burleigh.

What a soft, fresh, delicious evening it was! He had quitted his carriage at the lodge, and followed it across the small but picturesque park alone on foot. He had not seen the place since childhood—he had quite forgotten its aspect. He now wondered how he could have lived anywhere else. The trees did not stand in stately avenues, nor did the antlers of the deer wave above the sombre fern; it was not the domain of a grand seigneur, but of an old, long-descended English squire. Antiquity spoke in the moss-grown palings, in the shadowy groves, in the sharp gable-ends and heavy mullions of the house, as it now came in view, at the base of a hill covered with wood—and partially veiled by the shrubs of the neglected pleasure ground, separated from the park by the invisible ha-ha. There gleamed in the twilight the watery face of the oblong fish-pool, with its old-fashioned willows at each corner—there, grey and quaint, was the monastic dial—and there was the long terrace-walk, with discoloured and broken vases now filled with the orange or the aloe, which, in honour of his master's arrival, the gardener had extracted from the dilapidated green-house. The very evidence of neglect around, the very weeds and grass on the half-obliterated road, touched Maltravers with a sort of pitying and remorseful affection for his calm and sequestered residence. And it was not with his usual proud step and erect crest that he passed from the porch to the solitary library—through a line of his servants:—the two or three old retainers belonging to the place were utterly unfamiliar to him, and they had no smile for their stranger lord.

CHAPTER IV.

"*Lucian.*—He that is born to be a man, neither should nor can be anything nobler, greater, and better than a man.

Peregrine.—But, good Lucian, for the very reason that he may not become less than a man, he should be always striving to be more."—WIELAND's *Peregrinus Proteus.*

IT was two years from the date of the last chapter before Maltravers again appeared in general society. These two years had sufficed to produce a revolution in his fate. Ernest Maltravers had lost the happy rights of the private individual; he had given himself to the Public; he had surrendered his name to men's tongues, and was a thing that all had a right to praise, to blame, to scrutinise, to spy. Ernest Maltravers had become an author.

Let no man tempt Gods and Columns without weighing well the consequences of his experiment. He who publishes a book, attended with a moderate success, passes a mighty barrier. He will often look back with a sigh of regret at the land he has left for ever. The beautiful and decent obscurity of hearth and home is gone. He can no longer feel the just indignation of manly pride when he finds himself ridiculed or reviled. He has parted with the shadow of his life. His motives may be misrepresented, his character belied; his manners, his person, his dress, the "very trick of his walk," are all fair food for the cavil and the caricature. He can never go back, he cannot even pause; he has chosen his path, and all the natural feelings that make the nerve and muscle of the active being, urge him to proceed. To stop short is to fail. He has told the world that he will make a name; and he must be set down as a pretender, or toil on till the boast be fulfilled. Yet Maltravers thought nothing of all this when, intoxicated with his own dreams and aspirations, he desired to make the world his confidant; when from the living Nature, and the lore of books, and the mingled result of inward study and external observation, he sought to draw forth something that might interweave his name with the pleasurable associations of his kind. His easy fortune and lonely state gave him up to his own thoughts and contemplations; they suffused his mind, till it ran over upon the page which makes the channel that connects the solitary Fountain with the vast Ocean of Human Knowledge. The temperament of Maltravers was, as we have seen, neither irritable nor fearful. He formed himself, as a sculptor forms, with a model before his eyes, and an ideal in his heart. He endeavoured, with labour and patience, to approach nearer and nearer with every effort to the standard of such excellence as he thought might ultimately be attained by a reasonable ambition; and when, at last, his judgment was satisfied, he surrendered the product with a tranquil confidence to a more impartial tribunal.

His first work was successful; perhaps from this reason—that it bore the stamp of the Honest and the Real. He did not sit down to report of what he had never seen, to dilate on what he had never felt. A quiet and thoughtful observer of life, his descriptions were the more vivid, because his own first impressions were not yet worn away. His experience had sunk deep; not on the arid surface of matured age, but in the fresh soil of youthful emotions. Another reason, perhaps, that obtained success for his essay was, that he had more varied and more elaborate knowledge than young authors think it necessary to possess. He did not, like Cesarini, attempt to make a show of words upon a slender capital of ideas. Whether his style was eloquent or homely, it was still in him a faithful transcript of considered and digested thought. A third reason—and I dwell on these points not more to elucidate the career of Maltravers than as hints which may be useful to others—a third reason why Maltravers obtained a prompt and favourable reception from the public was, that he had not hackneyed his peculiarities of diction and thought in that worst of all schools for the literary novice—the columns of a magazine. Periodicals form an excellent mode of communication between the public and an author *already* established, who has lost the charm of novelty, but gained the weight of acknowledged reputation ; and who, either upon politics or criticism, seeks for frequent and continuous occasions to enforce his peculiar theses and doctrines. But, upon the young writer, this mode of communication, if too long continued, operates most injuriously both as to his future prospects and his own present taste and style. With respect to the first, it familiarises the public to his mannerism (and all writers worth reading have mannerism) in a form to which the said public are not inclined to attach much weight. He forestalls in a few months what ought to be the effect of years : namely, the wearying a world soon nauseated with the *toujours perdrix*. With respect to the last, it induces a man to write for momentary effects ; to study a false smartness of style and reasoning ; to bound his ambition of durability to the last day of the month ; to expect immediate returns for labour ; to recoil at the " hope deferred " of serious works on which judgment is slowly formed. The man of talent who begins young at periodicals, and goes on long, has generally something crude and stunted about both his compositions and his celebrity. He grows the oracle of small coteries ; and we can rarely get out of the impression that he is cockneyfied and conventional. Periodicals sadly mortgaged the claims that Hazlitt, and many others of his contemporaries, had upon a vast reversionary estate of Fame. But I here speak too politically ; to some, the *res angustæ domi* leave no option. And, as Aristotle and the Greek proverb have it, we cannot carve out all things with the knife of the Delphic cutler.

The second work that Maltravers put forth, at an interval of eighteen months from the first, was one of a graver and higher nature, it served to confirm his reputation ; and that is success enough for a second work, which is usually an author's "*pons asinorum.*" He who, after a triumphant first book, does not dissatisfy the public with a second, has a fair chance of gaining a fixed station in literature. But now commenced the pains and perils of the after-birth. By a maiden effort an author rarely makes enemies. His fellow-writers are not yet prepared to consider him as a rival ; if he be tolerably rich, they unconsciously trust that he will not become a regular, or, as they term it, "a professional" author : he did something just to be talked of ; he may write no more, or his second book may fail. But when that second book comes out, and does not fail, they begin to look about them ; envy wakens, malice begins. And all the old school—gentlemen who have retired on their pensions of renown—regard him as an intruder : then the sneer, then the frown, the caustic irony, the biting review, the depreciating praise. The novice begins to think that he is further from the goal than before he set out upon the race.

Maltravers had, upon the whole, a tolerably happy temperament ; but he was a very proud man, and he had the nice soul of a courageous, honourable, punctilious gentleman. He thought it singular that society should call upon him, as a gentleman, to shoot his best friend, if that friend affronted him with a rude word ; and yet that, as an author, every fool and liar might, with perfect impunity, cover reams of paper with the most virulent personal abuse of him.

It was one evening in the early summer that, revolving anxious and doubtful thoughts, Ernest sauntered gloomily along his terrace,

"And watched with wistful eyes the setting sun,"

when he perceived a dusty travelling carriage whirled along the road by the ha-ha, and a hand waved in recognition from the open window. His guests had been so rare, and his friends were so few, that Maltravers could not conjecture who was his intended visitant. His brother he knew was in London. Cleveland, from whom he had that day heard, was at his villa. Ferrers was enjoying himself at Vienna. Who could it be ? We may say of solitude what we please, but after two years of solitude a visitor is a pleasurable excitement. Maltravers retraced his steps, entered his house, and was just in time to find himself almost in the arms of De

CHAPTER V.

"Quid tam dextro pede concipis utile,
Conatus non pœnitet, votique peracti?"*—Juv.

"YES," said De Montaigne, "in my way *I* also am fulfilling my destiny. I am a member of the *Chambre de Députés*, and on a visit to England upon some commercial affairs. I found myself in your neighbourhood, and, of course, could not resist the temptation: so you must receive me as your guest."

"I congratulate you cordially on your senatorial honours. I have already heard of your rising name."

"I return the congratulations with equal warmth. You are bringing my prophecies to pass. I have read your works with increased pride at our friendship."

Maltravers sighed slightly, and half turned away.

"The desire of distinction," said he, after a pause, "grows upon us till excitement becomes disease. The child who is born with the Mariner's instinct laughs with glee when his paper bark skims the wave of a pool. By-and-by, nothing will content him but the ship and the ocean.—Like the child is the author."

"I am pleased with your simile," said De Montaigne, smiling. "Do not spoil it, but go on with your argument."

Maltravers continued—"Scarcely do we win the applause of a moment ere we summon the past and conjecture the future. Our contemporaries no longer suffice for competitors, our age for the Court to pronounce on our claims: we call up the Dead as our only true rivals—we appeal to Posterity as our sole just tribunal. Is this vain in us? Possibly. Yet such vanity humbles. 'Tis then only we learn all the difference between Reputation and Fame—between To-Day and Immortality!"

"Do you think," replied De Montaigne, "that the dead did not feel the same when they first trod the path that leads to the life beyond life? Continue to cultivate the mind, to sharpen by exercise the genius, to attempt to delight or to instruct your race; and even supposing you fall short of every model you set before you—supposing your name moulder with your dust, still you will have passed life more nobly than the unlaborious herd. Grant that you win

---

* What under such happy auspices do you conceive, that you may not repent of your endeavour and accomplished wish?

not that glorious accident, 'a name below,' how can you tell but what you may have fitted yourself for high destiny and employ in the world not of men, but of spirits? The powers of the mind are things that cannot be less immortal than the mere sense of identity; their acquisitions accompany us through the Eternal Progress; and we may obtain a lower or higher grade hereafter, in proportion as we are more or less fitted by the exercise of our intellect to comprehend and execute the solemn agencies of God. The wise man is nearer to the angels than the fool is. This may be an apocryphal dogma, but it is not an impossible theory."

"But we may waste the sound enjoyments of actual life in chasing the hope you justly allow to be 'apocryphal;' and our knowledge may go for nothing in the eyes of the Omniscient."

"Very well," said De Montaigne, smiling; "but answer me honestly. By the pursuits of intellectual ambition, *do* you waste the sound enjoyments of life? If so, you do not pursue the system rightly. Those pursuits ought only to quicken your sense for such pleasures as are the true relaxations of life. And this, with you peculiarly, since you are fortunate enough not to depend for subsistence upon literature :—did you do so, I might rather advise you to be a trunk-maker than an author. A man ought not to attempt any of the highest walks of Mind and Art as the mere provision of daily bread; not literature alone, but everything else of the same degree. He ought not to be a statesman, or an orator, or a philosopher, as a thing of pence and shillings : and usually all men, save the poor poet, feel this truth insensibly."

"This may be fine preaching," said Maltravers; "but you may be quite sure that the pursuit of literature is a pursuit apart from the ordinary objects of life, and you cannot command the enjoyments of both."

"I think otherwise," said De Montaigne; "but it is not in a country-house eighty miles from the capital, without wife, guests, or friends, that the experiment can be fairly made. Come, Maltravers, I see before you a brave career, and I cannot permit you to halt at the onset."

"You do not see all the calumnies that are already put forth against me, to say nothing of all the assurances (and many by clever men) that there is nothing in me!"

"Dennis was a clever man, and said the same thing of your Pope. Madame de Sévigné was a clever woman, but she thought Racine would never be very famous. Milton saw nothing in the first efforts of Dryden that made him consider Dryden better than a rhymester Aristophanes was a good judge of poetry, yet how ill he judged of Euripides! But all this is commonplace, and yet you bring arguments that a commonplace answers in evidence against yourself."

"But it is unpleasant not to answer attacks—not to retaliate on enemies."

"Then answer attacks, and retaliate on enemies."

"But would that be wise?"

"If it give you pleasure—it would not please *me*."

"Come, De Montaigne, you are reasoning Socratically. I will ask you plainly and bluntly, would you advise an author to wage war on his literary assailants, or to despise them?"

"Both; let him attack but few, and those rarely. But it is his policy to show that he is one whom it is better not to provoke too far. The author always has the world on his side against the critics, if he choose his opportunity. And he must always recollect that he is 'A STATE' in himself, which must sometimes go to war in order to procure peace. The time for war or for peace must be left to the State's own diplomacy and wisdom."

"You would make us political machines."

"I would make every man's conduct more or less mechanical; for system is the triumph of mind over matter; the just equilibrium of all the powers and passions may seem like machinery. Be it so. Nature meant the world—the creation—man himself, for machines."

"And one must even be in a passion mechanically, according to your theories.

"A man is a poor creature who is not in a passion sometimes; but a very unjust, or a very foolish one, if he be in a passion with the wrong person, and in the wrong place and time. But enough of this, it is growing late."

"And when will Madame visit England?"

"Oh, not yet, I fear. But you will meet Cesarini in London this year or next. He is persuaded that you did not see justice done to his poems, and is coming here as soon as his indolence will let him, to proclaim your treachery in a biting preface to some toothless satire."

"Satire!"

"Yes; more than one of your poets made their way by a satire, and Cesarini is persuaded he shall do the same. Castruccio is not as far-sighted as his namesake, the Prince of Lucca. Good night, my dear Ernest."

CHAPTER VI.

> "When with much pains this boasted learning's got,
> 'Tis an affront to those who have it not."
> —CHURCHILL: *The Author.*

THERE was something in De Montaigne's conversation, which, without actual flattery, reconciled Maltravers to himself and his career. It served less, perhaps, to excite than to sober and brace his mind. De Montaigne could have made no man rash, but he could have made many men energetic and persevering. The two friends had some points in common; but Maltravers had far more prodigality of nature and passion about him—had more of flesh and blood, with the faults and excellencies of flesh and blood. De Montaigne held so much to his favourite doctrine of moral equilibrium that he had really reduced himself, in much, to a species of clockwork. As impulses are formed from habits, so the regularity of De Montaigne's habits made his impulses virtuous and just, and he yielded to them as often as a hasty character might have done; but then those impulses never urged to anything speculative or daring. De Montaigne could not go beyond a certain defined circle of action. He had no sympathy for any reasonings based purely on the hypothesis of the imagination; he could not endure Plato, and he was dumb to the eloquent whispers of whatever was refining in poetry or mystical in wisdom.

Maltravers, on the contrary, not disdaining Reason, ever sought to assist her by the Imaginative faculty, and held all philosophy incomplete and unsatisfactory that bounded its inquiries to the limits of the Known and Certain. He loved the inductive process; but he carried it out to Conjecture as well as Fact. He maintained that, by a similar hardihood, all the triumphs of science, as well as art, had been accomplished—that Newton, that Copernicus, would have done nothing if they had not imagined as well as reasoned, guessed as well as ascertained. Nay, it was an aphorism with him, that the very soul of philosophy is conjecture. He had the most implicit confidence in the operations of the mind and the heart properly formed, and deemed that the very excesses of emotion and thought, in men well trained by experience and study, are conducive to useful and great ends. But the more advanced years, and the singularly practical character of De Montaigne's views, gave him a

superiority in argument over Maltravers, which the last submitted
to unwillingly. While, on the other hand, De Montaigne secretly
felt that his young friend reasoned from a broader base, and took
in a much wider circumference ; and that he was, at once, more
liable to failure and error, and more capable of new discovery and
of intellectual achievement. But their ways in life being different,
they did not clash; and De Montaigne, who was sincerely
interested in Ernest's fate, was contented to harden his friend's
mind against the obstacles in his way, and leave the rest to
experiment and to Providence. They went up to London together :
and De Montaigne returned to Paris. Maltravers appeared once
more in the haunts of the gay and great. He felt that his new
character had greatly altered his position. He was no longer
courted and caressed for the same vulgar and adventitious circumstances of fortune, birth, and connections, as before—yet for
circumstances that to him seemed equally unflattering. He was
not sought for his merit, his intellect, his talents ; but for his
momentary celebrity. He was an author in fashion, and run after
as anything else in fashion might have been. He was invited, less
to be talked to than to be stared at. He was far too proud in his
temper, and too pure in his ambition, to feel his vanity elated by
sharing the enthusiasm of the circles with a German prince or an
industrious flea. Accordingly he soon repelled the advances made
to him, was reserved and supercilious to fine ladies, refused to
be the fashion, and became very unpopular with the literary
exclusives. They even began to run down the works, because they
were dissatisfied with the author. But Maltravers had based his
experiments upon the vast masses of the general Public. He had
called the PEOPLE of his own and other countries to be his
audience and his judges ; and all the coteries in the world could
not have injured him. He was like the member for an immense
constituency, who may offend individuals, so long as he keep
his footing with the body at large. But while he withdrew himself
from the insipid and the idle, he took care not to become separated
from the world. He formed his own society according to his
tastes : took pleasure in the manly and exciting topics of the day ;
and sharpened his observation and widened his sphere as an
author, by mixing freely and boldly with all classes as a citizen.
But literature became to him as art to the artist—as his mistress
to the lover—an engrossing and passionate delight. He made it
his glorious and divine profession—he loved it *as* a profession—he

devoted to its pursuits and honours his youth, cares, dreams—his mind, and his heart, and his soul. He was a silent but intense enthusiast in the priesthood he had entered. From LITERATURE he imagined had come all that makes nations enlightened and men humane. And he loved Literature the more, because her distinctions were not those of the world—because she had neither ribands, nor stars, nor high places at her command. A name in the deep gratitude and hereditary delight of men—this was the title she bestowed. Hers was the Great Primitive Church of the world, without Popes or Muftis—sinecures, pluralities, and hierarchies. Her servants spoke to the earth as the prophets of old, anxious only to be heard and believed. Full of this fanaticism, Ernest Maltravers pursued his way in the great procession of the myrtle-bearers to the sacred shrine. He carried the thyrsus, and he believed in the god. By degrees his fanaticism worked in him the philosopy which De Montaigne would have derived from sober calculation; it made him indifferent to the thorns in the path, to the storms in the sky. He learned to despise the enmity he provoked, the calumnies that assailed him. Sometimes he was silent, but sometimes he retorted. Like a soldier who serves a cause, he believed that when the cause was injured in his person, the weapons confided to his hands might be wielded without fear and without reproach. Gradually he became feared as well as known. And while many abused him, none could contemn.

It would not suit the design of this work to follow Maltravers step by step in his course. I am only describing the principal events, not the minute details, of his intellectual life. Of the character of his works it will be enough to say, that whatever their faults, they were original—they were his own. He did not write according to copy, nor compile from commonplace books. He was an artist, it is true—for what is genius itself but art?—but he took laws, and harmony, and order, from the great code of Truth and Nature; a code that demands intense and unrelaxing study—though its first principles are few and simple: that study Maltravers did not shrink from. It was a deep love of truth that made him a subtle and searching analyst, even in what the dull world considers trifles; for he knew that nothing in literature is in itself trifling—that it is often but a hair's breadth that divides a truism from a discovery. He was the more original because he sought rather after the True than the New. No two minds are ever the same; and, therefore, any man who will give us fairly and frankly the results of his own impressions, uninfluenced by the servilities of imitation, will be original. But it was not from originality, which really made his predominant merit, that Maltravers derived his reputation, for his originality was not of that species which generally dazzles the vulgar—it was not extravagant nor *bizarre*—he affected no system and no school. Many authors of his day seemed more novel and *unique* to the superficial. Profound and durable invention proceeds by subtle and fine gradations—it has nothing to do with those jerks and starts, those convulsions and distortions, which belong not to the vigour and health, but to the epilepsy and disease of Literature.

CHAPTER VII.

"Being got out of town, the first thing I did was to give my mule her head."
—*Gil Blas.*

ALTHOUGH the character of Maltravers was gradually becoming more hard and severe—although as his reason grew more muscular, his imagination lost something of its early bloom, and he was already very different from the wild boy who had set the German youths in a blaze, and had changed into a Castle of Indolence the little cottage, tenanted with Poetry and Alice—he still preserved many of his old habits; he loved, at frequent intervals, to disappear from the great world—to get rid of books and friends, and luxury and wealth, and make solitary excursions, sometimes on foot, sometimes on horseback, through this fair garden of England.

It was one soft May-day that he found himself on such an expedition, slowly riding through one of the green lanes of ——shire. His cloak and his saddle-bags comprised all his baggage, and the world was before him "where to choose his place of rest." The lane wound at length into the main road, and just as he came upon it he fell in with a gay party of equestrians.

Foremost of this cavalcade rode a lady in a dark green habit, mounted on a thorough-bred English horse, which she managed with so easy a grace that Maltravers halted in involuntary admiration. He himself was a consummate horseman, and he had the quick eye of sympathy for those who shared the accomplishment.

He thought, as he gazed, that he had never seen but one woman whose air and mien on horseback were so full of that nameless elegance which skill and courage in any art naturally bestow—that woman was Valerie de Ventadour. Presently, to his great surprise, the lady advanced from her companions, neared Maltravers, and said, in a voice which he did not at first distinctly recognise—" Is it possible!—do I see Mr. Maltravers?"

She paused a moment, and then threw aside her veil, and Ernest beheld—Valerie de Ventadour! By this time a tall, thin gentleman had joined the Frenchwoman.

"Has *madame* met with an acquaintance?" said he; "and, if so, will she permit me to partake her pleasure?"

The interruption seemed a relief to Valerie; she smiled and coloured.

"Let me introduce you to Mr. Maltravers. Mr. Maltravers, this is my host, Lord Doningdale."

The two gentlemen bowed, the rest of the cavalcade surrounded the trio, and Lord Doningdale, with a stately yet frank courtesy, invited Maltravers to return with the party to his house, which was about four miles distant. As may be supposed, Ernest readily accepted the invitation. The cavalcade proceeded, and Maltravers hastened to seek an explanation from Valerie. It was soon given. Madame de Ventadour had a younger sister, who had lately married a son of Lord Doningdale. The marriage had been solemnised in Paris, and Monsieur and Madame de Ventadour had been in England a week on a visit to the English peer.

The *rencontre* was so sudden and unexpected that neither recovered sufficient self-possession for fluent conversation. The explanation given, Valerie sank into a thoughtful silence, and Maltravers rode by her side equally taciturn, pondering on the strange chance which, after the lapse of years, had thrown them again together.

Lord Doningdale, who at first lingered with his other visitors, now joined them, and Maltravers was struck with his highbred manner, and a singular and somewhat elaborate polish in his emphasis and expression. They soon entered a noble park, which attested far more care and attention than are usually bestowed upon these demesnes, so peculiarly English. Young plantations everywhere contrasted the venerable groves—new cottages of picturesque design adorned the outskirts—and obelisks and columns, copied from the antique, and evidently of recent workmanship, gleamed upon them as they neared the house—a large pile, in which the fashion of Queen Anne's day had been altered into the French roofs and windows of the architecture of the Tuileries. "You reside much in the country, I am sure, my lord," said Maltravers.

"Yes," replied Lord Doningdale, with a pensive air, "this place is greatly endeared to me. Here his Majesty Louis XVIII., when in England, honoured me with an annual visit. In compliment to him, I sought to model my poor mansion into an humble likeness of his own palace, so that he might as little as possible miss the rights he had lost. His own rooms were furnished exactly like those he had occupied at the Tuileries. Yes, the place is endeared to me—I think of the old times with pride. It is something to have sheltered a Bourbon in his misfortunes."

"It cost *milord* a vast sum to make these alterations," said Madame de Ventadour, glancing archly at Maltravers.

"Ah, yes," said the old lord; and his face, lately elated, became overcast—"nearly three hundred thousand pounds; but what then? —'*Les souvenirs, madame, sont sans prix!*'"

"Have you visited Paris since the restoration, Lord Doningdale?" asked Maltravers.

His lordship looked at him sharply, and then turned his eye to Madame de Ventadour.

"Nay," said Valerie, laughing, "I did not dictate the question."

"Yes," said Lord Doningdale, "I have been at Paris."

"His Majesty must have been delighted to return your lordship's hospitality."

Lord Doningdale looked a little embarrassed, and made no reply.

"You have galled our host," said Valerie, smiling. "Louis XVIII. and his friends lived here as long as they pleased, and as sumptuously as they could; their visits half ruined the owner, who is the model of a *gentilhomme* and *preux chevalier*. He went to Paris to witness their triumph; he expected, I fancy, the order of the St. Esprit. Lord Doningdale has royal blood in his veins. His Majesty asked him once to dinner, and, when he took leave, said to him, 'We are happy, Lord Doningdale, to have *thus* requited our obligations to your lordship.' Lord Doningdale went back in dudgeon, yet he still boasts of his *souvenirs*, poor man."

"Princes are not grateful, neither are republics," said Maltravers.

"Ah! who is grateful," rejoined Valerie, "except a dog and a woman?"

Maltravers found himself ushered into a vast dressing-room, and was informed by a French valet that, in the country, Lord Doningdale dined at six—the first bell would ring in a few minutes. While the valet was speaking, Lord Doningdale himself entered the room. His lordship had learned, in the meanwhile, that Maltravers was of the great and ancient commoners' house, whose honours were centred in his brother; and yet more, that he was the Mr. Maltravers whose writings every one talked of, whether for praise or abuse. Lord Doningdale had the two characteristics of a highbred gentleman of the old school—respect for birth and respect for talent; he was, therefore, more than ordinarily courteous to Ernest, and pressed him to stay some days with so much cordiality, that Maltravers could not but assent. His travelling toilet was scanty, but Maltravers thought little of dress.

CHAPTER VIII.

> "It is the soul that sees. The outward eyes
> Present the object, but the mind descries;
> And thence delight, disgust, or cool indifference rise."
>
> —CRABBE.

WHEN Maltravers entered the enormous saloon, hung with damask, and decorated with the ponderous enrichments and furniture of the time of Louis XIV. (that most showy and barbarous of all tastes, which has nothing in it of the graceful, nothing of the picturesque, and which, now-a-days, people who should know better imitate with a ludicrous servility), he found sixteen persons assembled. His host stepped up from a circle which surrounded him, and formally presented his new visitor to the rest. He was struck with the likeness which the sister of Valerie bore to Valerie herself; but it was a sobered and chastened likeness—less handsome, less impressive. Mrs. George Herbert—such was the name she now owned—was a pretty, shrinking, timid girl, fond of her husband, and mightily awed by her father-in-law. Maltravers sat by her, and drew her into conversation. He could not help pitying the poor lady when he found she was to live altogether at Doningdale Park—remote from all the friends and habits of her childhood—alone, so far as the affections

were concerned, with a young husband, who was passionately fond
of field sports, and who, from the few words Ernest exchanged with
him, seemed to have only three ideas—his dogs, his horses, and his
wife. Alas! the last would soon be the least in importance. It is
a sad position—that of a lively young Frenchwoman entombed in
an English country-house! Marriages with foreigners are seldom
fortunate experiments! But Ernest's attention was soon diverted
from the sister by the entrance of Valerie herself, leaning on her
husband's arm. Hitherto he had not very minutely observed what
change time had effected in her—perhaps he was half afraid. He
now gazed at her with a curious interest. Valerie was still extremely
handsome, but her face had grown sharper, her form thinner and
more angular; there was something in her eye and lip, discontented, restless, almost querulous. Such is the too common
expression in the face of those born to love, and condemned to be
indifferent. The little sister was more to be envied of the two—
come what may, she loved her husband, such as he was, and her
heart might ache, but it was not with a void.

Monsieur de Ventadour soon shuffled up to Maltravers—his nose
longer than ever.

"Hein—hein—how d'ye do—how d'ye do?—charmed to see you
—saw madame before me—hein—hein—I suspect—I suspect ——"

"Mr. Maltravers, will you give Madame de Ventadour your
arm?" said Lord Doningdale, as he stalked in to the dining-room,
with a duchess on his own.

"And you have left Naples," said Maltravers; "left it for good?"

"We do not think of returning."

"It was a charming place—how I loved it!—how well I remember it!" Ernest spoke calmly—it was but a general remark.

Valerie sighed gently.

During dinner, the conversation between Maltravers and Madame
de Ventadour was vague and embarrassed. Ernest was no longer
in love with her—he had outgrown that youthful fancy. She had
exercised influence over him—the new influences that he had
created had chased away her image. Such is life. Long absences
extinguish all the false lights, though not the true ones. The
lamps are dead in the banquet-room of yesterday; but a thousand
years hence and the stars we look on to-night will burn as brightly.
Maltravers was no longer in love with Valerie. But Valerie—ah,
perhaps *hers* had been true love!

Maltravers was surprised when he came to examine the state of his own feelings—he was surprised to find that his pulse did not beat quicker at the touch of one whose very glance had once thrilled him to the soul—he was surprised, but rejoiced. He was no longer anxious to seek but to shun excitement, and he was a better and a higher being than he had been on the shores of Naples.

CHAPTER IX.

"Whence that low voice, a whisper from the heart,
That told of days long past!"   —WORDSWORTH.

ERNEST stayed several days at Lord Doningdale's, and every day he rode out with Valerie, but it was with a large party; and every evening he conversed with her, but the whole world might have overheard what they said. In fact, the sympathy that had once existed between the young dreamer and the proud, discontented woman, had in much passed away. Awakened to vast and grand objects, Maltravers was a dreamer no more. Inured to the life of trifles she had once loathed, Valerie had settled down into the usages and thoughts of the common world—she had no longer the superiority of earthly wisdom over Maltravers, and his romance was sobered in its eloquence, and her ear dulled to its tone. Still Ernest felt a deep interest in her, and still she seemed to feel a sensitive pride in his career.

One evening Maltravers had joined a circle in which Madame de Ventadour, with more than her usual animation, presided—and to which, in her pretty, womanly, and thoroughly French way, she was lightly laying down the law on a hundred subjects—Philosophy, Poetry, Sèvres china, and the Balance of Power in Europe. Ernest listened to her, delighted, but not enchanted. Yet Valerie was not natural that night—she was speaking from forced spirits.

"Well," said Madame de Ventadour at last, tired, perhaps, of the part she had been playing, and bringing to a sudden close an animated description of the then French court—"well, see now if we ought not to be ashamed of ourselves—our talk has positively interrupted the music. Did you see Lord Doningdale stop it with a bow to me, as much as to say, with his courtly reproof—'It shall not disturb you, madame?' I will no longer be accessory to your crime of bad taste!"

With this the Frenchwoman rose, and gliding through the circle retired to the further end of the room. Ernest followed her with his eyes. Suddenly she beckoned to him, and he approached and seated himself by her side.

"Mr. Maltravers," said Valerie, then, with great sweetness in her voice—"I have not as yet expressed to you the delight I have felt from your genius. In absence you have suffered me to converse with you—your books have been to me dear friends; as we shall soon part again, let me now tell you of this, frankly and without compliment."

This paved the way to a conversation that approached more on the precincts of the past than any they had yet known. But Ernest was guarded, and Valerie watched his words and looks with an interest she could not conceal—an interest that partook of disappointment.

"It is an excitement," said Valerie, "to climb a mountain, though it fatigue; and though the clouds may even deny us a prospect from its summit—it is an excitement that gives a very universal pleasure, and that seems almost as if it were the result of a common human instinct, which makes us desire to rise—to get above the ordinary throughfares and level of life. Some such pleasure you must have in intellectual ambition, in which the mind is the upward traveller."

"It is not the *ambition* that pleases," replied Maltravers, "it is the following a path congenial to our tastes, and made dear to us in a short time by habit. The moments in which we look beyond our work, and fancy ourselves seated beneath the Everlasting Laurel, are few. It is the work itself, whether of action or literature, that interests and excites us. And at length the dryness of toil takes the familiar sweetness of custom. But in intellectual labour there is another charm—we become more intimate with our own nature. The heart and the soul grow friends, as it were, and the affections and aspirations unite. Thus, we are never without society—we are never alone; all that we have read, learned, and discovered, is company to us. This is pleasant," added Maltravers, "to those who have no dear connections in the world without."

"And is that your case?" asked Valerie, with a timid smile.

"Alas, yes! and since I conquered one affection, Madame de Ventadour, I almost think I have outlived the capacity of loving. I believe that when we cultivate very largely the reason or the imagination, we blunt, to a certain extent, our young susceptibilities to the fair impressions of real life. From 'idleness,' says the old Roman poet, 'Love feeds his torch.'*

"You are too young to talk thus."

"I speak as I feel."

Valerie said no more.

Shortly afterwards Lord Doningdale approached them, and proposed that they should make an excursion the next day to see the ruins of an old abbey, some few miles distant.

CHAPTER X.

*"If I should meet thee
After long years,
How shall I greet thee?"*—BYRON.

IT was a smaller party than usual the next day, consisting only of Lord Doningdale, his son George Herbert, Valerie, and Ernest. They were returning from the ruins, and the sun, now gradually approaching the west, threw its slant rays over the gardens and houses of a small, picturesque town, or, perhaps, rather village, on the high North Road. It is one of the prettiest places in England, that town or village, and boasts an excellent old-fashioned inn, with a large and quaint pleasure-garden. It was through the long and straggling street that our little party slowly rode, when the sky became suddenly overcast, and a few large hailstones falling, gave notice of an approaching storm.

"I told you we should not get safely through the day," said George Herbert. "Now we are in for it."

"George, that is a vulgar expression," said Lord Doningdale, buttoning up his coat. While he spoke, a vivid flash of lightning darted across their very path, and the sky grew darker and darker.

"We may as well rest at the inn," said Maltravers; "the storm is coming on apace, and Madame de Ventadour——"

"You are right," interrupted Lord Doningdale; and he put his horse into a canter.

They were soon at the door of the old hotel. Bells rang—dogs barked—ostlers ran. A plain, dark, travelling post chariot was before the inn-door; and roused perhaps by the noise below, a lady in the "first floor front, No. 2," came to the window. This lady owned the travelling-carriage, and was at this time alone in that apartment. As she looked carelessly at the party, her eyes rested on one form—she turned pale, uttered a faint cry, and fell senseless on the floor.

Meanwhile, Lord Doningdale and his guests were shown into the room next to that tenanted by the lady. Properly speaking, both the rooms made one long apartment for balls and county meetings, and the division was formed by a thin partition, removable at pleasure. The hail now came on fast and heavy, the trees groaned, the thunder roared; and in the large, dreary room there was a palpable and oppressive sense of coldness and discomfort. Valerie shivered—a fire was lighted—and the Frenchwoman drew near to it.

"You are wet, my dear lady," said Lord Doningdale. "You should take off that close habit, and have it dried."

"Oh, no; what matters it?" said Valerie, bitterly, and almost rudely.

"It matters everything," said Ernest; "pray be ruled."

"And do you care for me?" murmured Valerie.

"Can you ask that question?" replied Ernest, in the same tone, and with affectionate and friendly warmth.

Meanwhile, the good old lord had summoned the chambermaid, and, with the kindly imperiousness of a father, made Valerie quit the room. The three gentlemen, left together, talked of the storm, wondered how long it would last, and debated the propriety of sending to Doningdale for the carriage. While they spoke, the hail suddenly ceased, though clouds in the distant horizon were bearing heavily up to renew the charge. George Herbert, who was the most impatient of mortals, especially of rainy weather in a strange place, seized the occasion, and insisted on riding to Doningdale, and sending back the carriage.

"Surely a groom would do as well, George," said the father.

"My dear father, no; I should envy the rogue too much. I am bored to death here. Marie will be frightened about us. Brown Bess will take me back in twenty minutes. I am a hardy fellow, you know. Good-bye."

Away darted the young sportsman, and in two minutes they saw him spur gaily from the inn-door.

"It is very odd that *I* should have such a son," said Lord Doningdale, musingly—"a son who cannot amuse himself indoors for two minutes together. I took great pains with his education, too. Strange that people should weary so much of themselves that they cannot brave the prospect of a few minutes passed in reflection—that a shower and the resources of their own thoughts are evils so galling—very strange indeed. But it is a confounded climate this, certainly. I wonder when it will clear up."

Thus muttering, Lord Doningdale walked, or rather marched, to and fro the room, with his hands in his coat pockets, and his whip sticking perpendicularly out of the right one. Just at this moment the waiter came to announce that his lordship's groom was without, and desired much to see him. Lord Doningdale had then the pleasure of learning that his favourite grey hackney, which he had ridden, winter and summer, for fifteen years, was taken with shivers, and, as the groom expressed it, seemed to have "the collar [cholera?] in its bowels!"

Lord Doningdale turned pale, and hurried to the stables without saying a word.

Maltravers, who, plunged in thought, had not overheard the low and brief conference between master and groom, remained alone, seated by the fire, his head buried in his bosom, and his arms folded.

Meanwhile the lady, who occupied the adjoining chamber, had recovered slowly from her swoon. She put both hands to her temples, as if trying to recollect her thoughts. Hers was a fair, innocent, almost childish face; and now, as a smile shot across it, there was something so sweet and touching in the gladness it shed over that countenance, that you could not have seen it without strong and almost painful interest. For it was the gladness of a person who has known sorrow. Suddenly she started up, and said—" No—then! I do not dream. He is come back—he is here—all will be well again! Ha! it is his voice. Oh, bless him, it is *his* voice!" She paused, her finger on her lip, her face bent down. A low and indistinct sound of voices reached her straining ear through the thin door that divided her from Maltravers. She listened intently, but she could not overhear the import. Her heart beat violently. "He is not alone!" she murmured, mournfully. "I will wait till the sound ceases, and then venture in!"

And what was the conversation carried on in that chamber? We must return to Ernest. He was sitting in the same thoughtful posture when Madame de Ventadour returned. The Frenchwoman coloured when she found herself alone with Ernest, and Ernest himself was not at his ease.

"Herbert has gone home to order the carriage, and Lord Doningdale has disappeared, I scarce know whither. You do not, I trust, feel the worse for the rain?"

"No," said Valerie.

"Shall you have any commands in London?" asked Maltravers; "I return to town to-morrow."

"So soon!" and Valerie sighed. "Ah!" she added, after a pause, "we shall not meet again for years, perhaps. Monsieur de Ventadour is to be appointed ambassador to the —— Court—and so—and so——. Well, it is no matter. What has become of the friendship we once swore to each other?"

"It is here," said Maltravers, laying his hand on his heart. "Here, at least, lies the half of that friendship which was my charge; and more than friendship, Valerie de Ventadour—respect —admiration—gratitude. At a time of life, when passion and fancy, most strong, might have left me an idol and worthless voluptuary, you convinced me that the world has virtue, and that woman is too noble to be our toy—the idol of to-day, the victim of to-morrow. Your influence, Valerie, left me a more thoughtful man —I hope a better one."

"Oh!" said Madame de Ventadour, strongly affected; "I bless you for what you tell me: you cannot know—you cannot guess how sweet it is to me. Now I recognise you once more. What—what did my resolution cost me? Now I am repaid!"

Ernest was moved by her emotion, and by his own remembrances; he took her hand, and pressing it with frank and respectful tenderness—"I did not think, Valerie," said he, "when I reviewed the past, I did not think that you loved me—I was not vain enough for that; but if so, how much is your character raised in my eyes—how provident, how wise your virtue! Happier and better for both, our present feelings, each to each, than if we had indulged a brief and guilty dream of passion, at war with all that leaves passion without remorse, and bliss without alloy. Now——'

"Now," interrupted Valerie, quickly, and fixing on him her dark eyes—"now you love me no longer! Yet it is better so. Well, I will go back to my cold and cheerless state of life, and forget once more that heaven endowed me with a heart!"

"Ah, Valerie! esteemed, revered, still beloved, not indeed with the fires of old, but with a deep, undying, and holy tenderness, speak not thus to me. Let me not believe you unhappy; let me think that, wise, sagacious, brilliant as you are, you have employed your gifts to reconcile yourself to a common lot. Still, let me look up to you when I would despise the circles in which you live, and say,—'On that pedestal an altar is yet placed, to which the heart may bring the offerings of the soul.'"

"It is in vain—in vain that I struggle," said Valerie, half-choked with emotion, and clasping her hands passionately. "Ernest, I love you still—I am wretched to think you love me no more; I would give you nothing—yet I exact all; my youth is going—my beauty dimmed—my very intellect is dulled by the life I lead; and yet I ask from you that which your young heart once felt for me. Despise me, Maltravers, I am not what I seemed—I am a hypocrite—despise me."

"No," said Ernest, again possessing himself of her hand, and falling on his knee by her side. "No, never-to-be-forgotten, ever-to-be-honoured Valerie, hear me." As he spoke, he kissed the hand he held; with the other, Valerie covered her face and wept bitterly, but in silence. Ernest paused till the burst of her feelings had subsided, her hand still in his—still warmed by his kisses—kisses as pure as cavalier ever impressed on the hand of his queen.

At this time, the door communicating with the next room gently opened. A fair form—a form fairer and younger than that of Valerie de Ventadour, entered the apartment; the silence had deceived her—she believed that Maltravers was alone. She had entered with her heart upon her lips; love, sanguine, hopeful love, in every vein, in every thought—she had entered, dreaming that across that threshold life would dawn upon her afresh—that all would be once more as it had been, when the common air was rapture. Thus she entered; and now she stood spell-bound, terror-stricken, pale as death—life turned to stone—youth—hope—bliss were for ever over to her! Ernest kneeling to another was all she saw!—For this had she been faithful and true, amidst storm and desolation; for this had she hoped—dreamed—lived. They did not note her; she was unseen—unheard. And Ernest, who would have gone barefoot to the end of the earth to find her, was in the very room with her, and knew it not!

"Call me again *beloved!*" said Valerie, very softly.

"Beloved Valerie, hear me."

These words were enough for the listener; she turned noiselessly away: humble as that heart was, it was proud. The door closed on her—she had obtained the wish of her whole being—Heaven had heard her prayer—she had once more seen the lover of her youth; and thenceforth all was night and darkness to her. What matter what became of her? One moment, what an effect it produces upon years!—ONE MOMENT!—virtue, crime, glory, shame, woe, rapture, rest upon moments! Death itself is but a moment, yet Eternity is its successor!

"Hear me!" continued Ernest, unconscious of what had passed—"hear me; let us be what human nature and worldly forms seldom allow those of opposite sexes to be—friends to each other, and to virtue also—friends through time and absence—friends through all the vicissitudes of life—friends on whose affection shame and remorse never cast a shade—friends who are to meet hereafter! Oh, there is no attachment so true, no tie so holy, as that which is founded on the old chivalry of loyalty and honour; and which is what love would be, if the heart and the soul were unadulterated by clay."

There was in Ernest's countenance an expression so noble, in his voice a tone so thrilling, that Valerie was brought back at once to the nature which a momentary weakness had subdued. She looked at him with an admiring and grateful gaze, and then said, in a calm but low voice, "Ernest, I understand you; yes, your friendship is dearer to me than love."

At this time they heard the voice of Lord Doningdale on the stairs, Valerie turned away. Maltravers, as he rose, extended his hand; she pressed it warmly, and the spell was broken, the temptation conquered, the ordeal passed. While Lord Doningdale entered the room, the carriage, with Herbert in it, drove to the door. In a few minutes the little party were within the vehicle. As they drove away, the ostlers were harnessing the horses to the dark green travelling carriage. From the window, a sad and straining eye gazed upon the gayer equipage of the peer—that eye which Maltravers would have given his whole fortune to meet again. But he did not look up; and Alice Darvil turned away, and her fate was fixed!

CHAPTER XI.

"Strange fits of passion I have known,
And I will dare to tell."—WORDSWORTH.

". . . . The food of hope
Is meditated action."—WORDSWORTH.

MALTRAVERS left Doningdale the next day. He had no further conversation with Valerie; but when he took leave of her, she placed in his hand a letter, which he read as he rode slowly through the beech avenues of the park. Translated, it ran thus:—

"Others would despise me for the weakness I showed—but you will not! It is the sole weakness of a life. None can know what I have passed through—what hours of dejection and gloom—I, whom so many envy! Better to have been a peasant girl, with love, than a queen whose life is but a dull mechanism. You, Maltravers, I never forgot in absence: and your image made yet more wearisome and trite the things around me. Years passed, and your name was suddenly on men's lips. I heard of you wherever I went—I could not shut you from me. Your fame was as if you were conversing by my side. We met at last, suddenly and unexpectedly. I saw that you loved me no more, and that thought conquered all my resolves: anguish subdues the nerves of the mind as sickness those of the body. And thus I forgot, and humbled, and might have undone myself. Juster and better thoughts are once more awakened within me, and when we meet again I shall be worthy of your respect. I see how dangerous are that luxury of thought, that sin of discontent, which I indulged. I go back to life resolved to vanquish all that can interfere with its claims and duties. Heaven guide and preserve you, Ernest. Think of me as one whom you will not blush to have loved—whom you will not blush hereafter to present to your wife. With so much that is soft, as well as great, within you, you were not formed like me—to be alone.

"FAREWELL!"

Maltravers read and re-read this letter; and when he reached his home, he placed it carefully amongst the things he most valued. A lock of Alice's hair lay beside it—he did not think that either was dishonoured by the contact.

With an effort, he turned himself once more to those stern, yet high connections which literature makes with real life. Perhaps there was a certain restlessness in his heart which induced him ever to occupy his mind. That was one of the busiest years of his life—the one in which he did most to sharpen jealousy and confirm fame.

CHAPTER XII.

"In effect he entered my apartment."—*Gil Blas.*

"I am surprised, said he, at the caprice of fortune, who sometimes delights in loading an execrable author with favours, whilst she leaves good writers to perish for want."—*Gil Blas.*

IT was just twelve months after his last interview with Valerie, and Madame de Ventadour had long since quitted England, when one morning, as Maltravers sat alone in his study, Castruccio Cesarini was announced.

"Ah, my dear Castruccio, how are you?" cried Maltravers, eagerly, as the opening door presented the form of the Italian.

"Sir," said Castruccio, with great stiffness, and speaking in French, which was his wont when he meant to be distant—"sir, I do not come to renew our former acquaintance—you are a great man [here a bitter sneer], I an obscure one [here Castruccio drew himself up]—I only come to discharge a debt to you which I find I have incurred."

"What tone is this, Castruccio; and what debt do you speak of?"

"On my arrival in town yesterday," said the poet, solemnly, "I went to the man whom you deputed some years since to publish my little volume, to demand an account of its successs; and I found that it had cost one hundred and twenty pounds, deducting the sale of forty-nine copies which had been sold. *Your* books sell some thousands, I am told. It is well contrived—mine fell still-born, no pains were taken with it—no matter—[a wave of the hand]. You discharged this debt, I repay you: there is a cheque for the money. Sir, I have done! I wish you a good day, and health to enjoy *your* reputation."

"Why, Cesarini, this is folly."

"Sir——"

"Yes, it is folly; for there is no folly equal to that of throwing away friendship in a world where friendship is so rare. You insinuate that I am to blame for any neglect which your work experienced. Your publisher can tell you that I was more anxious about your book than I have ever been about my own."

"And the proof is, that forty-nine copies were sold!"

"Sit down, Castruccio; sit down and listen to reason;" and Maltravers proceeded to explain, and soothe, and console. He reminded the poor poet that his verses were written in a foreign tongue—that even English poets of great fame enjoyed but a limited sale for their works—that it was impossible to make the avaricious public purchase what the stupid public would not take an interest in —in short, he used all those arguments which naturally suggested themselves as best calculated to convince and soften Castruccio: and he did this with so much evident sympathy and kindness, that at length the Italian could no longer justify his own resentment. A reconciliation took place, sincere on the part of Maltravers, hollow on the part of Cesarini; for the disappointed author could not forgive the successful one.

"And how long shall you stay in London?"

"Some months."

"Send for your luggage, and be my guest."

"No; I have taken lodgings that suit me. I am formed for solitude."

"While you stay here, you will, however, go into the world?"

"Yes, I have some letters of introduction, and I hear that the English can honour merit, even in an Italian."

"You hear the truth, and it will amuse you, at least, to see our eminent men. They will receive you most hospitably. Let me assist you as a cicerone."

"Oh, your *valuable* time!"

"Is at your disposal; but where are you going?"

"It is Sunday, and I have had my curiosity excited to hear a celebrated preacher, Mr. ——, who, they tell me, is now more talked of than *any author* in London."

"They tell you truly—I will go with you—I myself have not yet heard him, but proposed to do so this very day."

"Are you not jealous of a man so much spoken of?"

"Jealous!—why, I never set up for a popular preacher!—*ce n'est pas mon métier.*"

"If I were a *successful* author, I should be jealous if the dancing-dogs were talked of."

"No, my dear Cesarini, I am sure you would not. You are a little irritated at present by natural disappointment; but the man who has as much success as he deserves is never morbidly jealous, even of a rival in his own line: want of success sours us; but a little sunshine smiles away the vapours. Come, we have no time to lose."

Maltravers took his hat, and the two young men bent their way to —— Chapel. Cesarini still retained the singular fashion of his dress, though it was now made of handsomer materials, and worn with more coxcombry and pretension. He had much improved in person—had been admired in Paris, and told that he looked like a man of genius—and with his black ringlets flowing over his shoulders, his long moustache, his broad Spanish-shaped hat, and eccentric garb, he certainly did not look like other people. He smiled with contempt at the plain dress of his companion. "I see," said he, "that you follow the fashion, and look as if you had passed your life with *élégans* instead of students. I wonder you condescend to such trifles as fashionably-shaped hats and coats."

"It would be worse trifling to set up for originality in hats and coats, at least in sober England. I was born a gentleman, and I dress my outward frame like others of my order. Because I am a writer, why should I affect to be different from other men?"

"I see that your are not above the weakness of your countryman, Congreve," said Cesarini, "who deemed it finer to be a gentleman than an author."

"I always thought that anecdote misconstrued. Congreve had a proper and manly pride, to my judgment, when he expressed a dislike to be visited merely as a raree-show."

"But is it policy to let the world see that an author is like other people? Would he not create a deeper personal interest if he showed that even in person alone he was unlike the herd? He ought to be seen seldom—not to stale his presence—and to resort to the arts that belong to the royalty of intellect as well as the royalty of birth."

"I dare say an author, by a little charlatanism of that nature, might be more talked of—might be more adored in the boarding-schools, and make a better picture in the exhibition. But I think, if his mind be manly, he would lose in self-respect at every quackery of the sort. And my philosophy is, that to respect one's self is worth all the fame in the world."

Cesarini sneered and shrugged his shoulders; it was quite evident that the two authors had no sympathy with each other.

They arrived at last at the chapel, and with some difficulty procured seats.

Presently the service began. The preacher was a man of unquestionable talent and fervid eloquence; but his theatrical arts, his affected dress, his artificial tones and gestures, and above all, the fanatical mummeries which he introduced into the House of God, disgusted Maltravers, while they charmed, entranced, and awed Cesarini. The one saw a mountebank and impostor—the other recognised a profound artist and an inspired prophet.

But while the discourse was drawing towards a close, while the preacher was in one of his most eloquent bursts—the ohs ! and ahs ! of which was the grand prelude to the pathetic peroration—the dim outline of a female form, in the distance, rivetted the eyes and absorbed the thoughts of Maltravers. The chapel was darkened, though it was broad daylight; and the face of the person that attracted Ernest's attention was concealed by her head-dress and veil. But that bend of the neck, so simply graceful, so humbly modest, recalled to his heart but one image. Every one has, perhaps, observed that there is a physiognomy (if the bull may be pardoned) of *form* as well as face, which it rarely happens that two persons possess in common. And this, with most, is peculiarly marked in the turn of the head, the outline of the shoulders, and the ineffable something that characterises the postures of each individual in repose. The more intently he gazed, the more firmly Ernest was persuaded that he saw before him the long-lost, the never-to-be-forgotten mistress of his boyish days, and his first love. On one side of the lady in question sat an elderly gentleman, whose eyes were fixed upon the preacher; on the other, a beautiful little girl, with long fair ringlets, and that cast of features which, from its exquisite delicacy and expressive mildness, painters and poets call the "angelic." These persons appeared to belong to the same party. Maltravers literally trembled, so great were his impatience and agitation. Yet still the dress of the supposed likeness of Alice, the appearance of her companions, were so evidently above the ordinary rank, that Ernest scarcely ventured to yield to the suggestions of his own heart. Was it possible that the daughter of Luke Darvil, thrown upon the wide world, could have risen so far

"IT IS SHE—IT IS—OH, HEAVENS, IT IS ALICE!" MURMURED MALTRAVERS.

beyond her circumstances and station? At length the moment came when he might resolve his doubts—the discourse was concluded—the extemporaneous prayer was at an end—the congregation broke up, and Maltravers pushed his way, as well as he could, through the dense and serried crowd. But every moment some vexatious obstruction, in the shape of a fat gentleman or three close-wedged ladies, intercepted his progress. He lost sight of the party in question amidst the profusion of tall bonnets and waving plumes. He arrived at last, breathless and pale as death (so great was the struggle within him), at the door of the chapel. He arrived in time to see a plain carriage with servants in grey undress liveries, driving from the porch—and caught a glimpse within the vehicle of the golden ringlets of a child. He darted forward, he threw himself almost before the horses. The coachman drew in, and with an angry exclamation, very much like an oath, whipped his horses aside and went off. But that momentary pause sufficed.—" It is she—it is! O heavens, it is Alice!" murmured Maltravers. The whole place reeled before his eyes, and he clung, overpowered and unconscious, to a neighbouring lamp-post for support. But he recovered himself with an agonising effort, as the thought struck upon his heart that he was about to lose sight of her again for ever. And he rushed forward, like one frantic, in pursuit of the carriage. But there was a vast crowd of other carriages, besides stream upon stream of foot-passengers—for the great and the gay resorted to that place of worship, as a fashionable excitement in a dull day. And after a weary and a dangerous chase, in which he had been nearly run over three times, Maltravers halted at last, exhausted and in despair. Every succeeding Sunday, for months, he went to the same chapel, but in vain ; in vain, too, he resorted to every public haunt of dissipation and amusement. Alice Darvil he beheld no more !

CHAPTER XIII.

> "Tell me, sir,
> Have you cast up your state, rated your land,
> And find it able to endure the charge?"
> —*The Noble Gentleman.*

BY degrees, as Maltravers sobered down from the first shock of that unexpected meeting, and from the prolonged disappointment that followed it, he became sensible of a strange kind of happiness or contentment. Alice was not in poverty, she was not eating the unhallowed bread of vice, or earning the bitter wages of laborious penury. He saw her in reputable, nay, opulent circumstances. A dark nightmare, that had often, amidst the pleasures of youth or the triumphs of literature, weighed upon his breast, was removed. He breathed more freely —he could sleep in peace. His conscience could no longer say to him, "She who slept upon thy bosom is a wanderer upon the face of the earth—exposed to every temptation, perishing, perhaps, for want." That single sight of Alice had been like the apparition of the injured Dead conjured up at Heraclea—whose sight could pacify the aggressor and exorcise the spectres of remorse. He was reconciled with himself, and walked on to the Future with a bolder step and statelier crest. Was she married to that staid and sober-looking personage whom he had beheld with her? was that child the offspring of their union? He almost hoped so—it was better to lose than destroy her. Poor Alice! could she have dreamed, when she sat at his feet gazing up into his eyes, that a time would come when Maltravers would thank heaven for the belief that she was happy with another?

Ernest Maltravers now felt a new man: the relief of conscience operated on the efforts of his genius. A more buoyant and elastic spirit entered into them—they seemed to breath as with a second youth.

Meanwhile, Cesarini threw himself into the fashionable world, and to his surprise was *fêted* and caressed. In fact, Castruccio was exactly the sort of person to be made a lion of. The letters of introduction that he had brought from Paris were addressed to those great personages in England, between whom and personages equally great in France, politics makes a bridge of connection.

Cesarini appeared to them as an accomplished young man, brother-in-law to a distinguished member of the French Chamber. Maltravers, on the other hand, introduced him to the literary dilettanti, who admire all authors that are not rivals. The singular costume of Cesarini, which would have revolted persons in an Englishman, enchanted them in an Italian. He looked, they said, like a poet. Ladies like to have verses written to them—and Cesarini, who talked very little, made up for it by scribbling eternally. The young man's head soon grew filled with comparisons between himself in London and Petrarch at Avignon. As he had always thought that fame was in the gift of lords and ladies, and had no idea of the multitude, he fancied himself already famous. And, since one of his strongest feelings was his jealousy of Maltravers, he was delighted at being told he was a much more interesting creature than that haughty personage, who wore his neckcloth like other people, and had not even those indispensable attributes of genius —black curls and a sneer. Fine society, which, as Madame de Staël well says, depraves the frivolous mind and braces the strong one, completed the ruin of all that was manly in Cesarini's intellect. He soon learned to limit his desire of effect or distinction to gilded saloons; and his vanity contented itself upon the scraps and morsels from which the lion heart of true ambition turns in disdain. But this was not all. Cesarini was envious of the greater affluence of Maltravers. His own fortune was in a small capital of eight or nine thousand pounds: but, thrown in the midst of the wealthiest society in Europe, he could not bear to sacrifice a single claim upon its esteem. He began to talk of the satiety of wealth, and young ladies listened to him with remarkable interest when he did so—he obtained the reputation of riches—he was too vain not to be charmed with it. He endeavoured to maintain the claim by adopting the extravagant excesses of the day. He bought horses—he gave away jewels—he made love to a marchioness of forty-two, who was very kind to him and very fond of *écarté*—he gambled—he was on the high road to destruction.

BOOK VI.

CHAPTER I.

"L'addresse et l'artifice ont passé dans mon cœur,
Qu'on a sous cet habit et d'esprit et de ruse."*—REGNARD.

IT was a fine morning in July, when a gentleman who had arrived in town the night before—after an absence from England of several years—walked slowly and musingly up that superb thoroughfare which connects the Regent's Park with St. James's.

He was a man who, with great powers of mind, had wasted his youth in a wandering, vagabond kind of life, but who had worn away the love of pleasure, and began to awaken to a sense of ambition.

"It is astonishing how this city is improved," said he to himself. "Everything gets on in this world with a little energy and bustle—and everybody as well as everything. My old cronies, fellows not half so clever as I am, are all doing well. There's Tom Stevens, my very fag at Eton—snivelling little dog he was, too!—just made under-secretary of state. Pearson, whose longs and shorts I always wrote, is now head-master to the human longs and shorts of a public school—editing Greek plays, and booked for a bishopric. Collier, I see by the papers, is leading his circuit—and Ernest Maltravers (but *he* had some talent!) has made a name in the world. Here am I, worth them all put together, who have done nothing but spend half my little fortune in spite of all my economy. Egad, this must have an end. I must look to the main chance; and yet, just when I want his help the most, my

* Subtlety and craft have taken possession of my heart, but under this habit one exhibits both shrewdness and wit.

worthy uncle thinks fit to marry again. Humph—I'm too good for this world."

While thus musing, the soliloquist came in direct personal contact with a tall gentleman, who carried his head very high in the air, and did not appear to see that he had nearly thrown our abstracted philosopher off his legs.

"Zounds, sir, what do you mean?" cried the latter.

"I beg your par——" began the other, meekly, when his arm was seized, and the injured man exclaimed, "Bless me, sir, is it indeed whom *you* I see?"

"Ha! Lumley?"

"The same; and how fares it, my dear uncle? I did not know you were in London. I only arrived last night. How well you are looking!"

"Why, yes, heaven be praised, I am pretty well."

"And happy in your new ties? You must present me to Mrs. Templeton."

"Ehem," said Mr. Templeton, clearing his throat, and with a slight but embarrassed smile, "I never thought I should marry again."

"*L'homme propose et Dieu dispose*," observed Lumley Ferrers, for it was he.

"Gently, my dear nephew," replied Mr. Templeton, gravely; "those phrases are somewhat sacrilegious; I am an old-fashioned person, you know."

"Ten thousand apologies."

"*One* apology will suffice; these hyperboles of phrases are almost sinful."

"Confounded old prig!" thought Ferrers; but he bowed sanctimoniously.

"My dear uncle, I have been a wild fellow in my day: but with years comes reflection; and under your guidance, if I may hope for it, I trust to grow a wiser and a better man."

"It is well, Lumley," returned the uncle; "and I am very glad to see you returned to your own country. Will you dine with me to-morrow? I am living near Fulham. You had better bring your carpet-bag, and stay with me some days; you will be heartily welcome, especially if you can shift without a foreign servant. I have a great compassion for papists, but——"

"Oh, my dear uncle, do not fear; I am not rich enough to have a foreign servant, and have not travelled over three-quarters of the globe without learning that it is possible to dispense with a valet."

"As to being rich enough," observed Mr. Templeton, with a calculating air, "seven hundred and ninety-five pounds ten shillings a-year will allow a man to keep *two* servants, if he pleases; but I am glad to find you economical at all events. We meet to-morrow, then, at six o'clock."

"*Au revoir*—I mean, God bless you."

"Tiresome old gentleman that," muttered Ferrers, "and not so cordial as formerly; perhaps his wife is *enceinte*, and he is going to do me the injustice of having another heir. I must look to this; for without riches, I had better go back and live *au cinquième* at Paris."

With this conclusion, Lumley quickened his pace, and soon arrived in Seamore Place. In a few moments more he was in the library, well stored with books, and decorated with marble busts and images from the studios of Canova and Thorwaldsen.

"My master, sir, will be down immediately," said the servant who admitted him; and Ferrers threw himself on a sofa, and contemplated the apartment with an air half envious and half cynical.

Presently the door opened, and "My dear Ferrers!" "Well, *mon cher*, how are you?" were the salutations hastily exchanged.

After the first sentences of inquiry, gratulation, and welcome, had cleared the way for more general conversation—"Well, Maltravers," said Ferrers, "so here we are together again, and after a lapse of so many years! both older, certainly; and you, I suppose, wiser. At all events, people think you so; and that's all that's important in the question. Why, man, you are looking as young as ever, only a little paler and thinner: but look at me—I am not very *much* past thirty, and I am almost an old man; bald at the temples, crow's feet, too, eh? Idleness ages one damnably."

"Pooh, Lumley, I never saw you look better. And are you really come to settle in England?"

"Yes, if I can afford it. But at my age, and after having seen so much, the life of an idle, obscure *garçon* does not content me. I feel that the world's opinion, which I used to despise, is growing necessary to me. I want to be something. What can I be? Don't look alarmed, I won't rival you. I dare say literary reputation is a fine thing, but I desire some distinction more substantial and worldly. You know your own country; give me a map of the roads to power."

"To Power? Oh, nothing but law, politics, and riches."

"For law, I am too old; politics, perhaps, might suit me; but riches, my dear Ernest—ah, how I long for a good account with my banker!"

"Well, patience and hope. Are you not a rich uncle's heir?"

"I don't know," said Ferrers, very dolorously; "the old gentleman has married again, and may have a family."

"Married!—to whom?"

"A widow, I hear; I know nothing more, except that she has a child already. So you see she has got into a cursed way of having children. And, perhaps, by the time I'm forty, I shall see a whole covey of cherubs flying away with the great Templeton property!"

"Ha, ha! your despair sharpens your wit, Lumley; but why not take a leaf out of your uncle's book, and marry yourself?"

"So I will, when I can find an heiress. If that is what you meant to say—it is a more sensible suggestion than any I could have supposed to come from a man who writes books, especially poetry; and your advice is not to be despised. For rich I will be; and as the fathers (I don't mean of the Church, but in Horace) told the rising generation, the first thing is to resolve to be rich—it is only the second thing to consider how."

"Meanwhile, Ferrers, you will be my guest."

"I'll dine with you to-day; but to-morrow I am off to Fulham, to be introduced to my aunt. Can't you fancy her?—grey gros de Naples gown; gold chain, with an eyeglass; rather fat; two pugs and a parrot! 'Start not, this is fancy's sketch!' I have not yet seen the respectable relative with my physical optics. What shall we have for dinner? Let *me* choose, you were always a bad caterer."

As Ferrers thus rattled on, Maltravers felt himself growing younger; old times and old adventures crowded fast upon him; and the two friends spent a most agreeable day together. It was only the next morning that Maltravers, in thinking over the various conversations that had passed between them, was forced reluctantly to acknowledge that the inert selfishness of Lumley Ferrers seemed now to have hardened into a resolute and systematic want of principle, which might, perhaps, make him a dangerous and designing man, if urged by circumstances into action.

CHAPTER II.

"*Dunelm. Sir, I must speak to you. I have been long your despised kinsman.*
"*Moross. Oh, what thou wilt, nephew.*"—EPICŒNE.

"*Her silence is dowry eno'*—exceedingly soft spoken; thrifty of her speech, that spends but six words a day."—*Ibid.*

THE coach dropped Mr. Ferrers at the gate of a villa about three miles from town. The lodge-keeper charged himself with the carpet-bag, and Ferrers strolled, with his hands behind him (it was his favourite mode of disposing of them), through the beautiful and elaborate pleasure-grounds.

"A very nice little box (jointure-house, I suppose)! I would not grudge that, I'm sure, if I had but the rest. But here, I suspect, comes madam's first specimen of the art of having a family." This last thought was extracted from Mr. Ferrers' contemplative brain by a lovely little girl, who came running up to him, fearless and spoilt as she was; and after indulging a tolerable stare, exclaimed, "Are you come to see papa, sir?"

"Papa!—the deuce!" thought Lumley; "and who is papa, my dear?"

"Why, mamma's husband. He is not my papa by rights."

"Certainly not, my love; not by rights—I comprehend."

"Eh!"

"Yes, I am going to your papa by wrongs—Mr. Templeton."

"Oh, this way then."

"You are very fond of Mr. Templeton, my little angel."

"To be sure I am. You have not seen the rocking-horse he is going to give me."

"Not yet, sweet child! And how is mamma?"

"Oh, poor, dear mamma," said the child, with a sudden change of voice, and tears in her eyes. "Ah, she is not well!"

"In the family-way, to a dead certainty!" muttered Ferrers, with a groan; "but here is my uncle. Horrid name! Uncles were always wicked fellows. Richard the Third, and the man who did something or other to the babes in the wood, were a joke to my hard-hearted old relation, who has robbed me with a widow! The lustful, liquorish, old—— My *dear* sir, I'm so glad to see you!"

Mr. Templeton, who was a man very cold in his manners, and

always either looked over people's heads or down upon the ground, just touched his nephew's outstretched hand, and telling him he was welcome, observed that it was a very fine afternoon.

"Very, indeed; sweet place this; you see, by the way, that I have already made acquaintance with my fair cousin-in-law. She is very pretty."

"I really think she is," said Mr. Templeton, with some warmth, and gazing fondly at the child, who was now throwing buttercups up in the air, and trying to catch them.—Mr. Ferrers wished in his heart that they had been brick-bats!

"Is she like her mother?" asked the nephew.

"Like whom, sir?"

"Her mother—Mrs. Templeton."

"No, not very; there is an air, perhaps, but the likeness is not remarkably strong. Would you not like to go to your room before dinner?"

"Thank you. Can I not first be presented to Mrs. Tem——"

"She is at her devotions, Mr. Lumley," interrupted Mr. Templeton, grimly.

"The she-hypocrite!" thought Ferrers. "Oh, I am delighted that your pious heart has found so congenial a helpmate!"

"It is a great blessing, and I am grateful for it. This is the way to the house."

Lumley, now formally installed in a grave bed-room, with dimity curtains, and dark-brown paper with light-brown stars on it, threw himself into a large chair, and yawned and stretched with as much fervour as if he could have yawned and stretched himself into his uncle's property. He then slowly exchanged his morning dress for a quiet suit of black, and thanked his stars that, amidst all his sins, he had never been a dandy, and had never rejoiced in a fine waistcoat—a criminal possession that he well knew would have entirely hardened his uncle's conscience against him. He tarried in his room till the second bell summoned him to descend; and then, entering the drawing-room, which had a cold look even in July, found his uncle standing by the mantel-piece, and a young, slight, handsome woman, half-buried in a huge but not comfortable *fauteuil*.

"Your aunt, Mrs. Templeton; madam, my nephew, Mr. Lumley Ferrers," said Templeton, with a wave of the hand. "John,—dinner!"

"I hope I am not late!"

"No," said Templeton, gently, for he had always liked his nephew, and began now to thaw towards him a little on seeing that Lumley put a good face upon the new state of affairs.

"No, my dear boy—no; but I think order and punctuality cardinal virtues in a well-regulated family."

"Dinner, sir," said the butler, opening the folding-doors at the end of the room.

"Permit me," said Lumley, offering his arm to the aunt. "What a lovely place this is!"

Mrs. Templeton said something in reply, but what it was Ferrers could not discover, so low and choked was the voice.

"Shy," thought he: "odd for a widow! but that's the way those husband-buriers take us in!"

Plain as was the general furniture of the apartment, the natural ostentation of Mr. Templeton broke out in the massive value of the plate, and the number of the attendants. He was a rich man, and he was proud of his riches: he knew it was respectable to be rich, and he thought it was moral to be respectable. As for the dinner, Lumley knew enough of his uncle's tastes to be prepared for viands and wines that even he (fastidious gourmand that he was) did not despise.

Between the intervals of eating, Mr. Ferrers endeavoured to draw his aunt into conversation, but he found all his ingenuity fail him. There was in the features of Mrs. Templeton an expression of deep but calm melancholy, that would have saddened most persons to look upon, especially in one so young and lovely. It was evidently something beyond shyness or reserve that made her so silent and subdued, and even in her silence there was so much natural sweetness, that Ferrers could not ascribe her manner to haughtiness, or the desire to repel. He was rather puzzled; "for though," thought he, sensibly enough, "my uncle is not a youth, he is a very rich fellow; and how any widow, who is married again to a rich old fellow, can be melancholy, passes my understanding!"

Templeton, as if to draw attention from his wife's taciturnity, talked more than usual. He entered largely into politics, and regretted that in times so critical he was not in parliament.

"Did I possess your youth and your health, Lumley, I would not neglect my country—Popery is abroad."

"I myself should like very much to be in parliament," said Lumley, boldly.

"I dare say you would," returned the uncle, drily. "Parliament is very expensive—only fit for those who have a large stake in the country. Champagne to Mr. Ferrers."

Lumley bit his lip, and spoke little during the rest of the dinner. Mr. Templeton, however, waxed gracious by the time the dessert was on the table ; and began cutting up a pine-apple, with many assurances to Lumley that gardens were nothing without pineries. "Whenever you settle in the country, nephew, be sure you have a pinery."

"Oh, yes," said Lumley, almost bitterly, "and a pack of hounds, and a French cook ; they will all suit my fortune very well."

"You are more thoughtful on pecuniary matters than you used to be," said the uncle.

"Sir," replied Ferrers, solemnly, "in a very short time I shall be what is called a middle-aged man."

"Humph!" said the host.

There was another silence. Lumley was a man, as we have said, or implied before, of great knowledge of human nature, at least the ordinary sort of it, and he now revolved in his mind the various courses it might be wise to pursue towards his rich relation. He saw that in delicate fencing his uncle had over him the same advantage that a tall man has over a short one with the physical sword-play ;—by holding his weapon in a proper position he kept the other at arm's length. There was a grand reserve and dignity about the man who had something to give away, of which Ferrers, however actively he might shift his ground and flourish his rapier, could not break the defence. He determined, therefore, upon a new game, for which his frankness of manner admirably adapted him. Just as he formed this resolution, Mrs. Templeton rose, and with a gentle bow, and soft, though languid smile, glided from the room. The two gentlemen resettled themselves, and Templeton pushed the bottle to Ferrers.

"Help yourself, Lumley ; your travels seem to have deprived you of your high spirits—you are pensive."

"Sir," said Ferrers, abruptly, "I wish to consult you."

"Oh, young man! you have been guilty of some excess—you have gambled—you have——"

"I have done nothing, sir, that should make me less worthy your esteem. I repeat, I wish to consult you ; I have outlived the hot days of my youth—I am now alive to the claims of the world. I have talents, I believe ; and I have application, I know. I wish to fill a position in the world that may redeem my past indolence, and do credit to my family. Sir, I set your example before me, and I now ask your counsel, with the determination to follow it."

Templeton was startled; he half shaded his face with his hand, and gazed searchingly upon the high forehead and bold eyes of his nephew. "I believe you are sincere," said he, after a pause.

"You may well believe so, sir."

"Well, I will think of this. I like an honourable ambition—not too extravagant a one—*that* is sinful; but a *respectable* station in the world is a proper object of desire, and wealth is a blessing; because," added the rich man, taking another slice of the pine-apple—"it enables us to be of use to our fellow-creatures!"

"Sir, then," said Ferrers, with daring animation—"then I avow that my ambition is precisely of the kind you speak of. I am obscure, I desire to be reputably known: my fortune is mediocre, I desire it to be great. I ask *you* for nothing—I know your generous heart; but I wish independently to work out my own career!"

"Lumley," said Templeton, "I never esteemed you so much as I do now. Listen to me—I will confide in you: I think the government are under obligations to me."

"I know it," exclaimed Ferrers, whose eyes sparkled at the thought of a sinecure—for sinecures *then* existed!

"And," pursued the uncle, "I intend to ask them a favour in return."

"Oh, sir!"

"Yes; I think—mark me—with management and address, I may——"

"Well, my dear sir!"

"Obtain a barony for myself and heirs; I trust I shall soon have a family!"

Had somebody given Lumley Ferrers a hearty cuff on the ear, he would have thought less of it than of this wind-up of his uncle's ambitious projects. His jaws fell, his eyes grew an inch larger, and he remained perfectly speechless.

"Ay," pursued Mr. Templeton, "I have long dreamed of this; my character is spotless, my fortune great. I have ever exerted my parliamentary influence in favour of ministers; and, in this commercial country, no man has higher claims than Richard Templeton to the honours of a virtuous, loyal, and religious state. Yes, my boy, I like your ambition—you see I have some of it myself; and since you are sincere in your wish to tread in my footsteps, I think I can obtain you a junior partnership in a highly respectable establishment. Let me see; your capital now is——"

"Pardon me, sir," interrupted Lumley, colouring with indignation, despite himself; "I honour commerce much, but my paternal relations are not such as would allow me to enter into trade. And permit me to add," continued he, seizing with instant adroitness the new weakness presented to him—"permit me to add, that those relations, who have been ever kind to me, would, properly managed, be highly efficient in promoting your own views of advancement; for your sake I would not break with them. Lord Saxingham is still a minister—nay, he is in the cabinet."

"Hem—Lumley—hem!" said Templeton, thoughtfully; "we will consider—we will consider. Any more wine?"

"No, I thank you, sir."

"Then I'll just take my evening stroll, and think over matters. You can rejoin Mrs. Templeton. And I say, Lumley—I read prayers at nine o'clock.—Never forget your Maker, and He will not forget you. The barony will be an excellent thing—eh?—an English peerage—yes—an English peerage! very different from your beggarly countships abroad!"

So saying, Mr. Templeton rang for his hat and cane, and stepped into the lawn from the window of the dining-room.

"'The world's mine oyster, which I with sword will open,'" muttered Ferrers; "I would mould this selfish old man to my purpose; for, since I have neither genius to write, nor eloquence to declaim, I will at least see whether I have not cunning to plot, and courage to act. Conduct—conduct—there lies my talent; and what is conduct but a steady walk from a design to its execution!"

With these thoughts Ferrers sought Mrs. Templeton. He opened the folding-doors very gently, for all his habitual movements were quick and noiseless, and perceived that Mrs. Templeton sat by the window, and that she seemed engrossed with a book which lay open on a little work-table before her.

"Fordyce's Advice to young Married Women, I suppose. Sly jade! However, I must not have her against me."

He approached; still Mrs. Templeton did not note him; nor was it till he stood facing her that he himself observed that her tears were falling fast over the page.

He was a little embarrassed, and, turning towards the window, affected to cough, and then said, without looking at Mrs. Templeton, "I fear I have disturbed you."

"No," answered the same low, stifled voice that had before replied to Lumley's vain attempts to provoke conversation; "it was a melancholy employment, and perhaps it is not right to indulge in it."

"May I inquire what author so affected you?"

"It is but a volume of poems, and I am no judge of poetry; but it contains thoughts which—which——." Mrs. Templeton paused abruptly, and Lumley quietly took up the book.

"Ah!" said he, turning to the title-page—"my friend ought to be much flattered."

"Your friend?"

"Yes; this, I see, is by Ernest Maltravers, a very intimate ally of mine."

"I should like to see him," cried Mrs. Templeton, almost with animation—"I read but little; it was by chance that I met with one of his books, and they are as if I heard a dear friend speaking to me. Ah! I should like to see him!"

"I'm sure, madam," said the voice of a third person, in an austere and rebuking accent, "I do not see what good it would do your immortal soul to see a man who writes idle verses, which appear to me, indeed, highly immoral. I just looked into that volume this morning, and found nothing but trash—love-sonnets and such stuff."

Mrs. Templeton made no reply, and Lumley, in order to change the conversation, which seemed a little too matrimonial for his taste, said, rather awkwardly, "You are returned very soon, sir."

"Yes, I don't like walking in the rain!"

"Bless me, it rains, so it does—I had not observed——"

"Are you wet, sir? had you not better——" began the wife, timidly.

"No, ma'am, I'm not wet, I thank you. By-the-by, nephew, this new author is a friend of yours. I wonder a man of his family should condescend to turn author. He can come to no good. I hope you will drop his acquaintance—authors are very unprofitable associates, I'm sure. I trust I shall see no more of Mr. Maltravers' books in my house."

"Nevertheless, he is well thought of, sir, and makes no mean figure in the world," said Lumley, stoutly; for he was by no means disposed to give up a friend who might be as useful to him as Mr. Templeton himself.

"Figure or no figure—I have not had many dealings with authors in my day; and when I had, I always repented it. Not sound, sir, not sound—all cracked somewhere. Mrs. Templeton, have the kindness to get the Prayer-book—my hassock must be fresh stuffed, it gives me quite a pain in my knee. Lumley, will you ring the bell? Your aunt is very melancholy. True religion is not gloomy; we will read a sermon on Cheerfulness."

"So, so," said Mr. Ferrers to himself, as he undressed that night —" I see that my uncle is a little displeased with my aunt's pensive face—a little jealous of her thinking of anything but himself: *tant mieux*. I must work upon this discovery; it will not do for them to live too happily with each other. And what with that lever, and what with his ambitious projects, I think I see a way to push the good things of this world a few inches nearer to Lumley Ferrers."

CHAPTER III.

> "The pride, too, of her step, as light
> Along the unconscious earth she went,
> Seemed that of one born with a right
> To walk some heavenlier element."—*Loves of the Angels*.
>
> . . . "Can it be
> That these fine impulses, these lofty thoughts,
> Burning with their own beauty, are but given
> To make me the low slave of vanity?"—*Erinna*.
>
> . . . "Is she not too fair
> Even to think of maiden's sweetest care?
> The mouth and brow are contrasts."—*Ibid*.

IT was two or three evenings after the date of the last chapter, and there was what the newspapers call "a select party" in one of the noblest mansions in London. A young lady, on whom all eyes were bent, and whose beauty might have served the painter for a model of a Semiramis or Zenobia, more majestic than became her years, and so classically faultless as to have something cold and statue-like in its haughty lineaments, was moving through the crowd that murmured applauses as she passed. This lady was Florence Lascelles, the daughter of Lumley's great relation, the Earl of Saxingham, and supposed to be the richest heiress in England. Lord Saxingham himself drew aside his daughter as she swept along.

"Florence," said he in a whisper, "the Duke of —— is greatly struck with you—be civil to him—I am about to present him."

So saying, the earl turned to a small, dark, stiff-looking man, of about twenty-eight years of age, at his left, and introduced the Duke of —— to Lady Florence Lascelles. The duke was unmarried; it was an introduction between the greatest match and the wealthiest heiress in the peerage.

"Lady Florence," said Lord Saxingham, "is as fond of horses as yourself, duke, though not quite so good a judge."

"I confess I *do* like horses," said the duke, with an ingenuous air.

Lord Saxingham moved away.

Lady Florence stood mute—one glance of bright contempt shot from her large eyes; her lip slightly curled, and she then half turned aside, and seemed to forget that her new acquaintance was in existence.

His grace, like most great personages, was not apt to take offence; nor could he, indeed, ever suppose that any slight towards the Duke of —— could be intended; still he thought it would be proper in Lady Florence to begin the conversation; for he himself, though not shy, was habitually silent, and accustomed to be saved the fatigue of defraying the small charges of society. After a pause, seeing, however, that Lady Florence remained speechless, he began—

"You ride sometimes in the Park, Lady Florence?"

"Very seldom."

"It is, indeed, too warm for riding at present."

"I did not say so."

"Hem—I thought you did."

Another pause.

"Did you speak, Lady Florence?"

"No."

"Oh! I beg pardon—Lord Saxingham is looking very well."

"I am glad you think so."

"Your picture in the exhibition scarcely does you justice, Lady Florence; yet Lawrence is usually happy."

"You are very flattering," said Lady Florence, with a lively and perceptible impatience in her tone and manner. The young beauty was thoroughly spoilt—and now all the scorn of a scornful nature was drawn forth by observing the envious eyes of the crowd were bent upon one whom the Duke of —— was actually talking to. Brilliant as were her own powers of conversation, she would not deign to exert them—she was an aristocrat of intellect rather than birth, and she took it into her head that the duke was an idiot. She was very much mistaken. If she had but broken up the ice, she would have found that the water below was not shallow. The Duke, in fact, like many other Englishmen, though he did not like the trouble of showing forth, and had an ungainly manner, was a man who had read a good deal, possessed a sound head and an honourable mind, though he did not know what it was to love anybody, to care much for anything, and was at once perfectly sated and yet perfectly contented ; for apathy is the combination of satiety and content.

Still, Florence judged of him as lively persons are apt to judge of the sedate; besides, she wanted to proclaim to him and to everybody else, how little she cared for dukes and great matches ; she, therefore, with a slight inclination of her head, turned away, and extended her hand to a dark young man, who was gazing on her with that respectful but unmistakable admiration which proud women are never proud enough to despise.

"Ah, Signor," said she, in Italian, " I am so glad to see you ; it is a relief, indeed, to find genius in a crowd of nothings."

So saying, the heiress seated herself on one of those convenient couches which hold but two, and beckoned the Italian to her side. Oh, how the vain heart of Castruccio Cesarini beat!—what visions of love, rank, wealth, already flitted before him!

"I almost fancy," said Castruccio, "that the old days of romance are returned, when a queen could turn from princes and warriors to listen to a troubadour."

"Troubadours are now more rare than warriors and princes," replied Florence, with gay animation, which contrasted strongly with the coldness she had manifested to the Duke of ——, "and therefore it would not now be a very great merit in a queen to fly from dulness and insipidity to poetry and wit."

"Ah, say not wit," said Cesarini ; " wit is incompatible with the grave character of deep feelings ;—incompatible with enthusiasm, with worship ;—incompatible with the thoughts that wait upon Lady Florence Lascelles."

Florence coloured and slightly frowned ; but the immense distinction between her position and that of the young foreigner, with her own inexperience, both of real life and the presumption of vain hearts, made her presently forget the flattery that would have offended her in another. She turned the conversation, however, into general channels, and she talked of Italian poetry with a warmth and eloquence worthy of the theme. While they thus conversed, a new guest arrived, who, from the spot where he stood engaged with Lord Saxingham, fixed a steady and scrutinising gaze upon the pair.

"Lady Florence has indeed improved," said this new guest. "I could not have conceived that England boasted any one half so beautiful."

"She certainly is handsome, my dear Lumley—the Lascelles cast of countenance," replied Lord Saxingham,—"and so gifted! She is positively learned—quite a *bas bleu*. I tremble to think of the crowd of poets and painters who will make a fortune out of her enthusiasm. *Entre nous*, Lumley, I could wish her married to a man of sober sense, like the Duke of ——; for sober sense is exactly what she wants. Do observe, she has been just half-an-hour flirting with that odd-looking adventurer, a Signor Cesarini, merely because he writes sonnets and wears a dress like a stage-player!"

"It is the weakness of the sex, my dear lord," said Lumley; "they like to patronise, and they dote upon all oddities, from China monsters to cracked poets. But I fancy, by a restless glance cast every now and then around the room, that my beautiful cousin has in her something of the coquette."

"There you are quite right, Lumley," returned Lord Saxingham, laughing; "but I will not quarrel with her for breaking hearts and refusing hands, if she do but grow steady at last, and settle into the Duchess of ——."

"Duchess of ——!" repeated Lumley, absently; "well, I will go and present myself. I see she is growing tired of the signor. I will sound her as to the ducal impressions, my dear lord."

"Do, *I* dare not," replied the father; "she is an excellent girl, but heiresses are always contradictory. It is very foolish to deprive me of all control over her fortune. Come and see me again soon, Lumley. I suppose you are going abroad?"

"No, I shall settle in England; but of my prospects and plans more hereafter."

With this, Lumley quietly glided away to Florence. There was something in Ferrers that was remarkable from its very simplicity. His clear, sharp features, with the short hair and high brow—the absolute plainness of his dress, and the noiseless, easy, self-collected calm of all his motions, made a strong contrast to the showy Italian, by whose side he now stood. Florence looked up at him with some little surprise at his intrusion.

"Ah, you don't recollect me!" said Lumley, with his pleasant laugh. "Faithless Imogen, after all your vows of constancy! Behold your Alonzo.

'The worms they crept in and the worms they crept out.'

Don't you remember how you trembled when I told you that true story, as we

'Conversed as we sat on the green!'"

"Oh!" cried Florence, "it is indeed you, my dear cousin—my dear Lumley! What an age since we parted!"

"Don't talk of age—it is an ugly word to a man of my years. Pardon, signor, if I disturb you."

And here Lumley, with a low bow, slid coolly into the place which Cesarini, who had shily risen, left vacant for him. Castruccio looked disconcerted: but Florence had forgotten him in her delight at seeing Lumley, and Cesarini moved discontentedly away, and seated himself at a distance.

"And I come back," continued Lumley, "to find you a confirmed beauty and a professional coquette—Don't blush!"

"Do they, indeed, call me a coquette?"

"Oh, yes—for once the world is just."

"Perhaps I do deserve the reproach. Oh, Lumley, how I despise all that I see and hear!"

"What, even the Duke of ——?"

"Yes, I fear even the Duke of —— is no exception!"

"Your father will go mad if he hear you."

"My father!—my poor father!—yes, he thinks the utmost that I, Florence Lascelles, am made for, is to wear a ducal coronet, and give the best balls in London."

"And, pray, what was Florence Lascelles made for?"

"Ah! I cannot answer the question. I fear for Discontent and Disdain."

"You are an enigma—but I will take pains and not rest till I solve you."

"I defy you."

"Thanks—better defy than despise."

"Oh, you must be strangely altered if I can despise *you*."

"Indeed! what do you remember of me?"

"That you were frank, bold, and therefore, I suppose, true!—that you shocked my aunts and my father, by your contempt for the vulgar hypocrisies of our conventional life. Oh, no! I cannot despise you."

Lumley raised his eyes to those of Florence—he gazed on her long and earnestly—ambitious hopes rose high within him.

"My fair cousin," said he, in an altered and serious tone, "I see something in your spirit kindred to mine; and I am glad that yours is one of the earliest voices which confirm my new resolves on my return to busy England!"

"And those resolves?"

"Are an Englishman's—energetic and ambitious."

"Alas, ambition! How many false portraits are there of the great original."

Lumley thought he had found a clue to the heart of his cousin, and began to expatiate with unusual eloquence on the nobleness of that daring sin which "lost angels heaven." Florence listened to him with attention, but not with sympathy. Lumley was deceived. His was not an ambition that could attract the fastidious but high-souled Idealist. The selfishness of his nature broke out in all the sentiments that he fancied would seem to her most elevated. Place —power—titles—all these objects were low and vulgar to one who saw them daily at her feet.

At a distance, the Duke of —— continued from time to time to direct his cold gaze at Florence. He did not like her the less for not seeming to court him. He had something generous within him, and could understand her. He went away at last, and thought seriously of Florence as a wife. Not a wife for companionship, for friendship, for love; but a wife who could take the trouble of rank off his hands—do him honour, and raise him an heir, whom he might flatter himself would be his own.

From his corner also, with dreams yet more vain and daring, Castruccio Cesarini cast his eyes upon the queen-like brow of the great heiress. Oh, yes, she had a soul—she could disdain rank and revere genius! What a triumph over De Montaigne—Maltravers —all the world, if he, the neglected poet, could win the hand for which the magnates of the earth sighed in vain! Pure and lofty as he thought himself, it was her birth and her wealth which Cesarini adored in Florence. And Lumley, nearer, perhaps, to the prize than either—yet still far off—went on conversing, with eloquent lips and sparkling eyes, while his cold heart was planning every word, dictating every glance, and laying out (for the most worldly are often the most visionary) the chart for a royal road to fortune. And Florence Lascelles, when the crowd had dispersed, and she sought her chamber, forgot all three; and with that morbid romance often peculiar to those for whom Fate smiles the most, mused over the ideal image of the one she *could* love—" in maiden meditation *not* fancy-free!"

CHAPTER IV.

"In mea vesanas habui dispendia vires,
Et valui pœnas fortis in ipse meas."*—OVID.

"Then might my breast be read within,
A thousand volumes would be written there."
—EARL OF STIRLING.

ERNEST MALTRAVERS was at the height of his reputation; the work which he had deemed the crisis that was to make or mar him was the most brilliantly successful of all he had yet committed to the public. Certainly, chance did as much for it as merit, as is usually the case with works that become instantaneously popular. We may hammer away at the casket with strong arm and good purpose, and all in vain; when some morning a careless stroke hits the right nail on the head, and we secure the treasure.

It was at this time, when in the prime of youth—rich, courted, respected, run after—that Ernest Maltravers fell seriously ill. It was no active or visible disease, but a general irritability of the nerves, and a languid sinking of the whole frame. His labours began, perhaps, to tell against him. In earlier life he had been as active as a hunter of the chamois, and the hardy exercise of his frame counteracted the effects of a restless and ardent mind. The change from an athletic to a sedentary habit of life —the wear and tear of the brain—the absorbing passion for knowledge which day and night kept all his faculties in a stretch, made strange havoc in a constitution naturally strong. The poor author! how few persons understand, and forbear with, and pity him! He sells his health and youth to a rugged taskmaster. And, oh blind and selfish world, you expect him to be as free

---

* I had the strength of a madman to my own cost, and employed that strength in my own punishment.

of manner, and as pleasant of cheer, and as equal of mood, as if he were passing the most agreeable and healthful existence that pleasure could afford to smooth the wrinkles of the mind, or medicine invent to regulate the nerves of the body! But there was, besides all this, another cause that operated against the successful man!—His heart was too solitary. He lived without the sweet household ties—the connections and amities he formed excited for a moment, but possessed no charm to comfort or to soothe. Cleveland resided so much in the country, and was of so much calmer a temperament, and so much more advanced in age, that with all the friendship that subsisted between them, there was none of that daily and familiar interchange of confidence which affectionate natures demand as the very food of life. Of his brother (as the reader will conjecture from never having been formally presented to him) Ernest saw but little. Colonel Maltravers, one of the gayest and handsomest men of his time, married to a fine lady, lived principally at Paris, except when, for a few weeks in the shooting season, he filled his country house with companions who had nothing in common with Ernest: the brothers corresponded regularly every quarter, and saw each other once a-year—this was all their intercourse. Ernest Maltravers stood in the world alone, with that cold but anxious spectre —Reputation.

It was late at night. Before a table covered with the monuments of erudition and thought sat a young man with a pale and worn countenance. The clock in the room told with a fretting distinctness every moment that lessened the journey to the grave. There was an anxious and expectant expression on the face of the student, and from time to time he glanced to the clock, and muttered to himself. Was it a letter from some adored mistress—the soothing flattery from some mighty arbiter of arts and letters—that the young man eagerly awaited? No; the aspirer was forgotten in the valetudinarian. Ernest Maltravers was waiting the visit of his physician, whom at that late hour a sudden thought had induced him to summon from his rest. At length the well-known knock was heard, and in a few moments the physician entered. He was one well versed in the peculiar pathology of book-men, and kindly as well as skilful.

"My dear Mr. Maltravers, what is this? How are we?—not seriously ill, I hope—no relapse—pulse low and irregular, I see, but no fever. You are nervous."

"Doctor," said the student, "I did not send for you at this time of night from the idle fear or fretful caprice of an invalid. But when I saw you this morning, you dropped some hints which have haunted me ever since. Much that it befits the conscience and the soul to attend to, without loss of time, depends upon my full knowledge of my real state. If I understand you rightly, I may have but a short time to live—is it so?"

"Indeed!" said the doctor, turning away his face; "you have exaggerated my meaning. I did not say that you were in what we technically call danger."

"Am I then likely to be a *long*-lived man?"

The doctor coughed—"That is uncertain, my dear young friend," said he, after a pause.

"Be plain with me. The plans of life must be based upon such calculations as we can reasonably form of its probable duration. Do not fancy that I am weak enough or coward enough to shrink from any abyss which I have approached unconsciously; I desire —I adjure—nay, I command you to be explicit."

There was an earnest and solemn dignity in his patient's voice and manner which deeply touched and impressed the good physician.

"I will answer you frankly," said he; "you over-work the nerves and the brain; if you do not relax, you will subject yourself to confirmed disease and premature death. For several months— perhaps for years to come—you should wholly cease from literary labour. Is this a hard sentence? You are rich and young—enjoy yourself while you can."

Maltravers appeared satisfied—changed the conversation—talked easily on other matters for a few minutes: nor was it till he had dismissed his physician that he broke forth with the thoughts that were burning in him.

"Oh!" cried he aloud, as he rose and paced the room with rapid strides; "now, when I see before me the broad and luminous path, am I to be condemned to halt and turn aside? A vast empire rises on my view, greater than that of Cæsars and conquerors—an empire durable and universal in the souls of men, that time itself cannot overthrow; and Death marches with me, side by side, and the skeleton hand waves me back to the nothingness of common men."

He paused at the casement—he threw it open, and leant forth and gasped for air. Heaven was serene and still, as morning came coldly forth amongst the waning stars, and the haunts of men, in their thoroughfare of idleness and of pleasure, were desolate and void. Nothing, save Nature, was awake.

"And if, O stars!" murmured Maltravers, from the depth of his excited heart—"if I have been insensible to your solemn beauty—if the heaven and the earth had been to me but as air and clay—if I were one of a dull and dim-eyed herd—I might live on, and drop into the grave from the ripeness of unprofitable years. It is because I yearn for the great objects of an immortal being, that life shrinks and shrivels up like a scroll. Away! I will not listen to these human and material monitors, and consider life as a thing greater than the things that I would live for. My choice is made; glory is more persuasive than the grave."

He turned impatiently from the casement—his eyes flashed—his chest heaved—he trod the chamber with a monarch's air. All the calculations of prudence, all the tame and methodical reasonings with which, from time to time, he had sought to sober down the impetuous man into the calm machine, faded away before the burst of awful and commanding passions that swept over his soul. Tell a man in the full tide of his triumphs that he bears death within him, and what crisis of thought can be more startling and more terrible!

Maltravers had, as we have seen, cared little for fame, till fame had been brought within his reach; then, with every step he took, new Alps had arisen. Each new conjecture brought to light a new truth that demanded enforcement or defence. Rivalry and competition chafed his blood, and kept his faculties at their full speed. He had the generous race-horse spirit of emulation. Ever in action ever in progress, cheered on by the sarcasms of foes even more than by the applause of friends, the desire of glory had become the habit of existence. When we have commenced a career, what stop is there till the grave?—where is the definite barrier of that ambition which, like the eastern bird, seems ever on the wing, and never rests upon the earth? Our names are not settled till our death; the ghosts of what we have done are made our haunting monitors—our scourging avengers—if ever we cease to do, or fall short of the younger past. Repose is oblivion; to pause is to unravel all the web that we have woven—until the tomb closes over us, and men, just when it is too late, strike the fair balance between ourselves and our rivals; and we are measured, not by the least, but by the greatest triumphs we have achieved. Oh, what a crushing sense of impotence comes over us, when we feel that our frame cannot support our mind—when the hand can no longer execute what the soul, actively as ever, conceives and desires!—the quick life tied to the dead form—the ideas fresh as immortality, gushing forth rich and golden, and the broken nerves, and the aching frame, and the weary eyes!—the spirit athirst for liberty and heaven—and the damning, choking consciousness that we are walled up and prisoned in a dungeon that must be our burial-place! Talk not of freedom—there is no such thing as freedom to a man whose body is the gaol, whose infirmities are the racks, of his genius!

Maltravers paused at last, and threw himself on his sofa, wearied and exhausted. Involuntarily, and as a half unconscious means of escaping from his conflicting and profitless emotions, he turned to several letters, which had for hours lain unopened on his table. Every one, the seal of which he broke, seemed to mock his state—every one seemed to attest the felicity of his fortunes. Some bespoke the admiring sympathy of the highest and the wisest—one offered him a brilliant opening into public life—another (it was from Cleveland) was fraught with all the proud and rapturous approbation of a prophet whose auguries are at last fulfilled. At that letter Maltravers sighed deeply, and paused before he turned to the others. The last he opened was in an unknown hand, nor was the name affixed to it. Like all writers of some note, Maltravers was in the habit of receiving anonymous letters of praise, censure, warning, and exhortation—especially from young ladies at boarding-schools, and old ladies in the country; but there was that in the first sentences of the letter, which he now opened with a careless hand, that rivetted his attention. It was a small and beautiful handwriting, yet the letters were more clear and bold than they usually are in feminine caligraphy.

"Ernest Maltravers," began this singular effusion, "have you weighed yourself?—are you aware of your capacities?—do you feel that for you there may be a more dazzling reputation than that which appears to content you? You who seem to penetrate into the subtlest windings of the human heart, and to have examined nature as through a glass—you, whose thoughts stand forth like armies marshalled in defence of truth, bold and dauntless, and without a stain upon their glittering armour;—are you, at your age, and with your advantages, to bury yourself amidst books and scrolls? Do you forget that action is the grand career of men who think as you do? Will this word-weighing and picture-writing—the cold eulogies of pedants—the listless praises of literary idlers, content all the yearnings of your ambition? You were not made solely for the closet; 'The Dreams of Pindus, and the Aonian Maids' cannot endure through the noon of manhood. You are too practical for the mere poet, and too poetical to sink into the dull tenor of a learned life. I have never seen you, yet I know you—I read your spirit in your page; that aspiration for something better and greater than the great and the good, which colours all your passionate revelations of yourself and others—cannot be satisfied merely by ideal images. You cannot be contented, as poets and historians mostly are, by becoming great only from delineating great men, or imagining great events, or describing a great era. Is it not worthier of you to *be* what you fancy or relate? Awake, Maltravers, awake! Look into your heart, and feel your proper destinies. And who am I that thus address you?—a woman whose soul is filled with you—a woman, in whom your eloquence has awakened, amidst frivolous and vain circles, the sense of a new existence—a woman who would make you yourself the embodied ideal of your own thoughts and dreams, and who would ask from earth no other lot than that of following you on the road of fame with the eyes of her heart. Mistake me not; I repeat that I have never seen you, nor do I wish it; you might be other than I imagine, and I should lose an idol, and be left without a worship. I am a kind of visionary Rosicrucian : it is a spirit that I adore, and not a being like myself. You imagine, perhaps, that I have some purpose to serve in this—I have no object in administering to your vanity; and, if I judge you rightly, this letter is one that might make you vain without a blush. Oh, the admiration that does not spring from holy and profound sources of emotion—how it saddens us or disgusts! I have had my share of vulgar homage, and it only makes me feel doubly alone. I am richer than you are—I have youth—I have what they call beauty. And neither riches, youth, nor beauty ever gave me the silent and deep happiness I experience when I think of you. This is a worship that might, I repeat, well make even you vain. Think of these words, I implore you. Be worthy, not of my thoughts, but of the shape in which they represent you; and every ray of glory that surrounds you will brighten my own way, and inspire me with a kindred emulation. Farewell.—I may write to you again, but you will never discover me; and in life I pray that we may never meet!"

CHAPTER V.

"Our list of nobles next let Amri grace."
—*Absalom and Achitophel.*

"Sine me vacivum tempus ne quod dem mihi Laboris." *—Ter.

"I CAN'T think," said one of a group of young men, loitering by the steps of a club-house in St. James's Street—"I can't think what has chanced to Maltravers. Do you observe (as he walks—there—the other side of the way) how much he is altered? He stoops like an old man, and hardly ever lifts his eyes from the ground. He certainly seems sick and sad!"

"Writing books, I suppose."

"Or privately married."

"Or growing too rich—rich men are always unhappy beings."

"Ha, Ferrers, how are you?"

"So—so! What's the news?" replied Lumley.

"Rattler pays forfeit."

"Oh, but in politics?"

"Hang politics!—are you turned politician?"

"At my age what else is there left to do?"

"I thought so by your hat; all politicians sport odd-looking hats: it is very remarkable, but that is the great symptom of the disease."

"My hat—*is* it odd?" said Ferrers, taking off the commodity in question, and seriously regarding it.

"Why, who ever saw such a brim?"

"Glad you think so."

"Why, Ferrers?"

"Because it is a prudent policy in this country to surrender something trifling up to ridicule. If people can abuse your hat, or your carriage, or the shape of your nose, or a wart on your chin, they let slip a thousand more important matters. 'Tis the wisdom of the camel-driver, who gives up his gown for the camel to trample on, that he may escape himself."

"How droll you are, Ferrers! Well, I shall turn in and read the papers; and you——"

* Suffer me to employ my spare time in some kind of labour.

"Shall pay my visits, and rejoice in my hat."

"Good day to you; by-the-by, your friend, Maltravers, has just passed, looking thoughtful, and talking to himself! What's the matter with him?"

"Lamenting, perhaps, that he, too, does not wear an odd hat for gentlemen like you to laugh at, and leave the rest of him in peace. Good day."

On went Ferrers, and soon found himself in the Mall of the Park. Here he was joined by Mr. Templeton.

"Well, Lumley," said the latter (and it may be here remarked, that Mr. Templeton now exhibited towards his nephew a greater respect of manner and tone that he had thought it necessary to observe before)—"well, Lumley, and have you seen Lord Saxingham?"

"I have, sir; and I regret to say——"

"I thought so—I thought it," interrupted Templeton; "no gratitude in public men—no wish, in high place, to honour virtue!"

"Pardon me; Lord Saxingham declares that he should be delighted to forward your views—that no man more deserves a peerage; but that——"

"Oh, yes; always '*buts!*'"

"But that there are so many claimants at present whom it is impossible to satisfy; and—and—but I feel I ought not to go on."

"Proceed, sir, I beg."

"Why, then, Lord Saxingham is (I must be frank) a man who has a great regard for his own family. Your marriage (a source, my dear uncle, of the greatest gratification to *me*) cuts off the probable chance of your fortune and title, if you acquire the latter, descending to——"

"Yourself!" put in Templeton, drily. "Your relation seems, for the first time, to have discovered how dear your interests are to him."

"For me, individually, sir, my relation does not care a rush—but he cares a great deal for any member of his house being rich and in high station. It increases the range and credit of his connections; and Lord Saxingham is a man whom connections help to keep great. To be plain with you, he will not stir in this business, because he does not see how his kinsman is to be benefited, or his house strengthened."

"Public virtue!" exclaimed Templeton.

"Virtue, my dear uncle, is a female: as long as she is private property, she is excellent; but Public Virtue, like any other public lady, is a common prostitute."

"Pshaw!" grunted Templeton, who was too much out of humour to read his nephew the lecture he might otherwise have done upon the impropriety of his simile; for Mr. Templeton was one of those men who hold it vicious to talk of vice as existing in the world; he was very much shocked to hear anything called by its proper name.

"Has not Mrs. Templeton some connections that may be useful to you?"

"No, sir!" cried the uncle, in a voice of thunder.

"Sorry to hear it—but we cannot expect all things; you have married for love—you have a happy home, a charming wife—this is better than a title and a fine lady."

"Mr. Lumley Ferrers, you must spare me your consolations. My wife——"

"Loves you dearly, I dare say," said the imperturbable nephew. "She has so much sentiment, is so fond of poetry. Oh, yes, she must love one who has done so much for her."

"Done so much; what do you mean?"

"Why, with your fortune—your station—your just ambition—you, who might have married any one—nay, by remaining unmarried, have conciliated all my interested, selfish relations, hang them—you have married a lady without connections—and what more could you do for her?"

"Pooh, pooh; you don't know all."

Here Templeton stopped short, as if about to say too much, and frowned; then, after a pause, he resumed, "Lumley, I have married, it is true. You may not be my heir, but I will make it up to you—that is, if you deserve my affection."

"My dear unc——"

"Don't interrupt me, I have projects for you. Let our interests be the same. The title may yet descend to you. I may have no male offspring—meanwhile, draw on me to any reasonable amount—young men have expenses—but be prudent, and if you want to get on in the world, never let the world detect you in a scrape. There, leave me now."

"My best, my heartfelt thanks!"

"Hush—sound Lord Saxingbam again; I must and will have this bauble—I have set my heart on it." So saying, Templeton waved away his nephew, and musingly pursued his path towards

Hyde Park Corner, where his carriage awaited him. As soon as he entered his demesnes, he saw his wife's daughter running across the lawn to greet him. His heart softened; he checked the carriage and descended; he caressed her, he played with her, he laughed as she laughed. No parent could be more fond.

"Lumley Ferrers has talent to do me honour," said he, anxiously, "but his principles seem unstable. However, surely that open manner is the sign of a good heart!"

Meanwhile, Ferrers, in high spirits, took his way to Ernest's house. His friend was not at home, but Ferrers never wanted a host's presence in order to be at home himself. Books were round him in abundance, but Ferrers was not one of those who read for amusement. He threw himself into an easy-chair, and began weaving new meshes of ambition and intrigue. At length the door opened, and Maltravers entered.

"Why, Ernest, how ill you are looking!"

"I have not been well, but I am now recovering. As physicians recommend change of air to ordinary patients—so I am about to try change of habit. Active I must be—action is the condition of my being; but I must have done with books for the present. You see me in a new character."

"How?"

"That of a public man—I have entered parliament."

"You astonish me!—I have read the papers this morning. I see not even a vacancy, much less an election."

"It's all managed by the lawyer and the banker. In other words, my seat is a close borough."

"No bore of constituents. I congratulate you, and envy. I wish I were in parliament myself."

"You! I never fancied you bitten by the political mania."

"Political!—no. But it is the most respectable way, with luck, of living on the public. Better than swindling."

"A candid way of viewing the question. But I thought at one time you were half a Benthamite, and that your motto was, 'The greatest happiness of the greatest number.'"

"The greatest number to me is number *one*. I agree with the Pythagoreans—unity is the perfect principle of creation! Seriously, how can you mistake the principles of opinion for the principles of conduct? I am a Benthamite, a benevolist, as a logician—but the moment I leave the closet for the world, I lay aside speculation for others, and act for myself."

"You are, at least, more frank than prudent in these confessions."

"There you are wrong. It is by affecting to be worse than we are that we become popular—and we get credit for being both honest and practical fellows. My uncle's mistake is to be a hypocrite in words: it rarely answers. Be frank in words, and nobody will suspect hypocrisy in your designs."

Maltravers gazed hard at Ferrers—something revolted and displeased his high-wrought Platonism in the easy wisdom of his old friend. But he felt, almost for the first time, that Ferrers was a man to get on in the world—and he sighed;—I hope it was for the world's sake.

After a short conversation on indifferent matters, Cleveland was announced; and Ferrers, who could make nothing out of Cleveland, soon withdrew. Ferrers was now becoming an economist in his time.

"My dear Maltravers," said Cleveland, when they were alone, "I am so glad to see you; for, in the first place, I rejoice to find you are extending your career of usefulness."

"Usefulness—ah, let me think so! Life is so uncertain and so short, that we cannot too soon bring the little it can yield into the great commonwealth of the Beautiful or the Honest; and both belong to and make up the useful. But in politics, and in a highly artificial state, what doubts beset us! what darkness surrounds! If we connive at abuses, we juggle with our own reason and integrity—if we attack them, how much, how fatally we may derange that solemn and conventional ORDER which is the mainspring of the vast machine! How little, too, can one man, whose talents may not be in that coarse road—in that mephitic atmosphere—be enabled to effect!"

"He may effect a vast deal even without eloquence or labour:—he may effect a vast deal, if he can set one example, amidst a crowd of selfish aspirants and heated fanatics, of an honest and dispassionate man. He may effect more, if he may serve among the representatives of that hitherto unrepresented thing—Literature; if he redeem, by an ambition above place and emolument, the character for subservience that court-poets have obtained for letters—if he may prove that speculative knowledge is not disjoined from the practical world, and maintain the dignity of disinterestedness that should belong to learning. But the end of a scientific morality is not to serve others only, but also to perfect and accomplish our individual selves; our own souls are a solemn trust to our own lives.

You are about to add to your experience of human motives and active men; and whatever additional wisdom you acquire will become equally evident and equally useful, no matter whether it be communicated through action or in books. Enough of this, my dear Ernest. I have come to dine with you, and make you accompany me to-night to a house where you will be welcome, and I think interested. Nay, no excuses. I have promised Lord Latimer that he shall make your acquaintance, and he is one of the most eminent men with whom political life will connect you."

And to this change of habits, from the closet to the senate, had Maltravers been induced by a state of health, which, with most men, would have been an excuse for indolence. Indolent he could not be; he had truly said to Ferrers, that "action was the condition of his being." If THOUGHT, with its fever and aching tension, had been too severe a task-master on the nerves and brain, the coarse and homely pursuit of practical politics would leave the imagination and intellect in repose, while it would excite the hardier qualities and gifts, which animate without exhausting. So, at least, hoped Maltravers. He remembered the profound saying in one of his favourite German authors, "that to keep the mind and body in perfect health, it is necessary to mix habitually and betimes in the common affairs of men." And the anonymous correspondent;—had her exhortations any influence on his decision? I know not. But when Cleveland left him, Maltravers unlocked his desk, and re-perused the last letter he had received from the Unknown. The *last* letter!—yes, those epistles had now become frequent.

CHAPTER VI.

. . . . " Le brillant de votre esprit donne un si grand éclat à votre teint et à vos yeux, que quoiqu'il semble que l'esprit ne doit toucher que les oreilles, il est pourtant certain que la vôtre éblouit les yeux."—*Lettres de Madame de Sévigné.**

AT Lord Latimer's house were assembled some hundreds of those persons who are rarely found together in London society: for business, politics, and literature draught off the most eminent men, and usually leave to houses that receive the

---

* The brilliance of your wit gives so great a lustre to your complexion and your eyes, that though it seems that wit should only reach the ears, it is together certain that yours dazzles the eyes.

world little better than indolent rank or ostentatious wealth. Even the young men of pleasure turn up their noses at parties now-a-days, and find society a bore. But there are some dozen or two of houses, the owners of which are both apart from and above the fashion, in which a foreigner may see, collected under the same roof, many of the most remarkable men of busy, thoughtful, majestic England. Lord Latimer himself had been a cabinet minister. He retired from public life on pretence of ill-health; but, in reality, because its anxious bustle was not congenial to a gentle and accomplished, but somewhat feeble, mind. With a high reputation and an excellent cook, he enjoyed a great popularity, both with his own party and the world in general; and he was the centre of a small, but distinguished, circle of acquaintance, who drank Latimer's wine, and quoted Latimer's sayings, and liked Latimer much better, because, not being author or minister, he was not in their way.

Lord Latimer received Maltravers with marked courtesy, and even deference, and invited him to join his own whist-table, which was one of the highest compliments his lordship could pay to his intellect. But when his guest refused the proffered honour, the earl turned him over to the countess, as having become the property of the womankind; and was soon immersed in his aspirations for the odd trick.

While Maltravers was conversing with Lady Latimer, he happened to raise his eyes, and saw opposite to him a young lady of such remarkable beauty, that he could scarcely refrain from an admiring exclamation. "And who," he asked, recovering himself, "is that lady? It is strange that even I, who go so little into the world, should be compelled to inquire the name of one whose beauty must already have made her celebrated."

"Oh, Lady Florence Lascelles—she came out last year. She is, indeed, most brilliant, yet more so in mind and accomplishments than face. I must be allowed to introduce you."

At this offer, a strange shyness, and as it were reluctant distrust, seized Maltravers—a kind of presentiment of danger and evil. He drew back, and would have made some excuse, but Lady Latimer did not heed his embarrassment, and was already by the side of Lady Florence Lascelles. A moment more, and beckoning to Maltravers, the countess presented him to the lady. As he bowed and seated himself beside his new acquaintance, he could not but observe that her cheeks were suffused with the most lively blushes, and that she received him with a confusion not common even in ladies just brought out, and just introduced to "a lion." He was rather puzzled than flattered by these tokens of an embarrassment somewhat akin to his own; and the first few sentences of their conversation passed off with a certain awkwardness and reserve. At this moment, to the surprise, perhaps to the relief, of Ernest, they were joined by Lumley Ferrers.

"Ah, Lady Florence, I kiss your hands—I am charmed to find you acquainted with my friend Maltravers."

"And Mr. Ferrers, what makes him so late to-night?" asked the fair Florence, with a sudden ease which rather startled Maltravers.

"A dull dinner, *voilà tout!*—I have no other excuse." And Ferrers, sliding into a vacant chair on the other side of Lady Florence, conversed volubly and unceasingly, as if seeking to monopolise her attention.

Ernest had not been so much captivated with the manner of Florence as he had been struck with her beauty, and now, seeing her apparently engaged with another, he rose and quietly moved away. He was soon one of a knot of men who were conversing on the absorbing topics of the day; and as by degrees the exciting subject brought out his natural eloquence and masculine sense, the talkers became listeners, the knot widened into a circle, and he himself was unconsciously the object of general attention and respect.

"And what think you of Mr. Maltravers?" asked Ferrers, carelessly; "does he keep up your expectations?"

Lady Florence had sunk into a reverie, and Ferrers repeated his question.

"He is younger than I imagined him—and—and—"

"Handsomer, I suppose, you mean."

"No! calmer and less animated."

"He seems animated enough now," said Ferrers; "but your lady-like conversation failed in striking the Promethean spark. 'Lay that flattering unction to your soul.'"

"Ay, you are right—he must have thought me very——"

"Beautiful, no doubt."

"Beautiful!—I hate the word, Lumley. I wish I were not handsome—I might then get some credit for my intellect."

"Humph!" said Ferrers, significantly.

"Oh, you don't think so, sceptic," said Florence, shaking her head with a slight laugh, and an altered manner.

"Does it matter what *I* think," said Ferrers, with an attempted touch at the sentimental, "when Lord This, and Lord That, and Mr. So-and-So, and Count What-d'ye-call-him, are all making their way to you, to dispossess me of my envied monopoly?"

While Ferrers spoke, several of the scattered loungers grouped around Florence, and the conversation, of which she was the cynosure, became animated and gay. Oh, how brilliant she was, that peerless Florence!—with what petulant and sparkling grace came wit and wisdom, and even genius, from those ruby lips! Even the assured Ferrers felt his subtle intellect as dull and coarse to hers, and shrank with a reluctant apprehension from the arrows of her careless and prodigal repartees. For there was a scorn in the nature of Florence Lascelles which made her wit pain more frequently than it pleased. Educated even to learning—courageous even to a want of feminacy—she delighted to sport with ignorance and pretension, even in the highest places; and the laugh that she excited was like lightning—no one could divine where next it might fall.

But Florence, though dreaded and unloved, was yet courted, flattered, and the rage. For this there was two reasons; first, she was a coquette, and secondly, she was an heiress.

Thus the talkers in the room were divided into two principal groups, over one of which Maltravers may be said to have presided; over the other, Florence. As the former broke up, Ernest was joined by Cleveland.

"My dear cousin," said Florence, suddenly, and in a whisper, as she turned to Lumley, "your friend is speaking of me—I see it. Go, I implore you, and let me know what he says!"

"The commission is not flattering," said Ferrers, almost sullenly.

"Nay, a commission to gratify a woman's curiosity is ever one of the most flattering embassies with which we can invest an able negotiator."

"Well, I must do your bidding, though I disown the favour." Ferrers moved away and joined Cleveland and Maltravers.

"She is, indeed, beautiful: so perfect a contour I never beheld; she is the only woman I ever saw in whom the aquiline features seem more classical than even the Greek."

"So, that is your opinion of my fair cousin!" cried Ferrers; "you are caught."

"I wish he were," said Cleveland. "Ernest is now old enough to settle, and there is not a more dazzling prize in England—rich, high-born, lovely, and accomplished."

"And what say you?" asked Lumley, almost impatiently, to Maltravers.

"That I never saw one whom I admire more or could love less," replied Ernest, as he quitted the rooms.

Ferrers looked after him, and muttered to himself; he then rejoined Florence, who presently rose to depart, and taking Lumley's arm, said, "Well, I see my father is looking round for me—and so for once I will forestall him. Come, Lumley, let us join him; I know he wants to see you."

"Well," said Florence, blushing deeply, and almost breathless, as they crossed the now half-empty apartments.

"Well, my cousin?"

"You provoke me—well, then, what said your friend?"

"That you deserved your reputation of beauty, but that you were not his style. Maltravers is in love, you know."

"In love!"

"Yes, a pretty Frenchwoman! quite romantic—an attachment of some years' standing."

Florence turned away her face, and said no more.

"That's a good fellow, Lumley," said Lord Saxingham; "Florence is never more welcome to my eyes than at half-past one o'clock A.M., when I associate her with thoughts of my natural rest, and my unfortunate carriage-horses. By-the-by, I wish you would dine with me next Saturday."

"Saturday: unfortunately, I am engaged to my uncle."

"Oh, he has behaved handsomely to you?"

"Yes."

"Mrs. Templeton pretty well?"

"I fancy so."

"As ladies wish to be, etc.?" whispered his lordship.

"No, thank heaven!"

"Well, if the old man could but make you his heir, we might think twice about the title."

"My dear lord, stop! one favour—write me a line to hint that delicately."

"No—no letters; letters always get into the papers."

"But cautiously worded—no danger of publication, on my honour."

"I'll think of it. Good night."

BOOK VII.

CHAPTER I.

"Deceit is the strong but subtile chain which runs through all the members of a society, and links them together; trick or be tricked, is the alternative; 'tis the way of the world, and without it intercourse would drop."—*Anonymous writer of* 1722.

"A lovely child she was, of looks serene,
And motions which o'er things indifferent shed
The grace and gentleness from whence they came."
                                                    PERCY BYSSHE SHELLEY.

"His years but young, but his experience old."—SHAKESPEARE.

"He after honour hunts, I after love."—*Ibid.*

LUMLEY FERRERS was one of the few men in the world who act upon a profound, deliberate, and organised system —he had done so even from a boy. When he was twenty-one he had said to himself, "Youth is the season for enjoyment: the triumphs of manhood, the wealth of age, do not compensate for a youth spent in unpleasurable toils." Agreeably to this maxim, he had resolved not to adopt any profession; and being fond of travel, and of a restless temper, he had indulged abroad in all the gratifications that his moderate income could afford him: that income went farther on the Continent than at home, which was another reason for the prolongation of his travels. Now, when the whims and passions of youth were sated; and, ripened by a consummate and various knowledge of mankind, his harder capacities of mind became developed and centred into such ambition as it was his nature to conceive, he acted no less upon a regular and methodical plan of conduct, which he carried into details. He had little or nothing within himself to cross his old theories by contradictory practice; for he was curbed by no principles, and regulated but by few tastes: and our tastes are often checks as powerful as our principles. Looking round the English world, Ferrers saw that at his age, and with an equivocal position, and no chances to throw away, it was necessary that he should cast off all attributes of the character of the wanderer and the *garçon*.

"There is nothing respectable in lodgings and a cab," said Ferrers to himself—that "*self*" was his grand confidant!—"nothing stationary. Such are the appliances of a here-to-day-gone-to-morrow kind of life. One never looks substantial till one pays rates and taxes, and has a bill with one's butcher!"

Accordingly, without saying a word to anybody, Ferrers took a long lease of a large house, in one of those quiet streets that proclaim the owners do not wish to be made by fashionable situations—streets in which, if you have a large house, it is supposed to be because you can afford one. He was very particular in its being a respectable street—Great George Street, Westminster, was the one he selected.

No frippery or baubles, common to the mansions of young bachelors—no buhl, and marquetrie, and Sévres china, and cabinet pictures, distinguished the large, dingy drawing-rooms of Lumley Ferrers. He bought all the old furniture a bargain of the late tenant—tea-coloured chintz curtains, and chairs, and sofas that were venerable and solemn with the accumulated dust of twenty-five years. The only things about which he was particular were a very long dining-table that would hold four-and-twenty, and a new mahogany sideboard. Somebody asked him why he cared about such articles. "I don't know," said he, "but I observe all respectable family-men do—there must be something in it—I shall discover the secret by-and-by."

In this house did Mr. Ferrers ensconce himself with two middle-aged maid-servants, and a man out of livery, whom he chose from a host of candidates, because the man looked especially well-fed.

Having thus settled himself, and told every one that the lease of his house was for sixty-three years, Lumley Ferrers made a little calculation of his probable expenditure, which he found, with good management, might be about one-fourth more than his income.

"I shall take the surplus out of my capital," said he, "and try the experiment for five years; if it don't do, and pay me profitably, why, then, either men are not to be lived upon, or Lumley Ferrers is much duller dog than he thinks himself!"

Mr. Ferrers had deeply studied the character of his uncle, as a prudent speculator studies the qualities of a mine in which he means to invest his capital, and much of his present proceedings was intended to act upon the uncle as well as upon the world. He saw that the more he could obtain for himself, not a noisy, social, fashionable reputation, but a good, sober, substantial one, the more highly Mr. Templeton would consider him, and the more likely he was to be made his uncle's heir—that is, provided Mrs. Templeton did not supersede the nepotal parasite by indigenous olive-branches. This last apprehension died away as time passed, and no signs of fertility appeared. And, accordingly, Ferrers thought he might prudently hazard more upon the game on which he now ventured to rely. There was one thing, however, that greatly disturbed his peace; Mr. Templeton, though harsh and austere in his manner to his wife, was evidently attached to her; and, above all, he cherished the fondest affection for his daughter-in-law. He was as anxious for her health, her education, her little childish enjoyments, as if he had been not only her parent, but a very doting one. He could not bear her to be crossed or thwarted. Mr. Templeton, who had never spoiled anything before, not even an old pen (so careful, and calculating, and methodical was he), did his best to spoil this beautiful child, whom he could not even have the vain luxury of thinking he had produced to the admiring world. Softly, exquisitely lovely was that little girl; and every day she increased in the charm of her person, and in the caressing fascination of her childish ways. Her temper was so sweet and docile, that fondness and petting, however injudiciously exhibited, only seemed yet more to bring out the colours of a grateful and tender nature. Perhaps the measured kindness of more reserved affection might have been the true way of spoiling one whose instincts were all for exacting and returning love. She was a plant that suns less warm might have nipped and chilled. But beneath an uncapricious and unclouded sunshine she sprang up in a luxurious bloom of heart and sweetness of disposition.

Every one, even those who did not generally like children, delighted in this charming creature, excepting only Mr. Lumley Ferrers. But that gentleman, less mild than Pope's Narcissa,

"To make a wash, had gladly stowed the child!"

He had seen how very common it is for a rich man, married late in life, to leave everything to a young widow and her children by her former marriage, when once attached to the latter; and he sensibly felt that he himself had but a slight hold over Templeton by the chain of the affections. He resolved, therefore, as much as possible, to alienate his uncle from his young wife; trusting, that as the influence of the wife was weakened, that of the child would be lessened also; and to raise in Templeton's vanity and ambition an ally that might supply to himself the want of love. He pursued his twofold scheme with masterly art and address. He first sought to secure the confidence and regard of the melancholy and gentle mother; and in this—for she was peculiarly unsuspicious and inexperienced—he obtained signal and complete success. His frankness of manner, his deferential attention, the art with which he warded off from her the spleen or ill-humour of Mr. Templeton, the cheerfulness that his easy gaiety threw over a very gloomy house, made the poor lady hail his visits and trust in his friendship. Perhaps she was glad of any interruption to *tête-à-têtes* with a severe and ungenial husband, who had no sympathy for the sorrows, of whatever nature they might be, which preyed upon her, and who made it a point of morality to find fault wherever he could.

The next step in Lumley's policy was to arm Templeton's vanity against his wife, by constantly refreshing his consciousness of the sacrifices he had made by marriage, and the certainty that he would have attained all his wishes had he chosen more prudently. By perpetually, but most judiciously, rubbing this sore point, he, as it were, fixed the irritability into Templeton's constitution, and it reacted on all his thoughts, aspiring or domestic. Still, however, to Lumley's great surprise and resentment, while Templeton cooled to his wife, he only warmed to her child. Lumley had not calculated enough upon the thirst and craving for affection in most human hearts; and Templeton, though not exactly an amiable man, had some excellent qualities; if he had less sensitively regarded the opinion of the world, he would neither have contracted the vocabulary of cant, nor sickened for a peerage—both his affectation of saintship, and his gnawing desire of rank, arose from an extraordinary and morbid deference to opinion, and a wish for worldly honours and respect, which he felt that his mere talents could not secure to him. But he was, at bottom, a kindly man—charitable to the poor, considerate to his servants, and had within him the want to love and be loved, which is one of the desires wherewith the atoms of the universe are cemented and harmonised.

Had Mrs. Templeton evinced *love* to *him*, he might have defied all Lumley's diplomacy, been consoled for worldly disadvantages, and been a good and even uxorious husband. But she evidently did not love him, though an admirable, patient, provident wife; and her daughter *did* love him—love him as well even as she loved her mother; and the hard worldling would not have accepted a kingdom as the price of that little fountain of pure and ever-refreshing tenderness. Wise and penetrating as Lumley was, he never could thoroughly understand this weakness, as he called it; for we never know men entirely, unless we have complete sympathies with men in all their natural emotions; and Nature had left the workmanship of Lumley Ferrers unfinished and incomplete, by denying him the possibility of caring for anything but himself.

His plan for winning Templeton's esteem and deference was, however, completely triumphant. He took care that nothing in his *ménage* should appear "*extravagant;*" all was sober, quiet, and well-regulated. He declared that he had so managed as to live within his income; and Templeton receiving no hint for money, nor aware that Ferrers had on the Continent consumed a considerable portion of his means, believed him. Ferrers gave a great many dinners, but he did not go on that foolish plan which has been laid down by persons who pretend to know life, as a means of popularity —he did not profess to give dinners better than other people. He knew that, unless you are a very rich or a very great man, no folly is equal to that of thinking that you soften the hearts of your friends by soups *à la bisque*, and Johannisberg at a guinea a bottle ! They all go away saying, "What right has that d—d fellow to give a better dinner than we do? What horrid taste! What ridiculous presumption!"

No; though Ferrers himself was a most scientific epicure, and held the luxury of the palate at the highest possible price, he dieted his friends on what he termed "*respectable* fare." His cook put plenty of flour into the oyster sauce; cod's-head and shoulders made his invariable fish; and four *entrées*, without flavour or pretence, were duly supplied by the pastry-cook, and carefully eschewed by the host. Neither did Mr. Ferrers affect to bring about him gay wits and brilliant talkers. He confined himself to men of substantial consideration, and generally took care to be himself the cleverest person present; while he turned the conversation on serious matters crammed for the occasion—politics, stocks, commerce, and the criminal code. Pruning his gaiety, though he retained his frankness, be sought to be known as a highly-informed, painstaking man, who would be sure to rise. His connections, and a certain nameless charm about him, consisting chiefly in a pleasant countenance, a bold yet winning candour, and the absence of all *hauteur* or pretence, enabled him to assemble round this plain table, which, if it gratified no taste, wounded no self-love, a sufficient number of public men of rank, and eminent men of business, to answer his purpose. The situation he had chosen, so near the Houses of Parliament, was convenient to politicians, and, by degrees, the large dingy drawing-rooms became a frequent resort for public men to talk over those thousand underplots by which a party is served or attacked. Thus, though not in parliament himself, Ferrers became insensibly associated with parliamentary men and things; and the ministerial party, whose politics he espoused, praised him highly, made use of him, and meant to do something for him.

While the career of this able and unprincipled man thus opened —and of course the opening was not made in a day—Ernest Maltravers was ascending, by a rough, thorny, and encumbered path, to that eminence on which the monuments of men are built. His success in public life was not brilliant nor sudden. For, though he had eloquence and knowledge, he disdained all oratorical devices; and though he had passion and energy, he could scarcely be called a warm partisan. He met with much envy, and many obstacles; and the gracious and buoyant sociality of temper and manners that had, in early youth, made him the idol of his contemporaries at school or college, had long since faded away into a cold, settled, and lofty, though gentle reserve, which did not attract towards him the animal spirits of the herd. But though he spoke seldom, and heard many, with half his powers, more enthusiastically cheered, he did not fail of commanding attention and respect; and though no darling of cliques and parties, yet in that great body of the people who were ever the audience and tribunal to which, in letters or in politics, Maltravers appealed, there was silently growing up, and spreading wide, a belief in his upright intentions, his unpurchasable honour, and his correct and well-considered views. He felt that his name was safely invested, though the return for the capital was slow and moderate. He was contented to abide his time.

Every day he grew more attached to that only true philosophy which makes a man, as far as the world will permit, a world to himself; and from the height of a tranquil and serene self-esteem, he felt the sun shine above him, when malignant clouds spread sullen and ungenial below. He did not despise or wilfully shock opinion, neither did he fawn upon and flatter it. Where he thought the world should be humoured, he humoured—where contemned, he contemned it. There are many cases in which an honest, well-educated high-hearted individual is a much better judge than the multitude of what is right and what is wrong; and in these matters he is not worth three straws if he suffer the multitude to bully or coax him out of his judgment. The Public, if you indulge it, is a most damnable gossip, thrusting its nose into people's concerns, where it has no right to make or meddle; and in those things, where the Public is impertinent, Maltravers scorned and resisted its interference as haughtily as he would the interference of any insolent member of the insolent whole. It was this mixture of deep love and profound respect for the eternal PEOPLE, and of calm, passionless disdain for that capricious charlatan, the momentary PUBLIC, which made Ernest Maltravers an original and solitary thinker; and an actor, in reality modest and benevolent, in appearance arrogant and unsocial. "Pauperism, in contradistinction to poverty," he was wont to say, "is the dependence upon other people for existence, not on our own exertions; there is a moral pauperism in the man who is dependent on others for that support of moral life—self-respect."

Wrapped in this philosophy, he pursued his haughty and lonesome way, and felt that in the deep heart of mankind, when prejudices and envies should die off, there would be a sympathy with his motives and his career. So far as his own health was concerned, the experiment had answered. No mere drudgery of business—late hours and dull speeches—can produce the dread exhaustion which follows the efforts of the soul to mount into the higher air of severe thought or intense imagination. Those faculties which had been overstrained now lay fallow—and the frame rapidly regained its tone. Of private comfort and inspiration Ernest knew but little. He gradually grew estranged from his old friend Ferrers, as their habits became opposed. Cleveland lived more and more in the country, and was too well satisfied with his quondam pupil's course of life and progressive reputation to trouble him with exhortation or advice. Cesarini had grown a literary lion, whose genius was vehemently lauded by all the reviews—on the same principle as that which induces us to praise foreign singers or dead men— we must praise something, and we don't like to praise those who jostle ourselves. Cesarini had therefore grown prodigiously conceited—swore that England was the only country for true merit,

and no longer concealed his jealous anger at the wider celebrity of
Maltravers. Ernest saw him squandering away his substance, and
prostituting his talents to drawing-room trifles, with a compassionate
sigh. He sought to warn him, but Cesarini listened to him with
such impatience that he resigned the office of monitor. He wrote
to De Montaigne, who succeeded no better. Cesarini was bent on
playing his own game. And to one game, without a metaphor, he
had at last come. His cravings for excitement vented itself at
Hazard, and his remaining guineas melted daily away.

But De Montaigne's letters to Maltravers consoled him for the
loss of less congenial friends. The Frenchman was now an eminent
and celebrated man; and his appreciation of Maltravers was sweeter
to the latter than would have been the huzzas of crowds. But, all
this while, his vanity was pleased and his curiosity roused by the
continued correspondence of his unseen Egeria. That correspondence (if so it may be called, being all on one side) had now gone on
for a considerable time, and he was still wholly unable to discover
the author: its tone had of late altered—it had become more sad
and subdued—it spoke of the hollowness as well as the rewards of
fame; and, with a touch of true womanly sentiment, often hinted
more at the rapture of soothing dejection, than of sharing triumph.
In all these letters there was the undeniable evidence of high
intellect and deep feeling; they excited a strong and keen interest
in Maltravers, yet the interest was not that which made him wish
to discover, in order that he might love, the writer. They were for
the most part too full of the irony and bitterness of a *man's* spirit,
to fascinate one who considered that gentleness was the essence of
a woman's strength. *Temper* spoke in them, no less than mind and
heart, and it was not the sort of temper which a man who loves
women to be womanly could admire.

"I hear you often spoken of" (ran one of these strange epistles),
"and I am almost equally angry whether fools presume to praise or
to blame you. This miserable world we live in, how I loathe and
disdain it!—yet I desire you to serve and to master it! Weak contradiction, effeminate paradox! Oh! rather a thousand times that
you would fly from its mean temptations and poor rewards!—if the
desert were your dwelling-place, and you wished one minister, I could
renounce all—wealth, flattery, repute, womanhood—to serve you.

. . . .

"I once admired you for your genius. My disease has fastened
on me, and I now almost worship you for yourself. I have seen

you, Ernest Maltravers—seen you often—and when you never suspected that these eyes were on you. Now that I have seen, I understand you better. We cannot judge men by their books and deeds. Posterity can know nothing of the beings of the past. A thousand books never written—a thousand deeds never done—are in the eyes and lips of the few greater than the herd. In that cold, abstracted gaze, that pale and haughty brow, I read the disdain of obstacles, which is worthy of one who is confident of the goal. But my eyes fill with tears when I survey you!—you are sad, you are alone! If failures do not mortify you, success does not elevate. Oh, Maltravers, I, woman as I am, and living in a narrow circle, I, even I, know at last, that to have desires nobler, and ends more august, than others, is but to surrender waking life to morbid and melancholy dreams.

. . . .

"Go more into the world, Maltravers, go more into the world, or quit it altogether. Your enemies must be met; they accumulate—they grow strong—you are too tranquil, too slow in your steps towards the prize which should be yours, to satisfy my impatience, to satisfy your friends. Be less refined in your ambition, that you may be more immediately useful. The feet of clay, after all, are the swiftest in the race. Even Lumley Ferrers will outstrip you if you do not take heed.

. . . .

"Why do I run on thus!—you—you love another, yet you are not less the ideal that I could love—if I ever loved any one. You love —and yet—well—no matter."

CHAPTER II.

"Well, but this is being only an official nobleman. No matter, 'tis still being a nobleman, and that's his aim."—*Anonymous writer of* 1772.

"Thus the slow ox would gaudy trappings claim."—HORACE.

MR. TEMPLETON had not obtained his peerage, and, though he had met with no direct refusal, nor made even a direct application to head-quarters, he was growing sullen. He had great parliamentary influence, not close borough, illegitimate influence, but very proper orthodox influence of character, wealth, and so forth. He could return one member at least for a city—he could almost return one member for a county, and in three boroughs any activity on his part could turn the scale in a close contest. The ministers were strong, but still they could not afford to lose supporters hitherto zealous—the example of desertion is contagious. In the town which Templeton had formerly represented, and which he now almost commanded, a vacancy suddenly occurred—a candidate started on the opposition side and commenced a canvass; to the astonishment and panic of the Secretary of the Treasury, Templeton put forward no one, and his interest remained dormant. Lord Saxingham hurried to Lumley.

"My dear fellow, what is this?—what can your uncle be about? We shall lose this place—one of our strongholds. Bets run even."

"Why, you see, you have all behaved very ill to my uncle—I am really sorry for it, but I can do nothing."

"What, this confounded peerage! Will that content him, and nothing short of it?"

"Nothing."

"He must have it, by Jove!"

"And even that may come too late."

"Ha! do you think so?"

"Will you leave the matter to me?"

"Certainly—you are a monstrous clever fellow, and we all esteem you."

"Sit down and write as I dictate, my dear lord."

"Well," said Lord Saxingham, seating himself at Lumley's enormous writing table—"well, go on."

"*My dear Mr. Templeton——*"

"Too familiar," said Lord Saxingham.

"Not a bit; go on."

"*My dear Mr. Templeton*

"*We are anxious to secure your parliamentary influence in C—— to the proper quarter, namely, to your own family, as the best defenders of the administration, which you honour by your support. We wish signally, at the same time, to express our confidence in your principles, and our gratitude for your countenance.*"

"D—d sour countenance!" muttered Lord Saxingham.

"*Accordingly,*" continued Ferrers, "*as one whose connection with you permits the liberty, allow me to request that you will suffer our joint relation, Mr. Ferrers, to be put into immediate nomination.*"

Lord Saxingham threw down the pen and laughed for two

minutes without ceasing. "Capital, Lumley, capital!—Very odd I did not think of it before."

"Each man for himself, and God for us all," returned Lumley, gravely: "pray go on, my dear lord."

"*We are sure you could not have a representative that would more faithfully reflect your own opinions and our interests. One word more. A creation of peers will probably take place in the spring, among which I am sure your name would be to his Majesty a gratifying addition; the title will of course be secured to your sons—and failing the latter, to your nephew.*

"*With great regard and respect,*

"*Truly yours,*

"SAXINGHAM."

"There, inscribe that 'Private and confidential,' and send it express to my uncle's villa."

"It shall be done, my dear Lumley—and this contents me as much as it does you. You are really a man to do us credit. You think it will be arranged?"

"No doubt of it."

"Well, good day. Lumley, come to me when it is all settled: Florence is always glad to see you; she says no one amuses her more. And I am sure that is rare praise, for she is a strange girl—quite a Timon in petticoats."

Away went Lord Saxingham.

"Florence glad to see me!" said Lumley, throwing his arms behind him, and striding to and fro the room—"Scheme the Second begins to smile upon me behind the advancing shadow of Scheme One. If I can but succeed in keeping away other suitors from my fair cousin until I am in a condition to propose myself, why I may carry off the greatest match in the three kingdoms. *Courage, mon brave Ferrers, courage!*"

It was late that evening when Ferrers arrived at his uncle's villa. He found Mrs. Templeton in the drawing-room, seated at the piano. He entered gently; she did not hear him, and continued at the instrument. Her voice was so sweet and rich, her taste so pure, that Ferrers, who was a good judge of music, stood in delighted surprise. Often as he had now been a visitor, even an inmate, at the house, he had never before heard Mrs. Templeton play any but sacred airs, and this was one of the popular songs of sentiment. He perceived that her feeling at last overpowered her voice, and

—16—

she paused abruptly, and turning round, her face was so eloquent of emotion, that Ferrers was forcibly struck by its expression. He was not a man apt to feel curiosity for anything not immediately concerning himself; but he did feel curious about this melancholy and beautiful woman. There was in her usual aspect that inexpressible look of profound resignation which betokens a lasting remembrance of a bitter past: a prematurely blighted heart spoke in her eyes, her smile, her languid and joyless step. But she performed the routine of her quiet duties with a calm and conscientious regularity which showed that grief rather depressed than disturbed her thoughts. If her burden were heavy, custom seemed to have reconciled her to bear it without repining; and the emotion which Ferrers now traced in her soft and harmonious features was of a nature he had only once witnessed before—viz., on the first night he had seen her, when poetry, which is the key of memory, had evidently opened a chamber haunted by mournful and troubled ghosts.

"Ah! dear madam," said Ferrers, advancing, as he found himself discovered, "I trust I do not disturb you. My visit is unseasonable; but my uncle—where is he?"

"He has been in town all the morning; he said he should dine out, and I now expect him every minute."

"You have been endeavouring to charm away the sense of his absence. Dare I ask you to continue to play? It is seldom that I hear a voice so sweet, and skill so consummate. You must have been instructed by the best Italian masters."

"No," said Mrs. Templeton, with a very slight colour in her delicate cheek—"I learned young, and of one that loved music and felt it; but who was not a foreigner."

"Will you sing me that song again?—you give the words a beauty I never discovered in them; yet they (as well as the music itself) are by my poor friend whom Mr. Templeton does not like—Maltravers."

"Are they his also?" said Mrs. Templeton, with emotion; "it is strange I did not know it. I heard the air in the streets, and it struck me much. I inquired the name of the song and bought it—it is very strange!"

"What is strange?"

"That there is a kind of language in your friend's music and poetry which comes home to me, like words I have heard years ago! Is he young, this Mr. Maltravers?"

"Yes, he is still young."

"And, and——"

Here Mrs. Templeton was interrupted by the entrance of her husband. He held the letter from Lord Saxingham—it was yet unopened. He seemed moody; but that was common with him. He coldly shook hands with Lumley, nodded to his wife, found fault with the fire, and throwing himself into his easy-chair, said, "So, Lumley, I think I was a fool for taking your advice—and hanging back about this new election. I see by the evening papers that there is shortly to be a creation of peers. If I had shown activity on behalf of the government, I might have shamed them into gratitude."

"I think I was right, sir," replied Lumley; "public men are often alarmed into gratitude, seldom shamed into it. Firm votes, like old friends, are most valued when we think we are about to lose them; but what is that letter in your hand?"

"Oh, some begging petition, I suppose."

"Pardon me—it has an official look."

Templeton put on his spectacles, raised the letter, examined the address and seal, hastily opened it, and broke into an exclamation very like an oath: when he had concluded—"Give me your hand, nephew—the thing is settled—I am to have the peerage. You were right—ha, ha!—my dear wife, you will be my lady, think of that—arn't you glad?—why don't your ladyship smile? Where's the child—where is she, I say?"

"Gone to bed, sir," said Mrs. Templeton, half frightened.

"Gone to bed! I must go and kiss her. Gone to bed, has she? Light that candle, Lumley." [Here Mr. Templeton rang the bell.] "John," said he, as the servant entered—"John, tell James to go the first thing in the morning to Baxter's, and tell him not to paint my chariot till he hears from me. I must go kiss the child—I must, really."

"D—— the child," muttered Lumley, as, after giving the candle to his uncle, he turned to the fire; "what the deuce has she got to do with the matter? Charming little girl—yours, madam! how I love her! My uncle dotes on her—no wonder!"

"He is, indeed, very, very fond of her," said Mrs. Templeton, with a sigh that seemed to come from the depth of her heart.

"Did he take a fancy to her before you were married?"

"Yes, I believe—oh yes, certainly."

"Her own father could not be more fond of her."

Mrs. Templeton made no answer, but lighted her candle, and wishing Lumley good night, glided from the room.

"I wonder if my grave aunt and my grave uncle took a bite at the apple before they bought the right of the tree. It looks suspicious; yet no, it can't be; there is nothing of the seducer or the seductive about the old fellow. It is not likely—here he comes."

In came Templeton, and his eyes were moist, and his brow relaxed.

"And how is the little angel, sir?" asked Ferrers.

"She kissed me, though I woke her up; children are usually cross when wakened."

"Are they?—little dears! Well, sir, so I was right, then; may I see the letter?"

"There it is."

Ferrers drew his chair to the fire, and read his own production with all the satisfaction of an anonymous author.

"How kind!—how considerate!—how delicately put!—a double favour! But perhaps, after all, it does not express your wishes."

"In what way?"

"Why—why—about myself."

"*You!*—is there anything about *you* in it?—I did not observe *that*—let me see."

"Uncles never selfish!—mem. for commonplace book!" thought Ferrers.

The uncle knit his brows as he reperused the letter. "This won't do, Lumley," said he, very shortly, when he had done.

"A seat in parliament is too much honour for a poor nephew, then, sir!" said Lumley, very bitterly, though he did not feel at all bitter; but it was the proper tone—"I have done all in my power to advance your ambition, and you will not even lend a hand to forward me one step in my career. But, forgive me, sir, I have no right to expect it."

"Lumley!" replied Templeton, kindly, "you mistake me. I think much more highly of you than I did—much: there is a steadiness, a sobriety about you most praiseworthy, and you shall go into parliament if you wish it; but not for C——. I will give my interest there to some other friend of the government, and in return they can give you a treasury borough! That is the same thing to you."

Lumley was agreeably surprised—he pressed his uncle's hand warmly, and thanked him cordially. Mr. Templeton proceeded to explain to him that it was inconvenient and expensive, sitting for places where one's family was known, and Lumley fully subscribed to all.

"As for the settlement of the peerage, that is all right," said Templeton; and then he sunk into a reverie, from which he broke joyously—"yes, that is all right. I have projects, objects—this may unite them all—nothing can be better—you will be the next lord—what—I say, what title shall we have?"

"Oh, take a sounding one—you have very little landed property, I think?"

"Two thousand a year in ——shire, bought a bargain."

"What's the name of the place?"

"Grubley."

"Lord Grubley!—Baron Grubley of Grubley—oh, atrocious! Who had the place before you?"

"Bought it of Mr Sheepshanks—very old family."

"But surely some old Norman once had the place?"

"Norman, yes! Henry the Second gave it to his barber—Bertram Courval."

"That's it!—that's it!—Lord de Courval—singular coincidence—descent from the old line. Heralds' College soon settle all that. Lord de Courval!—nothing can sound better. There must be a village or hamlet still called Courval about the property."

"I am afraid not. There is Coddle End!"

"Coddle End!—Coddle End!—the very thing, sir—the very thing—clear corruption from Courval!—Lord de Courval of Courval. Superb! Ha! ha!"

"Ha! ha!" laughed Templeton, and he had hardly laughed before since he was thirty.

The relations sat long and conversed familiarly. Ferrers slept at the villa, and his sleep was sound, for he thought little of plans once formed and half executed; it was the hunt that kept him awake, and he slept like a hound when the prey was down. Not so Templeton, who did not close his eyes all night.—"Yes, yes," thought he, "I must get the fortune and the title in one line, by a prudent management. Ferrers deserves what I mean to do for him. Steady, good-natured, frank, and will get on—yes, yes, I see it all. Meanwhile I did well to prevent his standing for C——; might pick up gossip about Mrs. T., and other things that might be unpleasant. Ah, I'm a shrewd fellow!"

CHAPTER III.

"Lauzun. There, Marquis, there, I've done it.
"Montespan. Done it ! yes ! Nice doings !"
—*The Duchess de la Vallière.*

LUMLEY hastened to strike while the iron was hot. The next morning he went straight to the Treasury—saw the managing secretary, a clever, sharp man, who, like Ferrers, carried off intrigue and manœuvre by a blunt, careless, bluff manner.

Ferrers announced that he was to stand for the free, respectable, open city of C——, with an electoral population of two thousand five hundred—a very showy place it was for a member in the old anti-reform times, and was considered a thoroughly independent borough. The secretary congratulated and complimented him.

"We have had losses lately in *our* elections among the larger constituencies," said Lumley.

"We have indeed—three towns lost in the last six months. Members do die so very unseasonably !"

"Is Lord Staunch yet provided for ?" asked Lumley. Now Lord Staunch was one of the popular show-fight great guns of the administration—not in office, but that most useful person to all governments, an out-an-out supporter upon the most independent principles—who was known to have refused place, and to value himself on independence—a man who helped the government over the stile when it was seized with a temporary lameness, and who carried "great weight with him in the country." Lord Staunch had foolishly thrown up a close borough in order to contest a large city, and had failed in the attempt. His failure was everywhere cited as a proof of the growing unpopularity of ministers.

"Is Lord Staunch yet provided for ?" asked Lumley.

"Why, he must have his old seat—Three-Oaks. Three-Oaks is a nice, quiet, little place; most respectable constituency—all Staunch's own family."

"Just the thing for him ; yet, 'tis a pity that he did not wait to stand for C——; my uncle's interest would have secured him."

"Ah, I thought so the moment C—— was vacant. However, it is too late now."

"It would be a great triumph if Lord Staunch could show that a large constituency volunteered to elect him as their representative without expense."

"Without expense!—Ah, yes, indeed!—It would prove that purity of election still exists—that British institutions are still upheld."

"It might be done, Mr. ———."

"Why, I thought that you——"

"Were to stand—that is true—and it will be difficult to manage my uncle; but he loves me much—you know I am his heir—I believe I could do it; that is, if you think it would be *a very great* advantage to the party, and *a very great service* to the government."

"Why, Mr. Ferrers, it would indeed be both."

"And in that case I could have Three-Oaks."

"I see—exactly so; but to give up so respectable a seat—really it is a sacrifice."

"Say no more, it shall be done. A deputation shall wait on Lord Staunch directly. I will see my uncle, and a despatch shall be sent down to C—— to-night; at least, I hope so. I must not be too confident. My uncle is an old man, nobody but myself can manage him; I'll go this instant."

"You may be sure your kindness will be duly appreciated."

Lumley shook hands cordially with the secretary, and retired. The secretary was not "humbugged," nor did Lumley expect he should be. But the secretary noted this of Lumley Ferrers (and that gentleman's object was gained), that Lumley Ferrers was a man who looked out for office, and if he did tolerably well in Parliament, that Lumley Ferrers was a man who ought to be *pushed*.

Very shortly afterwards, the *Gazette* announced the election of Lord Staunch for C——, after a sharp but decisive contest. The ministerial journals rang with exulting pœans; the opposition ones called the electors of C—— all manner of hard names, and declared that Mr. Stout, Lord Staunch's opponent, would petition; which he never did. In the midst of the hubbub, Mr. Lumley Ferrers quietly and unobservedly crept into the representation of Three-Oaks.

On the night of his election he went to Lord Saxingham's; but what there happened deserves another chapter.

CHAPTER IV.

"Je connois des princes du sang, des princes étrangers, des grands seigneurs, des ministres d'état, des magistrats, et des philosophes qui fileroient pour l'amour de vous. En pouvez-vous demander davantage?" *—*Lettres de Madame de Sévigné.*

"*Lindora.* I——I believe it will choke me. I'm in love. . . . Now hold your tongue. Hold your tongue, I say.
"*Dalner.* You in love! Ha! ha!
"*Lind.* There, he laughs.
"*Dal.* No; I am really sorry for you."—*German Play (False Delicacy).*

. . . What is here!
Gold."—SHAKESPEARE.

IT happened that that evening Maltravers had, for the first time, accepted one of many invitations with which Lord Saxingham had honoured him. His lordship and Maltravers were of different political parties, nor were they in other respects adapted to each other. Lord Saxingham was a clever man in his way, but worldly even to a proverb among worldly people. That "man was born to walk erect and look upon the stars," is an eloquent fallacy that Lord Saxingham might suffice to disprove. He seemed born to walk with a stoop; and if he ever looked upon any stars, they were those which go with a garter. Though of celebrated and historical ancestry, great rank, and some personal reputation, he had all the ambition of a *parvenu*. He had a strong regard for office, not so much from the sublime affection for that sublime thing—power over the destinies of a glorious nation, as because it added to that vulgar thing—importance in his own set. He looked on his cabinet uniform as a beadle looks on his gold lace. He also liked patronage, secured good things to distant connections, got on his family to the remotest degree of relationship; in short, he was of the earth, earthy. He did not comprehend Maltravers: and Maltravers, who every day grew prouder and prouder, despised him. Still, Lord Saxingham was told that Maltravers was a rising man, and he thought it well to be civil to rising men, of whatever party; besides, his vanity was

---

* I know princes of blood, foreign princes, great lords, ministers of state, magistrates, and philosophers who would even spin for love of you. What can you ask more?

flattered by having men who are talked of in his train. He was too busy and too great a personage to think Maltravers could be other than sincere, when he declared himself, in his notes, "very sorry," or "much concerned," to forego the honour of dining with Lord Saxingham on the, etc., etc.; and therefore continued his invitations, till Maltravers, from that fatality which undoubtedly regulates and controls us, at last accepted the proffered distinction.

He arrived late—most of the guests were assembled; and after exchanging a few words with his host, Ernest fell back into the general group, and found himself in the immediate neighbourhood of Lady Florence Lascelles. This lady had never much pleased Maltravers, for he was not fond of masculine or coquettish heroines, and Lady Florence seemed to him to merit both epithets; therefore, though he had met her often since the first day he had been introduced to her, he had usually contented himself with a distant bow or a passing salutation. But now, as he turned round and saw her—she was, for a miracle, sitting alone—and in her most dazzling and noble countenance there was so evident an appearance of illhealth, that he was struck and touched by it. In fact, beautiful as she was, both in face and form, there was something in the eye and the bloom of Lady Florence, which a skilful physician would have seen with prophetic pain. And, whenever occasional illness paled the roses of the cheek, and sobered the play of the lips, even an ordinary observer would have thought of the old commonplace proverb—"that the brightest beauty has the briefest life." It was some sentiment of this kind, perhaps, that now awakened the sympathy of Maltravers. He addressed her with more marked courtesy than usual, and took a seat by her side.

"You have been to the House, I suppose, Mr. Maltravers?" said Lady Florence.

"Yes, for a short time; it is not one of our field nights—no division was expected; and by this time, I daresay, the House has been counted out."

"Do you like the life?"

"It has excitement," said Maltravers, evasively.

"And the excitement is of a noble character?"

"Scarcely so, I fear—it is so made up of mean and malignant motives—there is in it so much jealousy of our friends, so much unfairness to our enemies;—such readiness to attribute to others the basest objects—such willingness to avail ourselves of the poorest stratagems!—The ends may be great, but the means very ambiguous."

"I knew *you* would feel this," exclaimed Lady Florence, with a heightened colour.

"Did you?" said Maltravers, rather interested as well as surprised. "I scarcely imagined it possible that you would deign to divine secrets so insignificant."

"You did not do *me* justice, then," returned Lady Florence, with an arch yet half-painful smile; "for—but I was about to be impertinent."

"Nay, say on."

"For—then—I do not imagine you to be one apt to do injustice to yourself."

"Oh, you consider me presumptuous and arrogant; but that is common report, and you do right, perhaps, to believe it."

"Was there ever any one unconscious of his own merit?" asked Lady Florence, proudly. "They who distrust themselves have good reason for it."

"You seek to cure the wound you inflicted," returned Maltravers, smiling.

"No; what I said was an apology for myself, as well as for you. You need no words to vindicate you; you are a man, and can bear out all arrogance with the royal motto—*Dieu et mon droit*. With you, deeds can support pretension; but I am a woman—it was a mistake of Nature!"

"But what triumphs that man can achieve bring so immediate, so palpable a reward as those won by a woman, beautiful and admired—who finds every room an empire, and every class her subjects?"

"It is a despicable realm."

"What!—to command—to win—to bow to your worship—the greatest, and the highest, and the sternest; to own slaves in those whom men recognise as their lords! Is such a power despicable? If so, what power is to be envied?"

Lady Florence turned quickly round to Maltravers, and fixed on him her large, dark eyes, as if she would read into his very heart. She turned away with a blush and a slight frown—"There is mockery on your lip," said she.

Before Maltravers could answer, dinner was announced, and a foreign ambassador claimed the hand of Lady Florence. Maltravers saw a young lady, with gold oats in her very light hair, fall to his lot, and descended to the dining-room, thinking more of Lady Florence Lascelles than he had ever done before.

He happened to sit nearly opposite to the young mistress of the house (Lord Saxingham, as the reader knows, was a widower, and Lady Florence an only child); and Maltravers was that day in one of those felicitous moods in which our animal spirits search, and carry up, as it were, to the surface, our intellectual gifts and acquisitions. He conversed generally and happily; but once, when he turned his eyes to appeal to Lady Florence for her opinion on some point in discussion, he caught her gaze fixed upon him with an expression that checked the current of his gaiety, and cast him into a curious and bewildered reverie. In that gaze there was earnest and cordial admiration; but it was mixed with so much mournfulness, that the admiration lost its eloquence, and he who noticed it was rather saddened than flattered.

After dinner, when Maltravers sought the drawing-rooms, he found them filled with the customary mob of good society. In one corner he discovered Castruccio Cesarini, playing on a guitar, slung across his breast with a blue riband. The Italian sang well; many young ladies were grouped round him, amongst others Florence Lascelles. Maltravers, fond as he was of music, looked upon Castruccio's performance as a disagreeable exhibition. He had a Quixotic idea of the dignity of talent; and though himself of a musical science, and a melody of voice that would have thrown the room into ecstasies, he would as soon have turned juggler or tumbler for polite amusement, as contended for the bravos of a drawing-room. It was because he was one of the proudest men in the world that Maltravers was one of the least *vain*. He did not care a rush for applause in small things. But Cesarini would have summoned the whole world to see him play at push-pin, if he thought he played it well.

"Beautiful! divine! charming!"—cried the young ladies, as Cesarini ceased; and Maltravers observed that Florence praised more earnestly than the rest, and that Cesarini's eyes sparkled, and his pale cheek flushed with unwonted brilliancy. Florence turned to Maltravers, and the Italian, following her eyes, frowned darkly.

"You know the Signor Cesarini," said Florence, joining Maltravers. "He is an interesting and gifted person."

"Unquestionably. I grieve to see him wasting his talents upon a soil that may yield a few short-lived flowers, without one useful plant or productive fruit."

"He enjoys the passing hour, Mr. Maltravers; and sometimes when I see the mortifications that await sterner labour, I think he is right."

"Hush!" said Maltravers; "his eyes are on us—he is listening breathlessly for every word you utter. I fear that you have made an unconscious conquest of a poet's heart; and if so, he purchases the enjoyment of the passing hour at a fearful price."

"Nay," said Lady Florence, indifferently, "he is one of those to whom the fancy supplies the place of the heart. And if I give him an inspiration, it will be an equal luxury to him whether his lyre be strung to hope or disappointment. The sweetness of his verses will compensate to him for any bitterness in actual life."

"There are two kinds of love," answered Maltravers—"love and self-love; the wounds of the latter are often most incurable in those who appear least vulnerable to the former. Ah, Lady Florence, were I privileged to play the monitor, I would venture on one warning, however much it might offend you."

"And that is——"

"To forbear coquetry."

Maltravers smiled as he spoke, but it was gravely—and at the same time he moved gently away. But Lady Florence laid her hand on his arm.

"Mr. Maltravers," said she, very softly, and with a kind of faltering in her tone, "am I wrong to say that I am anxious for your good opinion? Do not judge me harshly. I am soured, discontented, unhappy. I have no sympathy with the world. These men whom I see around me—what are they? the mass of them unfeeling and silken egotists—ill-judging, ill-educated, well-dressed: the few who are called distinguished—how selfish in their ambition, how passionless in their pursuits! Am I to be blamed if I sometimes exert a power over such as these, which rather proves my scorn of them than my own vanity?"

"I have no right to argue with you."

"Yes, argue with me, convince me, guide me—heaven know that, impetuous and haughty as I am, I need a guide"—and Lady Florence's eyes swam with tears. Ernest's prejudices against her were greatly shaken; he was even somewhat dazzled by her beauty, and touched by her unexpected gentleness; but still, his heart was not assailed, and he replied almost coldly, after a short pause—

"Dear Lady Florence, look round the world—who so much to be envied as yourself? What sources of happiness and pride are open to you! Why, then, make to yourself causes of discontent? —why be scornful of those who cross not your path? Why not look with charity upon God's less endowed children, beneath you as they may seem? What consolation have you in hurting the hearts or the vanities of others? Do you raise yourself even in your own estimation? You affect to be above your sex—yet what character do you despise more in women than that which you assume? Semiramis should not be a coquette! There now, I have offended you—I confess I am very rude."

"I am not offended," said Florence, almost struggling with her tears; and she added inly, "Ah, I am too happy!"—There are some lips from which even the proudest women love to hear the censure which appears to disprove indifference.

It was at this time that Lumley Ferrers, flushed with the success of his schemes and projects, entered the room; and his quick eye fell upon that corner, in which he detected what appeared to him a very alarming flirtation between his rich cousin and Ernest Maltravers. He advanced to the spot, and with his customary frankness, extended a hand to each.

"Ah, my dear and fair cousin, give me your congratulations, and ask me for my first frank, to be bound up in a collection of autographs by distinguished senators—it will sell high one of these days. Your most obedient, Mr. Maltravers;—how we shall laugh in our sleeves at the humbug of politics, when you and I, the best friends in the world, sit *vis-à-vis* on opposite benches. But why, Lady Florence, have you never introduced me to your pet Italian? *Allons!* I am his match in Alfieri, whom, of course, he swears by, and whose verses, by-the-way, seem cut out of boxwood—the hardest material for turning off that sort of machinery that invention ever hit on."

Thus saying, Ferrers contrived, as he thought, very cleverly, to divide a pair that he much feared were justly formed to meet by nature—and, to his great joy, Maltravers shortly afterwards withdrew.

Ferrers, with the happy ease that belonged to his complacent, though plotting character, soon made Cesarini at home with him; and two or three slighting expressions which the former dropped with respect to Maltravers, coupled with some outrageous compliments to the Italian, completely won the heart of the poet. The brilliant Florence was more silent and subdued than usual; and her voice was softer, though graver, when she replied to Castruccio's eloquent appeals. Castruccio was one of those men who *talk fine*. By degrees, Lumley lapsed into silence, and listened to what took place between Lady Florence and the Italian, while appearing to be deep in "The Views of the Rhine," which lay on the table.

"Ah," said the latter, in his soft, native tongue, "could you know how I watch every shade of that countenance which makes my heaven! Is it clouded! night is with me!—is it radiant! I am as the Persian gazing on the sun!"

"Why do you speak thus to me?—were you not a poet I might be angry."

"You were not angry when the English poet, that cold Maltravers, spoke to you perhaps as boldly."

Lady Florence drew up her haughty head. "Signor," said she, checking, however, her first impulse, and with mildness, "Mr. Maltravers neither flatters nor——"

"Presumes, you were about to say," said Cesarini, grinding his teeth. "But it is well—once you were less chilling to the utterance of my deep devotion."

"Never, Signor Cesarini, never—but when I thought it was but the common gallantry of your nation: let me think so still."

"No, proud woman," said Cesarini, fiercely, "no—hear the truth."

Lady Florence rose indignantly.

"Hear me," he continued. "I—I, the poor foreigner, the despised minstrel, dare to lift up my eyes to you! I love you!"

Never had Florence Lascelles been so humiliated and confounded. However she might have amused herself with the vanity of Cesarini, she had not given him, as she thought, the warrant to address her—the great Lady Florence, the prize of dukes and princes—in this hardy manner; she almost fancied him insane. But the next moment she recalled the warning of Maltravers, and felt as if her punishment had commenced.

"You will think and speak more calmly, sir, when we meet again," and so saying she swept away.

Cesarini remained rooted to the spot, with his dark countenance expressing such passions as are rarely seen in the aspect of civilised men.

"Where do you lodge, Signor Cesarini?" asked the bland, familiar voice of Ferrers. "Let us walk part of the way together—that is, when you are tired of these hot rooms."

Cesarini groaned. "You are ill," continued Ferrers; "the air will revive you—come." He glided from the room, and the Italian mechanically followed him. They walked together for some moments in silence, side by side, in a clear, lovely, moonlight night. At length Ferrers said, "Pardon me, my dear signor, but you may already have observed that I am a very frank, odd sort of fellow. I see you are caught by the charms of my cruel cousin. Can I serve you in any way?"

A man at all acquainted with the world in which we live would have been suspicious of such cordiality in the cousin of an heiress towards a very unsuitable aspirant. But Cesarini, like many indifferent poets (but like few good ones), had no common-sense. He thought it quite natural that a man who admired his poetry so much as Lumley had declared he did, should take a lively interest in his welfare; and he therefore replied warmly, "Oh, sir, this is indeed a crushing blow: I dreamed she loved me. She was ever flattering and gentle when she spoke to me, and in verse already I had told her of my love, and met with no rebuke."

"Did your verses really and plainly declare love, and in your own person?"

"Why, the sentiment was veiled, perhaps—put into the mouth of a fictitious character, or conveyed in an allegory."

"Oh!" ejaculated Ferrers, thinking it very likely that the gorgeous Florence, hymned by a thousand bards, had done little more than cast a glance over the lines that had cost poor Cesarini such anxious toil, and inspired him with such daring hope. "Oh! —and to-night she was more severe!—she is a terrible coquette, *la belle Florence!* But perhaps you have a rival."

"I feel it—I saw it—I know it."

"Whom do you suspect?"

"That accursed Maltravers! He crosses me in every path— my spirit quails beneath his whenever we encounter. I read my doom."

"If it be Maltravers," said Ferrers, gravely, "the danger cannot be great. Florence has seen but little of him, and he does not admire her much; but she is a great match, and he is ambitious. We must guard against this betimes, Cesarini—for know that I dislike Maltravers as much as you do, and will cheerfully aid you in any plan to blight his hopes in that quarter."

"Generous, noble friend!—yet he is richer, better-born than I."

"That may be; but to one in Lady Florence's position, all minor grades of rank in her aspirants seem pretty well levelled. Come, I don't tell you that I would not sooner she married a countryman and an equal—but I have taken a liking to you, and I detest Maltravers. She is very romantic—fond of poetry to a passion—writes it herself, I fancy. Oh, you'll just suit her; but, alas! how will you see her?"

"See her! What mean you?"

"Why, have you not declared love to-night? I thought I overheard you. Can you for a moment fancy that, after such an avowal, Lady Florence will again receive you—that is, if she means to reject your suit?"

"Fool that I was! But no—she must, she shall."

"Be persuaded: in this country violence will not do. Take my advice, write an humble apology, confess your fault, invoke her pity; and, declaring that you renounce for ever the character of a lover, implore still to be acknowledged as a friend. Be quiet now, hear me out; I am older than you: I know my cousin; this will pique her; your modesty will soothe, while your coldness will arouse her vanity. Meanwhile, you will watch the progress of Maltravers; I will be by your elbow; and between us, to use a homely phrase, we will do for him. Then you may have your opportunity, clear stage, and fair play."

Cesarini was at first rebellious; but, at length, even he saw the policy of the advice. But Lumley would not leave him till the advice was adopted. He made Castruccio accompany him to a club, dictated the letter to Florence, and undertook its charge. This was not all.

"It is also necessary," said Lumley, after a short but thoughtful silence, "that you should write to Maltravers."

"And for what?"

"I have my reasons. Ask him, in a frank and friendly spirit, his opinion of Lady Florence; state your belief that she loves you, and inquire ingenuously what he thinks of your chances of happiness in such a union."

"But why this?"

"His answer may be useful," returned Lumley, musingly. "Stay, I will dictate the letter."

Cesarini wondered and hesitated, but there was that about Lumley Ferrers which had already obtained command over the weak and passionate poet. He wrote, therefore, as Lumley dictated, beginning with some commonplace doubts as to the happiness of marriage in general, excusing himself for his recent coldness towards Maltravers, and asking him his confidential opinion, both as to Lady Florence's character and his own chances of success.

This letter, like the former one, Lumley sealed and despatched.

"You perceive," he then said, briefly, to Cesarini, "that it is the object of this letter to entrap Maltravers into some plain and honest avowal of his dislike to Lady Florence; we may make good use of such expressions hereafter, if he should ever prove a rival. And now go home to rest: you look exhausted. Adieu, my new friend."

"I have long had a presentiment," said Lumley to his counsellor SELF, as he walked to Great George Street, "that that wild girl has conceived a romantic fancy for Maltravers. But I can easily prevent such an accident ripening into misfortune. Meanwhile, I have secured a tool, if I want one. By Jove, what an ass that poet is! But so was Cassio; yet Iago made use of him. If Iago had been born now, and dropped that foolish fancy for revenge, what a glorious fellow he would have been! Prime minister at least!"

Pale, haggard, exhausted, Castruccio Cesarini, traversing a length of way, arrived at last at a miserable lodging in the suburb of Chelsea. His fortune was now gone; gone in supplying the poorest food to a craving and imbecile vanity; gone, that its owner might seem what nature never meant him for: the elegant Lothario, the graceful man of pleasure, the troubadour of modern life! gone in horses, and jewels, and fine clothes, and gaming, and printing unsaleable poems on gilt-edged vellum; gone, that he might be not a greater but a more fashionable man than Ernest Maltravers! Such is the common destiny of these poor adventurers who confine fame to boudoirs and saloons. No matter whether they be poets or dandies, wealthy *parvenus* or aristocratic cadets, all equally prove the adage that the wrong paths to reputation are strewed with the wrecks of peace, fortune, happiness, and too often honour! And yet this poor young man had dared to hope for the hand of Florence Lascelles! He had the common notion of foreigners, that English girls marry for love, are very romantic; that, within the three seas, heiresses are as plentiful as blackberries; and for the rest, his vanity had been so pampered, that it now insinuated itself into every fibre of his intellectual and moral system.

Cesarini looked cautiously round, as he arrived at his door; for he fancied that, even in that obscure place, persons might be anxious to catch a glimpse of the celebrated poet; and he concealed his residence from all; dined on a roll when he did not dine out, and left his address at "The Travellers." He looked round, I say, and he did observe a tall figure, wrapped in a cloak, that had indeed followed him from a distant and more populous part of the town. But the figure turned round, and vanished instantly. Cesarini mounted to his second floor. And about the middle of the next day a messenger left a letter at his door, containing one hundred pounds in a blank envelope. Cesarini knew not the writing of the address; his pride was deeply wounded. Amidst all his penury he had not even applied to his own sister. Could it come from her—from De Montaigne? He was lost in conjecture. He put the remittance aside for a few days, for he had something fine in him, the poor poet! but bills grew pressing, and necessity hath no law.

Two days afterwards, Cesarini brought to Ferrers the answer he had received from Maltravers. Lumley had rightly foreseen that the high spirit of Ernest would conceive some indignation at the coquetry of Florence in beguiling the Italian into hopes never to be realised; that he would express himself openly and warmly. He did so, however, with more gentleness than Lumley had anticipated.

"This is not exactly the thing," said Ferrers, after twice reading the letter; "still, it may hereafter be a strong card in our hands—we will keep it."

So saying, he locked up the letter in his desk, and Cesarini soon forgot its existence.

CHAPTER V.

"She was a phantom of delight,
When first she gleamed upon my sight;
A lovely apparition sent
To be a moment's ornament."—WORDSWORTH.

MALTRAVERS did not see Lady Florence again for some weeks; meanwhile, Lumley Ferrers made his *début* in parliament. Rigidly adhering to his plan of acting on a deliberate system, and not prone to overrate himself, Mr. Ferrers did not, like most promising new members, try the hazardous ordeal of a great first speech. Though bold, fluent, and ready, he was not eloquent; and he knew that on great occasions, when great speeches are wanted, great guns like to have the fire to themselves. Neither did he split upon the opposite rock of "promising young men," who stick to "the business of the House" like leeches, and quibble on details; in return for which labour they are generally voted bores, who can never do anything remarkable. But he spoke frequently, shortly, courageously, and with a strong dash of good-humoured personality. He was the man whom a minister could get to say something which other people did not like to say; and he did so with a frank fearlessness that carried off any seeming violation of good taste. He soon became a very popular speaker in the parliamentary clique; especially with the gentlemen who crowd the bar, and never want to hear the argument of the debate. Between him and Maltravers a visible coldness now existed; for the latter looked upon his old friend (whose principles of logic led him even to republicanism, and who had been accustomed to accuse Ernest of temporising with plain truths, if he demurred to their application to artificial states of society) as a cold-blooded and hypocritical adventurer; while Ferrers, seeing that Ernest could now be of no further use to him, was willing enough to drop a profitless intimacy. Nay, he thought it would be wise to pick a quarrel with him, if possible, as the best means of banishing a supposed rival from the house of his noble relation, Lord Saxingham. But no opportunity for that step presented itself; so Lumley kept a fit of convenient rudeness, or an impromptu sarcasm, in reserve, if ever it should be wanted.

The season and the session were alike drawing to a close, when Maltravers received a pressing invitation from Cleveland to spend a week at his villa, which he assured Ernest would be full of agreeable people; and as all business productive of debate or division was over, Maltravers was glad to obtain fresh air and a change of scene. Accordingly, he sent down his luggage and favourite books, and, one afternoon in early August, rode alone towards Temple Grove. He was much dissatisfied, perhaps disappointed, with his experience of public life; and with his high-wrought and over-refining views of the deficiencies of others more prominent, he was in a humour to mingle also censure of himself, for having yielded too much to the doubts and scruples that often, in the early part of their career, beset the honest and sincere in the turbulent whirl of politics, and ever tend to make the robust hues that should belong to action—

"Sicklied o'er with the pale cast of thought."

his mind was working its way slowly towards those conclusions, which sometimes form the best practical men out of the most errant theorists, and perhaps he saw before him the pleasing prospect flatteringly exhibited to another, when he complained of being too honest for party—viz. "becoming a very pretty rascal in time!"

For several weeks he had not heard from his unknown correspondent, and the time was come when he missed those letters, now continued for more than two years; and which, in their eloquent mixture of complaint, exhortation, despondent gloom, and declamatory enthusiasm, had often soothed him in dejection, and made him more sensible of triumph. While revolving in his mind thoughts connected with these subjects—and, somehow or other, with his more ambitious reveries were always mingled musings of curiosity respecting his correspondent—he was struck by the beauty of a little girl, of about eleven years old, who was walking with a female attendant on the footpath that skirted the road. I said that he was struck by her beauty, but that is a wrong expression; it was rather the charm of her countenance than the perfection of her features which arrested the gaze of Maltravers—a charm that might not have existed for others, but was inexpressively attractive to him, and was so much apart from the vulgar fascination of mere beauty, that it would have equally touched a chord at his heart, if coupled with homely features or a bloomless cheek. This charm was in a wonderful innocent and dove-like softness of expression. We all form to ourselves some *beau-idéal* of the "fair spirit" we desire as our earthly "minister," and somewhat capriciously gauge and proportion our admiration of living shapes according as the *beau-idéal* is more or less embodied or approached. Beauty, of a stamp that is not familiar to the dreams of our fancy, may win the cold homage of our judgment, while a look, a feature, a something that realises and calls up a boyish vision, and assimilates even distinctly to the picture we wear within us, has a loveliness peculiar to our eyes, and kindles an emotion that almost seems to belong to memory. It is this which the Platonists felt when they wildly supposed that souls attracted to each other on earth had been united in an earlier being and a diviner sphere; and there was in the young face on which Ernest gazed precisely this ineffable harmony with his preconceived notions of the beautiful. Many a nightly and noonday reverie was realised in those mild yet smiling eyes of the darkest blue; in that ingenuous breadth of brow, with its slightly pencilled arches, and the nose, not cut in that sharp and clear symmetry which looks so lovely in marble, but usually gives to flesh and blood a decided and hard character, that better becomes the sterner than the gentler sex—no; not moulded in the pure Grecian, nor in the pure Roman, cast; but small, delicate, with the least possible inclination to turn upward, that was only to be detected in one position of the head, and served to give a prettier archness to the sweet, flexile lips, which, from the gentleness of their repose, seemed to smile unconsciously, but rather from a happy constitutional serenity than from the giddiness of mirth. Such was the character of this fair child's countenance, on which Maltravers turned and gazed involuntarily and reverently, with something of the admiring delight with which we look upon the Virgin of a Raphael, or the sunset landscape of a Claude. The girl did not appear to feel any premature coquetry at the evident, though respectful, admiration she excited. She met the eyes bent upon her, brilliant and eloquent as they were, with a fearless and unsuspecting gaze, and pointed out to her companion, with all a child's quick and unrestrained impulse, the shining and raven gloss, the arched and haughty neck, of Ernest's beautiful Arabian.

Now, there happened between Maltravers and the young object of his admiration a little adventure, which served, perhaps, to fix in her recollection this short encounter with a stranger; for certain it is, that, years after, she did remember both the circumstances of the adventure and the features of Maltravers. She wore one of those large straw hats which look so pretty upon children, and the warmth of the day made her untie the strings which confined it. A gentle breeze arose, as, by a turn in the road, the country became more open, and suddenly wafted the hat from its proper post—almost to the hoofs of Ernest's horse. The child naturally made a spring forward to arrest the deserter, and her foot slipped down the bank, which was rather steeply raised above the road; she uttered a low cry of pain. To dismount—to regain the prize—and to restore it to its owner, was, with Ernest, the work of a moment; the poor girl had twisted her ankle, and was leaning upon her servant for support. But when she saw the anxiety, and almost the alarm, upon the stranger's face (and her exclamation of pain had literally thrilled his heart—so much and so unaccountably had she excited his interest), she made an effort at self-control, not common at her years, and, with a forced smile, assured him she was not much hurt—that it was nothing—that she was just at home.

"Oh, miss!" said the servant, "I am sure you are very bad. Dear heart, how angry master will be! It was not my fault; was it, sir?"

"Oh, no, it was not your fault, Margaret; don't be frightened—papa shan't blame you. But I'm much better now." So saying, she tried to walk; but the effort was vain—she turned yet more pale, and though she struggled to prevent a shriek, the tears rolled down her cheeks.

It was very odd, but Maltravers had never felt more touched—the tears stood in his own eyes; he longed to carry her in his arms, but, child as she was, a strange kind of nervous timidity forbade him. Margaret, perhaps, expected it of him, for she looked hard in his face, before she attempted a burthen, to which, being a small, slight person, she was by no means equal. However, after a pause, she took up her charge, who, ashamed of her tears, and almost overcome with pain, nestled her head in the woman's bosom, and Maltravers walked by her side, while his docile and well-trained horse followed at a distance, every now and then putting its forelegs on the bank, and cropping away a mouthful of leaves from the hedge-row.

"Oh, Margaret!" said the little sufferer, "I cannot bear it—indeed I cannot."

And Maltravers observed that Margaret had permitted the lamed foot to hang down unsupported, so that the pain must indeed have been scarcely bearable. He could restrain himself no longer.

"You are not strong enough to carry her," said he, sharply, to the servant; and the next moment the child was in his arms. Oh, with what anxious tenderness he bore her! and he was so happy when she turned her face to him and smiled, and told him she now scarcely felt the pain. If it were possible to be in love with a child of eleven years old, Maltravers was almost in love. His pulses trembled as he felt her pure breath on his cheek, and her rich beautiful hair was waved by the breeze across his lips. He hushed his voice to a whisper as he poured forth all the soothing and comforting expressions, which give a natural eloquence to persons fond of children—and Ernest Maltravers was the idol of children—he understood and sympathised with them; he had a great deal of the child himself, beneath the rough and cold husk of his proud reserve. At length they came to a lodge, and Margaret, eagerly inquiring "whether master and missus were at home," seemed delighted to hear they were not. Ernest, however, insisted on bearing his charge across the lawn to the house, which, like most suburban villas, was but a stone's throw from the lodge; and, receiving the most positive promise that surgical advice should be immediately sent for, he was forced to content himself with laying the sufferer on a sofa in the drawing-room; and she thanked him so prettily, and assured him she was so much easier, that he would have given the world to kiss her. The child had completed her conquest over him by being above the child's ordinary littleness of making the worst of things, in order to obtain the consequence and dignity of being pitied—she was evidently unselfish and considerate for others. He did kiss her, but it was the hand that he kissed, and no cavalier ever kissed his lady's hand with more respect; and then, for the first time, the child blushed—then, for the first time, she felt as if the day would come when she should be a child no longer! Why was this?—perhaps because it is an era in life—the first sign of a tenderness that inspires respect, not familiarity!

"If ever again I could be in love," said Maltravers, as he spurred on his road, "I really think it would be with that exquisite child. My feeling is more like that of love at first sight than any emotion which beauty ever caused in me. Alice—Valerie—no; the *first* sight of them did not;—but what folly is this!—a child of eleven—and I verging upon thirty!"

Still, however, folly as it might be, the image of that young girl haunted Maltravers for many days; till change of scene, the distractions of society, the grave thoughts of manhood, and, above all, a series of exciting circumstances about to be narrated, gradually obliterated a strange and most delightful impression. He had learned, however, that Mr. Templeton was the proprietor of the villa, which was the child's home. He wrote to Ferrers, to narrate the incident, and to inquire after the sufferer. In due time he heard from that gentleman that the child was recovered, and gone with Mr. and Mrs. Templeton to Brighton, for change of air and sea-bathing.

BOOK VIII.

CHAPTER I.

"*Notitiam primosque gradus vicinia fecit.*"*—OVID.

CLEVELAND'S villa *was* full, and of persons usually called agreeable. Amongst the rest was Lady Florence Lascelles. The wise old man had ever counselled Maltravers not to marry too young; but neither did he wish him to put off that momentous epoch of life till all the bloom of heart and emotion was passed away. He thought, with the old lawgivers, that thirty was the happy age for forming a connection, in the choice of which, with the reason of manhood, ought, perhaps, to be blended the passion of youth. And he saw that few men were more capable than Maltravers of the true enjoyments of domestic life. He had long thought, also, that none were more calculated to sympathise with Ernest's views, and appreciate his peculiar character, than the gifted and brilliant Florence Lascelles. Cleveland looked with toleration on her many eccentricities of thought and conduct—eccentricities which he imagined would rapidly melt away beneath the influence of that attachment which usually operates so great a change in women; and, where it is strongly and intensely felt, moulds even those of the most obstinate character into compliance or similitude with the sentiments or habits of its object.

The stately self-control of Maltravers was, he conceived, precisely that quality that gives to men an unconscious command over the very thoughts of the woman whose affection they win; while on the other hand, he hoped that the fancy and enthusiasm of Florence would tend to render sharper and more practical an ambition, which

* Neighbourhood caused the acquaintance and first introduction.

seemed to the sober man of the world too apt to refine upon the means, and to *cui bono* the objects, of worldly distinction. Besides, Cleveland was one who thoroughly appreciated the advantages of wealth and station; and the rank and the dower of Florence were such as would force Maltravers into a position in social life, which could not fail to make new exactions upon talents which Cleveland fancied were precisely those adapted rather to command than to serve. In Ferrers he recognised a man to *get* into power—in Maltravers one by whom power, if ever attained, would be wielded with dignity, and exerted for great uses. Something, therefore, higher than mere covetousness for the vulgar interests of Maltravers, made Cleveland desire to secure to him the heart and hand of the great heiress; and he fancied that, whatever might be the obstacle, it would not be in the will of Lady Florence herself. He prudently resolved, however, to leave matters to their natural course. He hinted nothing to one party or the other. No place for falling in love like a large country-house, and no time for it, amongst the indolent well-born, like the close of a London season, when, jaded by small cares, and sickened of hollow intimacies, even the coldest may well yearn for the tones of affection—the excitement of an honest emotion.

Somehow or other it happened that Florence and Ernest, after the first day or two, were constantly thrown together. She rode on horseback, and Maltravers was by her side—they made excursions on the river, and they sat in the same bench in the gliding pleasure-boat. In the evenings, the younger guests, with the assistance of the neighbouring families, often got up a dance, in a temporary pavilion built out of the dining-room. Ernest never danced. Florence did at first. But once, as she was conversing with Maltravers, when a gay guardsman came to claim her promised hand in the waltz, she seemed struck by a grave change in Ernest's face.

"Do you never waltz?" she asked, while the guardsman was searching for a corner wherein safely to deposit his hat.

"No," said he; "yet there is no impropriety in *my* waltzing."

"And you mean that there is in mine?"

"Pardon me—I did not say so."

"But you think it."

"Nay, on consideration, I am glad, perhaps, that you do waltz."

"You are mysterious."

"Well, then, I mean that you are precisely the woman I would never fall in love with. And I feel the danger is lessened, when I see you destroy any one of my illusions, or, as I ought to say, attack any one of my prejudices."

Lady Florence coloured; but the guardsman and the music left her no time for reply. However, after that night she waltzed no more. She was unwell—she declared she was ordered not to dance, and so quadrilles were relinquished as well as the waltz.

Maltravers could not but be touched and flattered by this regard for his opinion; but Florence contrived to testify it so as to forbid acknowledgment, since another motive had been found for it. The second evening after that commemorated by Ernest's candid rudeness they chanced to meet in the conservatory, which was connected with the ball-room; and Ernest, pausing to inquire after her health, was struck by the listless and dejected sadness which spoke in her tone and countenance as she replied to him.

"Dear Lady Florence," said he, "I fear you are worse than you will confess. You should shun these draughts. You owe it to your friends to be more careful of yourself."

"Friends!" said Lady Florence, bitterly—"I have no friends!—even my poor father would not absent himself from a cabinet dinner a week after I was dead. But that is the condition of public life—its hot and searing blaze puts out the lights of all lesser but not unholier affections. Friends! Fate that made Florence Lascelles the envied heiress denied her brothers, sisters; and the hour of her birth lost her even the love of a mother! Friends! where shall I find them?"

As she ceased, she turned to the open casement, and stepped out into the verandah, and by the trembling of her voice Ernest felt that she had done so to hide or to suppress her tears.

"Yet," said he, following her, "there is one class of more distant friends, whose interest Lady Florence Lascelles cannot fail to secure, however she may disdain it. Among the humblest of that class suffer me to rank myself. Come, I assume the privilege of advice—the night air is a luxury you must not indulge."

"No, no, it refreshes me—it soothes. You misunderstand me, I have no illness that still skies and sleeping flowers can increase."

Maltravers, as is evident, was not in love with Florence, but he could not fail, brought, as he had lately been, under the direct influence of her rare and prodigal gifts, mental and personal, to feel for her a strong and even affectionate interest—the very frankness with which he was accustomed to speak to her, and the many links of communion there necessarily were between himself and a mind so naturally powerful and so richly cultivated, had already established their acquaintance upon an intimate footing.

"I cannot restrain you, Lady Florence," said he, half smiling, "but my conscience will not let me be an accomplice. I will turn king's evidence, and hunt out Lord Saxingham to send him to you."

Lady Florence, whose face was averted from his, did not appear to hear him.

"And you, Mr. Maltravers," turning quickly round—"you—have you friends?—Do you feel that there are, I do not say public, but private affections and duties, for which life is made less a possession than a trust?"

"Lady Florence—no!—I have friends, it is true, and Cleveland is of the nearest; but the life within life—the second self, in whom we vest the right and mastery over our own being—I know not. But is it," he added, after a pause, "a rare privation? Perhaps it is a happy one. I have learned to lean on my own soul, and not look elsewhere for the reeds that a wind can break."

"Ah, it is a cold philosophy—you may reconcile yourself to its wisdom in the world, in the hum and shock of men: but in solitude with Nature—ah, no! While the mind alone is occupied, you may be contented with the pride of stoicism; but there are moments when the *heart* wakens as from a sleep—wakens like a frightened child—to feel itself alone and in the dark."

Ernest was silent, and Florence continued, in an altered voice—"This is a strange conversation—and you must think me indeed a wild, romance-reading person, as the world is apt to call me. But if I live—I—pshaw!—life denies ambition to women."

"If a woman like you, Lady Florence, should ever love, it will be one in whose career you may perhaps find that noblest of all ambitions—the ambition women only feel—the ambition for another!"

"Ah, but I shall never love," said Lady Florence, and her cheek grew pale as the starlight shone on it; "still, perhaps," she added quickly, "I may at least know the blessing of friendship. Why now," and here, approaching Maltravers, she laid her hand with a winning frankness on his arm—"why now, should not we be to each other as if love, as you call it, were not a thing for earth—and friendship supplied its place?—there is no danger of our falling in love with each other. You are not vain enough to expect it in me, and I, you know, am a coquette; let us be friends, confidants—at least till you marry, or I give another the right to control my friendships and monopolise my secrets."

Maltravers was startled—the sentiment Florence addressed to him, he, in words not dissimilar, had once addressed to Valerie.

"The world," said he, kissing the hand that yet lay on his arm, "the world will——"

"Oh, you men!—the world, the world!—Everything gentle, everything pure, everything noble, high-wrought and holy—is to be squared, and cribbed, and maimed to the rule and measure of the world! The world—are you, too, its slave? Do you not despise its hollow cant—its methodical hypocrisy?"

"Heartily!" said Ernest Maltravers, almost with fierceness. "No man ever so scorned its false gods and its miserable creeds—its war upon the weak—its fawning upon the great—its ingratitude to benefactors—its sordid league with mediocrity against excellence. Yes, in proportion as I love mankind, I despise and detest that worse than Venetian oligarchy which mankind set over them and call 'THE WORLD.'"

And then it was, warmed by the excitement of released feelings, long and carefully shrouded, that this man, ordinarily so calm and self-possessed, poured burningly and passionately forth all those tumultuous and almost tremendous thoughts, which, however much we may regulate, control, or disguise them, lurk deep within the souls of all of us, the seeds of the eternal war between the natural man and the artificial; between our wilder genius and our social conventionalities;—thoughts that from time to time break forth into the harbingers of vain and fruitless revolutions, impotent struggles against destiny;—thoughts that good and wise men would be slow to promulge and propagate, for they are of a fire which burns as well as brightens, and which spreads from heart to heart, as a spark spreads amidst flax;—thoughts which are rifest where natures are most high, but belong to truths that virtue dare not tell aloud. And as Maltravers spoke, with his eyes flashing almost intolerable light—his breast heaving, his form dilated, never to the eyes of Florence Lascelles did he seem so great: the chains that bound the strong limbs of his spirit seemed snapped asunder, and all his soul was visible and towering, as a thing that has escaped slavery, and lifts its crest to heaven, and feels that it is free.

That evening saw a new bond of alliance between these two persons;—young, handsome, and of opposite sexes; they agreed to be friends, and nothing more! Fools!

CHAPTER II.

"Idem velle, et idem nolle, ea demum firma amicitia est." *—SALLUST.

"*Carlos.*—That letter.
Princess Eboli.—Oh, I shall die. Return it instantly."
—SCHILLER: *Don Carlos.*

IT seemed as if the compact Maltravers and Lady Florence had entered into removed whatever embarrassment and reserve had previously existed. They now conversed with an ease and freedom not common in persons of different sexes before they have passed their grand climacteric. Ernest, in ordinary life, like most men of warm emotions and strong imagination, if not taciturn, was at least guarded. It was as if a weight were taken from his breast, when he found one person who could understand him best when he was most candid. His eloquence—his poetry—his intense and concentrated enthusiasm found a voice. He could talk to an individual as he would have written to the public—a rare happiness to the man of books.

Florence seemed to recover her health and spirits as by a miracle; yet was she more gentle, more subdued, than of old—there was less effort to shine, less indifference whether she shocked. Persons who had not met her before wondered why she was dreaded in society. But at times a great natural irritability of temper—a quick suspicion of the motives of those around her—an imperious and obstinate vehemence of will, were visible to Maltravers, and served, perhaps, to keep him heart-whole. He regarded her through the eyes of the intellect, not those of the passions—he thought not of her as a woman—her very talents, her very grandeur of idea and power of purpose, while they delighted him in conversation, diverted his imagination from dwelling on her beauty. He looked on her as something apart from her sex—a glorious creature spoilt by being a woman. He once told her so, laughingly, and Florence considered it a compliment. Poor Florence, her scorn of her sex avenged her sex, and robbed her of her proper destiny!

Cleveland silently observed their intimacy, and listened with a quiet smile to the gossips who pointed out *têtes-à-tête* by the terrace,

* To will the same thing and not to will the same thing, that at length is firm friendship.

and loiterings by the lawn, and predicted what would come of it all. Lord Saxingham was blind. But his daughter was of age, in possession of her princely fortune, and had long made him sensible of her independence of temper. His lordship, however, thoroughly misunderstood the character of her pride, and felt fully convinced she would marry no one less than a duke; as for flirtations, he thought them natural and innocent amusements. Besides, he was very little at Temple Grove. He went to London every morning, after breakfasting in his own room—came back to dine, play at whist, and talk good-humoured nonsense to Florence in his dressing-room, for the three minutes that took place between his sipping his wine-and-water and the appearance of his valet. As for the other guests, it was not their business to do more than gossip with each other; and so Florence and Maltravers went on their way unmolested, though not unobserved. Maltravers not being himself in love, never fancied that Lady Florence loved him, or that she would be in any danger of doing so. This is a mistake a man often commits—a woman, never. A woman always knows when she is loved, though she often imagines she is loved when she is not. Florence was not happy, for happiness is a calm feeling. But she was excited with a vague, wild, intoxicating emotion.

She had learned from Maltravers that she had been misinformed by Ferrers, and that no other claimed empire over his heart; and whether or not he loved her, still for the present they seemed all in all to each other; she lived but for the present day, she would not think of the morrow.

Since that severe illness, which had tended so much to alter Ernest's mode of life, he had not come before the public as an author. Latterly, however, the old habit had broken out again. With the comparative idleness of recent years, the ideas and feelings which crowd so fast on the poetical temperament, once indulged, had accumulated within him to an excess that demanded vent. For with some, to write is not a vague desire, but an imperious destiny. The fire is kindled and must break forth; the wings are fledged, and the birds must leave their nest. The communication of thought to man is implanted as an instinct in those breasts to which heaven has entrusted the solemn agencies of genius. In the work which Maltravers now composed, he consulted Florence: his confidence delighted her—it was a compliment she could appreciate. Wild, fervid, impassioned, was that work—a brief and holiday creation—the youngest and most beloved of the children of his brain. And as day by day the bright design grew into shape, and thought and imagination found themselves "local habitations," Florence felt as if she were admitted into the palace of the genii, and made acquainted with the mechanism of those spells and charms with which the preternatural powers of mind design the witchery of the world. Ah, how different in depth and majesty were those inter-communications of idea between Ernest Maltravers and a woman scarcely inferior to himself in capacity and acquirement, from that bridge of shadowy and dim sympathies which the enthusiastic boy had once built up between his own poetry of knowledge and Alice's poetry of love!

It was one late afternoon in September, when the sun was slowly going down its western way, that Lady Florence, who had been all that morning in her own room, paying off, as she said, the dull arrears of correspondence, rather on Lord Saxingham's account than her own; for he punctiliously exacted from her the most scrupulous attention to cousins fifty times removed, provided they were rich, clever, well off, or in any way of consequence:—it was one afternoon that, relieved from these avocations, Lady Florence strolled through the grounds with Cleveland. The gentlemen were still in the stubble-fields, the ladies out in barouches and pony phaetons, and Cleveland and Lady Florence were alone.

Apropos of Florence's epistolary employment, their conversation fell upon that most charming species of literature, which joins with the interest of a novel the truth of a history—the French memoir and letter-writers.

"Those agreeable and polished gossips," said Cleveland, "how well they contrived to introduce nature into art! Everything artificial seemed so natural to them. They even feel by a kind of clockwork, which seems to go better than the heart itself. Those pretty sentiments, those delicate gallantries, of Madame de Sévigné to her daughter, how amiable they are; but, somehow or other, I can never fancy them the least motherly. What an ending for a maternal epistle is that elegant compliment—'Songez que de tous les cœurs où vous régnez, il n'y en a aucun où votre empire soit si bien établi que dans le mien.'* I can scarcely fancy Lord Saxingham writing so to you, Lady Florence."

"No, indeed," replied Lady Florence, smiling. "Neither papas nor mammas in England are much addicted to compliment; but, I

* Think that of all hearts over which you reign, there is not one in which your empire can be so well established as in mine.

not again occur—and—but you know the man !—what shall we do ? I am sure he will not listen to me ; he looks on me as an interested rival for fame."

"Do you think I have any subtler eloquence ?" said Cleveland. "No, I am an author, too. Come, I think your ladyship must be the arch-negotiator."

"He has genius, he has merit," said Maltravers, pleadingly ; he wants nothing but time and experience to wean him from his foibles. *Will* you try to save him, Lady Florence ?"

"Why! nay, I must not be obdurate ; I will see him when I go to town. It is like you, Mr. Maltravers, to feel this interest in one——"

"Who does not like me, you would say ; but he will, some day or other. Besides, I owe him deep gratitude. In his weaker qualities I have seen many which all literary men might incur, without strict watch over themselves ; and let me add, also, that his family have great claims on me."

"You believe in the soundness of his heart, and in the integrity of his honour ?" said Cleveland, inquiringly.

"Indeed I do : these are, these must be, the redeeming qualities of poets."

Maltravers spoke warmly; and such at that time was his influence over Florence, that his words formed—alas, too fatally !—her estimate of Castruccio's character, which had at first been high, but which his own presumption had latterly shaken. She had seen him three or four times in the interval between the receipt of his apologetic letter and her visit to Cleveland, and he had seemed to her rather sullen than humbled. But she felt for the vanity she herself had wounded.

"And now," continued Maltravers, "for my second subject of consultation. But that is political ; will it weary Lady Florence ?"

"Oh, no ; to politics I am never indifferent : they always inspire me with contempt or admiration, according to the motives of those who bring the science into action. Pray say on."

"Well," said Cleveland, "one confidant at a time ; you will forgive me, for I see my guests coming across the lawn, and I may as well make a diversion in your favour. Ernest can consult *me* at any time."

Cleveland walked away ; but the intimacy between Maltravers and Florence was of so frank a nature that there was nothing embarrassing in the thought of a *tête-à-tête.*

—18—

"Lady Florence," said Ernest, "there is no one in the world with whom I can confer so cheerfully as with you. I am almost glad of Cleveland's absence, for, with all his amiable and fine qualities, 'the world is too much with him,' and we do not argue from the same data. Pardon my prelude—now to my position. I have received a letter from Mr. ——. That statesman, whom none but those acquainted with the chivalrous beauty of his nature can understand or appreciate, sees before him the most brilliant career that ever opened in this country to a public man not born an aristocrat. He has asked me to form one of the new administration that he is about to create. The place offered to me is above my merits, nor suited to what I have yet done, though, perhaps, it be suited to what I may yet do. I make that qualification, for you know," added Ernest, with a proud smile, "that I am sanguine and self-confident."

"You accept the proposal?"

"Nay—should I not reject it? Our politics are the same only for the moment, our ultimate objects are widely different. To serve with Mr. ——, I must make an unequal compromise—abandon nine opinions to promote one. Is not this a capitulation of that great citadel, one's own conscience? No man will call me inconsistent, for, in public life, to agree with another on a party question is all that is required; the thousand questions not yet ripened, and lying dark and concealed in the future, are not inquired into and divined; but I own I shall deem myself worse than inconsistent. For this is my dilemma—if I use this noble spirit merely to advance one object, and then desert him where he halts, I am treacherous to him; if I halt with him, but one of my objects is effected, I am treacherous to myself. Such are my views. It is with pain I arrive at them, for, at first, my heart beat with a selfish ambition."

"You are right, you are right," exclaimed Florence, with glowing cheeks; "how could I doubt you? I comprehend the sacrifice you make; for a proud thing is it to soar above the predictions of foes in that palpable road to honour which the world's hard eyes can see, and the world's cold heart can measure; but prouder is it to feel that you have never advanced one step to the goal which remembrance would retract. No, my friend, wait your time, confident that it must come, when conscience and ambition can go hand-in-hand—when the broad objects of a luminous and enlarged policy lie before you like a chart, and you can calculate every step of the way without peril of being lost. Ah, let them still call loftiness of purpose and whiteness of soul the dreams of a theorist—even if they be so, the Ideal in this case is better than the Practical. Meanwhile your position is not one to forfeit lightly. Before you is that throne in literature which it requires no doubtful step to win, if you have, as I believe, the mental power to attain it ; an ambition that may indeed be relinquished, if a more troubled career can better achieve those public purposes at which both letters and policy should aim, but which is not to be surrendered for the rewards of a placeman, or the advancement of a courtier."

It was while uttering these noble and inspiring sentiments that Florence Lascelles suddenly acquired in Ernest's eye a loveliness with which they had not before invested her.

"Oh," he said, as, with a sudden impulse, he lifted her hand to his lips, "blessed be the hour in which you gave me your friendship! These are the thoughts I have longed to hear from living lips, when I have been tempted to believe patriotism a delusion, and virtue but a name."

Lady Florence heard, and her whole form seemed changed—she was no longer the majestic sybil, but the attached, timorous, delighted woman.

It so happened that in her confusion she dropped from her hand the flower Maltravers had given her, and involuntarily glad of a pretext to conceal her countenance, she stooped to take it from the ground. In so doing, a letter fell from her bosom—and Maltravers, as he bent forwards to forestall her own movement, saw that the direction was to himself, and in the handwriting of his unknown correspondent. He seized the letter, and gazed in flattered and entranced astonishment, first on the writing, next on the detected writer. Florence grew deadly pale, and, covering her face with her hands, burst into tears.

"Oh, fool that I was," cried Ernest, in the passion of the moment, "not to know—not to have felt that there were not two Florences in the world ! But if the thought had crossed me, I would not have dared to harbour it."

"Go, go," sobbed Florence ; "leave me, in mercy, leave me !"

"Not till you bid me rise," said Ernest, in emotion scarcely less deep than hers, as he sank on his knee at her feet.

Need I go on ?—When they left that spot, a soft confession had been made—deep vows interchanged, and Ernest Maltravers was the accepted suitor of Florence Lascelles.

CHAPTER III.

"A hundred fathers would in my situation tell you that, as you are of noble extraction, you should marry a nobleman. But I do not say so. I will not sacrifice my child to any prejudice."—KOTZEBUE: *Lover's Vows.*

"Take heed, my lord; the welfare of us all
Hangs on the cutting short that fraudful man."
—SHAKESPEARE: *Henry VI.*

"Oh, how this spring of love resembleth
Th' uncertain glory of an April day;
Which now shows all the beauty of the sun,
And by-and-by a cloud takes all away!"
—SHAKESPEARE: *The Two Gentlemen of Verona.*

WHEN Maltravers was once more in his solitary apartment, he felt as in a dream. He had obeyed an impulse, irresistible, perhaps, but one with which the *conscience of his heart* was not satisfied. A voice whispered to him, "Thou hast deceived her and thyself—thou dost not love her!" In vain he recalled her beauty, her grace, her genius—her singular and enthusiastic passion for himself—the voice still replied, "Thou dost not love. Bid farewell for ever to thy fond dreams of a life more blessed than that of mortals. From the stormy sea of the future are blotted out eternally for thee—Calypso and her Golden Isle. Thou canst no more paint on the dim canvas of thy desires the form of her with whom thou couldst dwell for ever. Thou hast been unfaithful to thine own ideal—thou hast given thyself for ever and for ever to another—thou hast renounced hope—thou must live as in a prison, with a being with whom thou hast not the harmony of love."

"No matter," said Maltravers, almost alarmed, and starting from these thoughts, "I am betrothed to one who loves me—it is folly and dishonour to repent and to repine. I have gone through the best years of youth without finding the Egeria with whom the cavern would be sweeter than a throne. Why live to the grave a vain and visionary Nympholept? Out of the real world could I have made a nobler choice?"

While Maltravers thus communed with himself, Lady Florence passed into her father's dressing-room, and there awaited his return from London. She knew his worldly views—she knew also the pride of her affianced, and she felt that she alone could mediate between the two.

Lord Saxingham at last returned; busy, bustling, important, and good-humoured as usual. "Well, Flory, well?—glad to see you—quite blooming, I declare—never saw you with such a colour—monstrous like me, certainly. We always had fine complexions and fine eyes in our family. But I'm rather late—first bell rung—we *cidevant jeunes hommes* are rather long dressing, and you are not dressed yet, I see."

"My dearest father, I wished to speak with you on a matter of much importance."

"Do you !—what, immediately?"

"Yes."

"Well—what is it?—your Slingsby property, I suppose."

"No, my dear father—pray sit down and hear me patiently."

Lord Saxingham began to be both alarmed and curious—he seated himself in silence, and looked anxiously in the face of his daughter.

"You have always been very indulgent to me," commenced Florence, with a half-smile, "and I have had my own way more than most young ladies. Believe me, my dear father, I am most grateful, not only for your affection, but your esteem. I have been a strange, wild girl, but I am now about to reform; and as the first step, I ask your consent to give myself a preceptor and a guide——"

"A what !" cried Lord Saxingham.

"In other words, I am about to—to—well, the truth must out—to marry."

"Has the Duke of —— been here to-day?"

"Not that I know of. But it is no duke to whom I have promised my hand—it is a nobler and rarer dignity that has caught my ambition. Mr. Maltravers has——"

"Mr. Maltravers !—Mr. Devil !—the girl's mad !—don't talk to me, child; I won't consent to any such nonsense. A country gentleman—very respectable, very clever, and all that, but it's no use talking—my mind's made up. With your fortune, too !"

"My dear father, I will not marry without your consent, though my fortune is settled on me, and I am of age."

"There's a good child—and now let me dress—we shall be late."

"No, not yet," said Lady Florence, throwing her arm carelessly round her father's neck—"I shall marry Mr. Maltravers, but it will be with your full approval. Just consider; if I married the Duke of ——, he would expect all my fortune, such as it is. Ten thousand a-year is at my disposal: if I marry Mr. Maltravers, it will be settled on you—I always meant it—it is a poor return for your kindness, your indulgence—but it will show that your own Flory is not ungrateful."

"I wont hear."

"Stop—listen to reason. You are not rich—you are entitled but to a small pension if you ever resign office; and your official salary, I have often heard you say, does not prevent you from being embarrassed. To whom should a daughter give from her superfluities but to a parent?—from whom should a parent receive but from a child who can never repay his love?—Ah, this is nothing; but you—you who have never crossed her lightest whim—do not you destroy all the hopes of happiness your Florence can ever form."

Florence wept, and Lord Saxingham, who was greatly moved, let fall a few tears also. Perhaps it is too much to say that the pecuniary part of the proffered arrangement entirely won him over; but still the way it was introduced softened his heart. He possibly thought that it was better to have a good and grateful daughter in a country gentleman's wife, than a sullen and thankless one in a duchess. However that may be, certain it is that before Lord Saxingham began his toilet, he promised to make no obstacle to the marriage, and all he asked in return was, that at least three months (but that, indeed, the lawyers would require) should elapse before it took place; and on this understanding Florence left him, radiant and joyous as Flora herself, when the sun of spring makes the world a garden. Never had she thought so little of her beauty, and never had it seemed so glorious as that happy evening. But Maltravers was pale and thoughtful, and Florence in vain sought his eyes during the dinner, which seemed to her insufferably long. Afterwards, however, they met, and conversed apart the rest of the evening; and the beauty of Florence began to produce upon Ernest's heart its natural effect; and that evening—ah, how Florence treasured the remembrance of every hour, every minute of its annals!

It would have been amusing to witness the short conversation between Lord Saxingham and Maltravers, when the latter sought the earl at night in his lordship's room. To Lord Saxingham's surprise, not a word did Maltravers utter of his own subordinate pretensions to Lady Florence's hand. Coldly, drily, and almost haughtily, did he make the formal proposals, "as if [as Lord Saxingham afterwards said to Ferrers] the man were doing me the highest possible honour in taking my daughter, the beauty of London, with fifty thousand a-year, off my hands." But this was quite Maltravers!—if he had been proposing to the daughter of a country curate, without a sixpence, he would have been the humblest of the humble. The earl was embarrassed and discomposed—he was almost awed by the Siddons-like countenance and Coriolanus-like air of his future son-in-law—he even hinted nothing of the compromise as to time which he had made with his daughter. He thought it better to leave it to Lady Florence to arrange that matter. They shook hands frigidly, and parted. Maltravers went next into Cleveland's room, and communicated all to the delighted old man, whose congratulations were so fervid that Maltravers felt it would be a sin not to fancy himself the happiest man in the world. That night he wrote his refusal of the appointment offered him.

The next day Lord Saxingham went to his office in Downing Street as usual, and Lady Florence and Ernest found an opportunity to ramble through the grounds alone.

There it was that occurred those confessions, sweet alike to utter and to hear. Then did Florence speak of her early years—of her self-formed and solitary mind—of her youthful dreams and reveries. Nothing around her to excite interest or admiration, or the more romantic, the higher, or the softer qualities of her nature, she turned to contemplation and to books. It is the combination of the faculties with the affections, exiled from action, and finding no worldly vent, which produces Poetry, the child of passion and of thought. Hence, before the real cares of existence claim them, the young, who are abler yet lonelier than their fellows, are nearly always poets: and Florence was a poetess. In minds like this, the first book that seems to embody and represent their own most cherished and beloved trains of sentiment and ideas, ever creates a reverential and deep enthusiasm. The lonely, and proud, and melancholy soul of Maltravers, which made itself visible in all his creations, became to Florence like a revealer of the secrets of her own nature. She conceived an intense and mysterious interest in the man whose mind exercised so pervading a power over her own. She made herself acquainted with his pursuits, his career—she fancied she found a symmetry and harmony between the actual being and the breathing genius—she imagined she understood what seemed dark and obscure to others. He whom she had never seen grew to her a never-absent friend. His ambition, his reputation, were to her like a possession of her own. So at length, in the folly of her young romance, she wrote to him, and dreaming of no discovery, anticipating no result, the habit once indulged became to her that luxury which writing for the eye of the world is to an author oppressed with the burthen of his own thoughts. At length she saw him, and he did not destroy her illusion. She might have recovered from the spell if she had found him ready at once to worship at her shrine. The mixture of reserve and frankness—frankness of language, reserve of manner—which belonged to Maltravers, piqued her. Her vanity became the auxiliary to her imagination. At length they met at Cleveland's house; their intercourse became more unrestrained—their friendship was established, and she discovered that she had wilfully implicated her happiness in indulging her dreams; yet even then she believed that Maltravers loved her, despite his silence upon the subject of love. His manner, his words, bespoke his interest in her, and his voice was ever soft when he spoke to women; for he had much of the old chivalric respect and tenderness for the sex. What was general it was natural that she should apply individually—she who had walked the world but to fascinate and to conquer. It was probable that her great wealth and social position imposed a check on the delicate pride of Maltravers—she hoped so—she believed it—yet she felt her danger, and her own pride at last took alarm. In such a moment she had resumed the character of the unknown correspondent—she had written to Maltravers—addressed her letter to his own house, and meant the next day to have gone to London, and posted it there. In this letter she had spoken of his visit to Cleveland, of his position with herself. She exhorted him, if he loved her, to confess, and if not, to fly. She had written artfully and eloquently; she was desirous of expediting her own fate; and then, with that letter in her bosom, she had met Maltravers, and the reader has learned the rest. Something of all this the blushing and happy Florence now revealed: and when she ended with uttering the woman's soft fear that she had been too bold, is it wonderful that Maltravers, clasping her to his bosom, felt the gratitude, and the delighted vanity, which seemed even to himself like love? And into love those feelings rapidly and deliciously will merge, if fate and accident permit !

And now they were by the side of the water; and the sun was gently setting as on the eve before. It was about the same hour, the fairest of an autumn day; none were near—the slope of the hill hid the house from their view. Had they been in the desert they could not have been more alone. It was not silence that breathed around them, as they sat on that bench with the broad beech spreading over them its trembling canopy of leaves—but those murmurs of living nature which are sweeter than silence itself—the songs of birds—the tinkling bell of the sheep on the opposite bank —the wind sighing through the trees, and the gentle heaving of the glittering waves that washed the odorous reed and the water-lily at their feet. They had both been for some moments silent; and Florence now broke the pause, but in tones more low than usual.

"Ah!" said she, turning towards him, "these hours are happier than we can find in that crowded world whither your destiny must call us. For me, ambition seems for ever at an end. I have found all; I am no longer haunted with the desire of gaining a vague something—a shadowy empire, that we call fame or power. The sole thought that disturbs the calm current of my soul, is the fear to lose a particle of the rich possession I have gained."

"May your fears ever be as idle!"

"And you really love me! I repeat to myself ever and ever that one phrase. I could once have borne to lose you—now, it would be my death. I despaired of ever being loved for myself; my wealth was a fatal dower; I suspected avarice in every vow, and saw the base world lurk at the bottom of every heart that offered itself at my shrine. But you, Ernest—you, I feel, never could weigh gold in the balance—and you—if you love—love me for myself."

"And I shall love thee more with every hour."

"I know not that: I dread that you will love me less when you know me more. I fear I shall seem to you exacting—I am jealous already. I was jealous even of Lady T——, when I saw you by her side this morning. I would have your every look—monopolise your every word."

This confession did not please Maltravers, as it might have done if he had been more deeply in love. Jealousy, in a woman of so vehement and imperious a nature, was indeed a passion to be dreaded.

"Do not say so, dear Florence," said he, with a very grave smile; "for love should have implicit confidence as its bond and nature—and jealousy is doubt, and doubt is the death of love."

A shade passed over Florence's *too* expressive face, and she sighed heavily.

It was at this time that Maltravers, raising his eyes, saw the form of Lumley Ferrers approaching towards them from the opposite end of the terrace: at the same instant a dark cloud crept over the sky, the waters seemed overcast, and the breeze fell: a chill and strange presentiment of evil shot across Ernest's heart, and, like many imaginative persons, he was unconsciously superstitious as to presentiments.

"We are no longer alone," said he, rising; "your cousin has doubtless learned our engagement, and comes to congratulate your suitor."

"Tell me," he continued musingly, as they walked on to meet Ferrers, "are you very partial to Lumley? what think you of his character?—it is one that perplexes me; sometimes I think that it has changed since we parted in Italy—sometimes I think that it has not changed, but ripened."

"Lumley I have known from a child," replied Florence, "and see much to admire and like in him; I admire his boldness and candour, his scorn of the world's littleness and falsehood; I like his good-nature—his gaiety—and fancy his heart better than it may seem to the superficial observer."

"Yet he appears to me selfish and unprincipled."

"It is from a fine contempt for the vices and follies of men that he has contracted the habit of consulting his own resolute will—and believing everything done in this noisy stage of action a cheat, he has accommodated his ambition to the fashion. Though without what is termed genius, he will obtain a distinction and power that few men of genius arrive at."

"Because *genius* is essentially honest," said Maltravers. "However, you teach me to look on him more indulgently. I suspect the real frankness of men whom I know to be hypocrites in public life—but, perhaps, I judge by too harsh a standard."

"Third persons," said Ferrers, as he now joined them, "are seldom unwelcome in the country; and I flatter myself that I am the exact thing wanting to complete the charm of this beautiful landscape."

"You are ever modest, my cousin."

"It is my weak side, I know; but I shall improve with years and wisdom. What say you, Maltravers?" and Ferrers passed his arm affectionately through Ernest's.

"By-the-by, I am too familiar—I am sunk in the world. I am a thing to be sneered at by you old-family people. I am next heir to a bran-new Brummagem peerage. Gad, I feel brassy already!"

"What, is Mr. Templeton——?"

"Mr. Templeton no more; he is defunct, extinguished—out of the ashes rises the phœnix Lord Vargrave. We had thought of a more sounding title; De Courval has a nobler sound—but my good uncle has nothing of the Norman about him; so we dropped the De as ridiculous—Vargrave is euphonious and appropriate. My uncle has a manor of that name—Baron Vargrave of Vargrave."

"Ah—I congratulate you."

"Thank you. Lady Vargrave may destroy all my hopes yet. But nothing venture, nothing have. My uncle will be gazetted to-day. Poor man, he will be delighted; and as he certainly owes it much to me, he will, I suppose, be very grateful—or hate me ever afterwards—that is a toss up. A benefit conferred is a complete hazard between the thumb of pride and the forefinger of affection. Heads gratitude, tails hatred! There, that's a simile in the fashion of the old writers. 'Well of English undefiled!' humph!"

"So that beautiful child is Mrs. Templeton's, or rather Lady Vargrave's, daughter by a former marriage?" said Maltravers, abstractedly.

"Yes; it is astonishing how fond he is of her. Pretty little creature—confoundedly artful, though. By-the-way, Maltravers, we had an unexpectedly stormy night the last of the session—strong division—ministers hard pressed. I made quite a good speech for them. I suppose, however, there will be some change—the moderates will be taken in. Perhaps by next session I may congratulate you."

Ferrers looked hard at Maltravers while he spoke. But Ernest replied coldly, and evasively, and they were now joined by a party of idlers, lounging along the lawn in expectation of the first dinner bell. Cleveland was in high consultation about the proper spot for a new fountain; and he summoned Maltravers to give his opinion whether it should spring from the centre of a flower-bed or beneath the drooping shade of a large willow. While this interesting discussion was going on, Ferrers drew aside his cousin, and pressing her hand affectionately, said, in a soft and tender voice—

"My dear Florence—for in such a time permit me to be familiar —I understand from Lord Saxingham, whom I met in London, that you are engaged to Maltravers. Busy as I was, I could not rest without coming hither to offer my best and most earnest wish for your happiness. I may seem a careless, I am considered a selfish person; but my heart is warm to those who really interest it. And never did brother offer up for the welfare of a beloved sister prayers more anxious and fond than those that poor Lumley Ferrers breathes for Florence Lascelles."

Florence was startled and melted—the whole tone and manner of Lumley was so different from those he usually assumed. She warmly returned the pressure of his hand, and thanked him briefly, but with emotion.

"No one is great and good enough for you, Florence," continued Ferrers—"no one. But I admire your disinterested and generous choice. Maltravers and I have not been friends lately; but I respect him, as all must. He has noble qualities, and he has great ambition. In addition to the deep and ardent love that you cannot fail to inspire, he will owe you eternal gratitude. In this aristocratic country, your hand secures to him the most brilliant fortunes, the most proud career. His talents will now be measured by a very different standard. His merits will not pass through any subordinate grades, but leap at once into the highest posts; and as he is even more proud than ambitious, how he must bless one who raises him, without effort, into positions of eminent command!"

"Oh, he does not think of such worldly advantages—he, the too pure, the too refined!" said Florence, with trembling eagerness. "He has no avarice, nothing mercenary in his nature!"

"No; there you indeed do him justice—there is not a particle of baseness in his mind—I did not say there was. The very greatness of his aspirations, his indignant and scornful pride, lift him above the thought of your wealth, your rank—except as means to an end."

"You mistake still," said Florence, faintly smiling, but turning pale.

"No," resumed Ferrers, not appearing to hear her, and as if pursuing his own thoughts. "I always predicted that Maltravers would make a distinguished connection in marriage. He would not permit himself to love the low-born or the poor. His affections are in his pride as much as in his heart. He is a great creature—you have judged wisely—and may heaven bless you!"

With these words, Ferrers left her, and Florence, when she descended to dinner, wore a moody and clouded brow. Ferrers stayed three days at the house. He was peculiarly cordial to Maltravers, and spoke little to Florence. But that little never failed to leave upon her mind a jealous and anxious irritability, to which she yielded with morbid facility. In order perfectly to understand Florence Lascelles, it must be remembered that, with all her dazzling qualities, she was not what is called a loveable person. A certain hardness in her disposition, even as a child, had prevented her winding into the hearts of those around her. Deprived of her mother's care—having little or no intercourse with children of her own age—brought up with a starched governess, or female relations, poor and proud—she never had contracted the softness of manner which the reciprocation of household affections usually produces. With a haughty consciousness of her powers, her birth, her position—advantages always dinned into her ears—he grew up solitary, unsocial, and imperious. Her father was rather proud than fond of her—her servants did not love her—she had too little consideration for others, too little blandness and suavity to be loved by inferiors—she was too learned and too stern to find pleasure in the conversation and society of young ladies of her own age—she had no friends. Now, having really strong affections, she felt all this, but rather with resentment than grief—she longed to be loved, but did not *seek* to be so—she felt as if it was her fate not to be loved—she blamed Fate, not herself.

When, with all the proud, pure, and generous candour of her nature, she avowed to Ernest her love for him, she naturally expected the most ardent and passionate return; nothing less could content her. But the habit and experience of all the past made her eternally suspicious that she was not loved; it was wormwood and poison to her to fancy that Maltravers had ever considered her advantages of fortune, except as a bar to his pretensions and a check to his passion. It was the same thing to her, whether it was the pettiest avarice or the loftiest aspirations that actuated her lover, if he *had been* actuated in his heart by any sentiment *but* love; and Ferrers, to whose eyes her foibles were familiar, knew well how to make his praises of Ernest arouse against Ernest all her exacting jealousies and irritable doubts.

"It is strange," said he, one evening, as he was conversing with Florence, "how complete and triumphant a conquest you have effected over Ernest! Will you believe it?—he conceived a prejudice against you when he first saw you—he even said that you were made to be admired, not to be loved."

"Ha! did he so?—true, true—he has almost said the same thing to me."

"But now how he must love you! Surely he has all the signs."

"And what are the signs, most learned Lumley?" said Florence, forcing a smile.

"Why, in the first place, you will doubtless observe that he never takes his eyes from you—with whomsoever he converses, whatever his occupation, those eyes, restless and pining, wander around for one glance from you."

Florence sighed, and looked up—at the other end of the room her lover was conversing with Cleveland, and his eyes never wandered in search of her.

Ferrers did not seem to notice this practical contradiction of his theory, but went on.

"Then surely his whole character is changed—that brow has lost its calm majesty, that deep voice its assured and tranquil tone. Has he not become humble, and embarrassed, and fretful, living only on your smile, reproachful if you look upon another—sorrowful if your lip be less smiling—a thing of doubt, and dread, and trembling agitation—slave to a shadow—no longer lord of the creation!—Such is love, such is the love you should inspire—such is the love Maltravers is capable of—for I have seen him testify it to another. But," added Lumley, quickly, and as if afraid he had said too much, " Lord Saxingham is looking out for me to make up his whist-table. I go to-morrow—when shall you be in town?"

"In the course of the week," said poor Florence, mechanically; and Lumley walked away.

In another moment, Maltravers, who had been more observant than he seemed, joined her where she sat.

"Dear Florence," said he, tenderly, "you look pale—I fear you are not so well this evening."

"No affectation of an interest you do not feel, pray," said Florence, with a scornful lip but swimming eyes.

"Do not feel, Florence!"

"It is the first time, at least, that you have observed whether I am well or ill. But it is no matter."

"My dear Florence—why this tone?—how have I offended you? Has Lumley said——"

"Nothing but in your praise. Oh, be not afraid, you are one of those of whom all speak highly. But do not let me detain you here! let us join our host—you have left him alone."

Lady Florence waited for no reply, nor did Maltravers attempt to detain her. He looked pained, and when she turned round to catch a glance, that she hoped would be reproachful, he was gone. Lady Florence became nervous and uneasy, talked she knew not what, and laughed hysterically. She, however, deceived Cleveland into the notion that she was in the best possible spirits.

By-and-by she rose, and passed through the suite of rooms; her heart was with Maltravers—still he was not visible. At length she entered the conservatory, and there she observed him, through the open casements, walking slowly, with folded arms, upon the moonlit lawn. There was a short struggle in her breast between woman's pride and woman's love; the last conquered, and she joined him.

"Forgive me, Ernest," she said, extending her hand, "I was to blame."

Ernest kissed her fair hand, and answered touchingly—

"Florence, you have the power to wound me—be forbearing in its exercise. Heaven knows that I would not, from the vain desire of showing command over you, inflict upon you a single pang. Ah! I do not fancy that in lovers' quarrels there is any sweetness that compensates the sting."

"I told you I was too exacting, Ernest. I told you, you would not love me so well when you knew me better."

"And were a false prophetess. Florence, every day, every hour, I love you more—better than I once thought I could."

"Then," cried this wayward girl, anxious to pain herself, "then once you did not love me?"

"Florence, I will be candid—I did not. You are now rapidly obtaining an empire over me, greater than my reason should allow. But beware; if my love be really a possession you desire—beware how you arm my reason against you. Florence, I am a proud man. My very consciousness of the more splendid alliances you could form renders me less humble a lover than you might find in others. I were not worthy of you if I were not tenacious of my self-respect."

"Ah!" said Florence, to whose heart these words went home, "forgive me but this once. I shall not forgive myself so soon."

And Ernest drew her to his breast, and felt that with all her faults, a woman whom he feared he could not render as happy as her sacrifices to him deserved, was becoming very dear to him. In his heart he knew that she was not formed to render *him* happy; but that was not his thought, his fear. Her love had rooted out all thought of self from that generous breast. His only anxiety was to requite *her*.

They walked along the sward, silent, thoughtful; and Florence melancholy, yet blessed.

"That serene heaven, those lovely stars," said Maltravers at last, "do they not preach to us the Philosophy of Peace? Do they not tell us how much of calm belongs to the dignity of man, and the sublime essence of the soul. Petty distractions and self-wrought cares are not congenial to our real nature; their very disturbance is a proof that they are at war with our natures. Ah, sweet Florence, let us learn from yon skies, over which, in the faith of the Poets of old, brooded the wings of primeval and serenest Love, what earthly love should be—a thing pure as light, and peaceful as immortality, watching over the stormy world, that it shall survive, and high above the clouds and vapours that roll below. Let little minds introduce into the holiest of affections all the bitterness and tumult of common life! Let *us* love as beings who will one day be inhabitants of the stars!"

CHAPTER IV.

"A slippery and subtle knave; a finder out of occasions, that has an eye can stamp and counterfeit advantages."—*Othello*.

"Knavery's plain face is never seen till used."—*Ibid*.

"YOU see, my dear Lumley," said Lord Saxingham, as the next day the two kinsmen were on their way to London in the earl's chariot, "you see that, at the best, this marriage of Flory's is a cursed bore."

"Why, indeed, it has its disadvantages. Maltravers is a gentleman and a man of genius; but gentlemen are plentiful, and his genius only tells against us, since he is not even of our politics."

"Exactly, my own son-in-law voting against me!"

"A practicable, reasonable man would change; not so Maltraver—and all the estates, and all the parliamentary influence, and all the wealth that ought to go with the family and with the party, go out of the family and against the party. You are quite right, my dear lord—it is a cursed bore."

"And she might have had the Duke of ——, a man with a rental of £100,000 a-year. It is too ridiculous.—This Maltravers—d—d disagreeable fellow, too, eh?"

"Stiff and stately—much changed for the worst of late years—grown conceited and set up."

"Do you know, Lumley, I would rather, of the two, have had you for my son-in-law."

Lumley half started. "Are you serious, my lord? I have not Ernest's fortune—I cannot make such settlements; my lineage, too, at least on my mother's side, is less ancient."

"Oh, as to settlements, Flory's fortune ought to be settled on herself—and as compared with that fortune, what could Mr. Maltravers pretend to settle?—Neither she nor any children she may have could want his £4000 a-year, if he settled it all. As for family, connections tell more now-a-days than Norman descent—and for the rest, you are likely to be old Templeton's heir, to have a peerage (a large sum of ready money is always useful)—are rising in the House—one of our own set—will soon be in office—and, flattery apart, a devilish good fellow into the bargain. Oh, I would sooner a thousand times that Flory had taken a fancy to you!"

Lumley Ferrers bowed his head, but said nothing. He fell into a reverie, and Lord Saxingham took up his official box, became deep in its contents, and forgot all about the marriage of his daughter.

Lumley pulled the check-strings as the carriage entered Pall Mall, and desired to be set down at the "Travellers." While Lord Saxingham was borne on to settle the affairs of the nation, not being able to settle those of his own household, Ferrers was inquiring the address of Castruccio Cesarini. The porter was unable to give it him. The Signor generally called every day for his notes, but no one at the club knew where he lodged. Ferrers wrote, and left with the porter a line, requesting Cesarini to call on him as soon as possible, and bent his way to his house in Great George Street. He went straight into his library, unlocked his escritoir, and took out that letter which, the reader will remember, Maltravers had written to Cesarini, and which Lumley had secured; carefully did he twice read over this effusion, and the second time his face brightened and his eyes sparkled. It is now time to lay this letter before the reader. It ran thus:—

"*Private and confidential.*

"MY DEAR CESARINI,

"The assurance of your friendly feelings is most welcome to me. In much of what you say of marriage, I am inclined, though with reluctance, to agree. As to Lady Florence herself, few persons are more calculated to dazzle, perhaps to fascinate. But is she a person to make a home happy—to sympathise where she has been accustomed to command—to comprehend, and to yield to the waywardness and irritability common to our fanciful and morbid race—to content herself with the homage of a single heart? I do not know her enough to decide the question ; but I know her enough to feel deep solicitude and anxiety for your happiness, if centered in a nature so imperious and so vain. But you will remind me of her fortune, her station. You will say that such are the sources from which, to an ambitious mind, happiness may well be drawn! Alas! I fear that the man who marries Lady Florence must indeed confine his dreams of felicity to those harsh and disappointing realities. But, Cesarini, these are not the words which, were we more intimate, I would address to you. I doubt the reality of those affections which you ascribe to her, and suppose devoted to yourself. She is evidently fond of conquest. She sports with the victims she makes. Her vanity dupes others—perhaps to be duped itself at last. I will not say more to you.—Yours,

"E. MALTRAVERS."

"Hurrah!" cried Ferrers, as he threw down the letter, and rubbed his hands with delight. "I little thought, when I schemed for this letter, that chance would make it so inestimably serviceable. There is less to alter than I thought for—the clumsiest botcher in the world could manage it. Let me look again.—Hem, hem—the first phrase to alter is this :—' I know her enough to feel deep solicitude and anxiety for *your* happiness, if centered in a nature so imperious and vain '—scratch out ' your,' and put ' my.' All the rest good, good—till we come to ' affections which you ascribe to her, and suppose devoted to *yourself*'—for '*yourself*' write ' *my*self '—the rest will do. Now, then, the date—we must change it to the present month, and the work is done. I wish that Italian blockhead would come. If I can but once make an irreparable breach between her and Maltravers, I think I cannot fail in securing his place ; her pique, her resentment will hurry her into taking the first who offers, by way of revenge. And, by Jupiter, even if I fail (which I am sure I shall not), it will be something to keep Flory as lady paramount for a duke of our own party. I shall gain immensely by such a connection; but I lose everything and gain nothing by her marrying Maltravers—of opposite politics too—whom I begin to hate like poison. But no duke shall have her—Florence Ferrers, the only alliteration I ever liked—yet it would sound rough in poetry."

Lumley then deliberately drew towards him his inkstand—"No penknife !—Ah, true, I never mend pens—sad waste—must send out for one." He rang the bell, ordered a penknife to be purchased, and the servant was still out when a knock at the door was heard, and in a minute more Cesarini entered.

"Ah," said Lumley, assuming a melancholy air, "I am glad that you are arrived; you will excuse my having written to you so unceremoniously. You received my note—sit down, pray—and how are you ?—you look delicate—can I offer you anything ?"

"Wine," said Cesarini, laconically, "wine; your climate requires wine."

Here the servant entered with the penknife, and was ordered to bring wine and sandwiches. Lumley then conversed lightly on different matters till the wine appeared; he was rather surprised to observe Cesarini pour out and drink off glass upon glass, with an evident craving for the excitement. When he had satisfied himself, he turned his dark eyes to Ferrers, and said, "You have news to communicate, I see it in your brow. I am now ready to hear all."

"Well, then, listen to me; you were right in your suspicions; jealousy is ever a true diviner. I make no doubt Othello was quite right, and Desdemona was no better than she should be. Maltravers has proposed to my cousin, and been accepted."

Cesarini's complexion grew perfectly ghastly; his whole frame shook like a leaf—for a moment he seemed paralysed.

"Curse him !" said he, at last, drawing a deep breath, and betwixt his grinded teeth—"curse him, from the depths of the heart he has broken !"

"And after such a letter to you !—do you remember it ?—here it is. He warns you against Lady Florence, and then secures her to himself—is this treachery ?"

"Treachery, black as hell ! I am an Italian," cried Cesarini, springing to his feet, and with all the passions of his climate in his face, "and I will be avenged ! Bankrupt in fortune, ruined in hopes, blasted in heart—I have still the godlike consolation of the desperate—I have revenge."

"Will you call him out?" asked Lumley, musingly and calmly. "Are you a dead shot? If so, it is worth thinking about; if not, it is a mockery—your shot misses, his goes in the air, seconds interpose, and you both walk away devilish glad to get off so well. Duels are humbug."

"Mr. Ferrers," said Cesarini, fiercely, "this is not a matter of jest."

"I do not make it a jest; and what is more, Cesarini," said Ferrers, with a concentrated energy far more commanding than the Italian's fury, "what is more, I so detest Maltravers, I am so stung by his cold superiority, so wroth with his success, so loathe the thought of his alliance, that I would cut off this hand to frustrate that marriage! I do not jest, man; but I have method and sense in my hatred—it is our English way."

Cesarini stared at the speaker gloomily, clenched his hand, muttered, and strode rapidly to and fro the room.

"You would be avenged, so would I. Now what shall be the means?" said Ferrers.

"I will stab him to the heart—I will——"

"Cease these tragic flights. Nay, frown and stamp not; but sit down, and be reasonable, or leave me, and act for yourself."

"Sir," said Cesarini, with an eye that might have alarmed a man less resolute than Ferrers, "have a care how you presume on my distress."

"You are in distress, and you refuse relief; you are bankrupt in fortune, and you rave like a poet, when you should be devising and plotting for the attainment of boundless wealth. Revenge and ambition may both be yours; but they are prizes never won but by a cautious foot as well as a bold hand."

"What would you have me do? and what but his life would content me?"

"Take his life if you can—I have no objection—go and take it; only just observe this, that if you miss your aim, or he, being the stronger man, strike you down, you will be locked up in a madhouse for the next year or two, at least; and that is not the place in which I should like to pass the winter—but as you will."

"You!—you!—But what are you to me? I will go. Good day, sir."

"Stay a moment," said Ferrers, when he saw Cesarini about to leave the room; "stay, take this chair, and listen to me—you had better——"

Cesarini hesitated, and then, as it were, mechanically obeyed.

"Read that letter, which Maltravers wrote to you. You have finished—well—now observe—if Florence sees that letter, she will not and cannot marry the man who wrote it—you must show it to her."

"Ah, my guardian angel, I see it all! Yes, there are words in this letter no woman so proud could ever pardon. Give it me again, I will go at once."

"Pshaw! You are too quick; you have not remarked that this letter was written five months ago, before Maltravers knew much of Lady Florence. He himself has confessed to her that he did not then love her—so much the more would she value the conquest she has now achieved. Florence would smile at this letter, and say, 'Ah, he judges me differently now.'"

"Are you seeking to madden me? What do you mean? Did you not just now say that, did she see that letter, she would never marry the writer?"

"Yes, yes, but the letter must be altered. We must erase the date; we must date it from to-day—to-day—Maltravers returns to-day. We must suppose it written, not in answer to a letter from you, demanding his advice and opinion as to *your* marriage with Lady Florence, but in answer to a letter of yours in which you congratulate *him* on his approaching marriage to her. By the substitution of one pronoun for another, in two places, the letter will read as well one way as another. Read it again, and see; or stop, I will be the lecturer."

Here Ferrers read over the letter, which, by the trifling substitutions he proposed, might indeed bear the character he wished to give it.

"Does the light break in upon you now?" said Ferrers. "Are you prepared to go through a part that requires subtlety, delicacy, address, and, above all, self-control?—qualities that are the common attributes of your countrymen."

"I will do all, fear me not. It may be villainous, it may be base; but I care not; Maltravers shall not rival, master, eclipse me in all things."

"Where are you lodging?"

"Where?—out of town a little way."

"Take up your home with me for a few days. I cannot trust you out of my sight. Send for your luggage, I have a room at your service."

Cesarini at first refused; but a man who resolves on a crime feels the awe of solitude, and the necessity of a companion. He went himself to bring his effects, and promised to return to dinner.

"I must own," said Lumley, resettling himself at his desk, "this is the dirtiest trick that ever I played; but the glorious end sanctifies the paltry means. After all, it is the mere prejudice of a gentlemanlike education."

A very few seconds, and with the aid of the knife to erase, and the pen to re-write, Ferrers completed his task, with the exception of the change of date, which, on second thoughts, he reserved as a matter to be regulated by circumstances.

"I think I have hit off his *m*'s and *y*'s tolerably," said he, "considering I was not brought up to this sort of thing. But the alteration would be visible on close inspection. Cesarini must read the letter to her, then if she glances over it herself it will be with bewildered eyes and a dizzy brain. Above all, he must not leave it with her, and must bind her to the closest secrecy. She is honourable, and will keep her word; and so now that matter is settled. I have just time before dinner to canter down to my uncle's and wish the old fellow joy."

CHAPTER V.

"And then my lord has much that he would state,
All good to you."—CRABBE: *Tales of the Heart.*

LORD VARGRAVE was sitting alone in his library, with his account-books before him. Carefully did he cast up the various sums, which, invested in various speculations, swelled his income. The result seemed satisfactory—and the rich man threw down his pen with an air of triumph. "I will invest £120,000 in land—only £120,000, I will not be tempted to sink more. I will have a fine house—a house fitting for a nobleman—a fine old Elizabethan house—a house of historical interest. I must have woods and lakes—and a deer-park, above all. Deer are very gentlemanlike things, very. De Clifford's place is to be sold, I know; they ask too much money for it, but ready money is tempting. I can bargain—bargain; I am a good hand at a bargain. Should I be now Lord Baron Vargrave if I had always given people what they asked? I will double my subscriptions to the Bible

Society, and the Philanthropic, and the building of new churches. The world shall not say Richard Templeton does not deserve his greatness. I will——Come in. Who's there—come in."

The door gently opened—the meek face of the new peeress appeared. "I disturb you—I beg your pardon—I——"

"Come in, my dear, come in—I want to talk to you—I want to talk to your ladyship—sit down, pray."

Lady Vargrave obeyed.

"You see," said the peer, crossing his legs, and caressing his left foot with both hands, while he see-sawed his stately person to and fro in his chair—"you see that the honour conferred upon me will make a great change in our mode of life, Mrs. Temple——, I mean Lady Vargrave. This villa is all very well—my country-house is not amiss for a country-gentleman—but now, we must support our rank. The landed estate I already possess will go with the title—go to Lumley—I shall buy another at my own disposal, one that I can feel *thoroughly mine*—it shall be a splendid place, Lady Vargrave."

"This place is spendid to me," said Lady Vargrave, timidly.

"This place! nonsense—you must learn loftier ideas, Lady Vargrave; you are young, you can easily contract new habits, more easily perhaps than myself—you are naturally ladylike, though I say it—you have good taste, you don't talk much, you don't show your ignorance—quite right. You must be presented at court, Lady Vargrave—we must give great dinners, Lady Vargrave. Balls are sinful, so is the opera, at least I fear so—yet an opera-box would be a proper appendage to your rank, Lady Vargrave."

"My dear Mr. Templeton——"

"Lord Vargrave, if your ladyship pleases."

"I beg your pardon. May you live long to enjoy your honours; but I, my dear lord—I am not fit to share them: it is only in our quiet life that I can forget what—what I was. You terrify me, when you talk of court—of——"

"Stuff, Lady Vargrave! stuff; we accustom ourselves to these things. Do I look like a man who has stood behind a counter?—rank is a glove that stretches to the hand that wears it. And the child, dear child—dear Evelyn, she shall be the admiration of London, the beauty, the heiress, the—oh, she will do me honour!"

"She will, she will!" said Lady Vargrave, and the tears gushed from her eyes.

Lord Vargrave was softened.

"No mother ever deserved more from a child than you from Evelyn."

"I would hope I have done my duty," said Lady Vargrave drying her tears.

"Papa, papa!" cried an impatient voice, tapping at the window, "come and play, papa—come and play at ball, papa!"

And there by the window stood that beautiful child, glowing with health and mirth—her light hair tossed from her forehead, her sweet mouth dimpled with smiles.

"My darling, go on the lawn—don't over-exert yourself—you have not quite recovered that horrid sprain—I will join you immediately—bless you!"

"Don't be long, papa—nobody plays so nicely as you do;" and, nodding and laughing from very glee, away scampered the young fairy.

Lord Vargrave turned to his wife.

"What think you of my nephew—of Lumley?" said he, abruptly.

"He seems all that is amiable, frank, and kind."

Lord Vargrave's brow became thoughtful. "I think so too," he said, after a short pause; "and I hope you will approve of what I mean to do. You see Lumley was brought up to regard himself as my heir—I owe something to him, beyond the poor estate which goes with, but never can adequately support, *my* title. Family honours, hereditary rank, must be properly regarded. But that dear girl—I shall leave her the bulk of my fortune. Could we not unite the fortune and the title? It would secure the rank to her, it would incorporate all my desires—all my duties."

"But," said Lady Vargrave, with evident surprise, "if I understand you rightly, the disparity of years——"

"And what then, what then, Lady Vargrave? Is there no disparity of years between *us*—a greater disparity than between Lumley and that tall girl? Lumley is a mere youth, a youth still, five-and-thirty—he will be little more than forty when they marry; I was between fifty and sixty when I married you, Lady Vargrave. I don't like boy and girl marriages: a man should be older than his wife. But you are so romantic, Lady Vargrave. Besides, Lumley is so gay and good-looking, and wears so well. He has been very nearly forming another attachment: but that, I trust, is out of his head now. They must like each other. You will not gainsay me, Lady Vargrave, and if anything happens to me—life is uncertain."

"Oh, do not speak so—my friend, my benefactor!"

"Why, indeed," resumed his lordship, mildly, "thank heaven, I am very well—feel younger than ever I did—but still, life is uncertain; and if you survive me, you will not throw obstacles in the way of my grand scheme?"

"I—no, no—of course you have the right in all things over her destiny; but so young—so soft-hearted, if she should love one of her own years——"

"Love!—pooh! love does not come into girls' heads unless it is put there. We will bring her up to love Lumley. I have another reason—a cogent one—our secret!—to him it can be confided—it should not go out of our family. Even in my grave I could not rest if a slur were cast on my respectability—my name."

Lord Vargrave spoke solemnly and warmly; then muttering to himself, "Yes, it is for the best," he took up his hat and quitted the room. He joined his step-child on the lawn. He romped with her—he played with her—that stiff, stately man!—he laughed louder than she did, and ran almost as fast. And when she was fatigued and breathless, he made her sit down beside him, in a little summerhouse, and, fondly stroking down her disordered tresses, said, "You tire me out, child; I am growing too old to play with you. Lumley must supply my place. You love Lumley?"

"Oh, dearly, he is so good-humoured, so kind; he has given me such a beautiful doll, with *such* eyes!"

"You shall be his little wife—you would like to be his little wife."

"Wife! why, poor mamma is a wife, and she is not so happy as I am."

"Your mamma has bad health, my dear," said Lord Vargrave, a little discomposed. "But it is a fine thing to be a wife and have a carriage of your own, and a fine house, and jewels, and plenty of money, and be your own mistress; and Lumley will love you dearly."

"Oh yes, I should like all that."

"And you will have a protector, child, when I am no more."

The tone, rather than the words, of her stepfather struck a damp into that childish heart. Evelyn lifted her eyes, gazed at him earnestly, and then, throwing her arms around him, burst into tears.

Lord Vargrave wiped his own eyes, and covered her with kisses

"Yes, you shall be Lumley's wife, his honoured wife, heiress to my rank as to my fortunes."

"I will do all that papa wishes."

"You will be Lady Vargrave then, and Lumley will be your husband," said the stepfather, impressively. "Think over what I have said. Now let us join mamma. But, as I live, here is Lumley himself. However, it is not yet the time to sound him—I hope that he has no chance with that Lady Florence."

CHAPTER VI.

*"Fair encounter
Of two most rare affections."—Tempest.*

MEANWHILE the Betrothed were on their road to London. The balmy and serene beauty of the day had induced them to perform the short journey on horseback. It is somewhere said, that lovers are never so handsome as in each other's company, and neither Florence nor Ernest ever looked so well as on horseback. There was something in the stateliness and the grace of both, something even in the aquiline outline of their features, and the haughty bend of the neck, that made a sort of likeness between these young persons, although there was no comparison as to their relative degrees of personal advantage: the beauty of Florence defied all comparison. And as they rode from Cleveland's porch, where the other guests yet lingering were assembled to give the farewell greeting, there was a general conviction of the happiness destined to the affianced ones—a general impression that both in mind and person they were eminently suited to each other. Their position was that which is ever interesting, even in more ordinary people, and at that moment they were absolutely popular with all who gazed on them; and when the good old Cleveland turned away with tears in his eyes and murmured, "Bless them!" there was not one of the party who would have hesitated to join the prayer.

Florence felt a nameless dejection as she quitted a spot so consecrated by grateful recollections.

"When shall we be again so happy?" said she, softly, as she turned back to gaze upon the landscape, which, gay with flowers and shrubs, and the bright English verdure, smiled behind them like a garden.

"We will try and make my old hall, and its gloomy shades, remind us of these fairer scenes, my Florence."

"Ah! describe to me the character of your place. We shall live there principally, shall we not? I am sure I shall like it much better than Marsden Court, which is the name of that huge pile of arches and columns in Vanbrugh's heaviest taste, which will soon be yours."

"I fear we shall never dispose of all your mighty retinue, grooms of the chamber, and Patagonian footmen, and heaven knows who besides, in the holes and corners of Burleigh," said Ernest, smiling. And then he went on to describe the old place with something of a well-born country gentleman's not displeasing pride; and Florence listened, and they planned, and altered, and added, and improved, and laid out a map for the future. From that topic they turned to another, equally interesting to Florence. The work in which Maltravers had been engaged was completed, was in the hands of the printer, and Florence amused herself with conjectures as to the criticisms it would provoke. She was certain that all that had most pleased her would be *caviare* to the multitude. She never would believe that any one could understand Maltravers but herself. Thus time flew on, till they passed that part of the road in which had occurred Ernest's adventure with Mrs. Templeton's daughter. Maltravers paused abruptly in the midst of his glowing periods, as the spot awakened its associations and reminiscences, and looked round anxiously and inquiringly. But the fair apparition was not again visible; and whatever impression the place produced, it gradually died away as they entered the suburbs of the great metropolis. Two other gentlemen and a young lady of thirty-three (I had almost forgotten them) were of the party, but they had the tact to linger a little behind during the greater part of the road, and the young lady, who was a wit and a flirt, found gossip and sentiment for both the cavaliers.

"Will you come to us this evening?" asked Florence, timidly.

"I fear I shall not be able. I have several matters to arrange before I leave town for Burleigh, which I must do next week. Three months, dearest Florence, will scarcely suffice to make Burleigh put on its best looks to greet its new mistress; and I have already appointed the great modern magicians of draperies and ormolu to consult how we may make Aladdin's palace fit for the reception of the new princess. Lawyers, too!—in short, I expect to be fully occupied. But to-morrow at three I shall be with you, and we can ride out, if the day be fine."

"Surely," said Florence, "yonder is Signor Cesarini—how haggard and altered he appears!"

Maltravers, turning his eyes towards the spot to which Florence pointed, saw Cesarini emerging from a lane, with a porter behind him carrying some books and a trunk. The Italian, who was talking and gesticulating as to himself, did not perceive them.

"Poor Castruccio! he seems leaving his lodging," thought Maltravers. "By this time I fear he will have spent the last sum I conveyed to him—I must remember to find him out and replenish his stores.—Do not forget," said he aloud, "to see Cesarini, and urge him to accept the appointment we spoke of."

"I will not forget it—I will see him to-morrow before we meet. Yet it is a painful task, Ernest."

"I allow it. Alas! Florence, you owe him some reparation. He undoubtedly once conceived himself entitled to form hopes, the vanity of which his ignorance of our English world and his foreign birth prevented him from suspecting."

"Believe me, I did not give him the right to form such expectations."

"But you did not sufficiently discourage them. Ah, Florence, never underrate the pangs of hope crushed, of love contemned."

"Dreadful!" said Florence, almost shuddering. "It is strange, but my conscience never so smote me before. It is since I love that I feel, for the first time, how guilty a creature is——"

"A coquette!" interrupted Maltravers. "Well, let us think of the past no more; but if we can restore a gifted man, whose youth promised much, to an honourable independence and a healthful mind, let us do so. Me, Cesarini never can forgive; he will think I have robbed him of you. But we men—the woman we have once loved, even after she rejects us, ever has some power over us; and your eloquence, which has so often roused me, cannot fail to impress a nature yet more excitable."

Maltravers, on quitting Florence at her own door, went home, summoned his favourite servant, gave him Cesarini's address at Chelsea, bade him find out where he was, if he had left his lodgings; and leave at his present home, or (failing its discovery) at the "Travellers," a cover, which he made his servant address, enclosing a bank-note of some amount. If the reader wonder why Maltravers thus constituted himself the unknown benefactor of the Italian, I must tell him that he does not understand Maltravers. Cesarini was not the only man of letters whose faults he pitied, whose wants he relieved. Though his name seldom shone in the pompous list of public subscriptions—though he disdained to affect the Mæcenas and the patron, he felt the brotherhood of mankind, and a kind of gratitude for those who aspired to raise or to delight their species. An author himself, he could appreciate the vast debt which the world owes to authors, and pays but by calumny in life and barren laurels after death. He whose profession is the Beautiful succeeds only through the Sympathies. Charity and Compassion are virtues taught with difficulty to ordinary men; to true Genius they are but the instincts which direct it to the Destiny it is born to fulfil—viz., the discovery and redemption of new tracts in our common nature. Genius—the Sublime Missionary—goes forth from the serene Intellect of the Author to live in the wants, the griefs, the infirmities of others, in order that it may learn their language; and as its highest achievement is Pathos, so its most absolute requisite is Pity!

CHAPTER VII.

"*Don John.* How canst thou cross this marriage?
Borachio. Not honestly, my lord; but so covertly, that no dishonesty shall appear in me, my lord."—*Much Ado about Nothing.*

FERRERS and Cesarini were sitting over their wine, and both had sunk into silence, for they had only one subject in common, when a note was brought to Lumley from Lady Florence. "This is lucky enough!" said he, as he read it. "Lady Florence wishes to see you, and encloses me a note for you, which she asks me to address and forward to you. There it is."

Cesarini took the note with trembling hands: it was very short, and merely expressed a desire to see him the next day at two o'clock.

"What can it be?" he exclaimed; "can she want to apologise, to explain?"

"No, no, no! Florence will not do that; but, from certain words she dropped in talking with me, I guess that she has some offer to your worldly advantage to propose to you. Ha! by the way, a thought strikes me."

Lumley eagerly rang the bell. "Is Lady Florence's servant waiting for an answer?"

"Yes, sir."

"Very well—detain him."

"Now, Cesarini, assurance is made doubly sure. Come into the next room. There, sit down at my desk, and write, as I shall dictate, to Maltravers."

"I?"

"Yes, now *do* put yourself in my hands—write, write. When you have finished, I will explain."

Cesarini obeyed, and the letter was as follows:—

"MY DEAR MALTRAVERS—I have learned your approaching marriage with Lady Florence Lascelles. Permit me to congratulate you. For myself, I have overcome a vain and foolish passion, and can contemplate your happiness without a sigh.

"I have reviewed all my old prejudices against marriage, and believe it to be a state which nothing but the most perfect congeniality of temper, pursuits, and minds, can render bearable.—How rare is such congeniality! in your case it may exist. The affections of that beautiful being are doubtless ardent—and they are yours!

"Write me a line by the bearer to assure me of your belief in my sincerity.—Yours,   C. CESARINI."

"Copy out this letter, I want its ditto—quick. Now seal and direct the duplicate," continued Ferrers; "that's right; go into the hall, give it yourself to Lady Florence's servant, and beg him to take it to Seamore Place, wait for an answer, and bring it here; by which time you will have a note ready for Lady Florence. Say I will mention this to her ladyship—and give the man half-a-crown. There—begone."

"I do not understand a word of this," said Cesarini, when he returned; "will you explain?"

"Certainly; the copy of the note you have despatched to Maltravers I shall show to Lady Florence this evening, as a proof of your sobered and generous feelings; observe, it is so written that the old letter of your rival may seem an exact reply to it. Tomorrow a reference to this note of yours will bring out our scheme more easily; and if you follow my instructions, you will not seem to *volunteer* showing our handiwork as we at first intended; but rather to yield it to her eyes from a generous impulse, from an irresistible desire to save her from an unworthy husband and a wretched fate. Fortune has been dealing our cards for us, and has turned up the ace. Three to one now on the odd trick. Maltravers, too, is at home. I called at his house on returning from my uncle's, and learned that he would not stir out all the evening.

In due time came the answer from Ernest: it was short and hurried, but full of all the manly kindness of his nature; it expressed admiration and delight at the tone of Cesarini's letter; it revoked all former expressions derogatory to Lady Florence; it owned the harshness and error of his first impressions; it used every delicate argument that could soothe and reconcile Cesarini: and concluded by sentiments of friendship and desire of service, so cordial, so honest, so free from the affectation of patronage, that even Cesarini himself, half insane as he was with passion, was almost softened. Lumley saw the change in his countenance—snatched the letter from his hand—read it—threw it into the fire—and saying, "We must guard against accidents," clapped the Italian affectionately on the shoulder, and added, "Now you can have no remorse; for a more Jesuitical piece of insulting, hypocritical cant I never read. Where's your note to Lady Florence? Your compliments, you will be with her at two. There, now the rehearsal's over, the scenes arranged, and I'll dress, and open the play for you with a prologue."

CHAPTER VIII.

"Æstuat ingens
Imo in corde pudor, mixtoque insania luctu,
Et furiis agitatus amor, et conscia virtus." *—Virgil.

THE next day, punctual to his appointment, Cesarini repaired to his critical interview with Lady Florence. Her countenance, which, like that of most persons whose temper is not under their command, ever too faithfully expressed what was within, was unusually flushed. Lumley had dropped words and hints which had driven sleep from her pillow and repose from her mind.

* Deep in her inmost heart is stirred the immense shame, and madness with commingled grief, and love agitated by rage, and conscious virtue.

She rose from her seat with nervous agitation as Cesarini entered and made his grave salutation. After a short and embarrassed pause she recovered, however, her self-possession, and with all a woman's delicate and dexterous tact urged upon the Italian the expediency of accepting the offer of honourable independence now extended to him.

"You have abilities," she said, in conclusion, "you have friends, you have youth; take advantage of those gifts of nature and fortune, and fulfil such a career as," added Lady Florence, with a smile, "Dante did not consider incompatible with poetry."

"I cannot object to any career," said Cesarini, with an effort, "that may serve to remove me from a country that has no longer any charms for me. I thank you for your kindness; I will obey you. May you be happy; and yet—no, ah! no—happy you must be! Even *he*, sooner or later, must see you with my eyes."

"I know," replied Florence, falteringly, "that you have wisely and generously mastered a past illusion. Mr. Ferrers allowed me to see the letter you wrote to Er——, to Mr. Maltravers; it was worthy of you; it touched me deeply; but I trust you will outlive your prejudices against ——"

"Stay," interrupted Cesarini; "did Ferrers communicate to you the answer to that letter?"

"No, indeed."

"I am glad of it."

"Why?"

"Oh, no matter. Heaven bless you; farewell."

"No; I implore you, do not go yet; what was there in that letter that it could pain me to see? Lumley hinted darkly, but would not speak out; be more frank."

"I cannot; it would be treachery to Maltravers, cruelty to you; yet, would it be cruel?"

"No, it would not; it would be kindness and mercy; show me the letter—you have it with you."

"You could not bear it; you would hate me for the pain it would give you. Let me depart."

"Man, you wrong Maltravers. I see it now. You would darkly slander him whom you cannot openly defame. Go; I was wrong to listen to you—go!"

"Lady Florence, beware how you taunt me into undeceiving you. Here is the letter, it is his handwriting; will you read it? I warn you not."

"I will believe nothing but the evidence of my own eyes; give it me."

"Stay then; on two conditions. First, that you promise me sacredly that you will not disclose to Maltravers, without my consent, that you have seen this letter. Think not I fear his anger. No! but in the mortal encounter that must ensue if you thus betray me, your character would be lowered in the world's eyes, and even I (my excuse unknown) might not appear to have acted with honour in obeying your desire, and warning you, while there is yet time, of bartering love for avarice. Promise me."

"I do, I do, most solemnly."

"Secondly, assure me that you will not ask to keep the letter, but will immediately restore it to me."

"I promise it. Now then."

"Take the letter."

Florence seized and rapidly read the fatal and garbled document; her brain was dizzy, her eyes clouded, her ears rang as with the sound of water; she was sick and giddy with emotion; but she read enough. This letter was written, then, in answer to Castruccio's of last night; it avowed dislike of her character; it denied the sincerity of her love; it more than hinted the mercenary nature of his own feelings. Yes, even there, where she had garnered up her heart, she was not Florence, the lovely and beloved woman, but Florence, the wealthy and high-born heiress. The world which she had built upon the faith and heart of Maltravers crumbled away at her feet. The letter dropped from her hands; her whole form seemed to shrink and shrivel up; her teeth were set, and her cheek was as white as marble.

"O God!" cried Cesarini, stung with remorse. "Speak to me, speak to me, Florence! I did wrong; forget that hateful letter! I have been false—false!"

"Ah, false—say so again!—no, no, I remember *he* told me—he, so wise, so deep a judge of human character, that he would be sponsor for your faith—that your honour and heart were incorruptible. It is true; I thank you—you have saved me from a terrible fate."

"Oh, Lady Florence, dear—too dear—yet, would that—alas! she does not listen to me," muttered Castruccio, as Florence, pressing her hands to her temples, walked wildly to and fro the room; at length she paused opposite to Cesarini, looked him full in the face, returned him the letter without a word, and pointed to the door.

—20—

"No, no, do not bid me leave you yet," said Cesarini, trembling with repentant emotion, yet half beside himself with jealous rage at her love for his rival.

"My friend, go," said Florence, in a tone of voice singularly subdued and soft. "Do not fear me; I have more pride in me than even affection; but there are certain struggles in a woman's breast which she could never betray to any one—any one but a mother. God help me, I have none! Go; when next we meet I shall be calm."

She held out her hand as she spoke, the Italian dropped on his knee, kissed it convulsively, and, fearful of trusting himself further, vanished from the room.

He had not been long gone before Maltravers was seen riding through the street. As he threw himself from his horse, he looked up at the window, and kissed his hand at Lady Florence, who stood there, watching his arrival, with feelings indeed far different from those he anticipated. He entered the room lightly and gaily.

Florence stirred not to welcome him. He approached and took her hand; she withdrew it with a shudder.

"Are you not well, Florence?"

"I am well, for I have recovered."

"What do you mean? why do you turn from me?"

Lady Florence fixed her eyes upon him, eyes that literally blazed; her lip quivered with scorn.

"Mr. Maltravers, at length I know you. I understand the feelings with which you have sought a union between us. O God! why, why was I thus cursed with riches—why made a thing of barter, and merchandise, and avarice, and low ambition? Take my wealth, take it, Mr. Maltravers, since that is what you prize. Heaven knows I can cast it willingly away; but leave the wretch whom you long deceived, and who now, wretch though she be, renounces and despises you!"

"Lady Florence, do I hear aright? Who has accused me to you?"

"None, sir, none; I would have believed none. Let it suffice that I am convinced that our union can be happy to neither. Question me no further; all intercourse between us is for ever over!"

"Pause," said Maltravers, with cold and grave solemnity; "another word, and the gulf will become impassable. Pause."

"Do not," exclaimed the unhappy lady, stung by what she considered the assurance of a hardened hypocrisy—"do not affect this haughty superiority; it dupes me no longer. I was your slave while I loved you: the tie is broken. I am free, and I hate and scorn you! Mercenary and sordid as you are, your baseness of spirit revives the differences of our rank. Henceforth, Mr. Maltravers, I am Lady Florence Lascelles, and by that title alone will you know me. Begone, sir!"

As she spoke, with passion distorting every feature of her face, all her beauty vanished away from the eyes of the proud Maltravers as if by witchcraft; the angel seemed transformed into the fury; and cold, bitter, and withering was the eye which he fixed upon that altered countenance.

"Mark me, Lady Florence Lascelles," said he, very calmly, "you have now said what you can never recall. Neither in man nor in woman did Ernest Maltravers ever forget or forgive a sentence which accused him of dishonour. I bid you farewell for ever; and with my last words I condemn you to the darkest of all dooms—the remorse that comes too late!"

Slowly he moved away; and as the door closed upon that towering and haughty form, Florence already felt that his curse was working to its fulfilment. She rushed to the window—she caught one last glimpse of him as his horse bore him rapidly away. Ah! when shall they meet again?

CHAPTER IX.

"And now I live—Oh, wherefore do I live?
And with that pang I prayed to be no more."—WORDSWORTH.

IT was about nine o'clock that evening, and Maltravers was alone in his room. His carriage was at the door—his servants were arranging the luggage—he was going that night to Burleigh. London—society—the world—were grown hateful to him. His galled and indignant spirit demanded solitude. At this time Lumley Ferrers abruptly entered.

"You will pardon my intrusion," said the latter, with his usual frankness—"but——"

"But what, sir—I am engaged."

"I shall be very brief. Maltravers, you are my old friend. I retain regard and affection for you, though our different habits have of late estranged us. I come to you from my cousin—from Florence; there has been some misunderstanding between you. I called on her to-day after you left the house. Her grief affected me. I have only just quitted her. She has been told by some gossip or other, some story or other—women are credulous, foolish creatures;—undeceive her, and, I dare say, all may be settled."

"Ferrers, if a man had spoken to me as Lady Florence did, his blood or mine must have flowed. And do you think that words that might have plunged me into the guilt of homicide if uttered by a man I could ever pardon in one whom I had dreamed of for a wife? Never!"

"Pooh, pooh—women's words are wind. Don't throw away so splendid a match for such a trifle."

"Do you too, sir, mean to impute mercenary motives to me?"

"Heaven forbid! You know I am no coward, but I really don't want to fight you. Come, be reasonable."

"I dare say you mean well, but the breach is final—all recurrence to it is painful and superfluous. I must wish you good evening."

"You have positively decided?"

"I have."

"Even if Lady Florence made the *amende honorable!*"

"Nothing on the part of Lady Florence could alter my resolution. The woman whom an honourable man—an English gentleman—makes the partner of his life, ought never to listen to a syllable against his fair name; his honour is hers, and if her lips, that should breathe comfort in calumny, only serve to retail the lie—she may be beautiful, gifted, wealthy, and high-born, but he takes a curse to his arms. That curse I have escaped."

"And this I am to say to my cousin."

"As you will. And now stay, Lumley Ferrers, and hear me. I neither accuse nor suspect you, I desire not to pierce your heart, and in this case I cannot fathom your motives; but if it should so have happened that you have, in any way, ministered to Lady Florence Lascelles' injurious opinions of my faith and honour, you will have much to answer for, and sooner or later there will come a day of reckoning between you and me."

"Mr. Maltravers, there can be no quarrel between us, with my cousin's fair name at stake, or else we should not now part without preparations for a more hostile meeting. I can bear your language.

I, too, though no philosopher, can forgive. Come, man, you are heated—it is very natural—let us part friends—your hand."

"If you can take my hand, Lumley, you are innocent, and I have wronged you."

Lumley smiled, and cordially pressed the hand of his old friend.

As he descended the stairs, Maltravers followed, and just as Lumley turned into Curzon Street, the carriage whirled rapidly past him, and by the lamps he saw the pale and stern face of Maltravers.

It was a slow, drizzling rain—one of those unwholesome nights frequent in London towards the end of autumn. Ferrers, however, insensible to the weather, walked slowly and thoughtfully towards his cousin's house. He was playing for a mighty stake, and hitherto the cast was in his favour, yet he was uneasy and perturbed. His conscience was tolerably proof to all compunction, as much from the levity as from the strength of his nature; and (Maltravers removed) he trusted in his knowledge of the human heart, and the smooth speciousness of his manner, to win, at last, in the hand of Lady Florence, the object of his ambition. It was not on her affection, it was on her pique, her resentment, that he relied. "When a woman fancies herself slighted by the man she loves, the first person who proposes must be a clumsy wooer indeed if he does not carry her away." So reasoned Ferrers, but yet he was ruffled and disquieted; the truth must be spoken—able, bold, sanguine, and scornful as he was, his spirit quailed before that of Maltravers; he feared the lion of that nature when fairly aroused: his own character had something of a woman's—an unprincipled, gifted, aspiring, and subtle woman's, and in Maltravers—stern, simple, and masculine—he recognised the superior dignity of the "lords of the creation;" he was overawed by the anticipation of a wrath and revenge which he felt he merited, and which he feared might be deadly.

While gradually, however, his spirit recovered its usual elasticity, he came in the vicinity of Lord Saxingham's house, and suddenly, by a corner of the street, his arm was seized: to his inexpressible astonishment he recognised in the muffled figure that accosted him the form of Florence Lascelles.

"Good heavens!" he cried, "is it possible!—You, alone in the streets, at this hour, in such a night, too! How very wrong—how very imprudent!"

"Do not talk to me—I am almost mad as it is; I could not rest

—I could not brave quiet, solitude—still less the face of my father—I could not!—but quick, what says he?—what excuse has he? Tell me everything—I will cling to a straw."

"And is this the proud Florence Lascelles?"

"No—it is the humbled Florence Lascelles. I have done with pride—speak to me!"

"Ah, what a treasure is such a heart. How can he throw it away!"

"Does he deny?"

"He denies nothing—he expresses himself rejoiced to have escaped—such was his expression—a marriage in which his heart never was engaged. He is unworthy of you—forget him."

Florence shivered, and as Ferrers drew her arm in his own, her ungloved hand touched his, and the touch was like that of ice.

"What will the servants think?—what excuse can we make?" said Ferrers, when they stood beneath the porch.

Florence did not reply; but as the door opened, she said softly—"I am ill—ill," and clung to Ferrers with that unnerved and heavy weight which betokens faintness.

The light glared on her—the faces of the lackeys betokened their undisguised astonishment. With a violent effort Florence recovered herself, for she had *not* yet done with pride, swept through the hall with her usual stately step, slowly ascended the broad staircase, and gained the solitude of her own room, to fall senseless on the floor.

BOOK IX.

CHAPTER I.

> "There the action lies
> In its true nature   .   .   .   .
>   What then? What rests?
> Try what repentance can!"—*Hamlet.*
>
> "I doubt he will be dead or ere I come."—*King John.*

IT was a fine afternoon in December when Lumley Ferrers turned from Lord Saxingham's door. The knockers were muffled—the windows on the third story were partially closed. There was sickness in that house.

Lumley's face was unusually grave; it was even sad. "So young—so beautiful," he muttered. "If ever I loved woman, I do believe I loved her that love must be my excuse. . . . I repent of what I have done—but I could not foresee that a mere lover's stratagem was to end in such effects—the metaphysician was very right when he said, 'We only sympathise with feelings we know ourselves.' A little disappointment in love could not have hurt me much—it is d—d odd it should hurt her so. I am altogether out of luck: old Templeton—I beg his pardon, Lord Vargrave (by-the-by he gets heartier every day—what a constitution he has!) seems cross with me. He did not like the idea that I should marry Lady Florence—and when I thought that vision might have been realised, hinted that I was disappointing some expectations he had formed; I can't make out what he means. Then, too, the government have offered that place to Maltravers instead of to me. In fact, my star is not in the ascendant. Poor Florence, though—I would really give a great deal to know her restored to health!—I have done a villainous thing, but I thought it only a clever one. However, regret is a fool's passion. By Jupiter!—talking of fools, here comes Cesarini."

Wan, haggard, almost spectral, his hat over his brow, his dress neglected, his air reckless and fierce, Cesarini crossed the way, and thus accosted Lumley—

"We have murdered her, Ferrers; and her ghost will haunt us to our dying day!"

"Talk prose; you know I am no poet. What do you mean?"

"She is worse to-day," groaned Cesarini, in a hollow voice. "I wander like a lost spirit round the house; I question all who come from it. Tell me—oh, tell me, is there hope?"

"I do, indeed, trust so," replied Ferrers, fervently. "The illness has only of late assumed an alarming appearance. At first it was merely a severe cold, caught by imprudent exposure one rainy night. Now they fear it has settled on the lungs; but if we could get her abroad, all might be well."

"You think so, honestly?"

"I do. Courage, my friend; do not reproach yourself; it has nothing to do with us. She was taken ill of a cold, not of a letter, man!"

"No, no; I judge her heart by my own. Oh, that I could recall the past! Look at me; I am the wreck of what I was; day and night the recollection of my falsehood haunts me with remorse."

"Pshaw!—we will go to Italy together, and in your beautiful land, love will replace love."

"I am half resolved, Ferrers."

"Ha!—to do what?"

"To write—to reveal all to her."

The hardy complexion of Ferrers grew livid; his brow became dark with a terrible expression.

"Do so, and fall the next day by my hand; my aim, in slighter quarrel, never erred."

"Do you dare to threaten me?"

"Do you dare to betray me? Betray one who, if he sinned, sinned on your account—in your cause; who would have secured to you the loveliest bride, and the most princely dower in England; and whose only offence against you is that he cannot command life and health!"

"Forgive me," said the Italian, with great emotion—"forgive me, and do not misunderstand; I would not have betrayed *you*—there is honour among villains. I would have confessed only my own crime; I would never have revealed yours—why should I? it is unnecessary."

"Are you in earnest?—are you sincere?"

"By my soul!"

"Then, indeed, you are worthy of my friendship. You will assume the whole forgery—an ugly word, but it avoids circumlocution—to be your own?"

"I will."

Ferrers paused a moment, and then stopped suddenly short.

"You will swear this!"

"By all that is holy."

"Then, mark me, Cesarini; if to-morrow Lady Florence be worse, I will throw no obstacle in the way of your confession, should you resolve to make it; I will even use that influence which you leave me to palliate your offence, to win your pardon. And yet to resign your hopes—to surrender one so loved to the arms of one so hated—it is magnanimous—it is noble—it is above my standard! Do as you will."

Cesarini was about to reply, when a servant on horseback abruptly turned the corner, almost at full speed. He pulled in—his eye fell upon Lumley—he dismounted.

"Oh, Mr. Ferrers," said the man, breathlessly, "I have been to your house; they told me I might find you at Lord Saxingham's—I was just going there——"

"Well, well, what is the matter?"

"My poor master, sir—my lord, I mean——"

"What of him?"

"Had a fit, sir—the doctors are with him—my mistress—for my lord can't speak—sent me express for you."

"Lend me your horse—there, just lengthen the stirrups."

While the groom was engaged at the saddle, Ferrers turned to Cesarini. "Do nothing rashly," said he; "I would say, if I might, nothing at all, without consulting me: but mind, I rely, at all events, on your promise—your oath."

"You may," said Cesarini, gloomily.

"Farewell, then," said Lumley, as he mounted; and in a few moments he was out of sight.

CHAPTER II.

*"Oh world, thou wast the forest to this hart,
Dost thou here lie!"—Julius Cæsar.*

AS Lumley leapt from his horse at his uncle's door, the disorder and bustle of those demesnes, in which the severe eye of the master usually preserved a repose and silence as complete as if the affairs of life were carried on by clockwork, struck upon him sensibly. Upon the trim lawn the old women employed in cleaning and weeding the walks were all assembled in a cluster, shaking their heads ominously in concert, and carrying on their comments in a confused whisper. In the hall the housemaid (and it was the first housemaid whom Lumley had ever seen in that house, so invisibly were the wheels of the domestic machine carried on) was leaning on her broom, "swallowing with open mouth a footman's news." It was as if, with the first slackening of the rigid rein, human nature broke loose from the conventual stillness in which it had ever paced its peaceful path in that formal mansion.

"How is he?"

"My lord is better, sir; he has spoken, I believe."

At this moment a young face, swollen and red with weeping looked down from the stairs; and presently Evelyn rushed breathlessly into the hall.

"Oh, come up—come up, cousin Lumley; he cannot, cannot die in your presence; you always seem *so full* of life! He cannot die; you do not think he will die? Oh, take me with you, they won't let me go to him!"

"Hush, my dear little girl, hush; follow me lightly—that is right."

Lumley reached the door, tapped gently—entered; and the child also stole in unobserved, or at least unprevented. Lumley drew aside the curtains; the new lord was lying on his bed, with his head propped by pillows, his eyes wide open, with a glassy, but not insensible stare, and his countenance fearfully changed. Lady Vargrave was kneeling on the other side of the bed, one hand clasped in her husband's, the other bathing his temples, and her tears falling, without sob or sound, fast and copiously down her pale, fair cheeks.

Two doctors were conferring in the recess of the window; an apothecary was mixing drugs at a table; and two of the oldest female servants of the house were standing near the physicians, trying to overhear what was said.

"My dear, dear uncle, how are you?" asked Lumley.

"Ah, you are come then," said the dying man, in a feeble yet distinct voice; "that is well—I have much to say to you."

"But not now—not now—you are not strong enough," said the wife, imploringly.

The doctors moved to the bedside. Lord Vargrave waved his hand and raised his head.

"Gentlemen," said he, "I feel as if death were hastening upon me; I have much need, while my senses remain, to confer with my nephew. Is the present a fitting time?—if I delay, are you sure I shall have another?"

The doctors looked at each other.

"My lord," said one; "it may perhaps settle and relieve your mind to converse with your nephew; afterwards you may more easily compose yourself to sleep."

"Take this cordial, then," said the other doctor.

The sick man obeyed. One of the physicians approached Lumley and beckoned him aside.

"Shall we send for his lordship's lawyer?" whispered the leech.

"I am his heir-at-law," thought Lumley. "Why, *no*, my dear sir —no, I think not, unless he expresses a desire to see him; doubtless my poor uncle has already settled his worldly affairs. What is his state?"

The doctor shook his head. "I will speak to you, sir, after you have left his lordship."

"What is the matter there?" cried the patient, sharply and querulously. "Clear the room — I would be alone with my nephew."

The doctors disappeared; the old women reluctantly followed: when, suddenly, the little Evelyn sprang forward and threw herself on the breast of the dying man, sobbing as if her heart would break.

"My poor child!—my sweet child—my own, own darling!" gasped out Lord Vargrave, folding his weak arms round her; "bless you—bless you! and God *will* bless you. My wife," he added, with a voice far more tender than Lumley had ever before heard him address to Lady Vargrave, "if these be the last words I utter to you, let them express all the gratitude I feel for you, for duties never more piously discharged: you did not love me, it is true; and in health and pride that knowledge has often made me unjust to you. I have been severe—you have had much to bear—forgive me."

"Oh, do not talk thus; you have been nobler, kinder than my deserts. How much I owe you!—how little I have done in return!"

"I cannot bear this; leave me, my dear, leave me. I may live yet—I hope I may—I do not want to die. The cup may pass from me. Go—go—and you, my child."

"Ah, let *me* stay."

Lord Vargrave kissed the little creature, as she clung to his neck, with passionate affection, and then, placing her in her mother's arms, fell back exhausted on his pillow. Lumley, with handkerchief to his eyes, opened the door to Lady Vargrave, who sobbed bitterly, and carefully closing it, resumed his station by his uncle.

When Lumley Ferrers left the room, his countenance was gloomy and excited rather than sad. He hurried to the room which he usually occupied, and remained there for some hours while his uncle slept—a long and sound sleep. But the mother and the step-child (now restored to the sick-room) did not desert their watch.

It wanted about an hour to midnight when the senior physician sought the nephew.

"Your uncle asks for you, Mr. Ferrers; and I think it right to say that his last moments approach. We have done all that can be done."

"Is he fully aware of his danger?"

"He is; and has spent the last two hours in prayer—it is a Christian's death-bed, sir."

"Humph!" said Ferrers, as he followed the physician.

The room was darkened—a single lamp, carefully shaded, burned on a table, on which lay the Book of Life in death; and with awe and grief on their faces, the mother and the child were kneeling beside the bed.

"Come here, Lumley," faltered forth the fast-dying man. "There are none here but you three—nearest and dearest to me?—that is well. Lumley, then, you know all—my wife, he knows all. My child, give your hand to your cousin—so you are now plighted. When you grow up, Evelyn, you will know that it is my last wish and prayer that you should be the wife of Lumley Ferrers. In giving you this angel, Lumley, I atone to you for all seeming injustice. And to you my child, I secure the rank and honours to which I have painfully climbed, and which I am forbidden to enjoy. Be kind to her, Lumley—you have a good and frank heart—let it be her shelter—she has never known a harsh word. God bless you all and God forgive me—pray for me. Lumley, to-morrow you will be Lord Vargrave, and by-and-by" (here a ghastly but exultant smile flitted over the speaker's countenance) "you will be my Lady—Lady Vargrave. Lady—so—so—Lady Var——"

The words died on his trembling lips; he turned round, and though he continued to breathe for more than an hour, Lord Vargrave never uttered another syllable.

CHAPTER III.

"Hopes and fears
Start up alarmed, and o'er life's narrow verge
Look down—on what?—a fathomless abyss."—YOUNG.

"Contempt, farewell, and maiden pride, adieu!"
—*Much Ado about Nothing.*

THE wound which Maltravers had received was peculiarly severe and rankling. It is true that he had never been what is called violently in love with Florence Lascelles; but from the moment in which he had been charmed and surprised into the character of a declared suitor, it was consonant with his scrupulous and loyal nature to view only the bright side of Florence's gifts and qualities, and to seek to enamour his grateful fancy with her beauty, her genius, and her tenderness for himself. He had thus forced and formed his thoughts and hopes to centre all in one object; and Florence and the Future had grown words which conveyed the same meaning to his mind. Perhaps he felt more bitterly her sudden and stunning accusations, couched, as they were, in language so unqualified, because they fell upon his pride rather than his affection, and were not softened away by the thousand excuses and remembrances which a passionate love would have invented and recalled. It was a deep, concentrated sense of injury and insult that hardened and soured his whole nature—wounded vanity, wounded pride, and wounded honour. And the blow, too, came upon him at a time when he was most dissatisfied with all other prospects. He was disgusted with the littleness of the agents and springs of political life—he had formed a weary contempt of the barrenness of literary reputation. At thirty years of age he had necessarily outlived the sanguine elasticity of early youth, and he had already broken up many of those later toys in business and ambition, which afford the rattle and the hobby-horse to our maturer manhood. Always asking for something too refined and too exalted for human life, every new proof of unworthiness in men and things saddened or revolted a mind still too fastidious for that quiet contentment with the world as it is, which we must all learn before we can make our philosophy practical, and our genius as fertile of the harvest as it may be prodigal of the blossom. Haughty, solitary, and unsocial, the ordinary resources of mortified and disappointed men were not for Ernest Maltravers. Rigidly secluded in his country retirement, he consumed the days in moody wanderings, and in the evenings he turned to books, with a spirit disdainful and fatigued. So much had he already learned, that books taught him little that he did not already know. And the biographies of authors, those ghost-like beings who seem to have had no life but in the shadow of their own haunting and imperishable thoughts, dimmed the inspiration he might have caught from their pages. Those Slaves of the Lamp, those Silkworms of the Closet, how little had they enjoyed, how little had they lived! Condemned to a mysterious fate by the wholesale destinies of the world, they seemed born but to toil and to spin thoughts for the common crowd—and, their task performed in drudgery and in darkness, to die when no further service could be wrung from their exhaustion. Names had they been in life, and as names they lived for ever, in life as in death, airy and unsubstantial phantoms. It pleased Maltravers at this time to turn a curious eye towards the obscure and half-extinct philosophies of the ancient world. He compared the Stoics with the Epicureans—those Epicureans who had given their own version to the simple and abstemious utilitarianism of their master. He asked which was the wiser, to sharpen pain or to deaden pleasure—to bear all or to enjoy all—and, by a natural reaction, which often happens to us in life, this man, hitherto so earnest, active-spirited, and resolved on great things, began to yearn for the drowsy pleasures of indolence. The Garden grew more tempting than the Porch. He seriously revolved the old alternative of the Grecian demi-god—might it not be wiser to abandon the grave pursuits to which he had been addicted, to dethrone the august but severe Ideal in his heart—to cultivate the light loves and voluptuous trifles of the herd—and to plant the brief space of youth yet left to h.m with the myrtle and the rose? As water flows over water, so new schemes rolled upon new—sweeping away every momentary impression, and leaving the surface facile equally to receive and to forget. Such is a common state with men of imagination in those crises of life, when some great revolution of designs and hopes unsettles elements too susceptible of every changing wind. And thus the weak are destroyed, while the strong relapse, after terrible but unknown convulsions, into that solemn harmony and order from which Destiny and God draw their use to mankind.

It was from this irresolute contest between antagonistic principles that Maltravers was aroused by the following letter from Florence Lascelles:—

"For three days and three sleepless nights I have debated with myself whether or not I ought to address you. Oh, Ernest, were I what I was, in health, in pride, I might fear that, generous as you are, you would misconstrue my appeal; but that is now impossible. Our union never can take place, and my hopes bound themselves to one sweet and melancholy hope, that you will remove from my last hours the cold and dark shadow of your resentment. We have both been cruelly deceived and betrayed. Three days ago I discovered the perfidy that has been practised against us. And then, ah! then, with all the weak human anguish of discovering it too late (*your curse is fulfilled*, Ernest!), I had at least one moment of proud, of exquisite rapture. Ernest Maltravers, the hero of my dreams, stood pure and lofty as of old—a thing it was not unworthy to love, to mourn, to die for. A letter in your handwriting had been shown me, garbled and altered, as it seems—but I detected not the imposture—it was yourself, yourself alone, brought in false and horrible witness against yourself! And could you think that any other evidence, the words, the oaths of others, would have convicted you in my eyes? There you wronged me. But I deserved it—I had bound myself to secrecy—the seal is taken from my lips in order to be set upon my tomb. Ernest, beloved Ernest—beloved till the last breath is extinct—till the last throb of this heart is stilled!—write me one word of comfort and of pardon. You will believe what I have imperfectly written, for *you* ever trusted my faith, if you have blamed my faults. I am now comparatively happy—a word from you will make me blest. And Fate has, perhaps, been more merciful to both, than in our short-sighted and querulous human vision we might, perhaps, believe ; for now that the frame is brought low—and in the solitude of my chamber I can duly and humbly commune with mine own heart—I see the aspect of those faults which I once mistook for virtues, and feel, that had we been united, I, loving you ever, might not have constituted your happiness, and so have known the misery of losing your affection. May He who formed you for glorious and yet all-unaccomplished purposes, strengthen you when these eyes can no longer sparkle at your triumphs, nor weep at your lightest sorrow. You will go on in your broad and luminous career :—A few years, and my remembrance will have left but the vestige of a dream behind.— But, but—I can write no more. God bless you!"

CHAPTER IV.

"Oh, stop this headlong current of your goodness ;
It comes too fast upon a feeble soul."
—DRYDEN : *Sebastian and Doras.*

THE smooth physician had paid his evening visit ; Lord Saxingham had gone to a cabinet dinner, for Life must ever walk side by side with Death : and Lady Florence Lascelles was alone. It was a room adjoining her sleeping-apartment—a room in which, in the palmy days of the brilliant and wayward heiress, she had loved to display her fanciful and peculiar taste. There had she been accustomed to muse, to write, to study—there had she first been dazzled by the novel glow of Ernest's undiurnal and stately thoughts—there had she first conceived the romance of girlhood, which had led her to confer with him, unknown—there had she first confessed to herself that fancy had begotten love—there had she gone through love's short and exhausting progress of lone emotion ;—the doubt, the hope, the ecstasy; the reverse, the terror; the inanimate despondency, the agonised despair! And there now, sadly and patiently, she awaited the gradual march of inevitable decay. And books, and pictures, and marble busts, half-shadowed by classic draperies—

all the delicate elegancies of womanly refinement—still invested the chamber with a grace as cheerful as if youth and beauty were to be the occupants for ever—and the dark and noisome vault were not the only lasting residence for the things of clay!

Florence Lascelles was dying; but not, indeed, wholly of that common, if mystic malady, a broken heart. Her health, always delicate, because always preyed upon by a nervous, irritable, and feverish spirit, had been gradually and invisibly undermined, even before Ernest confessed his love. In the singular lustre of those large-pupilled eyes—in the luxuriant transparency of that glorious bloom—the experienced might long since have traced the seeds which cradled death. In the night, when her restless and maddened heart so imprudently drove her forth to forestall the communication of Lumley (whom she had sent to Maltravers, she scarce knew for what object, or with what hope), in that night she was already in a high state of fever. The rain and the chill struck the growing disease within—her excitement gave it food and fire—delirium succeeded; and in that most fearful and fatal of all medical errors, which robs the frame when it most needs strength of the very principle of life, they had bled her into a temporary calm, and into permanent and incurable weakness. Consumption seized its victim. The physicians who attended her were the most renowned in London, and Lord Saxingham was firmly persuaded that there was no danger. It was not in his nature to think that death would take so great a liberty with Lady Florence Lascelles, when there were so many poor people in the world whom there would be no impropriety in removing from it. But Florence knew her danger, and her high spirit did not quail before it. Yet, when Cesarini, stung beyond endurance by the horrors of his remorse, wrote and confessed all his own share of the fatal treason, though, faithful to his promise, he concealed that of his accomplice—then, ah, then, she did indeed repine at her doom, and long to look once more with the eyes of love and joy upon the face of the beautiful world. But the illness of the body usually brings out a latent power and philosophy of the soul, which health never knows; and God has mercifully ordained it as the customary lot of nature, that in proportion as we decline into the grave, the sloping path is made smooth and easy to our feet; and every day, as the films of clay are removed from our eyes, Death loses the false aspect of the spectre, and we fall at last into its arms as a wearied child upon the bosom of its mother.

—21—

It was with a heavy heart that Lady Florence listened to the monotonous clicking of the clock that announced the departure of moments few, yet not precious, still spared to her. Her face buried in her hands, she bent over the small table beside her sofa, and indulged her melancholy thoughts. Bowed was the haughty crest, unnerved the elastic shape that had once seemed born for majesty and command—no friends were near, for Florence had never made friends. Solitary had been her youth, and solitary were her dying hours.

As she thus sat and mused, a sound of carriage wheels in the street below slightly shook the room—it ceased—the carriage stopped at the door. Florence looked up. "No, no, it cannot be," she muttered; yet, while she spoke, a faint flush passed over her sunken and faded cheek, and the bosom heaved beneath the robe, "a world too wide for its shrunk proportions." There was a silence, which to her seemed interminable, and she turned away with a deep sigh and a chill sinking of the heart.

At this time her woman entered with a flurried look.

"I beg your pardon, my lady—but——"

"But what?"

"Mr. Maltravers has called, and asked for your ladyship—so, my lady, Mr. Burton sent for me, and I said, my lady is too unwell to see any one; but Mr. Maltravers would not be denied, and he is waiting in my lord's library, and insisted on my coming up and 'nouncing him, my lady."

Now, Mrs. Shinfield's words were not euphonistic, nor her voice mellifluous; but never had eloquence seemed to Florence so effective. Youth, love, beauty, all rushed back upon her at once, brightening her eyes, her cheek, and filling up ruin with sudden and deceitful light.

"Well," she said, after a pause, "let Mr. Maltravers come up."

"Come up, my lady? Bless me!—let me just 'range your hair—your ladyship is really in such dish-a-bill."

"Best as it is, Shinfield—he will excuse all.—Go."

Mrs. Shinfield shrugged her shoulders and departed. A few moments more—a step on the stairs, the creaking of the door—and Maltravers and Florence were again alone. He stood motionless on the threshold. She had involuntarily risen, and so they stood opposite to each other, and the lamp fell full upon her face. Oh, heaven, when did that sight cease to haunt the heart of Maltravers! When shall that altered aspect not pass as a ghost before his eyes!

—there it is, faithful and reproachful, alike in solitude and in crowds—it is seen in the glare of noon—it passes dim and wan at night, beneath the stars and the earth—it looked into his heart, and left its likeness there for ever and ever! Those cheeks once so beautifully rounded, now sunken into lines and hollows—the livid darkness beneath the eyes—the whitened lip—the sharp, anxious, worn expression, which had replaced that glorious and beaming *regard* from which all the life of genius, all the sweet pride of womanhood, had glowed forth, and in which not only the intelligence, but the eternity of the soul, seemed visibly wrought!

There he stood, aghast and appalled. At length a low groan broke from his lips—he rushed forward, sank on his knees beside her, and clasping both her hands, sobbed aloud as he covered them with kisses. All the iron of his strong nature was broken down, and his emotions, long silenced, and now uncontrollable and resistless, were something terrible to behold!

"Do not—do not weep so," murmured Lady Florence, frightened by his vehemence; "I am sadly changed, but the fault is mine—Ernest, it is mine; best, kindest, gentlest, how could I have been so mad!—and you forgive me? I am yours again—a little while yours. Ah, do not grieve while I am so blessed!"

As she spoke, her tears—tears from a source how different from that whence broke the scorching and intolerable agony of his own! fell soft upon his bended head, and the hands that still convulsively strained hers. Maltravers looked wildly up into her countenance, and shuddered as he saw her attempt to smile. He rose abruptly, threw himself into a chair, and covered his face. He was seeking by a violent effort to master himself, and it was only by the heaving of his chest, and now and then a gasp as for breath, that he betrayed the stormy struggle within.

Florence gazed at him a moment in bitter, in almost selfish penitence. "And this was the man who seemed to me so callous to the softer sympathies—this was the heart that I trampled upon—this the nature I distrusted!"

She came near him, trembling and with feeble steps—she laid her hand upon his shoulder, and the fondness of love came over her, and she wound her arms around him.

"It is our fate—it is my fate," said Maltravers, at last, awaking as from a hideous dream, and in a hollow but calm voice—"we are the things of destiny, and the wheel has crushed us. It is an awful state of being this human life!—What is wisdom—virtue—faith to men—piety to heaven—all the nurture we bestow on ourselves—all our desire to win a loftier sphere, when we are thus the tools of the merest chance—the victims of the pettiest villainy; and our very existence—our very senses almost, at the mercy of every traitor and every fool?"

There was something in Ernest's voice, as well as in his reflections, which appeared so unnaturally calm and deep, that it startled Florence with a fear more acute than his previous violence had done. He rose, and muttering to himself, walked to and fro, as if insensible of her presence—in fact he was so. At length he stopped short, and fixing his eyes upon Lady Florence, said, in a whispered and thrilling tone—

"Now, then, the name of our undoer?"

"No, Ernest, no—never, unless you promise me to forego the purpose which I read in your eyes. He has confessed—he is penitent—I have forgiven him—you will do so too!"

"His name!" repeated Maltravers, and his face, before very flushed, was unnaturally pale.

"Forgive him—promise me."

"His name, I say—his name?"

"Is this kind?—you terrify me—you will kill me!" faltered out Florence, and she sank on the sofa exhausted; her nerves, now so weakened, were perfectly unstrung by his vehemence, and she wrung her hands and wept piteously.

"You will not tell me his name?" said Maltravers, softly. "Be it so. I will ask no more. I can discover it myself. Fate the Avenger will reveal it."

At the thought he grew more composed; and as Florence wept on, the unnatural concentration and fierceness of his mind again gave way, and seating himself beside her, he uttered all that could soothe, and comfort, and console. And Florence *was* soon soothed! And there, while over their heads the grim skeleton was holding the funeral pall, they again exchanged their vows, and again, with feelings fonder than of old, spoke of love.

CHAPTER V.

> "Erichtho, then,
> Breathes her dire murmurs, which enforce him bear
> Her baneful secrets to the spirits of horror."—MARLOW.

WITH a heavy step Maltravers ascended the stairs of his lonely house that night, and with a suppressed groan did he sink upon the first chair that proffered rest.

It was intensely cold. During his long interview with Lady Florence his servant had taken the precaution to go to Seamore Place, and make some hasty preparations for the owner's return. But the bedroom looked comfortless and bare, the curtains were taken down, the carpets were taken up (a single man's housekeeper is wonderfully provident in these matters; the moment his back is turned she bustles, she displaces, she exults; "things can be put a little to rights!"). Even the fire would not burn clear, but gleamed sullen and fitful from the smothering fuel. It was a large chamber, and the lights imperfectly filled it. On the table lay parliamentary papers, and pamphlets, and bills, and presentation-books from younger authors—evidences of the teeming business of that restless machine of the world. But of all this Maltravers was not sensible: the winter frost numbed not his feverish veins. His servant, who loved him, as all who saw much of Maltravers did, fidgeted anxiously about the room, and plied the sullen fire, and laid out the comfortable dressing-robe, and placed wine on the table, and asked questions which were not answered, and pressed service which was not heeded. The little wheels of life go on, even when the great wheel is paralysed or broken. Maltravers was, if I may so express it, in a kind of mental trance. His emotions had left him thoroughly exhausted. He felt that torpor which succeeds, and is again the precursor of, great woe. At length he was alone, and the solitude half unconsciously restored him to the sense of his heavy misery. For it may be observed, that when misfortune has stricken us home, the presence of any one seems to interfere between the memory and the heart. Withdraw the intruder, and the lifted hammer falls at once upon the anvil! He rose as the door closed on his attendant—rose with a start, and pushed the hat from his gathered brows. He walked for some moments to and fro, and the air of the room, freezing as it was, oppressed him.

There are times when the arrow quivers within us—in which all space seems too confined. Like the wounded hart we could fly on for ever; there is a vague desire of escape—a yearning almost insane, to get out from our own selves: the soul struggles to flee away and take the wings of the morning.

Impatiently, at last, did Maltravers throw open his window; it communicated upon a balcony, built out to command the wide view which, from a certain height, that part of the park affords. He stepped into the balcony and bared his breast to the keen air. The uncomfortable and icy heavens looked down upon the hoar-rime that gathered over the grass, and the ghostly boughs of the death-like trees. All things in the world without brought the thought of the grave, and the pause of being, and the withering up of beauty, closer and closer to his soul. In the palpable and griping winter, death itself seemed to wind round him its skeleton and joyless arms. And as thus he stood, and, wearied with contending against, passively yielded to, the bitter passions that rung and gnawed his heart—he heard not a sound at the door below—nor the footsteps on the stairs—nor knew he that a visitor was in his room—till he felt a hand upon his shoulder, and turning round, he beheld the white and livid countenance of Castruccio Cesarini.

"It is a dreary night and a solemn hour, Maltravers," said the Italian, with a distorted smile—"a fitting night and time for my interview with you."

"Away!" said Maltravers, in an impatient tone. "I am not at leisure for these mock heroics."

"Ay, but you shall hear me to the end. I have watched your arrival—I have counted the hours in which you remained with her —I have followed you home. If you have human passions, humanity itself must be dried up within you, and the wild beast in his cavern is not more fearful to encounter. Thus, then, I seek and brave you. Be still. Has Florence revealed to you the name of him who belied you, and who betrayed herself to the death?"

"Ha!" said Maltravers, growing very pale, and fixing his eyes on Cesarini, "you are not the man—my suspicions lighted elsewhere."

"I am the man. Do thy worst."

Scarce were the words uttered, when with a fierce cry, Maltravers threw himself on the Italian;—he tore him from his footing—he grasped him in his arms as a child—he literally whirled him around and on high; and in that maddening paroxysm, it was, perhaps, but the balance of a feather, in the conflicting elements of revenge and reason, which withheld Maltravers from hurling the criminal from the fearful height on which they stood. The temptation passed—Cesarini leaned, safe, unharmed, but half senseless with mingled rage and fear, against the wall.

He was alone—Maltravers had left him—had fled from himself—fled into the chamber—fled for refuge from human passions—to the wing of the All-Seeing and All-Present. "Father," he groaned sinking on his knees, "support me, save me: without Thee I am lost!"

Slowly Cesarini recovered himself and re-entered the apartment. A string in his brain was already loosened, and, sullen and ferocious, he returned again to goad the lion that had spared him. Maltravers had already risen from his brief prayer. With locked and rigid countenance, with arms folded on his breast—he stood confronting the Italian, who advanced towards him with a menacing brow and arm, but halted involuntarily at the sight of that commanding aspect.

"Well, then," said Maltravers at last, with a tone preternaturally calm and low, "you then are the man. Speak on—what arts did you employ?"

"Your own letter! When, many months ago, I wrote to tell you of the hopes it was mine to conceive, and to ask your opinion of her I loved, how did you answer me? With doubts, with depreciation, with covert and polished scorn, of the very woman, whom, with a deliberate treachery, you afterwards wrested from my worshipping and adoring love. That letter I garbled—I made the doubts you expressed of my happiness seem doubts of your own. I changed the dates—I made the letter itself appear written, not on your first acquaintance with her, but subsequent to your plighted and accepted vows. Your own handwriting convicted you of mean suspicion and of sordid motives. These were my arts."

"They were most noble. Do you abide by them—or repent?"

"For what I have done to *thee* I have no repentance. Nay, I regard thee still as the aggressor. Thou hast robbed me of her who was all the world to me—and, be thine excuses what they may, I hate thee with a hate that cannot slumber—that abjures the abject name of remorse! I exult in the very agonies thou endurest. But for her—the stricken—the dying! O God, O God! The blow falls on mine own head!"

"Dying!" said Maltravers, slowly and with a shudder. "No,

no—not dying—or what art thou? Her murderer! And what must I be? Her avenger!"

Overpowered with his own passions, Cesarini sank down and covered his face with his clasped hands. Maltravers stalked gloomily to and fro the apartment. There was silence for some moments.

At length Maltravers paused opposite Cesarini, and thus addressed him—

"You have come hither, not so much to confess the basest crime of which man can be guilty, as to gloat over my anguish, and to brave me to revenge my wrongs. Go, man, go—for the present you are safe. While she lives, my life is not mine to hazard—if she recover, I can pity you and forgive. To me your offence, foul though it be, sinks below contempt itself. It is the consequences of that crime as they relate to—to—that noble and suffering woman, which can alone raise the despicable into the tragic, and make your life a worthy and a necessary offering—not to revenge, but justice —life for life—victim for victim! 'Tis the old law—'tis a righteous one."

"You shall not, with your accursed coldness, thus dispose of me as you will, and arrogate the option to smite or save! No," continued Cesarini, stamping his foot—"no; far from seeking forbearance at your hands—I dare and defy you! You think I have injured you—I, on the other hand, consider that the wrong has come from yourself. But for you she might have loved me—have been mine. Let that pass. But for you, at least, it is certain that I should neither have sullied my soul with a vile sin, nor brought the brightest of human beings to the grave. If she dies, the murder may be mine, but you were the cause—the devil that tempted to the offence. I defy and spit upon you—I have no softness left in me—my veins are fire—my heart thirsts for blood. You —you—have still the privilege to see—to bless—to tend her: and I—I, who loved her so—who could have kissed the earth she trod on—I—well, well, no matter—I hate you—I insult you—I call you villain and dastard—I throw myself on the laws of honour, and I demand that conflict you defer or deny!"

"Home, doter—home—fall on thy knees, and pray to heaven for pardon—make up thy dread account—repine not at the days yet thine to wash the black spot from thy soul. For, while I speak, I foresee too well that her days are numbered, and with her thread of life is entwined thine own. Within twelve hours from her last moment, we shall meet again: but now I am as ice and stone—thou canst not move me. Her closing life shall not be darkened by the aspect of blood—by the thought of the sacrifice it demands. Begone, or menials shall cast thee from my door: those lips are too base to breathe the same air as honest men. Begone, I say, begone!"

Though scarce a muscle moved in the lofty countenance of Maltravers—though no frown darkened the majestic brow—though no fire broke from the steadfast and scornful eye—there was a kingly authority in the aspect, in the extended arm, the stately crest, and a power in the swell of the stern voice, which awed and quelled the unhappy being whose own passions exhausted and unmanned him. He strove to fling back scorn to scorn, but his lips trembled and his voice died in hollow murmurs within his breast. Maltravers regarded him with a crushing and intense disdain. The Italian with shame and wrath wrestled against himself, but in vain: the cold eye that was fixed upon him was as a spell, which the fiend within him could not rebel against or resist. Mechanically he moved to the door, then turning round, he shook his clenched hand at Maltravers, and with a wild, maniacal laugh, rushed from the apartment.

CHAPTER VI

"On some fond breast the parting soul relies."—GRAY.

NOT a day passed in which Maltravers was absent from the side of Florence. He came early, he went late. He subsided into his former character of an accepted suitor, without a word of explanation with Lord Saxingham. That task was left to Florence. She doubtless performed it well, for his lordship seemed satisfied though grave, and almost for the first time in his life, sad. Maltravers never reverted to the cause of their unhappy dissension. Nor from that night did he once give way to whatever might be his more agonised and fierce emotions—he never affected to reproach himself—he never bewailed with a vain despair their approaching separation. Whatever it cost him, he stood collected and stoical in the intense power of his self-control. He had but one object, one desire, one hope—to save the last hours of Florence Lascelles from every pang—to brighten and smooth the passage across the Solemn Bridge. His forethought, his presence of mind, his care, his tenderness, never forsook him for an instant; they went beyond the attributes of men, they went into all the fine, the indescribable minutiæ by which woman makes herself, "in pain and anguish," the "ministering angel." It was as if he had nerved and braced his whole nature to one duty—as if that duty were more felt than affection itself—as if he were resolved that Florence should not remember that *she had no mother!*

And oh, then, how Florence loved him! how far more luxurious in its grateful and clinging fondness was that love than the wild and jealous fire of their earlier connection! Her own character, as is often the case in lingering illness, became incalculably more gentle and softened down as the shadows closed around it. She loved to make him read and talk to her—and her ancient poetry of thought now grew mellowed, as it were, into religion, which is indeed poetry with a stronger wing. . . . There was a world beyond the grave—there was life out of the chrysalis sleep of death—they would yet be united. And Maltravers, who was a solemn and intense believer in the GREAT HOPE, did not neglect the purest and highest of all the fountains of solace.

Often in that quiet room, in that gorgeous mansion, which had been the scene of all vain or worldly schemes—of flirtations and feastings, and political meetings and cabinet dinners, and all the bubbles of the passing wave—often there did these persons, whose position to each other had been so suddenly and so strangely changed—converse on those matters—daring and divine—which "make the bridal of the earth and sky."

"How fortunate am I," said Florence, one day, "that my choice fell on one who thinks as you do! How your words elevate and exalt me!—yet once I never dreamt of asking your creed on these questions. It is in sorrow or sickness that we learn why Faith was given as a soother to man—Faith, which is Hope with a holier name—hope that knows neither deceit nor death. Ah, how wisely do you speak of the *philosophy* of belief! It is, indeed, the telescope through which the stars grow large upon our gaze. And to you, Ernest, my beloved—comprehended and known at last—to you I leave, when I am gone, that monitor—that friend ;—you will know yourself what you teach to me. And when you look not on the heaven alone but in all space—on all the illimitable creation, you will know that I am there! For the home of the spirit is wherever spreads the Universal Presence of God. And to what numerous stages of being, what paths, what duties, what active and glorious tasks in other worlds may we not be reserved—perhaps to know and share them together, and mount age after age higher in the scale of being. For surely in heaven there is no pause or torpor—we do not lie down in calm and unimprovable repose. Movement and progress will remain the law and condition of existence; and there will be efforts and duties for us above as there have been below."

It was in this theory, which Maltravers shared, that the character of Florence, her overflowing life and activity of thought—her aspirations, her ambition, were still displayed. It was not so much to the calm and rest of the grave that she extended her unreluctant gaze, as to the light and glory of a renewed and progressive existence.

It was while thus they sat, the low voice of Ernest, tranquil yet half trembling with the emotions he sought to restrain—sometimes sobering, sometimes yet more elevating, the thoughts of Florence, that Lord Vargrave was announced, and Lumley Ferrers, who had now succeeded to that title, entered the room. It was the first time that Florence had seen him since the death of his uncle—the first time Maltravers had seen him since the evening so fatal to Florence. Both started—Maltravers rose and walked to the window. Lord Vargrave took the hand of his cousin and pressed it to his lips in silence, while his lips betokened feelings that for once were genuine.

"You see, Lumley, I am resigned," said Florence, with a sweet smile. "I am resigned and happy."

Lumley glanced at Maltravers, and met a cold, scrutinising, piercing eye, from which he shrank with some confusion. He recovered himself in an instant.

"I am rejoiced, my cousin, I *am* rejoiced," said he, very earnestly, "to see Maltravers here again. Let us now hope the best."

Maltravers walked deliberately up to Lumley, "Will you take my hand *now*, too?" said he, with deep meaning in his tone.

"More willingly than ever," said Lumley; and he did not shrink as he said it.

"I am satisfied," replied Maltravers, after a pause, and in a voice that expressed more than his words.

There is in some natures so great a hoard of generosity that it often dulls their acuteness. Maltravers could not believe that frankness could be wholly a mask—it was an hypocrisy he knew not of. He himself was not incapable, had circumstances so urged him, of great crimes; nay, the design of one crime lay at that moment deadly and dark within his heart, for he had some passions which in so resolute a character could produce dire and terrible effects. Even at the age of thirty, it was yet uncertain whether Ernest Maltravers might become an exemplary or an evil man. But he could sooner have strangled a foe than taken the hand of a man whom he had once betrayed.

"I love to think you friends," said Florence, gazing at them affectionately, "and to you, at least, Lumley, such friendship should be a blessing. I always loved you much and dearly, Lumley—loved you as a brother, though our characters often jarred."

Lumley winced. "For heaven's sake," he cried, "do not speak thus tenderly to me—I cannot bear it, and look on you and think——"

"That I am dying. Kind words become us best when our words are approaching to the last. But enough of this—I grieved for your loss."

"My poor uncle!" said Lumley, eagerly changing the conversation—"the shock was sudden; and melancholy duties have absorbed me so till this day, that I could not come even to you. It soothed me, however, to learn, in answer to my daily inquiries, that Ernest was here. For my part," he added, with a faint smile, "I have had duties as well as honours devolved on me. I am left guardian to an heiress and betrothed to a child."

"How do you mean?"

"Why, my poor uncle was so fondly attached to his wife's daughter, that he has left her the bulk of his property; a very small estate—not £2000 a year—goes with the title (a new title, too, which requires twice as much to carry it off and make its pinchbeck pass for gold). In order, however, to serve a double purpose, secure to his *protégé* his own beloved peerage, and atone to his nephew for the loss of wealth, he has left it a last request that I should marry the young lady over whom I am appointed guardian, when she is eighteen—alas! I shall then be at the other side of forty! If she does not take to so mature a bridegroom, she loses thirty—only thirty of the £200,000 settled upon her, which goes to me as a sugar-plum after the nauseous draught of the young lady's 'No.' Now, you know all. His widow, really an exemplary young woman, has a jointure of £1500 a-year and the villa. It is not much, but she is contented."

The lightness of the new peer's tone revolted Maltravers, and he turned impatiently away. But Lord Vargrave, resolving not to suffer the conversation to glide back to sorrowful subjects, which he always hated, turned round to Ernest, and said, "Well, my dear Ernest, I see by the papers that you are to have N——'s late appointment—it is a very rising office. I congratulate you."

"I have refused," said Maltravers, drily.

"Bless me !—indeed !—why ?"

Ernest bit his lip and frowned; but his glance wandering unconsciously at Florence, Lumley thought he detected the true reply to his question, and became mute.

The conversation was afterwards embarrassed and broken up; Lumley went away as soon as he could, and Lady Florence that night had a severe fit, and could not leave her bed the next day. That confinement she had struggled against to the last; and now, day by day, it grew more frequent and inevitable. The steps of Death became accelerated. And Lord Saxingham, wakened at last to the mournful truth, took his place by his daughter's side, and forgot that he was a cabinet minister.

CHAPTER VII.

"Away, my friends, why take such pains to know
What some brave marble soon in church shall show ?"—CRABBE.

IT may seem strange, but Maltravers had never loved Lady Florence as he did now. Was it the perversity of human nature, that makes the things of mortality dearer to us in proportion as they fade from our hopes, like birds whose hues are only unfolded when they take wing and vanish amidst the skies; or was it that he had ever doted more on loveliness of mind than that of form, and the first bloomed out the more, the more the last decayed? A thing to protect, to soothe, to shelter—oh, how dear it is to the pride of man! The haughty woman who can stand alone and requires no leaning-place in our heart loses the spell of her sex.

I pass over those stages of decline gratuitously painful to record; and which, in this case, mine cannot be the cold and technical hand to trace. At length came that time when physicians could define within a few days the final hour of release. And latterly the mocking pruderies of rank had been laid aside, and Maltravers had, for some hours at least in the day, taken his watch beside the couch to which the admired and brilliant Florence Lascelles was now almost constantly reduced. But her high and heroic spirit was with her to the last. To the last she could endure love and hope. One day when Maltravers left his post, she besought him, with more solemnity than usual, to return that evening. She fixed the precise hour, and she sighed heavily when he departed. Maltravers paused in the hall to speak to the physician, who was just quitting Lord Saxingham's library. Ernest spoke to him for some moments calmly, and when he heard the fiat, he betrayed no other emotion than a slight quiver of the lip! "I must not weep for her yet," he muttered, as he turned from the door. He went thence to the house of a gentleman of his own age, with whom he had formed that kind of acquaintance which never amounts to familiar friendship, but rests upon mutual respect, and is often more ready than professed friendship itself to confer mutual service. Colonel Danvers was a man who usually sat next to Maltravers in parliament; they voted together, and thought alike on principles, both of politics and honour: they would have lent thousands to each other without bond or memorandum ; and neither ever wanted a warm and indignant advocate when he was abused behind his back in the presence of the other. Yet their tastes and ordinary habits were not congenial; and when they met in the streets, they never said, as they would to companions they esteemed less, " Let us spend the day together!" Such forms of acquaintance are not uncommon among honourable men who have already formed habits and pursuits of their own, which they cannot surrender even to friendship. Colonel Danvers was not at home—they believed he was at his club, of which Ernest also was a member. Thither Maltravers bent his way. On arriving, he found that Danvers had been at the club an hour ago, and left word that he should shortly return. Maltravers entered and sat down. The room was full of its daily loungers; but he did not shrink from, he did not even heed the crowd. He felt not the desire of solitude—there was solitude enough within him. Several distinguished public men were there, grouped around the fire, and many of the hangers-on and satellites of political life; they were talking with eagerness and animation, for it was a season of great party-conflict. Strange as it may seem, though Maltravers was then scarcely sensible of their conversation, it all came back vividly and faithfully on him afterwards, in the first hours of reflection on his own future plans, and served to deepen and consolidate his disgust of the world. They were discussing the character of a great statesman whom, warmed but by the loftiest and purest motives, they were unable to understand. Their gross suspicions, their coarse jealousies, their calculations of patriotism by place, all that strips the varnish from the face of that fair harlot—Political Ambition—sank like caustic into his spirit. A gentleman, seeing him sit silent, with his hat over his moody brows, civilly extended to him the paper he was reading.

"It is the second edition; you will find the last French express."

"Thank you," said Maltravers; and the civil man started as he heard the brief answer; there was something so inexpressibly prostrate and broken-spirited in the voice that uttered it.

Maltravers' eyes fell mechanically on the columns, and caught his own name. That work which, in the fair retirement of Temple Grove, it had so pleased him to compose—in every page and every thought of which Florence had been consulted—which was so inseparably associated with her image, and glorified by the light of her kindred genius—was just published. It had been completed long since; but the publisher had, for some excellent reason of the craft, hitherto delayed its appearance. Maltravers knew nothing of its publication; he had meant, after his return to town, to have sent to forbid its appearance; but his thoughts of late had crushed everything else out of his memory—he had forgotten its existence. And now, in all the pomp and parade of authorship, it was sent into the world! *Now, now,* when it was like an indecent mockery of the Bed of Death—a sacrilege, an impiety! There is a terrible disconnection between the author and the man—the author's life and the man's life—the eras of visible triumph may be those of the most intolerable, though unrevealed and unconjectured anguish. The book that delighted us to compose may first appear in the hour when all things under the sun are joyless. This had been Ernest Maltravers' most favoured work. It had been conceived in a happy hour of great ambition—it had been executed with that desire of truth which, in the mind of genius, becomes ART. How little in the solitary hours stolen from sleep had he thought of self, and that labourer's hire called "fame!" how had he dreamt that he was promulgating secrets to make his kind better, and wiser, and truer to the great aims of life! How had Florence, and Florence alone, understood the beatings of his heart in every page! *And not* —it so chanced that the work was reviewed in the paper he r it was not only a hostile criticism, it was a personally abusive diatribe, a virulent invective. All the motives that can darken or defile were ascribed to him. All the mean spite of some mean mind was sputtered forth. Had the writer known the awful blow that awaited Maltravers at that time, it is not in man's nature but that he would have shrunk from this petty gall upon the wrung withers; but, as I have said, there is a terrible disconnection between the author and the man. The first is always at our mercy—of the last we know nothing. At such an hour Maltravers could feel none of the contempt that proud, none of the wrath that vain, minds feel at these stings. He could feel nothing but an undefined abhorrence of the world, and of the aims and objects he had pursued so long. Yet that even he did not *then* feel. He was in a dream; but as men remember dreams, so when he awoke did he loathe his own former aspirations, and sicken at their base rewards. It was the first time since his first year of inexperienced authorship that abuse had had the power even to vex him for a moment. But here, when the cup was already full, was the drop that overflowed. The great column of his past world was gone, and all else seemed crumbling away.

At length Colonel Danvers entered. Maltravers drew him aside, and they left the club.

"Danvers," said the latter, "the time in which I told you I should need your services is at hand; let me see you to-night."

"Certainly—I shall be at the House till eleven. After that hour you will find me at home."

"I thank you."

"Cannot this matter be arranged amicably?"

"No; it is a quarrel of life and death."

"Yet the world is really growing too enlightened for these old mimicries of single combat."

"There are some cases in which human nature and its deep wrongs will be ever stronger than the world and its philosophy. Duels and wars belong to the same principle; both are sinful on light grounds and poor pretexts. But it is not sinful for a soldier to defend his country from invasion, nor for man, with a man's heart, to vindicate truth and honour with his life. The robber that asks me for money I am allowed to shoot. Is the robber that tears from me treasures never to be replaced to go free? These are the inconsistencies of a pseudoethics, which, as long as we are made of flesh and blood, we can never subscribe to."

"Yet the ancients," said Danvers, with a smile, "were as passionate as ourselves, and they dispensed with duels."

"Yes, because they resorted to assassination!" answered Maltravers, with a gloomy frown. "As in revolutions all law is suspended, so are there stormy events and mighty injuries in life which are as revolutions to individuals. Enough of this—it is no time to argue like the schoolmen. When we meet you shall know all, and you will judge like me. Good day!"

"What, are you going already? Maltravers, you look ill, your hand is feverish—you should take advice."

Maltravers smiled—but the smile was not like his own—shook his head, and strode rapidly away.

Three of the London clocks, one after the other, had told the hour of nine, as a tall and commanding figure passed up the street towards Saxingham House. Five doors before you reach that mansion there is a crossing, and at this spot stood a young man, in whose face youth itself looked sapless and blasted. It was then March; the third of March; the weather was unusually severe and biting, even for that angry month. There had been snow in the morning, and it lay white and dreary in various ridges along the street. But the wind was not still in the keen but quiet sharpness of frost; on the contrary, it howled almost like a hurricane through the desolate thoroughfares, and the lamps flickered unsteadily in the turbulent gusts. Perhaps it was these blasts which increased the haggardness of aspect in the young man I have mentioned. His hair, which was much longer than is commonly worn, was tossed wildly from cheeks preternaturally shrunken, hollow, and livid; and the frail, thin form, seemed scarcely able to support itself against the rush of the winds.

As the tall figure, which, in its masculine stature and proportions, and a peculiar and nameless grandeur of bearing, strongly contrasted that of the younger man, now came to the spot where the streets met, it paused abruptly.

"You are here once more, Castruccio Cesarini; it is well!" said the low but ringing voice of Ernest Maltravers. "This, I believe, will not be our last interview to-night."

"I ask you, sir," said Cesarini, in a tone in which pride struggled with emotion—"I ask you to tell me how she is; whether you know —I cannot speak——"

"Your work is nearly done," answered Maltravers. "A few hours more, and your victim, for she is yours, will bear her tale to the Great Judgment Seat. Murderer as you are, tremble, for your own hour approaches!"

"She dies, and I cannot see her! and you are permitted that last glimpse of human perfectness; *you* who never loved her as I did; you—hated and detested! you——"

Cesarini paused, and his voice died away, choked in his own convulsive gaspings for breath.

Maltravers looked at him from the height of his erect and lofty form with a merciless eye; for in this one quarter Maltravers had shut out pity from his soul.

"Weak criminal!" said he, "hear me. You received at my hands forbearance, friendship, fostering and anxious care. When your own follies plunged you into penury, mine was the unseen hand that plucked you from famine or the prison. I strove to redeem, and save, and raise you, and endow your miserable spirit with the thirst and the power of honour and independence. The agent of that wish was Florence Lascelles; you repaid us well! a base and fraudulent forgery, attaching meanness to me, fraught with agony and death to her. Your conscience at last smote you; you revealed to her your crime—one spark of manhood made you reveal it also to myself. Fresh as I was in that moment from the contemplation of the ruin you had made, I curbed the impulse that would have crushed the life from your bosom. I told you to live on while life was left to *her*. If she recovered, I could forgive; if she died, I must avenge. We entered into that solemn compact, and in a few hours the bond will need the seal: it is the blood of one of us. Castruccio Cesarini, there is justice in heaven. Deceive yourself not: you will fall by my hand. When the hour comes you will hear from me. Let me pass—I have no more now to say."

Every syllable of this speech was uttered with that thrilling distinctness which seems as if the depth of the heart spoke in the voice. But Cesarini did not appear to understand its import. He seized Maltravers by the arm, and looked in his face with a wild and menacing glare.

"Did you tell me she was dying?" he said. "I ask you that question: why do you not answer me? Oh, by-the-way, you threaten me with your vengeance. Know you not that I long to meet you front to front, and to the death? Did I not tell you so—did I not try to move your slow blood—to insult you into a conflict in which I should have gloried? Yet then you were marble."

"Because *my* wrong I could forgive, and *hers*—there was then a hope that *hers* might not need atonement. Away!"

Maltravers shook the hold of the Italian from his arm and passed on. A wild, sharp yell of despair rang after him, and echoed in his ear as he strode the long, dim, solitary stairs that led to the deathbed of Florence Lascelles.

Maltravers entered the room adjoining that which contained the sufferer—the same room, still gay and cheerful, in which had been his first interview with Florence since their reconciliation.

Here he found the physician dozing in a fauteuil. Lady Florence had fallen asleep during the last two or three hours. Lord Saxingham was in his own apartment, deeply and noisily affected; for it was not thought that Florence could survive the night.

Maltravers sat himself quietly down. Before him, on a table, lay several manuscript books, gaily and gorgeously bound; he mechanically opened them. Florence's fair, noble, Italian characters met his eye in every page. Her rich and active mind, her love for poetry, her thirst for knowledge, her indulgence of deep thought, spoke from those pages like the ghosts of herself. Often, underscored with the marks of her approbation, he chanced upon extracts from his own works, sometimes upon reflections by the writer herself, not inferior in truth and depth to his own; snatches of wild verse never completed, but of a power and energy beyond the delicate grace of lady-poets; brief, vigorous criticisms on books, above the common holiday studies of the sex; indignant and sarcastic aphorisms on the real world, with high and sad bursts of feeling upon the ideal one; all chequering and enriching the various volumes told of the rare gifts with which this singular girl was endowed—a herbal, as it were, of withered blossoms that might have borne Hesperian fruits. And sometimes in these outpourings of the full mind and laden heart were allusions to himself, so tender and so touching—the pencilled outline of his features, traced by memory in a thousand aspects—the reference to former interviews and conversations—the dates and hours marked with a woman's minute and treasuring care!—all these tokens of genius and of love spoke to him with a voice that said, "And this creature is lost to you for ever; you never appreciated her till the time for her departure was irrecoverably fixed!"

Maltravers uttered a deep groan; all the past rushed over him. Her romantic passion for one yet unknown—her interest in his glory—her zeal for his life of life, his spotless and haughty name.

It was as if with her Fame and Ambition were dying also, and henceforth nothing but common clay and sordid motives were to be left on earth.

How sudden—how awfully sudden had been the blow! True, there had been an absence of some months in which the change had operated. But absence is a blank, a nonentity. He had left her in apparent health, in the tide of prosperity and pride. He saw her again—stricken down in body and temper—chastened—humbled—dying. And this being, so bright and lofty, how had she loved him! Never had he been so loved, except in that morning dream, haunted by the vision of the lost and dim-remembered Alice. Never on earth could he be so loved again. The air and aspect of the whole chamber grew to him painful and oppressive. It was full of her—the owner! There the harp, which so well became her muse-like form that it was associated with her like a part of herself! There the pictures, fresh and glowing from her hand—the grace—the harmony—the classic and simple taste everywhere displayed!

Rousseau has left to us an immortal portrait of the lover waiting for the first embraces of his mistress. But to wait with a pulse as feverish, a brain as dizzy, for her last look—to await the moment of despair, not rapture—to feel the slow and dull time as palpable a load upon the heart, yet to shrink from your impatience, and wish that the agony of suspense might endure for ever—this, oh, this is a picture of intense passion—of flesh and blood reality—of the rare and solemn epochs of our mysterious life—which had been worthier the genius of that "Apostle of Affliction!"

At length the door opened; the favourite attendant of Florence looked in.

"Is Mr. Maltravers there? Oh, sir, my lady is awake and would see you."

Maltravers rose, but his feet were glued to the ground, his sinking heart stood still—it was a mortal terror that possessed him. With a deep sigh he shook off the numbing spell, and passed to the bedside of Florence.

She sat up, propped by pillows, and as he sank beside her, and clasped her wan, transparent hand, she looked at him with a smile of pitying love.

"You have been very, very kind to me," she said, after a pause, and with a voice which had altered even since the last time he heard it. "You have made that part of life from which human nature shrinks with dread the happiest and the brightest of all my short and vain existence. My own dear Ernest — heaven reward you!"

A few grateful tears dropped from her eyes, and they fell on the hand which she bent her lips to kiss.

"It was not here—nor amidst streets and the noisy abodes of anxious, worldly men—nor was it in this harsh and dreary season of the year, that I could have wished to look my last on earth. Could I have seen the face of Nature—could I have watched once more with the summer sun amidst those gentle scenes we loved so well, Death would have had no difference from sleep. But what matters it? With you there are summer and Nature everywhere!"

Maltravers raised his face, and their eyes met in silence—it was a long, fixed gaze, which spoke more than all words could. Her head dropped on his shoulder, and there it lay, passive and motionless, for some moments. A soft step glided into the room—it was the unhappy father's. He came to the other side of his daughter, and sobbed convulsively.

She then raised herself, and even in the shades of death a faint blush passed over her cheek.

"My good, dear father, what comfort will it give you hereafter to think how fondly you spoiled your Florence!"

Lord Saxingham could not answer: he clasped her in his arms and wept over her. Then he broke away—looked on her with a shudder—

"O God!" he cried, "she is dead—she is dead!"

Maltravers started. The physician kindly approached, and taking Lord Saxingham's hand, led him from the room—he went mute and obedient like a child.

But the struggle was not yet past. Florence once more opened her eyes, and Maltravers uttered a cry of joy. But along those eyes the film was darkening rapidly, as still through the mist and shadow they sought the beloved countenance which hung over her, as if to breathe life into waning life. Twice her lips moved, but her voice failed her; she shook her head sadly.

Maltravers hastily held to her mouth a cordial which lay ready on the table near her, but scarce had it moistened her lips, when her whole frame grew heavier and heavier in his clasp. Her head once more sank upon his bosom—she thrice gasped wildly for breath—and at length, raising her hand on high, life struggled into its expiring ray.

"*There*—above!—Ernest—that name—Ernest!"

Yes, that name was the last she uttered; she was evidently conscious of that thought, for a smile, as her voice again faltered—a smile sweet and serene—that smile never seen but on the faces of the dying and the dead—borrowed from a light that is not of this world—settled on her brow, her lips, her whole countenance; still she breathed, but the breath grew fainter; at length, without murmur, sound, or struggle, it passed away—the head drooped from his bosom—the form fell from his arms—all was over!

CHAPTER VIII.

" .   .   Is this the promised end!"—*Lear*.

IT was two hours after that scene before Maltravers left the house. It was then just on the stroke of the first hour of morning. To him, while he walked through the streets, and the sharp winds howled on his path, it was as if a strange and wizard life had passed into and supported him—a sort of drowsy, dull existence. He was like a sleep-walker, unconscious of all around him; yet his steps went safe and free; and the one thought that possessed his being—into which all intellect seemed shrunk—the thought, not fiery nor vehement, but calm, stern, and solemn—the thought of revenge—seemed, as it were, grown his soul itself. He arrived at the door of Colonel Danvers, mounted the stairs, and as his friend advanced to meet him, said calmly, "Now, then, the hour has arrived."

"But what would you do now?"

"Come with me, and you shall learn."

"Very well, my carriage is below. Will you direct the servants?"

Maltravers nodded, gave his orders to the careless footman, and the two friends were soon driving through the less known and courtly regions of the giant city. It was then that Maltravers concisely stated to Danvers the fraud that had been practised by Cesarini.

"You will go with me now," concluded Maltravers, "to his house. To do him justice, he is no coward; he has not shrunk from giving me his address, nor will he shrink from the atonement I demand. I shall wait below while you arrange our meeting—at day-break for to-morrow."

Danvers was astonished and even appalled by the discovery made to him. There was something so unusual and strange in the whole affair. But neither his experience, nor his principles of honour, could suggest any alternative to the plan proposed. For though not regarding the cause of quarrel in the same light as Maltravers, and putting aside all question as to the right of the latter to constitute himself the champion of the betrothed, or the avenger of the dead, it seemed clear to the soldier that a man whose confidential letter had been garbled by another for the purpose of slandering his truth and culumniating his name, had no option but contempt, or the sole retribution (wretched though it be) which the customs of the higher class permit to those who live within its pale. But contempt for a wrong that a sorrow so tragic had followed—was *that* option in human philosophy?

The carriage stopped at a door in a narrow lane in an obscure suburb. Yet, dark as all the houses around were, lights were seen in the upper windows of Cesarini's residence, passing to and fro; and scarce had the servant's loud knock echoed through the dim thoroughfare, ere the door was opened. Danvers descended, and entered the passage—"Oh, sir, I am so glad you are come!" said an old woman, pale and trembling; "he do take on so!"

"There is no mistake?" asked Danvers, halting; "an Italian gentleman named Cesarini lodges here?"

"Yes, sir, poor cretur—I sent for you to come to him—for says I to my boy, says I——"

"Whom do you take me for?"

"Why, la, sir, you be's the doctor, ben't you?"

Danvers made no reply. He had a mean opinion of the courage of one who could act dishonourably; he thought there was some design to cheat his friend out of his revenge. With this idea he accordingly ascended the stairs, motioning the woman to precede him.

He came back to the door of the carriage in a few minutes. "Let us go home, Maltravers," said he, "this man is not in a state to meet you."

"Ha!" cried Maltravers, frowning darkly, and all his long-smothered indignation rushing like fire through every vein of his body; "would he shrink from the atonement?" he pushed Danvers

impatiently aside, leapt from the carriage, and rushed excitedly
upstairs.

Danvers followed.

Heated, wrought-up, furious, Ernest Maltravers burst into a small
and squalid chamber, from the closed doors of which, through
many chinks, had gleamed the light that told him Cesarini was
within. And Cesarini's eyes, blazing with horrible fire, were the
first object that met his gaze. Maltravers stood still, as if frozen
into stone.

"Ha! ha!" laughed a shrill and shrieking voice, which contrasted dreadly with the accents of the soft Tuscan, in which the
wild words were strung—"who comes here with garments dyed in
blood? You cannot accuse me—for *my* blow drew no blood, it
went straight to the heart—it tore no flesh by the way; we Italians
poison our victims! Where art thou—where art thou, Maltravers?
I am ready. Coward, you do not come! Oh, yes, yes, here you
are!—the pistols—I will not fight so. I am a wild beast. Let us
rend each other with our teeth and talons!"

Huddled up like a heap of confused and jointless limbs in the
furthest corner of the room lay the wretch, a raving maniac;—
two men keeping their firm grip on him, which, ever and anon, with
the mighty strength of madness, he shook off, to fall back senseless
and exhausted; his strained and bloodshot eyes starting from their
sockets, the slaver gathering round his lips, his raven hair standing
on end, his delicate and symmetrical features distorted into a
hideous and Gorgon aspect. It was, indeed, an appalling and
sublime spectacle, full of an awful moral, the meeting of the foes!
Here stood Maltravers, strong beyond the common strength of
men, in health, power, conscious superiority, premeditated vengeance—wise, gifted—all his faculties ripe, developed, at his command—the complete and all-armed man, prepared for defence and
offence against every foe—a man who once roused in a righteous
quarrel would not have quailed before an army; and there and
thus was his dark and fierce purpose dashed from his soul, shivered
into atoms at his feet. He felt the nothingness of man and man's
wrath in the presence of the madman on whose head the mighty
thunderbolt of a greater curse than human anger ever breathes had
fallen. In his horrible affliction the Criminal triumphed over the
Avenger!

"Yes! yes!" shouted Cesarini again; "they tell me she is dying;
but he is by her side—pluck him thence—he shall not touch her

hand—she shall not bless him—she is mine—if I killed her, I have saved her from him—she is mine in death! Let me in, I say—I will come in—I will, I will see her, and strangle him at her feet!" With that, by a tremendous effort, he tore himself from the clutch of his holders, and with a sudden and exultant bound sprang across the room, and stood face to face to Maltravers. The proud brave man turned pale, and recoiled a step—"It is he! it is he!" shrieked the maniac, and he leaped like a tiger at the throat of his rival. Maltravers quickly seized his arm, and whirled him round. Cesarini fell heavily on the floor, mute, senseless, and in strong convulsions.

"Mysterious Providence!" murmured Maltravers, "thou hast justly rebuked the mortal for deeming he might arrogate to himself thy privilege of vengeance. Forgive the sinner, O God, as I do—as thou teachest this stubborn heart to forgive—as she forgave who is now with thee, a blessed saint in heaven!"

When, some minutes afterwards, the doctor who had been sent for arrived, the head of the stricken patient lay on the lap of his foe, and it was the hand of Maltravers that wiped the froth from the white lips, and the voice of Maltravers that strove to soothe, and the tears of Maltravers that were falling on that fiery brow.

"Tend him, sir, tend him as my brother," said Maltravers, hiding his face as he resigned the charge. "Let him have all that can alleviate and cure—remove him hence to some fitter abode—send for the best advice. Restore him, and—and——" He could say no more, but left the room abruptly.

It was afterwards ascertained that Cesarini had remained in the streets after his short interview with Ernest; that at length he had knocked at Lord Saxingham's door just in the very hour when death had claimed its victim. He heard the announcement—he sought to force his way upstairs—they thrust him from the house, and nothing more of him was known till he arrived at his own door, an hour before Danvers and Maltravers came, in raging frenzy. Perhaps by one of the dim erratic gleams of light which always chequer the darkness of insanity, he retained some faint remembrance of his compact and assignation with Maltravers, which had happily guided his steps back to his abode.

. . . .

It was two months after this scene, a lovely Sabbath morning in the earliest May, as Lumley, Lord Vargrave, sat alone by the window in his late uncle's villa, in his late uncle's easy-chair—his eyes were resting musingly on the green lawn on which the windows opened, or rather on two forms that were seated upon a rustic bench in the middle of the sward. One was the widow in her weeds, the other was that fair and lovely child destined to be the bride of the new lord. The hands of the mother and daughter were clasped each in each. There was sadness in the faces of both—deeper if more resigned on that of the elder, for the child sought to console her parent, and grief in childhood comes with a butterfly's wing.

Lumley gazed for some time on them both, and on the child more earnestly.

"She is very lovely," he said; "she will be very rich. After all, I am not to be pitied. I am a peer, and I have enough to live upon at present. I am a rising man—our party wants peers; and though I could not have had more than a subaltern's seat at the Treasury Board six months ago, when I was an active, zealous, able commoner, now that I am a lord, with what they call a stake in the country, I may open my mouth and—bless me! I know not how many windfalls may drop in! My uncle was wiser than I thought in wrestling for this peerage, which he won and I wear!—Then, by-and-by, just at the age when I want to marry and have an heir (and a pretty wife saves one a vast deal of trouble), £200,000 and a young beauty! Come, come, I have strong cards in my hands if I play them tolerably. I must take care that she falls desperately in love with me. Leave me alone for that—I know the sex, and have never failed except in——ah, that poor Florence! Well, it is no use regretting! Like thrifty artists, we must paint out the unmarketable picture, and call luckier creations to fill up the same canvas!"

Here the servant interrupted Lord Vargrave's meditation by bringing in the letters and the newspapers which had just been forwarded from his town house. Lord Vargrave had spoken in the Lords on the previous Friday, and he wished to see what the Sunday newspapers said of his speech. So he took up one of the leading papers before he opened the letters. His eyes rested upon two paragraphs in close neighbourhood with each other: the first ran thus—

"The celebrated Mr. Maltravers has abruptly resigned his seat for the —— of ——, and left town yesterday on an extended tour on the Continent. Speculation is busy on the causes of the singular and unexpected self-exile of a gentleman so distinguished—in the very zenith of his career."

"So, he has given up the game!" muttered Lord Vargrave; "he was never a practical man—I am glad he is out of the way. But what's this about myself?"

"We hear that important changes are to take place in the government—it is said that ministers are at last alive to the necessity of strengthening themselves with new talent. Among other appointments confidently spoken of in the best-informed circles, we learn that Lord Vargrave is to have the place of ——. It will be a popular appointment. Lord Vargrave is not a holiday orator—a mere declamatory rhetorician—but a man of clear, business-like views, and was highly thought of in the House of Commons. He has also the art of attaching his friends, and his frank, manly character cannot fail to have its due effect with the English public. In another column of our journal our readers will see a full report of his excellent maiden speech in the House of Lords on Friday last: the sentiments there expressed do the highest honour to his lordship's patriotism and sagacity."

"Very well, very well, indeed!" said Lumley rubbing his hands; and turning to his letters, his attention was drawn to one with an enormous seal, marked "Private and confidential." He knew before he opened it that it contained the offer of the appointment alluded to in the newspaper. He read, and rose exultantly; passing through the French windows, he joined Lady Vargrave and Evelyn on the lawn, and as he smiled on the mother and caressed the child, the scene and the group made a pleasant picture of English domestic happiness.

Here ends the First Portion of this work: it ends in the view that bounds us when we look on the practical world with the outward unspiritual eye—and see life that dissatisfies justice—for life is so seen but in fragments. The influence of fate seems so small on the man who, in erring, but errs as the egoist, and shapes out of ill some use that can profit himself. But Fate hangs a shadow so vast on the heart that errs but in venturing abroad, and knows only in others the sources of sorrow and joy.

Go alone, Oh Maltravers, unfriended, remote—thy present a waste, and thy past life a ruin, go forth to the future! Go, Ferrers, light cynic—with the crowd take thy way—complacent, elated—no cloud upon conscience, for thou seest but sunshine on fortune.—Go forth to the Future!

Human life is compared to the circle—Is the simile just? All lines that are drawn from the centre to touch the circumference, by the law of the circle, are equal. But the lines that are drawn from the heart of the man to the verge of his destiny—do they equal each other?—Alas! some seem so brief, and some lengthen on as for ever.

END OF THE FIRST PART OF ERNEST MALTRAVERS.

Printed by WALTER SCOTT, "*The Kenilworth Press,*" *Felling, Newcastle.*

www.ingramcontent.com/pod-product-compliance
Lightning Source LLC
Chambersburg PA
CBHW020221240426
43672CB00006B/375